INTRODUCTION TO EDUCATION
Series Editor: Jonathan Solity

PROMOTING EQUALITY IN PRIMARY SCHOOLS

D0240867

PROMOTING EQUALITY IN PRIMARY SCHOOLS

Edited by Mike Cole, Dave Hill and
Sharanjeet Shan

CASSELL

London and Washington

Cassell
Wellington House   PO Box 605
125 Strand   Herndon
London WC2R 0BB   VA 20172

First published in 1997

British Library Cataloguing in Publication Data
A catalogue record for this book is available from the British Library

ISBN 0-304-33307-7 (hardback)
    0-304-33308-5 (paperback)

Typeset by Action Typesetting Limited
Printed and bound in Great Britain by
Redwood Books, Trowbridge, Wiltshire

Contents

Part 2 Foundation subjects Key Stages 1 and 2: the core subjects

Part 3 Foundation subjects Key Stages 1 and 2: the non-core subjects

Part 4 Religious education, sex education and cross-curricular issues Key Stages 1 and 2

Notes on contributors

Jackie Barnes has taught at Culloden Primary School in Tower Hamlets for five years. Previous to this she was a secondary maths teacher and has taught in Sussex, Essex and Merseyside.

Ros Bayley is currently working as Deputy Headteacher at Culloden Primary School. She has been a teacher in Poplar, East London, since 1972.

Fiona Bellet was raised and educated in East London, where she has taught for the past four years at Culloden Primary School.

Terry Brown is a former special needs teacher, advisory teacher and Health Education Coordinator. Since 1993, he has been an independent consultant, and has worked for LEAs, Health Authorities, Channel 4 and SCAA.

Gill Clarke lectures in PE and Curriculum Studies at the University of Southampton. Prior to this she taught PE in a variety of schools in Hampshire and was Field Leader for PE at Chichester Institute of Higher Education. Her research interests are in equity and sexuality, and she has published articles on discourse analysis, research methods and lesbian students and teachers.

Mike Cole teaches at the University of Brighton and has written extensively on 'race' and anti-racism and on equality and schooling. With Dave Hill he co-founded the Hillcole Group of Radical

Left Educators. His most recent book is *Education for Equality: Some Guidelines for Good Practice.*

Tarsem Singh Cooner is a social worker and obtained two research degrees. Since 1989 he has been working for the Children and Families team at Sandwell Social Services. His particular interest is in the theoretical and practical developments of interactive multimedia in enhancing the self-esteem of children and adults, particularly those from minority ethnic communities.

Margaret Cox is a Senior Lecturer in the School of Education at King's College London, and Director of the MODUS (computer-based modelling across the curriculum project). She was the director of the Computers in the Curriculum project (1982–1991) which published over 200 educational software packages for schools. She is a founder member of the London Mental Models Group and the National Energy Education Forum.

Jenny Ellwood is a class teacher with responsibility for co-ordinating art and technology at Red Barn County Primary School, Hants. She is committed to promoting equality of access to all areas of the curriculum.

Dave Hill is Head of Initial Teacher Training for the Crawley Primary BEd course for mature and non-standard entry students run by Chichester Institute of Higher Education. He has advised the Labour Party on teacher education from a radical Left perspective, and is a former Labour group leader and parliamentary candidate and a regional chair of NATFHE, the lecturers' union. With Mike Cole he co-founded the Hillcole Group of Radical Left Educators.

Sheila Humbert is a primary teacher, Science Coordinator and Equal Opportunities Coordinator at Bewbush Middle School, Crawley, West Sussex.

Gianna Knowles currently lectures in geography and primary education at Chichester Institute of Higher Education. She spent eleven years teaching primary aged children in North-West London and the Midlands, in a variety of schools and with children from a variety of backgrounds, including travellers' children.

Ray Leigh lectures in PE and Sports Science at Chichester Institute of Higher Education. He has previously taught in both secondary and primary schools in Surrey and Merseyside.

Avril Loveless is a lecturer in IT in Education at the University of Brighton. She is concerned with the development of IT capability in student teachers and the use of IT in learning and teaching. Her book, *The Role of IT: Practical Issues for Primary Teachers*, is published by Cassell.

Derek Lovell has taught in primary and middle schools in four local authorities. For some years he was a language co-ordinator in an Oxford middle school and for the last six years he has been the Head of Gossops Green Middle School in Crawley, West Sussex.

Ruth Mantin is a Senior Lecturer in Religious Studies at Chichester Institute of Higher Education. Prior to this she was a secondary school teacher of religious education for seven years. She has written articles on religious education and has co-authored a book on teaching Christianity. Her research interest is in the feminist study of religion.

Tig O'Hearn taught in primary schools in the Inner London Education Authority for many years. She currently works in Broadfield East Middle School, Crawley, where she is responsible for Equal Opportunities, Drama and Personal, Social and Health Education.

Lina Patel was born in Kenya and raised in Kenya and England. She completed her education in England. She taught in an east London school for six years, before moving to the University of London, Institute of Education as a teacher fellow. Since then, she has worked with the Television and Publishing Centre, ILEA, and has co-ordinated an Equal Opportunities project for seven outer London boroughs. She was Co-ordinator for Multicultural Education in Haringey and is currently teaching on the BEd and PGCE courses at the University of North London.

Gillean Paterson has worked in London schools for twenty years, four of which were as acting headteacher at Culloden Primary School, Tower Hamlets, in East London.

Rod Paton is a composer, arranger, horn player and improvising musician. He studied music and philosophy at Southampton University and in the Czech Republic. He has worked as a teacher, lecturer and community musician with a wide range of ages and abilities and is currently Senior Lecturer in Music at the Chichester Institute of Higher Education.

Sara Reed lectures in Dance at the University of Surrey. Formerly she lectured at Chichester Institute of Higher Education. She studied dance at the Laban Centre, and has taught in primary and secondary schools and a sixth form college as well as teaching dance freelance in the community. Her areas of interest include dancers' training, health, safety and fitness.

Janet Sang is a Senior Lecturer in Art at Chichester Institute of Higher Education, and previously taught in schools in Wakefield, West Yorkshire. Her areas of interest include gender and cultural studies, and critical theory.

Sharanjeet Shan is Director of the Maths Centre for Primary Teachers in Johannesburg, South Africa, working with teachers from the townships. Prior to that she was general advisor for mathematics in Sandwell. She has written widely, in particular, on Mathematics Education.

Claudette Williams currently teaches on the BEd, PGCE, Articled and Licensed Teachers Programmes in the School of Teaching Studies at the University of North London.

To Khushvant Jabble and Cameroon Shan-Makanaki; and to Joshua Akehurst Hill and Clare Louise Coogan Cole, aged five years and one month, respectively, and their generation everywhere.

Preface

A society divided

Mike Cole, Dave Hill and Sharanjeet Shan

The contributors to this book are educators who deplore the way in which radical Right economic and social policies have dramatically increased inequalities in Britain. For example while we would distance ourselves from his overall (New Labour) political project Will Hutton[1] has written powerfully of the effects of the new 30/30/40 society – which, in reverse order, means that just over 40 per cent have stable and secure jobs, 30 per cent have work, but work which is frequently part-time and insecure, and a massive 30 per cent of the population live on the margins of society. In our schools we meet children from these varied economic backgrounds – in many cases, alienation starts in the primary years.

The current radical Right project, in Britain, has, as in other countries, almost succeeded in wiping issues of equality off the political, social, economic and ideological agenda. But it has not succeeded completely. In the world of education, for example, tens of thousands of primary school teachers are, against the odds, actively promoting equal opportunities and equality.

This book is an attempt to use the options and spaces that exist in one National Curriculum, namely that of England and Wales, in the pursuit of a more equal society. In considering, one by one, the subjects of the school curriculum of 5- to 12-year-olds, the book should be of interest to teachers, head teachers, school managers, parents, students, teacher educators and trainers; indeed to all those who have an interest in and/or a commitment to the promotion of more equality, more social justice and less discrimination, both within schools and within the larger society. Its relevance extends far beyond the confines of the UK. In these times, when equality in education is under grave threat, the issues raised are pertinent to the rest of Europe, to North America, to South Africa[2] and indeed to the world at large.

NOTES

1   Will Hutton has become somewhat of a guru to the 'New Labour' project of Tony Blair. While his analysis and critique of the ravages wrought on society by Thatcherism and its aftermath are very powerful, his own political project entails a rejection of socialism and an acceptance of market capitalism. As socialists, it is in this crucial sense that we would distance ourselves from Hutton.

2   In April 1995 Mike Cole and Dave Hill went to South Africa, in part to give a series of talks on transformative teacher education and schooling, and in part to visit Sharanjeet Shan, who works with primary school teachers in the townships of Johannesburg. In South Africa, we witnessed the ongoing demolition of the apartheid state. Accompanying this we experienced a dignity of spirit among those who have been exploited and oppressed for so long, and a euphoric sense of hope for, and commitment to a more equal society, by many, if not all sections of society.

In formal legal terms apartheid has been dismantled and everyone has the right, for example, to equal job entitlement and to attend the same school. In reality, however, the inequalities are still firmly intact. While there are now black millionaires alongside white ones in the plush suburbs, the poverty and economic deprivation of the homelands and the townships and the horrors of the squatter-camps remain. While every child is entitled to schooling, there are still gross inequalities of provision.

REFERENCE

Hutton, W. (1995) *The State We're In*. London: Jonathan Cape.

Introduction

Dave Hill and Mike Cole

THE THATCHER LEGACY

Although Margaret Thatcher took a somewhat minimalist interest in matters of education, the major educational changes, in particular, the advent of the Education Reform Act and the National Curriculum, cannot be understood without reference to Thatcherism.

We are still suffering from the legacy of Thatcherism, which may be thought of as having three broad phases, corresponding roughly to her three terms of office (cf. Cole, 1990:9). The first phase was characterized by appeals to all families to 'tighten their belts' and prepare for individual sacrifice, coupled with the beginnings of that sacrifice for the working class (lower wages, for example) and for the steadily increasing army of the unemployed. The beginnings of the attacks on trade union power and rights came in this first term.

The second phase was mainly about privatization and so-called 'popular capitalism'; the birth of the Nationality Act of 1981, designed to restrict Asian and black immigration further, and the limiting of the power of the unions.

The third phase initiated a frontal assault on the Welfare State (the UK is the only European Union member not to sign the

Social Chapter – designed to provide some basic rights for workers).

THE WELFARE STATE, THE EDUCATION REFORM ACT AND THE NATIONAL CURRICULUM

There are three aspects to radical Right education policy. First, there is the run-down of the welfare state, with state education a major target in this process. In practice, this means that class sizes in state schools are rising significantly (see Chapter 1), further widening the difference in provision between them and the private sector. While the radical Right clamours for ever more spending cuts, in the UK social spending as a proportion of Gross Domestic Product (GDP), the total value of goods produced and services provided in a country in one year, is by international standards low, with Portugal the only European Union country spending a lower percentage of GDP on welfare than the UK. Indeed the UK ranks only marginally above the USA, a country not renowned for having a recognisable welfare state (Joseph Rowntree Foundation 1995).

Second, the Education Reform Act of 1988 created a market in schooling in line with the radical Right obsession with the free reign of market forces in virtually every sector of society. This is discussed in great detail in Chapter 1. Here, Dave Hill shows how, overall, the effects of the Education Reform Act have been to increase inequalities, particularly for those children with special needs, working-class and Asian and black children. Causal factors include the demise of local education authority powers, the setting up of a hierarchy of types of school (with the introduction of grant maintained/opted out/independent state schools/CTCs) and the creation of a graded hierarchy within the various school sectors caused by the imposition of competitive gloss marketing of schools (in turn caused by per capita funding under Local Management of Schools and by the publication of league tables and results).

Third, the same Act created, for the first time this century, a National Curriculum in England and Wales. This Curriculum was the brainchild of the radical Right, and, in particular, of the Hillgate Group (1987). Strong representations from various sectoral organizations such as NATE (National Association for the Teaching of English) and the CRE (Commission for Racial Equality) have served to highlight just how political and ideological the National Curriculum is (see Chapters 1, 2 and 4).

In essence the National Curriculum embodies the Thatcherite agenda of nationalism (British history and the Christian religion); the discouraging of critical thought (with an increased emphasis on facts to be learnt and the learning tested); coercive order and discipline (with exhortations to have children in rows and whole class teaching); and individualism (with children encouraged to compete on an individual basis, rather than work co-operatively). Prior to the Education Reform Act, these 'traditional values' were felt to be threatened by both liberal child-centred progressivism and by radical Left educators and militant (teacher) trade unions (see Chapter 1 for an analysis).

THE NATIONAL CURRICULUM AND THE PROMOTION OF EQUALITY

We see this book as vigorously contesting Conservative schooling. This has two aspects. First, we oppose the view that the only way to run societies is to let loose an unbridled free market on the economy in general, on social provision, and, with particular respect to the concerns of this book, on schooling.

Second, while we believe that, in the longer term, a new Education Act and a new Common Curriculum are called for,[1] we are convinced that it is possible to promote equality within the confines of the present National Curriculum.[2]

The editors approached a number of specialists in various areas of the education of school students from the ages of 5 to 11 and asked them to suggest ways forward in the present climate to promote both equal opportunity (in the short-term) and equality (in the longer term). The authors were asked to address themselves to social class, 'race', gender, disability and special needs and sexuality, and also to issues of ecology.

The principal aim of the book is to provide practical guidelines for the promotion of equality in primary schools. Contributors to the book believe that the way forward is not simply to seek a return to the status quo of the late 1970s and early 1980s, which witnessed the success of the extremely gradual diminution of social inequality under the Labour governments of the 1960s and 1970s. While we welcome that progress in terms, for example, of the comprehensivisation of schooling, and of more equal opportunities in schooling and society in general, we do not see the 'equal opportunities' approach as being sufficient.

EQUAL OPPORTUNITIES AND EGALITARIAN POLICIES: WHAT IS THE DIFFERENCE?

We make a distinction between equal opportunities and equality. While we welcome equal opportunities policies in schools and elsewhere, we also see their limitations. When equal opportunity policies are advocated outside the framework of a longer-term commitment to equality, the assumption has been made that there is a 'level playing field', on which we all compete as equals. In addition, promoting equal opportunity policies alone, indicates a failure to recognize how deep are the divisions in our society, due to such factors as class, 'race', gender, disability and sexuality. This is because, in reality, equal opportunity policies seek to enhance social mobility within structures, which are essentially unequal. In other words, they seek a meritocracy, where people rise (or fall) on merit, but to grossly unequal levels or strata in society – unequal in terms of income, wealth, lifestyle, life chances and power.

To reiterate; we fully support equal opportunity policies in schools and elsewhere but we believe that they need to be considered within an overall framework of equality. Most children leave school with the belief that the class system is inevitable. Many consider that women should have different roles in society than men; many think that Asian, black and other minority ethnic groups are odd or peculiar or alien; that gays and lesbians are not normal; that disabled people are to be pitied. Teachers are failing to promote equality unless they challenge these beliefs.

A commitment to 'equality' means going further than equal opportunity policies. First, there is the need for an understanding that inequalities are structural and institutional, both at the level of an individual school, and in society at large. Second, egalitarians are committed to a transformed economy, and a more socially just society, where wealth and ownership and political power are shared far more equally, and where citizens (whether young citizens or teachers in schools, economic citizens in the workplace or political citizens in the polity) exercise democratic controls over their lives and the structures of the societies of which they are part/to which they contribute.

A HOLISTIC APPROACH TO THE CURRICULUM

One of the specific and deliberate features of this book is that we attempt to present a holistic approach to equal opportunities and equality and social justice issues in the curriculum. This is unusual but, we believe, highly necessary. It is unusual in that there are many books and articles written on aspects of gender equality, or 'race' equality or support for children with special educational needs. Very few are written on issues of social class and sexuality.

This is also true of local education authority and school policies. Probably a majority of schools, and certainly a majority of local education authorities, have anti-racist and anti-sexist policies (or at least multicultural and non-sexist policies). The number of schools with a policy relating to social class (or, as it is sometimes termed, social background), or sexuality is minimal. The Inner London Education Authority was virtually alone in commissioning a major report on how best to combat the underachievements of working-class girls and boys in primary schools (the 'Thomas Report', ILEA, 1985). The thrust of this report both in terms of its curriculum proposals and its hidden curriculum proposals is markedly different to current government policy. Curriculum proposals, for example, were far more eclectic in their cultural canon, far less culturally elitist, far more reflective of the variety of cultures and subcultures that characterize children in schools today.

Hence we feel that, in books and articles published to date, and in school and local education authority policy and overall national education policy guidelines, there is a lack of advice to teachers which might better enable them to challenge a more complete range of inequalities in schooling.

Issues of gender, 'race' and special educational needs tend to be perceived as far less controversial than issues of sexuality and class. With respect to sexuality, among the radical Right 'cultural restorationists' (who want to preserve what they see as traditional British culture), there is a special loathing of the 'unnaturalness' of homosexuality and what is perceived to be its threat to conventional morality, the family and social structure – and indeed its threat to the economic structure.

As far as the issues raised by social class are concerned (for example, major differences in income, life chances, lifestyle and power, as well as theoretical perspectives, as discussed in Chapter 2), these can be seen as a fundamental assault on the perpetuation of the capitalist economy. To put it bluntly, existing economic and social relationships (i.e. exploitation of labour by capital) can progress and continue in the face of more 'race' and gender equality[3] and more equality for lesbians and gays and for the disabled. Indeed, this much is recognized by the neo-liberal/free marketeer wing of the radical Right. However, by its very nature, the undermining or eradication of class inequality implies extremely radical, or indeed revolutionary, change: the end, or the transformation, of capitalism itself. Capitalism is predicated upon exploitative as opposed to co-operative relationships and upon inequalities of power, wealth and income (see Chapter 2 for a discussion). Hence social egalitarianism is, for the radical Right, and indeed for liberal progressives (when the chips are down), too dangerous to allow. Government legislation renders dealing with social class and capitalism (and with issues of sexuality) particularly problematic (see Chapters 2 and 15).

The second reason for our holistic approach is that, as Mike Cole points out in Chapter 2 (see also Hessari and Hill, 1989; Hill, 1994), while inequalities can be separate or discreet, they can also be experienced in a multiple sense. While at any one time individuals might be discriminated against, stereotyped, harassed or attacked solely on grounds of one of their presenting characteristics (as in the case of 'Paki bashing', 'gay bashing' or rape) people do have multiple identities and features which impact on one another. To take one example, in a brief discussion of 'the genderquake thesis' (the theory that it is now boys rather than girls who are failing in the education system) in Chapter 1, Dave Hill, in accord with the views of many socialist feminists, points out the differences in treatment afforded in general to working-class, middle-class and upper-class young women.

Although in various places we have undertaken critiques of the currently fashionable academic fad of postmodernism (e.g. Cole and Hill, 1995 and 1996), we do recognize that its foregrounding of the multiplicity of identities and the complexity of subjectivity has, together with developments of neo-Marxism in the 1970s and 1980s, served to point out that forms of oppression and exploitation (and indeed forms of privilege) are multifaceted. Hence teachers, student teachers and others need to address the various formations of children's subjectivity (see Chapter 2 for a discussion).

The third reason for the holistic approach in curriculum intervention and developments is that an understanding of any one of these aspects of oppression and discrimination can inform understanding of the others. Thus in many schools, the development of anti-racist policies has informed the development of anti-sexist policies and vice versa. Policies and procedures for the curriculum, for the hidden curriculum, for staffing can, in general, productively inform each other (Hill, 1994).

STRUCTURE OF THE BOOK

The format of the book is as follows. Part 1 looks at the 'The Wider Context'. In Chapter 1, Dave Hill examines the policy context of the radical Right reforms of the education system in England and Wales since 1979 and offers a critique of the conservative government's hostility to equality and equal opportunities in schooling. We consider it important for teachers and student teachers to become more aware of the wider contexts of pupils' schooling – aware of the big picture, of the place of the restructuring of primary schooling and of the National Curriculum within the context of the fullness of Conservative education policies.

In Chapters 1 and 4, the ideological differences between radical Right, liberal progressive and social democratic and radical Left policies are set out in some detail. As editors and contributors, we think it important for students, teachers and others with an interest in the educational community to understand and be able to critique not only what is happening in schooling and the National Curriculum but also why it is happening, and arguments for changing it.

In order to do this they also need an awareness of conceptual issues. Thus, in Chapter 2, Mike Cole looks in turn at the central conceptual issues of the book. First, the concepts of 'race' and racism are examined, in the context of three forms of education possible in a multicultural society. Second, the issue of sexuality, now firmly on the political, religious, social and academic agendas, is analysed, and its relationship to young children assessed. Third, the chapter looks at gender, at patriarchy and at types of feminism, in order to assess the implications for primary school practice. Fourth, the issue of disability and special needs is addressed. Different models of disability are assessed and educational implications drawn. Finally, the salience of social class is defended against postmodernism and others who deny its existence, and the relevance of social class demonstrated to children of primary age.

In Chapter 3, Ros Bayley and Gillean Paterson describe aspects of recent history which occurred at Culloden School, Tower Hamlets under the Thatcher government. This school has provided a good example of egalitarian schooling. For its pains, it was subjected to a right-wing press and government campaign of vilification.

Teacher education has a vital role to play in the promotion and understanding of conceptual and theoretical issues. However, Dave Hill, Mike Cole and Claudette Williams show in Chapter 4 how a Conservative government, intent on ideological conformity to its current project, is taking the theory and the wider awareness out of initial teacher training education. The teacher educators among us and, increasingly, school teachers are noticing, with some considerable concern the differences in contextual awareness, the differences in the degree to which trainee teachers, trained/educated under the new criteria for teacher training/teacher education (Circular 14/93), question what is going on as compared to students who followed courses validated under the 1989 CATE (Council for Accreditation of Teacher Education) criteria.

Indeed a number of surveys of headteachers, experienced

teachers, newly qualified teachers and student teachers make it clear that there is overwhelming opposition to the scope and nature of the Conservative restructuring of Initial Teacher Education (Hill, 1993 and 1994; Carrington and Tymms, 1993; SCOP, 1994; Blake and Hill, 1995; UWE/NUT, 1995; Hill and Cole, 1996). The authors of Chapter 4 suggest, therefore, that all undergraduate and postgraduate courses in teacher education/training should seriously consider theoretical, contextual and conceptual issues, as outlined above.

Parts 2 and 3 examine equality and equal opportunity issues with respect to the core and non-core foundation subjects respectively. In Part 2, Derek Lovell looks at English and Sharanjeet Shan addresses herself to Mathematics and Science. In Part 3, Shan and Margaret Cox look at Design and Technology, Lina Patel at History, Jackie Barnes, Fiona Bellet and Gianna Knowles at Geography, Rod Paton at Music, Janet Sang and Jenny Ellwood at Art and Gill Clarke, Ray Leigh and Sara Reed at Physical Education.

Part 4 considers Religious Education (Ruth Mantin), Sex Education (Terry Brown), cross-curricular Information Technology (Tarsem Singh Cooner and Avril Loveless) and Drama (Tig O'Hearn). The book concludes with a discussion of one school's approach to promoting and monitoring equal opportunities by Sheila Humbert.

As is to be expected, there are some differences in perception, opinion and emphasis between contributors, and individual chapters should stand in their own right and should not be read off as the precise academic or political views of the editors, either individually or collectively. However, all of us are committed to the resuscitation and extension of equal opportunities work in schools and in education for social justice and equality.

All the issues dealt with remain controversial in the present climate, but we believe that social class, 'race', gender, sexuality and disability and special needs issues should, inter alia, be central concerns of the primary school.

ACKNOWLEDGEMENTS

We would like to thank Helen Haji-Alexandrou and Raf Salkie

for their comments on this chapter. Any inadequacies, of course, remain ours.

NOTES

1 Such a curriculum, as part of the development of knowledge, skills, abilities and attitudes, should both encourage critical thinking, and promote issues of equality, as outlined in this book (for a discussion, see Hillcole Group, 1991; Hillcole Group, 1996).

2 Prior to 1988, there had been little change in the Primary Curriculum since the 1960s. A common view prevailed that curricula were relatively value-free and not embodiments of particular philosophies or ideologies. We would distance ourselves from this proposition. Any curriculum, whether written individually or collectively by teachers, or prescribed nationally, is not neutral. Curricula are ideological selections of what it is believed that children should learn or, more importantly, what they should not learn – what knowledge should be denied, suppressed or displaced (see Chapter 2; see also Whitty, 1985; Apple, 1988, 1993).

3 Having said that, it is important to point out that women traditionally have been and still are essential to the maintenance of capitalism, both as a source of free labour in the patriarchal household (servicing the needs of male partners and reproducing and nurturing future workers and capitalists) and as cheap and casual labour in the workforce. Similarly, Asian, black and other minority ethnic workers, especially women, have historically served as a source of cheap and excessively exploited labour. Thus, the degree of equality afforded to women in general and to Asian, black and other minority ethnic women and men is extremely problematic for capitalism (see Chapter 2 for a discussion of some of the defining features of capitalism, of patriarchy and of racism).

REFERENCES

Apple, M. (1988) *Teachers and Texts: A Political Economy of Class and Gender Relations in Education*. London: Routledge.

Apple, M. (1993) *Official Knowledge: Democratic Education in A Conservative Age.* London: Routledge.

Blake, D. and Hill, D. (1995) The newly qualified teacher in school. *Research Papers in Education,* 10, 3:309–39.

Carrington, B. and Tymms, P. (1993) *For Primary Heads, Mum's Not the Word.* Newcastle: School of Education, University of Newcastle upon Tyne.

Cole, M. (1990) *Education for Equality: Some Guidelines for Good Practice.* London: Routledge.

Cole, M. and Hill, D. (1995) Games of despair and rhetorics of resistance: postmodernism, education and reaction. *British Journal of Sociology of Education,* 16 (8).

Cole, M. and Hill, D. (1996) Resistance postmodernism: emancipation politics for a new era and academic chic for a defeatist intelligentsia? In K. Gill (ed.) *Information Society: New Media, Ethics and Postmodernism.* London: Springer.

Hessari, R. and Hill, D. (1989) *Practical Ideas for Multicultural Learning and Teaching in the Primary Classroom.* London: Routledge.

Hill, D. (1993) *What Teachers? School-Basing and Critical Reflection in Teacher Education and Training.* Brighton: Institute of Education Policy Studies.

Hill, D. (1994) Cultural diversity and initial teacher education. In G. Verma and P. Pumfrey (eds) *Cultural Diversity and the Curriculum, vol. 4, Cross-Curricular Contexts, Themes and Dimensions in Primary Schools.* London: Falmer Press.

Hill, D. and Cole, M. (1996) Initial teacher education and the irrelevance of theory: mainstream thinking or ideological dogma? In K. Watson, C. Modgil and S. Modgil (eds) *Educational Dilemmas: Debate and Diversity.* London: Cassell.

Hillcole Group (1991) *Changing the Future: Redprint for Education.* London: Tufnell Press.

Hillcole Group (1996) *2020 Vision: Education for the 21st Century.* London: Tufnell Press.

Hillgate Group (1987) *The Reform of British Education: From Principles to Practice.* London: The Claridge Press.

Inner London Education Authority (ILEA) (1985) *Committee on Primary Education – Improving Primary Schools: Report of the Committee on Primary Schools* ('Thomas Report'). London: ILEA.

Joseph Rowntree Foundation (1995).

Standing Conference of Principles (SCOP) (Teacher Education Group) (1994) *Education Bill: Primary ITT Questionnaire: Commentary on Findings.* London: SCOP.

University of the West of England/National Union of Teachers (UWE/NUT) (1995) *Learning the Lessons: Reform in Initial Teacher Education.* Bristol: UWE.

Whitty, G. (1985) *Sociology and School Knowledge: Curricular Theory, Research and Politics.* London: Methuen.

PART 1

THE WIDER CONTEXT

CHAPTER 1

Equality in primary schooling

The policy context, intentions and effects of the Conservative 'reforms'

Dave Hill

This chapter places the Primary School National Curriculum in its ideological and policy contexts and evaluates the various intentions and effects of wider Conservative policy for schools on issues of equality and equal opportunities. I begin by analysing two strands of Conservative ideology and education policy, the free market, neo-liberal position and the moral/social authoritarian, neo-conservative one. I point out what is distinctive about them in relation to education policy, and then what they have in common.

I then go on to examine the impact of the radical Right on the restructuring of schooling in England and Wales since 1979. Particular attention is paid to the effects of the Education Reform Act of 1988 in setting up of a competitive market in schooling and in reducing the powers of local education authorities (LEAs), and to the establishment of the National Curriculum. In doing so, I critique Conservative government policy for its 'equiphobia' (Myers, 1990, in Troyna, 1995), its hostility to equality and equal opportunities in schooling, as elsewhere.

RADICAL RIGHT IDEOLOGY AND EDUCATION

John Major, Prime Minister and Leader of the Conservative
Party, pronounced to the 1992 Conservative Party Conference:

> When it comes to education, my critics say I'm 'old fashioned'. Old
> fashioned? Reading and writing? Old fashioned? Spelling and
> sums? Great literature – and standard English Grammar? Old fash-
> ioned? Tests and tables? British history? A proper grounding in
> science? Discipline and self respect? Old fashioned? I also want
> reform of teacher training. Let us return to basic subject teaching,
> not courses in the theory of education. Primary teachers should
> learn to teach children how to read, not waste their time on the
> politics of race, gender and class.
>
> (Major, 1993:144)

John Patten, then Secretary of State for Education, speaking to
the same conference proclaimed that: 'All too often the problems
in education lie – not with parents, not with teachers – but with
1960s theorists, with the trendy left and with the teachers union
bosses' (Patten, 1993:146). Conservative policy on
schooling and on education generally, can be seen as classically
'Thatcherite' (Hall & Jacques, 1983; Gamble, 1988; Jessop,
1990), that is to say, a populist amalgam of neo-liberal and neo-
conservative ideology and policy.[1]

At the micro-policy level, of policy towards schools, both neo-
liberals and neo-conservatives have common views on some
policies, but disagree on others.[2] For example a number of free
marketeers do actually consider the National Curriculum to be
unwarranted intervention by the state, (c.f. Flew, 1991), opposing any state legislation for and control over the school
curriculum as being inconsistent with the rolling back of the
state and with the full free play of market forces. However,

> In formal terms these two tendencies are contradictory and at
> points these contradictions have recognisable effects at the level of
> policy and action. In reality however, they generally complement
> each other, even to the extent of inhabiting the mind of the same
> individual.... Jointly they have popularised the most powerful
> theme of right-wing educational discourse: that the decades long
> quest for equality has resulted only in the lowering of standards.
> Cultural analysis of what Scruton has called 'the impractical
> utopian values that will destroy all that is most valuable in our
> culture', and free market assertion about 'the evils of state mono-
> poly combine' in an anti-egalitarian crusade.
>
> (Jones, 1989:38; c.f. Lawton, 1994)

At the macro-policy level it can be argued that both strands of radical Right ideology seek to perpetuate the interests of capital, untrammelled by strong trade unions, by professional restrictive practices, by an inclusivist welfare state, and by what they see as a permissive, non-work-orientated, unproductive culture. 'For both traditions the good society is best understood in terms of a strong state, free economy and stable families' (Barton *et al.*, 1994:532; see also Gamble, 1983:31–60; Hill, 1994a). In Gamble's words, 'If the New right has a unity and if it deserves to be distinguished from previous "rights" what sets it apart is the combination of a traditional liberal defence of state authority' (Gamble, 1983:28).[3]

The radical Right of the Conservative Party has viscerally abhorred two types of ideology, their associated school developments and their institutional support bases. The first target of their attack over a long period has been the liberal, progressivist ideology and credo most famously set out in the Plowden Report of 1967 (CACE, 1967), which was for so long, the claimed 'bible' of progressive primary education. This was commonly understood by both its protagonists and its antagonists to have espoused child-centredness, 'the integrated day', topic work, 'readiness' (e.g. reading readiness), 'relevance' (e.g. of the curriculum to working-class children in general and to Asian, black and other minority ethnic group children in general), the teacher as a guide to educational experiences rather than a distributor of knowledge, 'discovery learning', with little competitive testing, and an emphasis on co-operation and group work rather than competitiveness.[4]

The second target of radical Right wrath has been, and remains, the socialist, radical Left with its anti-elitism, support for comprehensive primary and secondary schooling, stress on democracy within classrooms and schools, and its stress on overtly critiquing and confronting racism, sexism, homophobia and social class inequalities in schooling and society.

Terms of abuse such as 'trendy', 'permissive' and 'caring' as features of 'The Blue Peter Curriculum' (O'Keeffe, 1990a, b, 1992; c.f. Anderson, 1982) are applied indiscriminately to both liberal progressive and to social egalitarian schooling. These frequently conflated attacks on liberal progressivism, on the one hand, and socialist ideas and policies in education, on the other, have a history stretching from 'The Black Papers' of the 1960s and 1970s (see Cox and Dyson, 1971, 1975; Cox and Boyson, 1977) through to the Hillgate Group publications of 1986, 1987 and 1989.[5]

The publication of *Quality and Equality* (Maude, 1968) and the Black Papers (the first three Black Papers are in Cox and Dyson, 1971) saw an aggressive attack on all aspects of progressive and comprehensive education:

> with horror stories about 'free play' in primary schools, the absence of control in comprehensive schools.
> They contained both a defence of the elitist, traditional liberal curriculum and an attack on the destabilising effects of progressivism – the discourse being generated here links education with traditional social and political values and with social order.
>
> (Ball, 1990b:24)

These onslaughts have been supplemented in the 1980s and 1990s by radical Right academics such as Dennis O'Keeffe, Anthony O'Hear, Antony Flew, Sheila Lawlor and Stuart Sexton. Their proscriptions and prescriptions have not only appeared, in books and pamphlets, at the academic level of ideological discourse, they have also been articulated at the media level of discourse – they have been given plenty of pretty much uncontested space in the right-wing broadsheet, middle-brow and tabloid press. They also had what appears to have been easy and frequent access, for a time in the late 1980s and early 1990s, to the *Times Educational Supplement.* These levels of discourse are in addition to the Ministerial level of discourse, examples of which started this chapter and when Chris Woodhead became Chief Inspector of schools, an official level of discourse.

Elsewhere in this book (chapter 4) the restructuring of schooling and the wider education system (especially teacher education and training) has been seen as a determined assault by a radical Right government on opposition ideologies in an attempt, as part of the 'culture wars' (Shor, 1986) to reassert its ideologically hegemonic position (see also Hill, 1989, 1990; Cole and Hill, 1995; Hill and Cole, 1995). In short, as far as the radical Right were concerned, some local education authorities (and institutions of teacher education and schools) were simply appearing to be too successful in developing, disseminating and reproducing liberal progressive values, or socialist egalitarian values. Much ire was expressed in particular against 'loony left' councils, in particular Brent, Haringey, Lambeth and the Inner London Education Authority (ILEA) with their anti-racist, anti-sexist, in the cases of Haringey and Brent, anti-heterosexist policies, and, in the case of the ILEA, anti-classist policies.[6]

In Chapter 3 some of the teachers from Culloden Hamlets set out some of their beliefs and school practices. These are teachers from Culloden Primary School in Tower Hamlets, a school which was pilloried by the *Daily Mail* and the *Mail on Sunday*, and by the then Minister of Education Kenneth Clarke, as an example of a progressive and egalitarian school failing its children. The school's policies and practice had previously been widely praised for the six-part television series in 1991 entitled 'Culloden – a year in the life of a Primary School'.

The neo-liberals

With its emphasis on the social morality of individual choice, competition, inequality, and neo-liberal economic policies, the 'free marketeers', the neo-liberal section of the radical Right in Britain, has been influenced in particular by the philosophy of Friedrich von Hayek (Gamble, 1983; Ball, 1990a). Neo-liberals stress the efficiency and increased production of wealth and profit that they believe results from competition. They therefore attack any group which stands in restraint of trade, believing that the application of market forces, competition, diversity of provision and freedom of choice by consumers will raise standards in areas of public social provision such as health and education as well as in the commercial sector.

The influence of Hayek on radical Right thinking in Britain, and the transmogrification of the educational implications of Hayek's theory into the 1988 Education Reform Act have been discussed in depth (Jones, 1989; Ball, 1990a, 1990b; Lawton, 1994; Whitty, 1994). Hayek's privatizing, marketeering, competitive, hierarchicalizing philosophy heavily influenced a whole range of policies of the radical Right Conservative governments in Britain (1979–95) through the use of neo-liberal think tanks such as the Centre for Policy Studies, the Adam Smith Institute, the Social Affairs Unit, and the Institute for Economic

Affairs. As Ken Jones points out, *The Omega File*, produced by the Adam Smith Institute in 1983–84, was 'the most systematic and influential work of the free market right' (Jones, 1989:46) and presented a blueprint for a reorganization of schooling based on market principles. It developed on the generally neo-conservative cultural restorationist anti-progressivism of the Black Papers on Education.[7]

The introduction of a diversity in schools, the setting up of a competitive market place in schools, the funding support given to private schools via the Assisted Places Scheme,[8] open enrolment, and the transference of a substantial percentage of funding and of powers away from local education authorities to 'consumers' are classic manifestations of neo-liberal, free market ideology. 'Ostensibly, at least, these represent a "rolling back" of central and local government's influence on what goes on in schools (Troyna, 1995:141). Whitty notes that,

> For the neo-liberal politicians who dominated educational policy making in Britain during much of the 1980s, social affairs are best organised according to the 'general principle of consumer sovereignty', which holds that each individual is the best judge of his or her needs and wants, and of what is in their best interests. The preference for introducing market mechanisms into education, partly from a predilection for freedom of choice as a good in itself, is also grounded in the belief that competition produces improvements in the quality of services on offer which in turn enhance the wealth producing potential of the economy, thereby bringing about gains for the least well off as well as for the socially advantaged.
>
> (Whitty, 1994:xx)

The neo-conservatives

The second radical right strain is neo-conservatism, which is socially and morally authoritarian, has an agenda of returning to some aspects of Victorian values and espouses a 'back to basics' philosophy. Apple refers to neo-conservatives as 'cultural restorationists' (Apple, 1989a, b). Luminaries include Roger Scruton, Caroline (Baroness) Cox, Rhodes Boyson, Frank Palmer and Ray Honeyford. They stress traditional values such as respect for authority and 'the nation', 'Britishness', the values of a social elite and the importance of a common culture, that of the elite. Neo-conservatives seek a disciplined society, a strong government, a Britain that veers selectively between Victoriana, and John Major's childhood recollections of a time of warm beer, cricket matches on the village green and golden sunsets. These ideologues criticize what they see as the destruction of 'traditional educational values', indeed, of 'traditional Britain'. The Hillgate Group (1986, 1987, 1988) have been strikingly influential, or, at least, predictive of government legislation – in particular on the National Curriculum.[9]

What is now becoming apparent is that there is a fourth level of discourse attacking progressive schooling and egalitarian schooling. This is at the level of official discourse. One example of this was the 'Three Wise Men's Report' on primary schooling (Alexander *et al.*, 1992), one of whose conclusions was that 'there is a persistent and damaging belief that teachers must never point out when a pupil is wrong' (quoted in Clarke, 1992). This was grist to the mill for the then Secretary of State for Education, Kenneth Clarke, whose response was to criticize,

the anti-academic, anti-intellectual eccentric views have permeated too many of our schools and must have contributed to the unacceptable variations in standards that our league tables are to expose.[10]

(Clarke, 1992)

The tone of comments by Chris Woodhead, since his appointment as the Chief Inspector of schools, is clearly different, more acerbic, and more in tune with Conservative government thinking than that of his predecessors. One example is his (unwarranted) assertion in 1995 that 'class size does not matter' in terms of teaching effectiveness.[11]

THE RADICAL RIGHT AND EDUCATION POLICY

This section will examine the effects on equality and inequality in British schooling resulting from the Education Reform Act of 1988 and other Conservative legislation since 1979. It will be argued that:

the last decade has seen some major changes in both the philosophy and implementation of an education appropriate for all children ... the national policy objectives of the early 1980s ... embodied an idealistic preoccupation with social justice ... but by the beginning of the 1990s they had been by-passed by a broader, mainstream drive to raise educational productivity through a return to the market place, and by a weakening of the advocacy of equal opportunities.

(Tomlinson and Craft, 1995a: Foreword)

Jones' view is typical of many (e.g. Simon, 1987, 1992; Davies *et al.*, 1992) when he suggests that the 1988 Act can be seen as, 'a fundamental attack on the policies of equal opportunity which developed in the thirty five years following the Education Act of 1944' (Jones, 1989:185).

Parental choice, and the market in schooling

In effect the introduction of a great diversity of types of school has resulted in the introduction of a market in children – the ability, in effect, of some schools (both grant maintained and LEA) to choose their type of intake. Two new types of school were introduced, grant maintained (or opted out) schools and city technology colleges. This was accompanied, in the Educational Reform Act (ERA) of 1988, by what was proclaimed to be 'parental choice' of schools through Open Enrolment of pupils and by Local Management of Schools, with its increased powers for school governors and head teachers.

Brian Simon (1987) suggested that the effect of the Education Reform Act would be to establish a more rigid three-tier hierarchy of schooling than already existed (Simon, 1987; reprinted in 1992). This hierarchy, he suggested, would now consist of public schools at the top (by and large for the children of the upper class); 'opted out' or grant maintained schools and city technology colleges (for the aspiring and the achievers, in particular for the middle class and those with what is assumed to be the gumption to escape from the clutches of bureaucratized, inefficient, and 'loony left' councils); and the bottom tier of schooling, the council estate, local authority schools for the majority. What choice would there be in this school marketplace – and for whom?

Richard Hatcher has pointed out that what is emerging is a more graded system than simply these three tiers. The market also exacerbates the already competitive hierarchy within categories or tiers of schooling. So, for example, church schools in working-class areas often become the highest status schools (Hatcher, 1995). Also, some grant maintained schools and city technology colleges are not in leafy suburban middle-class areas but in working-class areas – indeed CTCs were envisaged as being in the 'cities' (or at least, large towns). Here, just as with the Assisted Places scheme, the intention, and the effect of these schooling developments is to siphon off a key layer from the working class in a new structural way of separating out 'the deserving' from 'the undeserving' working class.

In his Education Bill of 1992, the serving Secretary of State for Education, John Patten, spoke of the problem of those who did not gain access to the school of their choice: 'Corresponding to the right for parents to opt out is the requirement that parents should be free to choose. I am not pretending that every parent or pupil can without waiting get the school of his or her choice – life is not like that' (DFE, 1992:2). He omitted, however, to articulate a response to parents and pupils who find themselves in such a position as he outlined. The Commission for Racial Equality (CRE) has commented on the effects of the 1988 ERA and GMS in particu-lar on Asian, black and other minority ethnic pupils, as follows:

> grant maintained schools might, once they were established, intro-
> duce discriminatory admissions criteria that exclude ethnic
> minority pupils; financial delegation to schools might result in a
> neglect of the particular needs of ethnic minority pupils, such as
> English as a second language; LEA equal opportunity and multi-
> racial education policies would no longer apply to schools that opt
> out.
>
> (CRE 1987; see also Davies *et al.*, 1992)

Since the implementation of the Act a considerable number of writers have highlighted inegalitarian and anti-egalitarian effects of the new schooling system. For example, Fitz *et al.* (1991:36–38) have pointed out that those actually making a choice within the new choice-driven system are the middle classes who have the money, transport and knowledge of the education system effectively to choose their children's schools. They also suggest that rather than producing and delivering parental choice, those schools which originally chose to opt out were already disproportionately academically selective. Their research suggests that grant maintained schooling has preserved and consolidated existing patterns of school choice rather than providing either new alternatives or wider consumer empower-ment (Fitz *et al.*, 1993; Power *et al.*, 1994).[12]

The abolition of the power of the local education authorities in determining admission to schools applies both to opted out schools and to those which have remained with the local education authority. In both cases Local Management of Schools (LMS) has included, for oversubscribed schools, the power to choose their new intake on grounds which, in some cases, have included obvious discrimination against working-class, African-Caribbean children and children with special needs. In the quest by schools to climb higher up in the assessment league tables, such children and their parents seem to lose out with uncanny statistical frequency.

The results of a five-year study in Scotland show that parental choice does little to improve the quality of education. The findings do show, however, that parental choice has increased segregation between working-class and middle-class children, concluding that it is probably having a detrimental effect on the school system (Young, 1992). This 'parental right of choice of school, embodied in the 1980 and 1988 Education Acts, is exacerbating "white flight" from schools attended by minority children' (Tomlinson and Craft, 1995a:4).

The reduction of LEA powers

For Troyna (1995) the 'two distinctive channels' of Conservative education policy, centralization and devolution, 'coalesce around the ... weakening, and ultimately dismantling of LEA influence' (Troyna 1995:142). One of the major results has been the 'systematic erosion of LEA responsibilities for providing the policy (and financial) co-ordinates for what takes place in schools' (ibid:140). Troyna is referring in particular to LEA policy frameworks for anti-racism. The same can be said of anti-sexist, anti-classist and anti-homophobic policy.

Turner *et al.* in their 1995 research report (for the Equal Opportunities Commission on the impact of recent educational reforms on gender equality in Scottish schools) emphasize the effects of the reduction of LEA policy-making, policy implementing and policy monitoring powers in more radical urban LEAs. They show that gender equal opportunities policies in the more radical LEAs, those whose policies they describe as 'transformative', have, in general, been put on the back burner by schools' governing bodies, who are less radical on such issues.

A further major anti-egalitarian result of the Education Reform Act has been the considerable diminution of Local Education Authorities' autonomy and freedom to decide their own spending priorities. This has considerably reduced funding (staff courses, resources) for policy advising, implementation and monitoring for curricular, cross-curricular and extra-curricular developments, as indeed for most other developments. It has also diminished LEA financial capability for assisting those schools in greatest need. Since the ERA was implemented, funding for schools has been overwhelmingly on a per capita basis with children at the plushest schools receiving the same per capita funding as schools in the poorest areas. Prior to the 1988 Act, LEAs were able to fund schools according to who needed it most with schools in socially and economically deprived areas receiving some extra funding. Prior to 1988, LEAs were able to supplement the number of teachers, and 'plussages' for ancillary help, books and repairs to buildings, for less favoured schools. The capacity for LEAs to give 'plussages',[13] to give extra cash to 'sink' schools and schools in areas of particular social need, has been substantially abolished. Under the legislative provisions for financial devolution to schools, schools have had what appears, at first sight only, to be equality of funding provision.[14]

Even disallowing for the special needs of some schools, LEAs can no longer, to any noticeable extent, supplement the income of the primary school which raises £300 per annum through the Parent-Teachers' Association and fund raising, compared to the primary school which raises £3,000 per annum. From 1995, 90 per cent of a school's budget is determined directly by the numbers and ages of its pupils. Such a result of LMS, the disallowing of major preferential funding, is 'disproportionately damaging to inner urban schools' (Guy and Menter, 1992:65).[15]

THE NATIONAL CURRICULUM[16]

The ERA involved the establishment of the National Curriculum so that no matter the levels to which market-driven educational inequality would rise, cultural uniformity in the state sector would be maintained. The National Curriculum itself (both the 1988 and the Dearing 1995 revised version) can be seen as 'a bureaucratic device for exercising control over what goes on in schools' (Lawton and Chitty, 1987:5). It asserts the centrality of particular definitions of national culture – against the increasing tendencies to both ethnic and social class pluralism/ multiculturalism[17] that were at work in schools.

The DES blueprint for the curriculum, hastily devised in 1987, is subject based. Any area of educational experience which falls outside its subject framework has faced neglect: thus careers and health education, or multi-culturalism, let alone more radical forms of egalitarian education, have found it difficult to secure a stable place. The National Curriculum is driven more by a project of cultural homogeneity that by the rhetoric of equal opportunity. It is now more and more plainly the embodiment of a Conservative vision of a national culture. This shift owes much to the work done by the radical Right since the Education Reform Act of 1988. Having originally found itself excluded from influence on curriculum and testing arrangements, the radical Right has since been able to work itself into a central, powerful position. Activists of the radical Right – such as Martin Turner, John Marenbon and John Marks – were appointed to the National Curriculum Council and SEAC or its sub-committees and to its replacement Schools Curriculum and Assessment Authority (SCAA) (see Simon, 1992; Graham, 1992, 1993a and 1993b; Lawton, 1994). Ministers such as Tim Eggar, Michael Fallon and John Patten adopted many of the points of view on the curriculum associated with the Right.

This particular shift of emphasis achieved by the radical Right required a consistent and controversial overruling of 'professional' opinion (Jones, 1989; Graham, 1992; Lawton, 1994; Tomlinson and Craft, 1995b). In this conflict, the arbitrary powers awarded to the Secretary of State by the 1988 Act became all too visible. History has been brought to a stop at 1972, lest more recent history become a licence for radical approaches (Graham, 1992); Science has been redefined in a way that jettisons curricular attention to the social implications of scientific activity (Dobson, 1992); English has been reorganized so as to give priority to the Right's main cultural themes, which involve making fetishes out of 'Standard English', a literary canon, 'traditional grammar' and spelling. Indeed various of the chapters in this book refer to this political selection of knowledge in particular subject areas.

The dominant curriculum approach, moreover, is not only subject-based, it is content led: issues connected with the learning process are not adequately explored. One of the several debilitating consequences of this method is that issues which had implications for the ways in which different groups of students related to the formal, organized knowledge of the school are not explored: 'equal opportunities' issues, whether related to 'race', gender, class, disability and special needs, and to sexuality have never been prominent. The result is not simply that particular areas of content are incomplete, but that quite basic issues concerning the relationship between curriculum and learner, formal education and student cultures are left unexplored. Yet without such a development, progress towards 'higher educational standards' by large numbers of school pupils/students is likely to be impeded.

THE REVISED NATIONAL CURRICULUM OF 1995

Have the 1995 Dearing revisions of the National Curriculum, the 'slimming down', and the five-year moratorium on further changes to the National Curriculum, served to allay curriculum concern? They do not answer the detailed criticisms made in the various subject by subject chapters of this book. It is worth emphasizing this point. In terms of the analyses put forward by the various chapters the Dearing revisions of the national Curriculum have not improved it. Furthermore, though superficially attractive, the Dearing proposals do, in fact, create problems of their own.

> The emphasis on a core curriculum and on the essentials of foundation subjects brings the danger that the curriculum will become even more traditional and safe. That is, unless schools and teachers can be persuaded to use these promised reductions in the compulsory curriculum to pursue multi-cultural and anti-racist goals. Significantly, the final Dearing Report makes no mention of multicultural education at all.
>
> (King and Mitchell, 1995:20)

Thus, the changes the radical Right have sponsored have introduced strong elements of instability into important areas of the curriculum. The writings of modern radical Right Conservatives make much of their commitment to 'community', 'history', 'culture' and 'identity'. But these terms are constructed in a highly selective way, which tends to overlook present conflicts and diversity in favour of an imagined cultural unity. Their stress on 'pastness' makes it difficult for them to offer an educational response to the 'modern' aspects of contemporary culture. The whole area of media studies, for instance, is virtually a closed book to Conservatives, except for a curious refusal to allow the study of 'Neighbours' (Patten, 1993). The cultural plurality of contemporary society is likewise an issue from which the Right recoils – yet it is a fact that thousands of schools are scarcely able to avoid.

ASSESSMENT

The problem is made more acute by the place assumed by assessment in the overall shape of the National Curriculum. From the beginning, the structure of the National Curriculum has been strongly influenced by the need to allow frequent testing and to communicate test results in a very simplified way, so that they can provide the data to construct a 'league table' of school performance. It is now plain that testing has assumed not just an important but a dominant role in determining the shape of the whole. The complex activity-based approach initially suggested by the Task Group on Attainment and Testing (TGAT) was replaced by a model which assigns little importance to teachers' continuous assessment of students, and a great deal of importance to end-of-term, 'pencil and paper' testing. It is unlikely that these changes will benefit groups of students traditionally disadvantaged by 'formal' methods of teaching and testing.

There is a genuine concern that testing at the age of 11 will encourage the reintroduction (or intensification) of streaming arrangements for 7- to 11-year-olds, thereby marking a return to the immediate post-war period when the eleven-plus examination sorted children into grammar schools, secondary modern schools or (a few) technical schools.

It is also noteworthy that the Dearing Report fails to clarify the purposes of testing, the issue over which many teachers have carried out one of the most successful pieces of industrial action in recent years. Many classroom teachers believe strongly that the school curriculum should not be determined by testing arrangements. Assessment of pupils is necessary to diagnose and facilitate the progress of each individual, but it seems clear that current testing arrangements are intended more to monitor schools and teachers than to support pupils.

However the introduction of the National Curriculum and assessment has had some positive effects. Gipps and Stobart (1993) point out that the summer 1991 tests for 7-year-olds had beneficial effects in many schools in raising teachers' expectations of their pupils and improving lessons. Most teachers did learn more about their pupils and were able to adjust their classroom teaching methods accordingly. They discovered gaps in the curriculum, with areas such as capital letters and simple punctuation discovered to have been neglected. The government has always claimed that the tests would uncover shortcomings and enable them to be rectified. In most schools the SAT experience had given the staff food for thought, and many teachers were seriously considering changing their practice in some way. This was only rarely 'teaching to the test', more often it was the result of being offered a wider model of teaching and the curriculum. The government's view is that:

> Providing access to performance information on a consistent basis is essential to inform choice and drive up standards. None of us should underestimate the way in which the information revolution spearheaded by performance tables has helped to focus us all on achievement and outcomes.
>
> Arguably, openness on performance data is one of the most important prerequisites for school improvement. Last year's British Social Attitudes survey reported that the overwhelming majority of people supported the publication of secondary school exam results. Performance tables are here to stay.
>
> (DFEE, 1995)

However, Jo Boaler has pointed out 'the performance of pupils on tests is being used to judge schools, without any consideration of the intake of schools. Thus the wealthiest state schools with the highest ability intakes are appearing as better schools, even though they may have done nothing to enhance the performance of pupils' (personal communication, 1995).

The cumulative effect of this dogma-driven system is to make the National Curriculum vulnerable to the very danger which its original invention was designed to avoid: the perpetuation of low levels of achievement and becoming the object of permanent controversy. Traditional curricula, formal testing, a hostility to child-centred education and a preference for early selection are a sort of fantasy solution to the problems of mass education. They will probably lead to various forms of what could broadly be termed pupil 'resistance' by those relatively disfranchised and excluded: disenchantment, a sense of failure expressing itself in passive or actual withdrawal from lessons, 'disobedience'. They will also tend to lead to a further decline in the morale of teachers, as their commitments are frustrated, their autonomy reduced and their conflicts with students sharpened. Far from being an authoritative, hegemonic solution to long-standing curriculum problems, the National Curriculum will be seen, overall, as the imposition of a narrow, partisan and regressive programme.

Intentions and effects of the Education Reform Act of 1988 and subsequent Conservative policy on schooling

I would argue that the essential intention of Government policy is to increase class differentiation, that is, to increase differences between and within the social classes. In this enterprise I would argue that it is not essentially the intention to demarcate and intensify gender and racial differentiation more rigidly. A caveat here regarding 'race' is the linking of African-Caribbean with working-class location, and some South Asian (though not Bangladeshi ethnicity) with potential or actual middle-class location. In other words the racialized nature of the class system needs to be recognized. I recognize that since most members of Asian, black and other minority ethnic group communities are working class in socio-economic terms, then they are thereby disproportionately affected by increased social class differentiation. They are, of course, also affected, by personal and structural racism, just as girls and women are affected by personal and structural sexism.

Whether or not there has been a 'genderquake' in education and at work is a matter of current controversy. With regard to girls' education there have been undeniable improvements in examination performance relative to boys at GCSE and A level.[18] Girls in general are now getting better academic results than boys. Weiner (1995) and Arnot *et al.* (1995) emphasize that changes in girls' exam results are not reflected in the economy and in the labour market. In this they are partially, but only partially, correct (as they would recognize). Girls are finding it easier than boys to get jobs in unskilled and semi-skilled occupations (Panorama, 1995), in particular work which is part-time and low paid.[19] In full-time, highly paid work, there is a 'glass ceiling' on women achieving positions of power in most sectors of the labour market. Indeed, there are many facets of sexism in schools, too, within the hidden curriculum, for example, see Measor and Sikes, 1992, with recent specific data given in Cole *et al.* (1994) and Grima and Smith (1993).

To look at intention of any policy or series of policies is not the same as looking at actual or likely effects. I would argue that the actual and likely effects of the 1988 Education Reform Act and Conservative schools policy since 1979 are indeed to increase social class differentiation, but that, with regard to (declassed) gender, the effect, not least of the legally enforceable National Curriculum (with Maths, Science and Technology being compulsory and assessed, for girls as well as for boys) is actually to reduce gender differentiation. On a declassed basis (once the class factor has been removed), by diminishing race-based stereotyping of subject choices, it may also serve to reduce race differentiation. However, there are other race-related aspects/effects of government schools policy. As Chris Gaine has pointed out:

> schools choosing pupils not only operates against working class children but also against other groups often stereotyped as 'difficult' (such as African-Caribbean boys) or 'expensive' (such as pupils for whom English is a second language). This together with 'white flight' from 'black' or 'Asian' schools, can combine a racialised hierarchy of schools with the class based hierarchy referred to throughout this chapter. In connection with this it is worth noting the cultural effects of the National Curriculum. In effect success is offered to middle class Asian and black pupils in a white nationalist curriculum.
>
> (personal communication, 1995)

However, it is important to place the effects of the Education Reform Act and National Curriculum in the context of what else is going on in schooling – such as the major increase in class sizes during the 1990s. Duncan Graham, formerly chair and chief executive of the National Curriculum Council, has (among many others) claimed that the National Curriculum could not be delivered properly in classes of more than 35, and that when the National Curriculum was introduced in 1988 in England and Wales the assumption was that classes would be around 25 (Macleod, 1995).[20]

It is also important to place the positive effects of the National Curriculum in the context of the big picture of what else is going on in social policy and society generally (c.f. Hill and Cole, 1995),[21] that is to say, within the context of the increased impoverishment of the poorest in society, the increased enrichment, in particular, of the richest, and the assaults on the social wage and the welfare state set out in the Introduction.[22]

Resistance: subverting/converting the National Curriculum

King and Mitchell note that: 'There are many places where enterprising teachers are using the National curriculum to help pupils explore the riches and deficiencies of our complex social world, and to increase the life chances of all their pupils. Yet there is a fundamental difference between what is mandatory and what is obligatory and what is permissive and optional' (King and Mitchell 1995:29). There is no doubt that equal opportunities work and radical egalitarian work in primary schools has been constrained. As Richard Hatcher has noted:

> What was crucial about equal opportunities in the 70s/80s was that a 'vanguard' of progressive teachers had been able to reach a much wider layer of teachers in the 'middle ground' – the role of *LEAs* and *school* policies was important here, and so was the prevalence of *working groups* on equal opportunities as school and LEA levels – these were the key organisational form feeding equal opportunities into the wider arena. ERA has drastically attenuated this *link* between 'vanguard' and masses [sic!] and one key way has been work overhauled. Once we had equal opportunities working groups in schools, now we have National Curriculum or SATs working groups, or none. This has been a major material factor – many equal opportunity activists have become preoccupied with other

issues now deemed more important or are suffering from National Curriculum and Assessment overload.

> (personal communication, 1995; c.f. Turner *et al.*, 1995 specifically in respect of gender)

The Dearing model of 1995 pays even less importance to cross-curricular issues such as equal opportunities work. In addition to being ascribed cross-curricular status, equal opportunities work remains non-mandatory and is often ill-defined. Sharing cross-curricular space with a number of other themes such as Economic and Industrial Awareness squeezes the potential of equal opportunities work. The Dearing Review – the revised National Curriculum – does, however, open up more space for such work by cutting back on the time demands of the formal National Curriculum, and there are sources of legitimation for such as this.

A number of the cross-curricular themes (Health Education, Careers and Guidance Education, Environmental Education, Citizenship Education and Economic and Industrial Awareness) in fact, can serve as a powerful legitimation of equal opportunities work in primary schools (c.f. Verma and Pumfrey, 1994). So too can the Office for Standards in Education (OFSTED). The following extract from the OFSTED *Handbook for the Inspection of Schools* (1993) gives some indication of the degree of Equal Opportunities organisation and planning now required from schools:

7.3 (ii) Equality of Opportunity

Evaluation criteria

The school's arrangements for equality of opportunity are evaluated by the extent to which:

- all pupils, irrespective of gender, ability (including giftedness), ethnicity and social circumstance, have access to the curriculum and make the greatest progress possible;
- the school meets the requirements of the Sex Discrimination Act (1975) and the Race Relations Act (1976).

Evidence should include:

a standards of achievement of individuals and groups;
b assessment of pupils' needs within the curriculum;
c the school's stated policy for equal opportunity;

d admission policies, intake, exclusions;
e curriculum content and access;
f class organisation and management, teaching and differentiation;
g the use made of support teachers, bilingual assistants and other
   provision under section 11 of the Local Government Act 1966;
h pupils' relationships.

(OFSTED, 1994)[23]

However, the Runnymede Trust among others has issued a 'state-ment of concern' about 'equal opportunities and the inspection of schools'. Its work in compiling *Equality Assurance in Schools* (1993) and from a research study of the first fifty OFSTED reports published in 1994, gives cause for concern about the efficacy of this aspect of OFSTED's work. The Runnymede Trust's judgement is that 'Ofsted reports were very unsatisfactory in their treatment of equality issues in the schools inspected' (Runnymede Trust, 1995:2). Despite this caveat about OFSTED inspections, there is no doubt that its impending visit and printed requirements, such as those set out above, can act as a powerful tool for equal opportunities work in schools.

CONCLUSION

The National Curriculum and other 'equiphobic' Conservative legislation and campaigns have not stopped teachers 'doing equal opportunities' and 'teaching social justice and equality'. Spaces are still there and tens of thousands of primary school teachers are still 'doing it'. The various chapters in this book and its companion (Hill *et al.*, 1997), books such as those by Gaine (1987, 1995a), Cole (1989a, b), the Hillcole Group (1991, 1996), Runnymede Trust (1993), George (1993) and hundreds of short articles in journals such as *Forum* (for the promotion of 3–19 comprehensive education) *Multicultural Teaching, Education for Today and Tomorow, Socialist Teacher* and *NUT Education Review* are testimony to the work being carried out. So too, for example, are the local Equal Opportunities Support Group meetings of teachers, such as that in Crawley (in which some of the contributors to this book have been involved), and local conferences such as the 1995 confer-ence on education 'Success in the City', organized by Rehana

Minhas and colleagues for Haringey LEA. Egalitarian teachers have not disappeared, nor has the need for them and for social justice in primary schools and in society.

This book is both an attempt to use the options and spaces that exist in the current National Curriculum, in the pursuit of a more egalitarian schooling and society. It is also an attempt to render issues of equal opportunities and equality both mandatory and obligatory. It is also, in effect, a call for a subsequent consultative rewriting of a national Common Curriculum to replace the existing Conservative Curriculum.

ACKNOWLEDGEMENTS

I would like to thank Jo Boaler, Clyde Chitty, Mike Cole, Chris Gaine, Richard Hatcher, Ken Jones, Michele Lloyd and Gaby Weiner for their comments on/assistance with this chapter. Any inadequacies are, however, mine and these acknowledgements do not necessarily signify total agreement with this chapter.

NOTES

1 There have been many books and articles describing, analysing and critiquing the effect of Thatcherism and the radical Right on schooling, the wider education system and teacher education. (See, for example, Chitty, 1989; Chapter 2 in Hessari and Hill, 1989; Hill, 1989, 1990, 1994b, 1994c; Jones, 1989; Ball, 1990a; Knights, 1990; Wragg, 1991; Whitty, 1993, 1994; Barton *et al.*, 1994; Hillcole Group, 1994, 1996; Lawton, 1994). Knights analyses radical Right influence on education policy from a radical Right perspective.

2 Not only is there tension between these two wings of the radical Right, but there is also tension between these two strains and 'the moderate right'. The moderate right includes the Conservative Education Association, a number of leading local education authority Conservatives who have opposed the marketization of schooling and some moderate Conservative MPs such as Sir Malcolm Thornton, Chair of the House of Commons Select Committee on Education.

Lawton calls this group 'the pluralists', as opposed to the neo-liberal 'privatizers' and the authoritarian 'minimalists' (Lawton, 1994). However, such 'moderate' views on schooling 'reforms' have, effectively, been sidelined. The views of Conservative MP Sir Malcolm Thornton on grant maintained schools are scathing. 'The concept of Grant-Maintained schools owes more, in my view, to the antipathy of national government to local authorities than to finding the best way to improve education in this country' (Thornton, 1993:172). The defection to Labour by former Conservative Junior Education Minister Alan Howarth, in October 1995, was occasioned by his disquiet at radical Right control over social policy such as education.

3 This is discussed and examined, for example, in Gamble (1983); Jones (1989); Chitty (1989); *TES* (1989); Menter (1992); Elliott and MacLennan (1994).

4 Neville Bennett contrasted characteristics of 'progressive' (he might well have used the term 'liberal-progressive') and 'traditional' (he might well have used the term 'conservative') schooling in his *Teaching Styles and Pupil Progress* (Bennett, 1975:30).

5 This genealogy is charted, for example, in Jones (1989), Cole (1992) and in Lawton (1994).

6 The ILEA produced two major reports in the 1980s investigating the extent of working-class underachievement and detailing policy responses to combat it. As the then largest local education authority in Western Europe its resources were substantial and the 'Thomas Report' on Primary Schooling (ILEA, 1985) (and the 'Hargreaves Report' on Secondary Schooling (ILEA, 1984)) may be regarded as a major contribution to the debate on and proposals for a schooling system that is more egalitarian in terms of social class. The 'Thomas Report' on primary schools was summarized in the *Times Educational Supplement*, 18 Janury 1985. (The 'Hargreaves Report' was summarized in the *TES*, 23 March 1984). The recommendations of the 'Thomas Report' are radically different from those enacted by Conservative governments – in particular with its concern that schools should be community schools.

7 The Black Papers are described by Jones as 'the first popular

and effective critique of the post-war welfare state' (Jones, 1989:41).

8 The Assisted Places Scheme (APS) was introduced as part of the 1980 Education Act. It gave and continues to give public funding subsidies to some (public) private schools for 'academic' pupils whose parents cannot afford the full fees. It has been evaluated in Whitty *et al.* (1989b). Doubling the number of children on the APS was the main educational initiative announced by Prime Minister John Major at the October 1995 Conservative Party Conference.

9 See Hessari and Hill (1989); Jones (1989); Menter (1992); Massey (1991); Cole (1992); Hill (1994b).

10 Rhodes Boyson, in a *Sunday Times* reaction to this 'Three Wise Men's Report' which demonized the Plowden Report [CACE, 1967] as 'The Great Betrayal', commented:

> The whole emphasis on individual learning and children discovering things for themselves was wrong. If children could discover things for themselves, then what's the point in having schools? It destroyed the status of the teacher. If children can discover things for themselves, then the teacher becomes a group leader rather than someone who has to pass on knowledge.
> *(Sunday Times,* 1992)

11 This assertion, and reactions to it are set out in the *Times Educational Supplements,* 10 November 1995 and 17 November 1995. See in particular Passmore (1995), Bassey (1995) and the letters pages.

12 They also suggest that (at least thus far) opting out is not at the moment resulting in the new hierarchy of institutions predicted by Simon (1987) and Walford and Miller (1991). Edwards and Whitty (1992) had suggested that a market in schooling would reflect and reinforce existing patterns of socio-economic stratification. Power *et al.* (1994:31) have found no evidence of this. My own evaluation of Power *et al.*'s research is that it is early days yet and that other research over a longer term does indeed show not simply a consolidation of existing patterns of school choice but, instead, the likelihood of increased stratification of schooling over the long term. The market in education per se has had the various other negative effects on equality set out below in the main text.

13 'Plussages' are extra funding (for example, for staff or for

other resources which LEAs would allocate to schools on the basis of indicators of socio-economic deprivation and educational need. Such factors included the percentage of children in receipt of free school meals and the percentage of children whose mother tongue was not English. While LEAs retain some such redistributive ability, their financial scope for so doing is far more limited than before the ERA.

14 This allocation of funding to schools based on a universalizing principle, 'derives from a commitment to "horizontal equity" [Dixon, 1991], characteristic of liberal versions of equality of opportunity. Here, rules which are procedurally just and equitable are established, and inequality of outcome is predominant and inevitable [Turner, 1986]' (Troyna, 1995).

15 In Hill (1990b) I suggest that Local Management of Schools (LMS) could actually be used as a form of democratic workers control, through staff decision-making, to empower education workers. At the moment there is not much sign of this happening. Large pay rises for headteachers appear far more common.

16 This section on the National Curriculum draws on the section of the same name in the 1993 Hillcole Group booklet, *Falling Apart: The Coming Crisis of Conservative Education.* Ken Jones was the key influence on that section.

17 Although it is not common to do so I am using this term 'ethnic and social class pluralism/multiculturalism' to emphasize that social class cultures and subcultures are pluralistic and differ from each other as well as the cultures of different ethnic/religious groups – themselves fractured into different social classes.

18 The 1995 GCSE and A level results show that 'Girls race ahead in the classroom' (Brace, 1995). Among girls 43.8 per cent achieved five or more grades A* to C compared with 33.8 per cent of boys. 'Girls are even holding their own in the traditionally male dominated areas of maths and science. In science they were only half a percent behind and in maths they were level pegging' (ibid.). In some subjects girls' performance is far better than boys'. For example in English Language GCSE 65.9 per cent of girls achieved a top grade (A* to C) compared to 41.3 per cent of boys. At A level 68 per cent of girl entrants gained two or more A levels compared

with 63.5 per cent of boys (ibid.).

19 The extent of the 'genderquake', with girls now outperform-
ing boys at GCSE, A level and university have been widely
referred to. The think tank 'Demos' talks of an historic
change in relations between men and women due to structural change in the labour market – the decline of
manufacturing (traditionally men's) jobs from 31 per cent of
workers in 1979 to 20 per cent in 1993, and the growth in
service industry (traditionally women's) jobs from 58 per
cent to 67 per cent in the same period. However this 'restructuring of British Capitalism' has entailed a shift from
full-time and secure jobs to part-time and insecure ones.
Women part-timers in manual jobs earn 73 per cent of the
hourly rate of equivalent full-time women workers. It is
mainly because women are segregated in low-paid, part-time
jobs that they still only earn 72 per cent of men's wages,
£100 a week in money terms (data from *Militant
International Review*, 1995). This has recently led the Equal
Opportunities Commission's report *Targeting Potential
Discrimination* to call again for employers to introduce equal
opportunities. *Militant International Review* has pointed out:

> For some better qualified women the 'genderquake' has meant
> opportunities to break into higher skilled, higher paid jobs
> previously dominated by men. Women in their early 30s now
> earn 90% of the wages of men of the same age, although once
> they start to have children, the gap begins to widen again.
> However, for the vast majority of working class women equal-
> ity is not, unfortunately, just around the corner.
>
> (*Militant International Review*, 1995:10)

See also Moore, 1996.

20 The number of primary age children in England taught by a
single teacher in classes of more than 40 went up from
14,057 in January 1994 to 18,223 in Janury 1995. In January
1995 the number in classes of 36 or more taught by a single
teacher rose by 11 per cent over the year to 107,985 while
1,155,726 primary children were in classes of 31 or more
(Carvel and Wintour, 1995).

21 The analysis of Cole and Hill is an attempt to amend cultur-
alist/humanist Marxist analyses of schooling and economic/
social/ideological reproduction, which were prominent in the

1980s (Hill, 1994c; Cole and Hill, 1995; Hill and Cole, 1995). Cole and Hill seek to revert to a more structuralist analysis of the 1970s drawing, though not uncritically, on Louis Althusser and his essay *Schooling as Ideological State Apparatus* (1971). Such accounts as those of Hill and Cole recognize the structural constraints on effective oppositional egalitarian action but also recognize spaces for human agency and 'resistance'. Hill, following, to an extent, Giroux (1983, 1988) and Giroux and McLaren (1989) calls for teachers to act as 'transformative intellectuals'. See Chapter 4 of this book for a development of this concept (also Hill 1994b, 1996).

22 This polarization of society, with its increased class differentiation, has been described as a 'two-nation hegemonic project'. As part of this project the Conservative government has, in effect, ceased claiming to be pursuing a 'one-nation-project' and, instead, vilifies, scapegoats, and punishes the 'undeserving outsiders' (Gamble, 1983, 1988; Hall, 1983, 1985; Jessop, 1990). In this project, the ideological state apparatuses of education (Althusser, 1971) can be seen as but one of a set of ideological and repressive state apparatuses, albeit an important set (see Hill, 1994a; Hill and Cole, 1995).

23 There are many sources of legitimation for teaching, just as there are many sources of delegitimation. The agencies of the state do not always run in harmony with each other. There are disarticulations and resistances at various sites in the vertical 'chain of command' from Ministry to classroom. Indeed horizontal disarticulations and disagreements between, for example, different parts of the educational state apparatuses (c.f. Dale, 1989; Jessop, 1990; Whitty, 1993; Hill, 1994a; Hill and Cole, 1995). One agency which can confer considerable legitimation for progressive and radical egalitarian work in schools is OFSTED.

REFERENCES

Alexander, R., Woodhead, C. and Rose, J. (1992) *The Three Wise Men's Report*. London: DES.

Althusser, L. (1971) Ideology and Ideological state apparatuses. In L. Althusser (ed.) *Lenin and Philosophy and other Essays.* London: New Left Books.

Anderson, D. (1982) *Detecting Bad Schools: A Guide for Normal Parents.* London: Social Affairs Unit.

Apple, M. (1989a) Critical introduction: ideology and the state in educational policy. In R. Dale (ed.), *The State and Education Policy.* Milton Keynes: Open University Press.

Apple, M. (1989b) How equality has been redefined in the conservative restoration. In W. Secada (ed.), *Equity in Education.* London: Falmer Press.

Arnot, M., David, M. and Weiner, G. (1995) A new era? New contexts for gender equality in school, part 1. Paper delivered to the British Educational Association Annual Conference, University of Bath.

Ball, S. (1990a) *Markets, Morality and Equality in Education.* London: Tufnell Press.

Ball, S. (1990b) *Politics and Policy Making in Education: Explorations in Policy Sociology.* London: Routledge.

Ball, S. and Bowe, R. with Gold, A. (1991) *Reforming Education and Changing Schools.* London: Routledge.

Barton, L., Barrett, E., Whitty, G., Miles, S. and Furlong, J. (1994) Teacher education and teacher professionalism in England: some emerging issues. *British Journal of Sociology of Education*, 15(4):529–44.

Bassey, M. (1995) Inspectors ask the wrong questions. *Times Educational Supplement.* 17 November.

Bennett, S. N. (1976) *Teaching Styles and Pupil Progress.* London: Open Books.

Black, P. (1993) The shifting scenery of the National Curriculum. In C. Chitty and B. Simon (eds) *Education Answers Back: Critical Responses to Government Policy.* London: Lawrence and Wishart.

Brace, A. (1995) Girls race ahead in the classroom. *Mail on Sunday*, 19 November.

CACE (Central Advisory Council for Education) (1967) *Children and their Primary Schools* (The Plowden Report). London: HMSO.

Carvel, J. and Wintour, P. (1995) Huge rise in primary classes of 40-plus. *Guardian*, 25 October.

Chitty, C. (1989) *Towards a New Education System: The Victory of the New Right.* London: Lawrence and Wishart.

Chitty, C. (1995) Comments on a draft of this chapter.

Clarke, K. (1992) Education's insane bandwagon finally goes into the ditch: an ideology's demise allows common sense to return to schools. *Sunday Times*, 26 January.

Cole, A., Conlon, T., Jackson, S. and Welch, D. (1994) Information technology and gender: problems and proposals. *Gender and Education*, 6(1):77–85.

Cole, M. (ed.) (1989a) *Education for Equality: Some Guidelines for Good Practice.* London: Routledge.

Cole, M. (ed.) (1989b) *The Social Contexts of Schooling.* London: Falmer Press.

Cole, M. (1992) Racism, history and educational policy: from the origins of the Welfare State to the rise of the radical Right. Unpublished PhD thesis, Department of Sociology, University of Essex.

Cole, M. and Hill, D. (1995) Games of despair and rhetorics of resistance: postmodernism, education and reaction. *British Journal of Sociology of Education* 16(2).

Commission for Racial Equality (1987) *Press Release 264.* London: CRE.

Cox, B. and Dyson, A. (1971) *The Black Papers on Education – A Revised Edition.* London: Maurice Temple Smith.

Cox, B. and Boyson, R. (eds) (1977) *Black Paper 1977.* London: Maurice Temple Smith.

Cox, B. (1992) *The Great Betrayal.* London: Chapmans.

Dale, R. (1989a) *The State and Education Policy.* Milton Keynes: Open University Press.

Davies, A.M., Holland, J. and Minhas, R. (1992) *Equal Opportunities in the New Era*, second edn. London: Tufnell Press.

Department for Education (DFE) (1992) Secretary of State's Second Reading speech. *DFE News*, 363/92, 9 November.

Department for Education and Employment (DFEE) (1995) Schools Minister Robin Squire addresses the Secondary Heads Association. *DFEE News*, 234/95, 18 October.

Dixon, R. (1991) Repercussions of LMS. *Educational Management and Administration* 19(1).

Dobson, K. (1992) *Guardian*, 21 March.

Edwards, T. and Whitty, G. (1992) Parental choice and educational reform in Britain and the United States. *British Journal of Educational Studies* 50(2):101–17.

Elliot, G. and MacLennan, D. (1994) Education, modernity and neo-Conservative school reform in Canada, Britain and the USA. *British Journal of Sociology of Education*, 15(2):165–86.

Equal Opportunities Commission (1995) *Targeting Potential Discrimination.* Manchester: EOC.

Fitz, J. Halpin, D. and Power, S. (1991) Grant maintained schools: a third force in education. *Forum* 33(2).

Fitz, J., Power, S. and Halpin, D. (1993) Opting for grant-maintained studies: a study of policy making in Britain. *Policy Studies Journal* 14(1):4–20.

Flew, A. (1991) Educational services: independent competition or maintained monopoly. In D. Green (ed.) *Empowering the Parents: How to Break the Schools Monopoly.* London: Institute of Economic Awareness Health and Welfare Unit.

Gaine, C. (1987) *No Problem Here.* London: Hutchinson.

Gaine, C. (1995) *Still No Problem Here.* Stoke-on-Trent: Trentham Books.

Gamble, A. (1983) Thatcherism and conservative politics. In S. Hall and M. Jacques (eds) *The Politics of Thatcherism.* London: Macmillan.

Gamble, A. (1988) *The Free Economy and the Strong State: The Politics of Thatcherism.* London: Macmillan

George, R. (1993) *A Handbook on Equal Opportunities in Schools: Principles, Policy and Practice.* Harlow: Longman.

Gipps, C. and Stobart, G. (1993) *Assessment: A Teacher's Guide to the Issues.* London: Hodder and Stoughton.

Giroux, H. (1983) *Theory and Resistance in Education: A Pedagogy for the Opposition.* London: Heinemann

Giroux, H. (1988) *Teachers as Intellectuals: Towards a Critical Pedagogy of Learning.* Granby, Massachusetts: Bergin and Garvey.

Giroux, H. and McLaren, P. (1989) *Critical Pedagogy, the State and Cultural Struggle.* New York: State University of New York Press.

Graham, D. (1992) *Guardian*, 13 October.

Graham, D. (1993a) *A Lesson For Us All: The Making of the National Curriculum.* London: Routledge.

Graham, D. (1993b) Reflections on the first four years. In M. Barber and D. Graham (eds) *Sense, Nonsense and the National Curriculum.* London: Falmer Press.

Grima, G. and Smith, A. (1993) Participation in home economics. *Gender and Education* 5(3):251–68.

Guy, W. and Menter, I. (1992) Local management: who benefits? In D. Gill, B. Mayor and M. Blair (eds) *Racism and Education: Structures and Strategies.* London: Sage.

Hall, S. (1983) The great moving right show. In S. Hall and M. Jacques (eds) *The Politics of Thatcherism.* London: Lawrence and Wishart.

Hall, S. and Jacques, M. (eds) (1983) *The Politics of Thatcherism.* London: Lawrence and Wishart in association with *Marxism Today.*

Hart, D. (1994) Speech report. *Times Educational Supplement,* 10 June.

Hessari, R. and Hill, D. (1989) *Practical Approaches to Multicultural Learning and Teaching in the Primary Classroom.* London: Routledge.

Hill, D. (1989) *Charge of the Right Brigade.* Brighton: Institute for Education Policy Studies.

Hill, D. (1990a) *Something Old, Something New, Something Borrowed, Something Blue.* London: Tufnell Press.

Hill, D. (1990b) A little local difficulty – local management of schools. *New Socialist,* 69.

Hill, D. (1994a) *Britain Today: Capitalist (Teacher-) Education or Postmodern (Teacher-) Education.* Paper presented at the British Educational Association Annual Conference, Oxford University.

Hill, D. (1994b) Initial Teacher Education and Cultural Diversity. In G. Verma and P. Pumfrey (eds) *Cultural Diversity and the Curriculum, vol. 4: Cross-Curricular Contexts, Themes and Dimensions in Primary Schools.* London: Falmer Press.

Hill, D. (1994c) Teacher education, radical right and radical left. *Forum for the Promotion of 3–18 Comprehensive Education,* 36(3).

Hill, D. (1996) Reflection in teacher education. In K. Watson, C. Modgil and S. Modgil (eds) *Education Dilemmas: Debate and Diverstiy, vol. 1: Teacher Education and Training.* London: Cassell.

Hill, D. and Cole, M. (1995) Marxist state theory and state autonomy theory: the case of 'race' education in initial teacher education. *Journal of Education Policy,* 10(2).

Hill, D., Cole, M. and Shan, S. (eds) (1997) *Promoting Equality in Secondary Schools.* London: Cassell.

Hillcole Group (1991) *Changing the Future: Redprint for Education.* London: Tufnell Press.

Hillcole Group (1993) *Falling Apart: The Coming Crisis in Conservative Education.* London: Tufnell Press.

Hillcole Group (1996) *20/20 Vision: Education for the Twenty-First Century.* London: Tufnell Press.

Hillgate Group (1986) *Whose Schools? – A Radical Manifesto.* London: The Hillgate Group.

Hillgate Group (1987) *The Reform of British Education – From Principles to Practice.* London: The Claridge Press.

Hillgate Group (1989) *Learning to Teach.* London: The Claridge Press.

Inner London Education Authority (ILEA) (1984) *Improving Secondary Schools, Report of the Committee on the Curriculum and Organisation of Secondary Schools* (known as the 'Hargreaves Report'). London: ILEA.

Inner London Education Authority (ILEA) (1985) *Improving Primary Schools, Report of the Committee on Primary Education* (known as the 'Thomas Report'). London: ILEA.

Jessop, B. (1990) *State Theory: Putting the Capitalist State in its Place*. London: Polity Press.

Jones, K. (1989) *Right Turn: The Conservative Revolution in Education*. London: Hutchinson Radius.

King, A. and Mitchell, P. (1995) The national curriculum and ethnic relations. In S. Tomlinson and M. Craft (eds) *Ethnic Relations and Schooling*. London: Athlone.

Knights, C. (1990) *The Making of Tory Education Policy in Post-War Britain 1950–1986*. London: Falmer Press.

Lawton, D. (1992) *Education and Politics in the 1990s*. London: Falmer Press.

Lawton, D. (1994) *The Tory Mind on Education 1979–94*. London: Falmer Press.

Lawton, D. and Chitty, C. (1987) Towards a national curriculum. *Forum*, 30(1):4–6.

Levitas, R. (1987) *Ideology of the New Right*. Cambridge: Polity Press.

Macleod, D. (1995) Big classes 'hit curriculum'. *Guardian*, 16 October.

Major, J. (1993) Extract from speech to the 1992 Conservative party conference. In C. Chitty and B. Simon (eds) *Education Answers Back: Critical Responses to Government Policy*. London: Lawrence and Wishart.

Massey, I. (1991) *More Than Skin Deep: Developing Anti-Racist Multicultural Education in Schools*. London: Hodder and Stoughton.

Maude, A. (1968) *Education Quality and Equality*. London: Conservative Political Centre.

McGavin, H. (1995) National tests a 'waste of time'. *Times Educational Supplement*, 20 October.

Measor, L. and Sikes, P. (1992) *Gender and Schools*. London: Cassell.

Menter, I. (1992) The New Right, racism and teacher education. some recent developments. *Multicultural Teaching*, 10 (2):6–10.

Militant International Review (1995) Has there been a 'genderquake'? 60:9–16.

Moore, R. (1996) Back to the future: the problem of change and the possibilities of advance in the sociology of education. *British Journal of Sociology of Education*, 17(2).

Morris, M. and Griggs, C. (1988) Thirteen wasted years. In M. Morris, and C. Griggs (eds) *Education – The Wasted Years?*

1973–1986. Lewes: Falmer Press.

Myers, K. (1990) Review of 'equal opportunities in the new era'. *Education,* 5 October.

National Commission on Education (1992) *Learning to Succeed: Report of the Paul Hamlyn Foundation.* London: Heinemann.

Office for Standards in Education (OFSTED) (1993) *Handbook for the Inspection of Schools.* London: HMSO.

O'Hear, A. and Ranson, S. (1988) Of primary concern. *Daily Telegraph,* 10 October 1988.

O'Hear, P. (1994) An alternative national curriculum. In S. Tomlinson (ed.) *Educational Reform and the Consequences.* London: Rivers Oram Press.

O'Keeffe, D. (1990a) The real lesson to be learned in our schools. *Daily Mail,* 9 March.

O'Keeffe, D. (1990b) *The Wayward Elite: A Critique of British Teacher Education.* London: Adam Smith Institute.

O'Keeffe, D. (1992) Diligence abandoned: the dismissal of traditional virtues in school. In D. Anderson (ed.) *The Loss of Virtue: Moral Confusion and Social Disorder in Britain and America.* London: Social Affairs Unit.

Panorama (1995) Men aren't working: a report from Darlington on demoralised and underachieving men who were once guaranteed industrial jobs for life but now face a future on the dole. BBC 1, 16 October.

Passmore, B. (1995) Small is best, but not for everyone. *Times Educational Supplement,* 17 November.

Patten, J. (1993) Extract from speech to the 1992 Conservative Party Conference. In C. Chitty, and B. Simon *Education Answers Back: Critical Responses to Government Policy.* London: Lawrence and Wishart.

Power, S., Halpin, D. and Fitz, J. (1994) Underpinning choice and diversity? The grant maintained schools policy in context. In S. Tomlinson (ed.) *Educational Reform and Its Consequences.* London: Cassell.

Runnymede Trust (1993) *Equality Assurance.* London: Runnymede Trust.

Runnymede Trust (1995) *Equal Opportunities and the Inspection of Schools: A Statement of Concern.* London: Runnymede Trust.

Shor, I. (1986) *Culture Wars: School and Society in the Conservative Restoration 1969–1984.* London: Routledge.

Simon, B. (1987) 'Lessons in Elitism', *Marxism Today,* September.

Simon, B. (1992) *What Future for Education?* London: Lawrence and Wishart.

Sunday Times (1992) The great betrayal. 26 January.

Taylor, W. (1995) Ethnic relations in all-white schools'. In S. Tomlinson and M. Craft (eds) *Ethnic Relations and Schooling.* London: Athlone.

Thornton, M. (1993) The Role of the Government in Education. In C. Chitty and B. Simon (eds) *Education Answers Back: Critical Responses to Government Policy.* London: Lawrence and Wishart.

Tomlinson, S. (ed.) (1994) *Educational Reform and Its Consequences.* London: Cassell.

Tomlinson, S. and Craft, M. (1995a) *Ethnic Relations and Schooling.* London: Athlone.

Tomlinson, S. and Craft, M. (1995b) Education for all in the 1990s. In S. Tomlinson, and M. Craft (1995) *Ethnic Relations and Schooling.* London: Athlone.

Troyna, B. (1995) The local management of schools and racial equality. In S. Tomlinson and M. Craft (eds) *Ethnic Relations and Schooling.* London: Athlone.

Turner, B. (1986) *Equality.* London: Methuen.

Turner, E., Riddell, S. and Brown, S. (1995) *Gender Equality in Scottish Schools: The Impact of Recent Educational Reforms.* Manchester: Equal Opportunities Commission.

Verma, G. and Pumfrey, P. (eds) (1994) *Cultural Diversity and the Curriculum, vol. 4: Cross-Curricular Contexts, Themes and Dimensions in Primary Schools.* London: Falmer Press.

Walford, G. and Miller, H. (1991) *City Technology Colleges.* Milton Keynes: Open University Press.

Weiner, G. (1995) Comments on a draft of this chapter.

Whitty, G. (1989a) The new right and the national curriculum: state control or market forces. *Journal of Education Policy*, 4(4).

Whitty, G. (1989b) Assisting whom? Benefits and costs of the assisted places scheme. In A. Hargreaves and D. Reynolds (eds) *Educational Policies: Controversies and Critiques.* London: Falmer Press.

Whitty, G. (1993) Education reform and teacher education in England in the 1990s. In P. Gilroy and M. Smith (eds) *International Analyses of Teacher Education.* Abingdon: Carfax Publishing Company.

Whitty, G. (1994) *Consumer Rights versus Citizen Rights in Contemporary Education Policy.* Draft paper to conference on 'Education, Democracy and Reform'. University of Auckland, New Zealand.

Wragg, T. (1991) *Mad Curriculum Disease.* Stoke-on-Trent: Trentham Books.

Young, S. (1992) Choice widens class divide, *Times Educational Supplement*, 2 October.

CHAPTER 2

Equality and primary education
What are the conceptual issues?

Mike Cole

*Education is a meaningless process unless it is con-
cerned with the struggle against all forms of tyranny,
whether based on ignorance, oppression, inequality or
exploitation.*
(*Chris Mullard. Talk to the Faculty of Education,
Brighton Polytechnic, 29 June 1988*)

INTRODUCTION

This book is premised on the conviction that all those connected
with the education of children should have a sound awareness of
equality and equal opportunity issues (for a discussion of the
differences between these two terms, see the Introduction). This
chapter has two aims; first to provide a conceptual overview of
the issues of 'race', sexuality, gender, disability and special needs
and social class in relation to society in general; second to draw
out some implications for primary schooling.

Four important points need to be made at the outset. First,
these equality issues are all social constructs, which reflect
particular social systems; they are not inevitable features of any
society, but rather crucial terrains of struggle between conflicting

social forces in any given society. In other words, I do not believe that societies need to be class-based, to have 'racialized' hierarchies, to have one sex dominating another. I refuse to accept that people are naturally homophobic or prone to marginalizing the needs of disabled people. On the contrary, I would argue that we are socialized into accepting the norms, values and customs of the social systems in which we grow up, and schools have traditionally played an important part in that process.

Where these social systems exhibit inequalities of any form, those at the receiving end of exploitation, oppression or discrimination have, along with their supporters, historically resisted and fought back in various ways. Primary schools do not have to be places where children are encouraged to think in one-dimensional ways. Indeed, were this the case, there would be no point in this book. They can and should be arenas for the encouragement of critical thought, where young people are provided with a number of ways of interpreting the world, not just the dominant ones.

Second, each of the issues under consideration in this chapter has a material and institutional parameter (differences in wealth and power, laws which disfavour certain groups) and a socio/psychological parameter (modes of thinking and acting both by the exploiters and discriminators and those on the receiving end of exploitation and discrimination).

Third, as we argue in the Introduction, and as the chapters of this book bear witness, these inequalities are interrelated and need to be considered in a holistic way. This in turn has at least two dimensions. First, every human being has multiple identities. To take a case in point: there are, of course, lesbians, gays and bisexuals in all social classes, among the Asian, black and other minority ethnic communities and among the white communities. There are gays, lesbians and bisexuals with disabilities and with special needs. Second (and again, the chapters of this book testify to this) all of the curriculum subject areas lend themeselves to a serious consideration of all equality issues, often in an interrelated way.

Fourth, equalities are also separate. As will become clear in this chapter, not only are people exploited and oppressed in similar ways, they are also exploited and oppressed in different ways. For this reason, and for the sake of conceptual clarity, the issues will be dealt with one by one.

'RACE' AND RACISM

Robert Miles has argued cogently against the notion that there exist distinct 'races' (1982:9–16). After a review of the literature, and following Bodmer, he gives three reasons for this. First, the extent of genetic variation within any population is usually greater than the average difference between populations; second, while the frequency of occurrence of possible forms taken by genes does vary from one so-called 'race' to another, any particular genetic combination can be found in almost any 'race'; third, owing to interbreeding and large scale migrations, the distinctions between 'races', identified in terms of dominant gene frequencies, are often blurred (Miles, 1982:16).

If 'race' has no genetic validity, it still has use as an analytic concept (in comparing and contrasting 'race' with other equality issues, for example). In addition, it does, of course, also exist as 'a social construct' in discourse. Therefore, it is still necessary to use the term. When this is the case, for the reasons outlined above, I would argue that it should be put in inverted commas.

The (false) belief that there exist distinct 'races' is the genesis of the concept of racism. Racism has traditionally referred to a situation, where people are seen as causing negative consequences for other groups or as possessing certain negatively evaluated characteristics because of their biology. While this has seemingly been the dominant form of racism throughout history, I would argue that it is necessary to extend this definition in two major ways. First, there is a need to include 'seemingly positive characteristics' in any definition of racism (c.f. Cole, 1996a, b). Second, it is necessary to enlarge the definition to include cultural factors (c.f. Cope and Poynting, 1989; Modood, 1992,[1] 1994; Cole, 1996a, b). I will deal with each in turn.

Evaluated characteristics

Negatively evaluated characteristics include such instances of racist discourse as 'black children are not as clever as white children', but exclude such seemingly positive statements as 'black children are good at sports'.[2] While such assertions can lead to individual and/or short-term group enhancement (an unmerited place in the school football team for the individual or enhanced status for the group as a whole in an environment where prowess at sport is highly regarded), it is potentially racist and likely to have racist consequences. This is because, like most stereotypes, it is distorted and misleading and typically appears as part of a discourse which works to justify black children's exclusion from academic activities.

Distinguishing between 'seemingly positive' and 'ultimately damaging' discourse is important. Nazi propaganda portrayed Jewish people as alien and morally subhuman and, therefore, a threat to the Aryan 'race'; a description which was part of a process that led eventually to the Holocaust. However, Jews were also characterized as a clever 'race' and (at least implicitly) superior in terms of ability. Thus, along with perceived threats of German 'racial degeneration' were fears that, through having superordinate skills of organization, the ability to dominate and act collectively as one entity, the Jews were able to control the world. This 'clever', 'super-able' stereotype, a perception which, on the surface, could seem positive, led to allegations that Jewish people were part of a conspiracy to take over the world, a notion which was also in part responsible for the Holocaust.

To take another example, people of Asian origin tend to be stereotyped as having a 'strong culture', an attribute which is used to pathologize people of African-Caribbean origin, who are in turn stereotyped as having a weak culture or as having no culture at all. While this may serve to enhance the status of the former at the expense of the latter, in the context of racist discourse it can result in accusations that people of Asian origin are failing to integrate or are 'taking over', which can lead to violence and other forms of hostility.

Cultural racism

David Mason has argued that 'new racisms' depend for their power on the continued influence of biologically determinist modes of conceptualizing human difference (1994:845–58). While I agree that a belief in a biological notion of 'race' lies at the root of much contemporary racism, I do not believe that it provides a full explanation. Perhaps contemporary racism might best be thought of as a matrix of biological and cultural racism (c.f. Cole, 1996b). In that matrix, I would suggest that racism can be based purely on biology (e.g. such statements as 'blacks are not as intelligent as whites'), or purely on culture (e.g. in Peregrine Worsthorne's (1991) words: 'Islam ... has degenerated into a primitive enemy' (cited in Richardson, 1992:xi)).

Quite often, it is not easily identifiable as either. The racist term 'Paki' is a curious case in point. Relatively unrelated to Pakistan, it has become a generic term for anyone who is perceived to be from a specific alien stock and/or is believed to engage in certain alien cultural practices, based, for example, around religion, dress or food. The fact that it is being written by racists as 'packy' in the singular and 'packies' in the plural (*Guardian*, 1995) is indicative of how far it has become removed from the geographical area of Pakistan. Even when 'Pakistani' is used in racist discourse, it is highly unlikely that it is used in a knowledgeable way to refer to an (ex-)inhabitant of that particular South Asian country.

The issue of nomenclature is important and is a hotly contested issue. The first point to make is that it is perhaps easier to establish terms that are not acceptable, than those which are preferred. The nomenclature 'coloured', for example, is unacceptable to most people in Britain. The second point to make is that there are no accurate and fixed definitions of a minority ethnic group. As Floya Anthias has succinctly put it: 'the notion of where and how the boundary [between groups] is constructed is diverse, contextual and relational', with the boundaries often changing 'over time, and in response to concrete economic, political or ideological conditions' (1992: 423). Ideally, I believe in ethnic self-definition. However, there is, inevitably, disagreement over what is and is not appropriate (e.g. Modood, 1988, 1994; Mama, 1992). Since many people of Asian and other minority ethnic origin do not self-describe as 'black' and because the use of the term 'ethnic minority' has, in practice, meant that members of the dominant majority group are not referred to in terms of their ethnicity, with the implication that they do not have ethnicity (Leicester, 1989:17), I would suggest that, at the present time in Britain, the formulation 'Asian, black and other minority ethnic' is preferable (the sequencing of 'minority' before 'ethnic' does not carry the implication referred to by Leicester above).[3] 'Ethnic' or 'ethnics' should not be used in isolation and need to be prefigured by 'minority' (or 'majority') and followed by a noun such as community (-ies) or group(s).

The educational implications

There are three broadly identifiable approaches to education in multicultural Britain: monocultural, multicultural and anti-racist education respectively. Monocultural education attempts to make everyone 'socially and culturally British'. It is the traditional and most practised form of education in Britain and in many ways has been given a boost by the National Curriculum. Multicultural education, on the other hand, starts from the premise that education should use the rich cultural heritage of Britain and celebrate difference. Multicultural educators set out to teach about other people's cultures, other people's ways of life, thereby hoping to improve Asian, black and other minority ethnic people's self-image and instil respect for minority ethnic cultures. Finally, anti-racist education's starting-point is that Britain is a fundamentally racist society, that racism cannot be understood without reference to economic, political and ideological factors, nor without reference to other inequality issues, and that education should play a role in attempting to dismantle that racism. Advocates of the three approaches share the conviction that their preferred approach should be adopted in *all* schools, irrespective of ethnic composition.

The main problem with monocultural education is that it has the tendency to reinforce biological and cultural racism, by implicitly and explicitly championing British colonial history and by exalting the supposed superiority of British cultural institutions and 'the British character'. Multicultural education, in concentrating on safe 'cultural sites' – the arts, religion and food – allows the teacher to avoid examining her/his own racism and has a tendency to be patronizing. How can the vast majority of a predominantly white teaching force be capable of teaching about the dynamic and multifaceted cultures of Britain? Elsewhere (Cole, 1992), I have attempted an extended critique of monocultural and multicultural education and an appraisal of anti-racist education. Here one brief practical example of the different approaches will suffice. Several years ago primary school teachers attempted projects on the Australian bicentennial. Assuming all teachers would pass on some basic information – where Australia is, climate, size, population and so on, the ensuing emphases might then be very different.

In the monocultural classroom the emphasis might be as follows. Australia was discovered two hundred years ago by the British. The country is geographically very different from Britain, but Australia has inherited 'our parliamentary system', 'our legal system' and 'our culture'. It would tend to reinforce a view of Australia as portrayed in some 'soaps', where most characters are of British origin.

Multiculturalists would probably stress the multicultural nature of Australia and the way in which the different cultural groups, including the Aboriginal community, have contributed to the society, producing an interesting variety of musical styles, of art and music. Children might be encouraged to challenge the interpretation of Australian life which stresses 'Britishness'. Here, an attempt is made to celebrate difference and to present positive images of minority ethnic communities. The main problem, however, is a marked tendency to stereotype (Cole, 1992).

In the anti-racist classroom children would learn that while some people view what happened two hundred years ago as 'a discovery', Aboriginal people and their supporters view it as an invasion. Given access to a comprehensive range of resources pertaining to life in Australia, children would discover that, in reality, multicultural Australia is a society rigidly stratified on lines of class, 'race' and gender, with women of the numerous Aboriginal communities at the very bottom of the hierarchy, eking out existences in conditions approximating those of 'the developing world'. They would learn about 'land rights' and the economic and ecological arguments pertaining to these rights. They would consider these issues in the light of the more traditional classroom interpretations of Australian life outlined in the two other approaches.[4] With the anti-racist approach there is a marked emphasis on social justice rather than cultural artefacts.

SEXUALITY

Here again the issue of nomenclature is important. The term 'gay' seems generally acceptable to gay men and to some gay women. Other gay women prefer to be referred to as lesbians. The term 'bisexual' or 'bi' is still in common usage for those people attracted to both sexes. Recently, former terms of abuse like 'queer', 'bent' and 'dyke' have been reclaimed as positive and assertive by some gay and lesbian activists and artists (in a similar way some rap artists, for example, particularly in the USA, have retrieved negative terms like 'nigger'). The golden rule, once again, is that we should take note of self-definitions but be aware of disagreements and different preferences and that we should bear in mind changing modes of self-referral.

Sexuality is firmly on the political, religious, social and academic agendas. I will deal with each agenda in turn. As far as politics is concerned, there have been a number of campaigns for lesbian and gay rights (the one concerning the age of consent being an ongoing issue). In addition, British 'municipal socialism' in the 1980s (especially in London and Manchester) took the issues on board and there are varying degrees of commitment to lesbian and gay rights from local authorities today.

With respect to religion, a number of clergy in the Christian Church have decided to 'come out' or have been 'outed' and Christianity has been reinterpreted to encompass a love of all humankind, not just heterosexuals (for a discussion, see Babuscio, 1988:74–92).

As far as the social scene is concerned, there are now numerous lesbian, gay and bisexual clubs, pubs and other social venues. There is lesbian and gay theatre, cinema and music, and lesbian and gay publications can be bought in the local newsagents and at high street bookshops. In addition, other issues of sexual diversity such as transvestism and transsexualism are being more openly discussed.

Finally, academic publishers are marketing many books on sexuality and there are degrees in lesbian and gay studies at British universities.

All this indicates most forcefully that lesbians and gays and bisexuals are here to stay and a full acceptance of their inalienable right to their sexuality will increasingly become the norm in communities, including the community of the primary school.

On the negative side, gay sexuality is, in the popular imagination, very much associated with HIV infection and AIDS. However, as Epstein (1994) points out, there are at least two key agendas in operation here. The first, dominant agenda, as spelt out in the popular press, has been that of the 'moral majority', with an emphasis on 'normal' family life, as opposed to 'unnatural' homosexuality and the accompanying 'gay plague'. The second, counter-agenda, promoted by voluntary bodies such as the Terrence Higgins Trust, has celebrated diverse formations of sexuality (ibid., 1994:3). Indeed, while the issue of sexuality is clearly here to stay, it abounds with contradtions. Epstein provides a couple of pertinent examples.

> The contradictions, and even polarizations ... are manifold, in public policy, between different people and even within the same person. For example, the government is currently restating Section 28 ... but John Major has entertained gay activist and actor, Ian McKellen, at 10 Downing Street. The same police force may be simultaneously engaged in harassing gay men and appointing community liaison officers to work with the lesbian and gay community.
>
> (Epstein, 1994:7)

The extent to which such contradictions are apparent at present, Epstein concludes, can be taken as an indication that now is a critical time in which to challenge lesbian and gay inequalities in education.

The educational implications

In primary schools, lesbians, gays and bisexuals may be members of the teaching profession and other workers in the school. Guardians and parents of children may be lesbian, gay or bisexual. It is estimated, for example, that about one-third of all lesbians are mothers and a smaller, but none the less significant, proportion of gay men are fathers (Harris, 1990:46). Furthermore, there is evidence that some children identify as gay or lesbian in the primary years (NUT, 1991:7; Epstein, 1994: 49–56).

Most primary age children will have encountered gay and lesbian issues and, to a lesser extent, issues of bisexuality, from newspapers and from other organs of the media, particularly television. They may also have come across transvestism and transsexualism, both of which are issues that come under the broad heading of sexuality.

How the teacher deals with such issues will depend greatly on the context and on the age of the children. Given that there is a marked tendency for schools not to deal openly with issues of sexuality (Epstein and Johnson, 1994; Redman, 1994; Rogers, 1994), especially lesbian and gay sexuality and bisexuality, it is a particularly problematic issue for teachers, but one which should not be swept under the carpet.

The difficulty has been exacerbated by legislation. First, the Education Act (No. 2) 1986 gives school governors the duty of laying down sex education policies. Bearing in mind the fact that school governors are not, in general, likely to be very well informed about equal opportunity policies and practices (Deem *et al.*, 1992, cited in Rogers, 1994:32), they are unlikely to adopt policies which challenge heterosexism and homophobia (Rogers, 1994:33). Second, Section 28 of the Local Government Act 1988 prohibited local education authorities 'intentionally promoting homosexuality' or promoting 'the teaching in any maintained school of the acceptability of homosexuality as a pretended family relationship'. As Rogers points out, Section 28 had contradictory effects; on the one hand, it legitimated heterosexism and homophobia; on the other hand, it put the issue of homosexuality in schools firmly on the agenda (1994:33).

Two caveats need to be stressed: Section 28 applies only to local education authorities (Rogers, 1994:33); it does not apply to individual schools. Circular 11/87 acknowledged this by stating that the Act 'does not impose any direct responsibilities' on schools (DFE, 1993, cited in Redman, 1994:139). However, the fact that Section 28 was restated indicates the continuing favour in government circles of what Redman refers to as 'moral traditionalist thinking' (1994:139; see also Epstein, 1994:2). Moreover, the official OFSTED *Handbook* states categorically that 'promoting homosexuality through resources or teaching is prohibited' (cited in Epstein, 1994:2). As Epstein notes, this is even stronger than the original prohibition of intentional promotion.

The advice of the National Union of Teachers on Section 28, and on gay and lesbian issues in general, is that Section 28 'should not be interpreted as a prohibition on objective factual teaching about homosexuality, and teachers should feel confident that if they follow Union advice, and their school governors' policy on sex education, the process of educating against prejudice and discrimination is clearly within the law' (National Union of Teachers, 1991:6).

GENDER

Whereas sex refers to basic physiological differences between females and males, gender relates to social and cultural differences, relative to time and place. For example, what is considered the norm with respect to 'acceptable modes of dress' or body language for males and females varies dramatically through history and according to geographical location. (This is not to say, of course, that everyone conforms to such norms.)

There are a number of competing theories about how gender roles become established. First, there are those who argue that biology accounts for gender differences in society, that human beings possess a genetically based programme, a 'biogrammar', which predisposes them to behave in certain ways (c.f. Tiger and Fox, 1972). The main problem with these explanations is that they fail to account for geographical and historical variations. If our gender roles are biologically determined, why is there not one universal form for each sex? (Measor and Sikes, 1992:7; see also La Fontaine, 1978).

Other explanations are based around socialization and can be grouped under the headings: 'social learning theory' (roles learned from parents, peers and teachers); 'cognitive development theory' (roles established in the child's quest for competence in a world where such competence is linked to being 'male' or 'female'); and psychoanalytic theories. This last field focuses on the emotional aspects of a child's life. Rooted in a feminist critique of the work of Freud, specifically a challenge to Freud's deficit view of women, feminist psychoanalytic theory has emphasized femininity in a positive sense. In place of female/male inferiority/dominance, has come 'difference' and complementarity. It has been suggested too that boys can be jealous of girls' femininity, whereas Freud emphasized only girls' envy of boys. It has also been suggested that, unlike girls with respect to their femininity, boys have to struggle to become 'masculine' and this can involve the attacking of things that are feminine and the devaluing of girls and women (Measor and Sikes, 1992:11–12).

Measor and Sikes suggest that socialization might best be seen as a combination of the above non-biological approaches (1992:10, 12). What they have in common is a belief that gender is *by definition* a social construct, unlike sex, which is a biological construct; that is to say appropriate gender roles are learned through socialization rather than genetically given.

As far as nomenclature is concerned, while the radical Right, in general, and others refuse to listen, a growing number of people now accept the right of women to decide how they wish to be referred to, whether it is a preference for 'woman' over other forms of address, or a preference for 'Ms' over more traditional titles, or vice versa.

That there are a much larger number of derogatory terms in popular discourse, in the English language, to describe women than men is indicative of the patriarchal nature of the societies in which we live. Patriarchy has been defined by Adrienne Rich as:

> the power of the fathers: a familial–social, ideological, political system in which men – by force, direct pressure, or through ritual, tradition, law, and language, customs, etiquette, education, and the division of labour, determine what part women shall or shall not play, and in which the female is everywhere subsumed under the male.
>
> (Cited in Eisenstein, 1981:18–19)

Just how true this is can be gleaned from a cursory glance at who, in general, at national and international level, controls big business and finance, politics, the military, the police, technology, science and education.

Gender inequalities are reproduced, in large part, through the institution of the family, where gender roles, with respect to expectations, dress, household chores or lack of such chores, chosen toys and comics, and so on, are constructed through the socialization process. Inequalities are also reproduced through, for example, peer pressure (often an effective counter to an enlightened family socialization), the media (c.f. Cole *et al.*, 1995), leisure and sport (c.f. Tomlinson, 1995) and by the education system (discussed below).

So how have feminists and their supporters challenged gender inequalities? Traditional feminist perspectives have ranged from those of radical or revolutionary feminists (who see patriarchy as the principal form of oppression), through the views of socialist feminists (targeting both capitalism and patriarchy), black feminists (an important corrective to those feminists who tended to be colour blind), to the perspectives of those liberal feminists favouring reform, who envisage full equality for women under capitalism (something which socialists would see as not feasible, because of capitalism's reliance on the cheap labour of women in the workforce and the free labour of women in the household).

Unfortunately, the interests of girls and women are not served by the current spate of feminist theory based on poststructuralism or postmodernism (see, for example, Butler, 1990; Lather, 1991). Dave Hill and I have written at length elsewhere on what we see as the dangers of the extensive appropriation of feminism by postmodernism (see, for example, Cole and Hill, 1995a, b; see also Kelly, 1992, 1994). Briefly, consistent with our general critique of postmodernism (see below), we argue that in its rejection of a metanarrative of social change, in its concentration on the local, rather than the national and international, in its implicit acceptance of *all* voices as equally valid, postmodernism is not able to theorize, nor to advance the causes of women in the modern world.

In particular, as socialist feminist Jane Kelly (1994) has argued, postmodern feminists have nothing to say about the situation of working-class women in the 1990s. Without an 'overarching' theory, they are unable to explain the ways in which women's oppression, centred in the family, determines their entry into the workforce; unable to analyse why the majority of women workers are confined within a segregated labour market, are paid less and work in worse conditions than men; unable to understand the ways in which part-time work, seen as 'appropriate' for women, whose primary responsibilities are viewed as domestic, has been used in the restructuring of the workforce in Britain in the last decade; unable, finally, to decide which women's issues should take priority in campaigning.

Educational implications

Gender inequality is reproduced in primary schooling in a myriad number of ways, including the organization of the school, the organization and management of classrooms and lessons, children's experience of the curriculum, both actual or formal and hidden, and in teacher's activities and actions (c.f. Measor and Sikes, 1992:53). Strategies to promote anti-sexism (actions or behaviours which consciously seek to redress the current sexist nature of society (George, 1993:88)) would entail a careful consideration of some of the following issues.[5]

To begin with, as far as the school as a whole is concerned, pupils in primary schools are often divided into single-sex groups for activities where gender is irrelevant. Sports teams are an obvious example. In the individual classroom, girls are often encouraged to compete against boys (Measor and Sikes, 1992:55). In addition, gender roles are constructed and boys become sexist at a very early age. Teachers must take steps to counter these tendencies.

In the formal curriculum, history, for example, can give the impression that it is all about white ruling-class men, 'his-story' rather than 'her-story'. Indeed, as is shown throughout the various chapters of this book, the positive ways in which women and girls have contributed to societies should be stressed across the curriculum. Women and girls should not be marginalized and the perpetuation of stereotypes should be avoided.

Through the hidden curriculum, via the expectations of teachers and other school staff, by the respective roles of staff in the schools, schooling often reflects and reinforces the patriarchal hierarchy of the wider society. Again, this is an area which needs careful consideration by all those involved in the education of primary school children.

With respect to teachers' activities and actions, numerous research studies have shown that boys are more disruptive and demanding of attention than girls (Fuller, 1980; Walkerdine, 1981; Stanworth, 1983; Measor and Sikes, 1992:63–4). The teacher's common response is to give more attention to boys. This is something which all teachers need to consider most seriously (for a critical analysis of teacher attention, see Wolpe, 1988).

DISABILITY AND SPECIAL NEEDS

Through history, disabled people have generally been seen as unclean and polluting. This is apparent, for example, in the Old

Testament of the Bible. In the New Testament, however, charity is counselled for disabled people (Rieser, 1990:12–13). With the emergence of medical knowledge in the mid-nineteenth century, disabled people became individual objects to be 'treated', 'changed', 'improved', 'cured', made more 'normal'. 'The overall picture is that the human being is flexible and "alterable" whilst society is fixed and unalterable' (Mason and Rieser, 1990:14; see also Ford *et al.*, 1982; Tomlinson, 1982; Barton and Tomlinson, 1984; Slee, 1993).

In place of the 'religious model' and the 'medical model', a 'social model' has been suggested. Disability, according to this model, is seen as 'the complex system of economic and social constraints imposed on people with impairments by the organisation of society' (Barton *et al.*, 1993:110). Mason and Rieser spell out the implications of such a view:

> whilst we may have medical conditions which hamper us and which may or may not need medical treatment, human knowledge, technology and collective resources are already such that our physical or mental impairments need not prevent us from being able to live perfectly good lives. It is society's unwillingness to employ these means to altering *itself* rather than *us*, which cause our disabilities.
>
> (Mason and Rieser, 1990:15)

As is the case with other issues of equality, nomenclature is of great importance with respect to disability and special needs (terms now more or less universally used, rather than 'handicap').[6] Mason (1990:88) gives some suggestions of both offensive and preferred terminology (as always, this should be read in the context of a cultural climate, subject to constant change and revision). In addition, Jonathan Solity has alerted us to certain problems inherent in assumptions arising from the way terminology relating to disability and special needs is used. An example is the myth, deriving from the Warnock Report of 1978, that it is learning difficulties *themselves* which ultimately determine relative success or failure in schools, rather than the nature of the learning environment and general learning opportunities (Solity, 1991, 1995). In his 1995 paper he is critical of the widely used phrase, 'special educational needs'. He suggests that the term is the result of an increasingly sophisticated use of labels. As he puts it, '[c]ould it be that children deemed "idiots" through government legislation in 1913, who were then described as "severely subnormal" in 1945, and became "educationally subnormal" in 1962, are now known as "children with special needs"?' (1991:16).

Taking a more benign interpretation of the genesis of this term, Micheline Mason has argued that 'special educational needs' came about as an attempt to demedicalize the labelling of children with disabilities; in other words to replace offensive terms, such as 'retarded', 'maladjusted' and so on, with what was hoped to be less negative labelling based on educational need. Disabled people welcome the spirit in which this was done but the political dimension is overlooked (Mason, 1990:88):

> We do *not* consider ourselves to be special. We consider disability to be a norm within every society, born out by statistics, and we want our needs to be taken into account as normal human beings. It seems questionable that even 20% of young people can have 'special needs'. It seems ridiculous that 45% of young people within inner city areas can have 'special needs'. Surely the question is how does the education system fail to answer the needs of 45% of its users?
>
> (Mason, 1990:88)

Educational implications

Mason suggests retaining the official terminology of 'special needs' for the present and for it to include disabled children, children with learning difficulties and children with emotional and behavioural problems; in fact, in the context of the compulsory school years, to include all young people with any physical and/or mental condition, be it permanent or temporary, who are affected in some way by the wider society's attitudes towards disability (Mason, 1990:89).

The 1981 Education Act decreed that children with special educational needs should be educated in mainstream schools, wherever possible. This was reinforced by the Code of Practice for the implementation of the 1993 Act which stated that '[t]he special educational needs of most children can be met effectively in mainstream schools, with outside specialist help if necessary' (DFE, 1994:ii).

In the last five years, the emphasis on the idea of *integration*, with its assumption that extra arrangements will be made to accommodate exceptional pupils in largely unchanged schools, has given way to the concept of *inclusive education*, where the aim is to restructure all schools in order to respond to the needs of all children (Clark *et al.*, 1995). According to the UNESCO Statement of 1994, regular schools with an inclusive orientation are:

> the most effective means of combating discriminatory attitudes, creating welcoming communities, building an inclusive society and achieving education for all; moreover they provide an effective education to the majority of children and improve the efficiency and ultimately the cost-effectiveness of the entire education system.
> (UNESCO, cited in Ainscow, 1995:147)

Experience of disabled children, Mason argues, is that they do better educationally and socially as long as the school responds in a positive way to their 'special needs'. Able-bodied children also report that it is a positive experience for them, as do their teachers (Mason, 1990:148). At this point, it is worth stressing that, as with all the other issues outlined in this chapter, whatever the proportion of disabled to able-bodied children or whatever the proportion of children with special educational needs, it is the teacher's responsibility to increase all children's awareness of the relevant issues. This will include not only increasing knowledge of such issues, but also promoting positive images of disabled people and people with special educational needs throughout the curriculum.

This requires a serious and considered deployment of resources, including perhaps the employment of non-teaching assistants (NTAs). However, crucial though this is, inclusive education necessitates in addition, again as with all the issues of equality discussed in this chapter, the engagement of teachers in critical reflection on their pedagogical repertoire, their assumptions about curriculum and classroom and school organization, along with the ideologies that inform these components of schooling (Slee, 1993:351. Ainscow, 1995; see also Hill, 1994, 1996). Only then will they be in a position to begin to provide appropriate educational experiences to include *all* children.

SOCIAL CLASS

Almost the whole world is currently run on market capitalist lines. All pupils, I would insist, have a right to know that this is only one way of running economies, nationally and globally. Economic and industrial understanding should form an essential part of the curriculum of every school pupil/student, including primary school children. Indeed, as we shall see, the National Curriculum Council endorses this view.

In order to begin to understand the changes occurring in industry and in the economy and society in general, in addition to an awareness of the issue of ecology (something recognized in various National Curriculum documents), an awareness is needed of the crucial relevance of the concept of social class.

As we have seen in the Introduction, and as I hope to demonstrate in this chapter, despite John Major's rhetoric about a classless society, Britain continues to be rigidly stratified according to social class. Nevertheless, there exists an influential world view which poses a serious challenge to the salience of the notion of social class. *Postmodernism* has infiltrated or is infiltrating virtually every discipline within the social sciences, to the extent that it is rapidly becoming an orthodoxy, both in research and in undergraduate and postgraduate texts. Student teachers, teachers and others concerned with the education of primary children are increasingly likely to be confronted with the ideas of postmodernism. There is a need, therefore, for a theoretical consideration of its fundamental tenets.

Postmodernists argue that we live in 'new times', that we are in a postmodern (some say post-capitalist) era, that social class is not a central issue any more, that socialism is no longer a viable proposition. With Dave Hill, I have elsewhere attempted an extended critique of such postmodernist arguments (Cole and Hill, 1995a, b; see also Callinicos, 1989). Here I will summarize our views on the postmodern position on social class.

SOCIAL CLASS AND 'NEW TIMES'

The 'New Times' project began with a seminar in May 1988, organized by the editorial board of the now defunct journal, *Marxism Today*. The 'New Times' argument is that the world has changed, both quantitatively and qualitatively, and that the advanced capitalist countries are 'increasingly characterised by diversity, differentiation and fragmentation' (Hall and Jacques,

1989:11). The 'New Times' thesis has a number of recurring themes: the decline of mass production and of the traditional industrial proletariat, the rise of myriad political and social struggles, and individualism, style and consumption as a replacement for human solidarity.

In addition to Hall and Jacques' book, *New Times: The Changing Face of Politics in the 1990s*, and the Communist Party's *Manifesto for New Times*, Paul Gilroy's influential book, *There Ain't No Black in the Union Jack*, has done much to further the cause of 'New Times'. Gilroy suggests that, along with mass unemployment, 'consumer-oriented people's capitalism' has 'undermined both the theory and practice of the left' (1989:18). He queries whether working-class unification 'is still possible or even desirable' (1989:19), submits that we should dispense with the vocabulary of class analysis created during the industrial era or at least ruthlessly modernize it (1989:225) and wonders whether 'the political languages of class and socialism ... may be completely beyond resuscitation' (1989:245). Not surprisingly, he prioritizes individual autonomy (1989:233) and new social movements over class struggle (1989:224–6; 245–6).

Issues of nomenclature are crucial in understanding the nature of social class. For example, the use of the terms 'upper class' and 'lower class' can imply a justification for the existence of differentiated social classes and says nothing about the relationship between these classes. 'Ruling' and/or 'capitalist class', on the one hand, and 'working class', on the other, however, implies a specific relationship between them. What, then, is the nature and composition of the working class in contemporary Britain?

Arguing that the working class has changed, rather than declined, John Kelly has suggested that there are two definitions of that class in common usage: (1) a narrow definition which includes only those workers directly exploited by capital in the production process, where actual goods are produced, *workers whose surplus labour yields surplus value*;[7] and (2) a wider definition which includes all those who are obliged to sell their labour in order to survive (the majority of whom, but not all, are *indirectly* exploited, i.e. not actually producing goods).[8] On the latter definition, the working class is growing both absolutely and relatively (1989:26; see also Ainley, 1994).

Justifying this wider definition of the working class in the context of Britain, Kelly argues, first, that an increasing section of the workfroce is employed in business services which directly contribute to the production of surplus value by helping capitalists extract ever more out of workers (such businesses include research and development, industrial engineering, computer hardware and software and other branches of consultancy).

Second, there is a growing service sector (retail stores, hotels, the leisure industry and personal services such as hairdressing – Kelly fails to mention the sex industry). The antagonistic relationship between, say, a supermarket check-out assistant or burger-chain worker and her/his boss is analogous to that of a factory worker and her/his boss, since both bosses have a vested interest in keeping wages and salaries down, and therefore profits up.

Third, there are workers in the central state and in the local state who are essential for the political stability of capitalism, even though they are not directly exploited for surplus value, such as civil servants and local authority office workers/bureaucrats.

Finally, there is a large section of the workforce engaged in producing new workers and/or maintaining the working class, particularly in the health and education services. Teachers of course fall into this last category. The devolution of budgets, the marketization of schools, the setting-up of hierarchical management structures, league tables and performance-related pay mean that working in schools more and more resembles working for big business (for a fuller discussion, see Chapter 1).

If it is the case that there has been a *recomposition*, rather than the demise of the working class, could it still be that there has been a change in class *identification*? Is Eric Hobsbawm correct in arguing that everywhere solidaristic forms of consciousness have given way to 'the values of consumer-society, individualism and the search for private and personal satisfaction above all else' (cited in Marshall *et al.* 1989:1)? In a comprehensive survey of social class in Britain, Marshall *et al.* show that 'social class is still the most common source of social identity and retains its salience as such' (1989:143).[9]

The postmodern denial of social class is part of a wider denial of solidarity, of people joining together to effect major changes in society, part of their stress on the local, rather than the national and international. Countering the postmodern position, I would refer postmodernists to a relatively recent example of mass human solidarity, namely the overthrow of the self-proclaimed 'socialist' states of Eastern Europe. If such regulated and dictatorial regimes can be destroyed by collective human agency, then the possibilities for major structural change remain firmly on the agenda. Ironically, there are currently indications that the new brutal market economies created in the former Eastern bloc are being met with growing resistance, with many even preferring and voting for a return to aspects of the old way of life under 'communism'. In Britain, the revolt aginst the poll tax and the subsequent demise of Thatcher, if not Thatcherism, show that human beings will only take so much before they are prepared to join together to try to effect change. At the time of writing (December 1995), France is witnessing mass unrest by workers (protesting primarily against cuts in welfare), unprecedented since 1968.

The educational implications

The National Curriculum Council states that education for economic and industrial understanding is 'an essential part of every pupil's curriculum ... needed in all stages of their education' (National Curriculum Council, 1991: Foreword) and that such understanding should be based on 'a broad and balanced programme' which includes 'the exploration of values and beliefs, both the pupils' own and those of others' and which 'involves the study of controversial issues' (ibid.:7, 15). The danger is that the combined effect of the current ascendancy of 'the market' (for an extended analysis, see Chapter 1), upheld at worst, not effectively challenged at best, by postmodernism (as it trickles down into everyday consciousness), will stifle alternative ways of thinking about social class or about a radically more equal society. Are we not doing young people a disservice if, through our teaching, market capitalism is presented as natural and uncontested; if possible alternative systems, such as forms of socialism (e.g. 'state interventionist' on the one hand and 'workers control' on the other) are not fully addressed?

Egalitarians and others who seek to avoid indoctrination will want to make sure that children are made aware of all the major possible ways that have been suggested to run local, national and international economies. The Primary Education Curriculum has for too long been structured so as to exclude, repress and prevent certain issues being addressed (Young, 1984:236; Carrington and Troyna, 1988:208). This exclusionary ethos was reinforced by the 1986 Education Reform Act, which forbids 'the pursuit of partisan political activities by any of those registered pupils at the school who are junior pupils' (DES, 1986: para 44). Drawn up by the radical Right (see Chapter 1), the primary aim of this clause is, I would suggest, to forestall consideration of views hostile to capitalism, or, indeed, a consideration of arguments in favour of radically reforming capitalism. Thus individual teachers who discuss capitalism in an uncritical way have nothing to fear. Those who do not, need to tread warily. This book is written in the spirit of challenging the restrictive ethos of current Conservative developments in primary schools and replacing it with one that encourages rather than obstructs critical thinking.

ACKNOWLEDGEMENTS

I would like to thank Len Barton, Clyde Chitty, Rosalyn George, Carol Gray, Tom Hickey, Dave Hill, Raf Salkie, Jonathan Solity and Sue Yearley for their helpful comments on various drafts this chapter. As always, any inadequacies remain mine.

NOTES

1   While I agree with Modood's arguments for racism's having a cultural dimension, I am not in sympathy with his overall project in this book, which entails the wholesale rejection of historical materialism, and the privileging of functionalist analysis and a liberal concept of 'ethnic pluralism' (Cole, 1993a:23).
2   I am indebted to Smina Akhtar for the following discussion of positively evaluated characteristics.
3   For a fuller discussion of nomenclature in Britain, see Cole

(1993b). For a discussion of nomenclature with respect to Britain and to some other (selected) countries in Europe, see Cole (1996b).

4 Some writers have suggested that multicultural and anti-racist education are compatible (see, for example, Hessari and Hill, 1989: Leicester 1992). For arguments that they are not compatible see Cole (1992); see also the works of Barry Troyna (e.g. Troyna, 1993). (At the end of Cole, 1992, there is an interchange of views between Leicester and myself as to whether or not the two approaches are compatible.)

5 Issues of academic success are more complicated and a British television programme (*Panorama*, 24 October 1994), suggested that, based on examination success, women are more successful in the educational system and the 'future is female'. In addition, a study by Harris *et al.* (1993) showed that Year 11 boys in three semi-rural schools under study in one LEA were all underachieving in terms of coursework and examination grades (see also Chapter 1 for a discussion). It is too early, at the time of writing, to assess to what extent these findings are generalizable and, if so, how this might relate to attempts at challenging patriarchy. What seems clear is that whatever the apparent success of girls at GCSE and A level, young women's chosen destinations suggest that stereotypical choices are still being made in terms of occupation and entry into further and higher education.

6 Barton *et al.* unanimously agreed to change the title of their journal *Disability, Handicap and Society* to *Disability and Society* as from No. 1 1994, because of the overtly negative and oppressive implications of the term 'handicap', used in relation to disabled people (Barton *et al.*, 1993:110).

7 For a discussion of the concept of surplus value, see Marx, 1976.

8 Kelly's analysis is an attempt to defend Karl Marx's concept of social class, where relationship to the sphere of production is the determining factor. The sociologist, Max Weber, whose work is often cited as providing an alternative to Marxist theory, argued that it is differential life chances, distributed by the capitalist market, rather than relationship to production, that distinguish social classes. In Government censuses and other surveys, and in academic and other empirical

research, social class is defined by occupation, ranked according to what are perceived to be a hierarchy of skills (for a
critical discussion, see Marshall *et al.*, 1989, chapter 2; see
also Marx, 1976 and Weber, 1968).

9   Sixty per cent of their sample calimed that they thought of
themselves as belonging to one particular class, and well over
ninety per cent could place themselves in a *specific* class
category, when asked the follow-up question, 'suppose you
were asked to say which class you belonged to, what would
you say?' (1989:143, 166). Respondents placed themselves in
the categories, 'upper', 'upper middle', 'middle', 'lower
middle', 'upper working', 'working' and 'lower working' class
respectively (1989:144). Marshall *et al* conclude that
'modern Britain is a society shaped predominantly by class
... no matter whether the phenomena under scrutiny are
structural or cultural in nature' (1989:183).

REFERENCES

Ainley, P. (1994) *Degrees of Difference: Higher Education in the
1990s*. London: Lawrence and Wishart.

Ainscow, M. (1995) Education for all. *Support for Learning*,
10(4):147–55.

Anthias, F. (1992) Connecting 'race' and ethnic phenomena.
Sociology, 26(3):421–38.

Babuscio, J. (1988) *We Speak for Ourselves: The Experiences of
Gay Men and Lesbians*. London: SPCK.

Barton, L. and Tomlinson, S. (eds) (1984) *Special Education and
Social Interest*. London: Croom Helm.

Barton, L. *et al.* (1993) Editorial. *Disability, Handicap and
Society*, 8(2):109–10.

Butler, J. (1990) *Gender Trouble: Gender and the Subversion of
Identity*. London: Routledge.

Callinicos, A. (1989) *Against Postmodernism: A Marxist
Critique*. Cambridge: Polity Press.

Carrington, B. and Troyna, B. (1988) Combating racism through
political education. In B. Carrington, and B. Troyna (eds)
*Children and Controversial Issues: Strategies for the Early and
Middle Years of Schooling*. Lewes: Falmer Press.

Clark, C., Dyson, A. and Millward, A. (eds) (1995) *Towards
Inclusive Schooling*. Fulton: London.

Cole, M. (ed.) (1988) *Bowles and Gintis Revisited: Correspondence and Contradiction in Educational Theory.* Lewes: Falmer Press.

Cole, M. (1992) British values, liberal values or values of justice and equality: three approaches to education in multicultural Britain. In J. Lynch, C. Modgil and S. Modgil (eds) *Cultural Diversity and the Schools, vol. 3: Equity or Excellence? Education and Cultural Reproduction.* London: Falmer Press.

Cole, M. (1993a) Widening the cricket test. *The Times Higher Education Supplement,* 26 March.

Cole, M. (1993b) 'Black and Ethnic Minority' or 'Asian, Black and other Minority Ethnic': a further note on nomenclature. *Sociology,* 27(4): 671–3.

Cole, M. (1996a) 'Race' and racism. In M. Payne (ed.) *A Dictionary of Cultural and Critical Theory.* Oxford: Blackwell Publishers.

Cole, M. (1996b) 'Race', racism and nomenclature: a conceptual analysis'. In U. Merkel (ed.) *Racism and Xenophobia in European Football.* Aachen: Meyer & Meyer.

Cole, M. and Hill, D. (1995a) Postmodernism, education and contemporary capitalism: a materialist critique. In O. Valente, A. Barrios and V. Teodoro (eds) *Values and Education vol. 1.* Lisbon: University of Lisbon Press.

Cole, M. and Hill, D. (1995b) Games of despair and rhetorics of resistance: postmodernism, education and reaction. *British Journal of Sociology of Education,* 16(8):165–82.

Cole, M., Maguire, P. and Bosowski, J. (1995) Radio 1 in the 1980s: day-time DJs and the cult of masculinity. In A. Tomlinson (ed.) *Gender, Sport and Leisure: Continuities and Challenges.* Brighton: Chelsea School Research Centre, University of Brighton.

Communist Party (1990) *Manifesto for New Times.* London: Communist Party of Great Britain/Lawrence and Wishart.

Cope, B. and Poynting, S. (1989) Class, gender and ethnicity as influences on Australian schooling: an overview. In M. Cole (ed.) *The Social Contexts of Schooling.* Lewes: Falmer Press.

Department of Education and Science (DES) (1986) *Education Act (No. 2).* London: HMSO.

Department for Education (DFE) (1994) *Code of Practice on the Identification and Assessment of Special Educational Needs.* London: HMSO.

Eisenstein, Z. (1981) *The Radical Future of Liberal Feminism.* New York: Longman.

Epstein, D. (ed.) (1994) *Challenging Lesbian and Gay Inequalities in Education.* Buckingham: Open University Press.

Epstein, D. and Johnson, P. (1994) On the straight and narrow: the heterosexual presumption, homophobia and schools. In D. Epstein (ed.) *Challenging Lesbian and Gay Inequalities in Education.* Buckingham: Open University Press.

Ford, J., Mongon, D. and Whelan, T. (1982) *Invisible Disasters: Special Education and Social Control.* London: Routledge & Kegan Paul.

Fuller, M. (1980) Black girls in a London comprehensive school. In R. Deem (ed.) *Co-Education Reconsidered.* Milton Keynes: Open University Press.

George, R. (1993) *A Handbook on Equal Opportunities in Schools: Principles, Policy and Practice.* Harlow: Longman.

Gilroy, R. (1987) *There Ain't No Black in the Union Jack.* London: Hutchinson.

Guardian (1995) News report, 17 February.

Hall, S. and Jacques, M. (eds) (1989) *New Times: The Changing Face of Politics in the 1990s.* London: Lawrence and Wishart.

Harris, S. (1990) *Lesbian and Gay Issues in the English Classroom.* Milton Keynes: Open University Press.

Harris, S., Nixon, J. and Ruddock, J. (1993) School work, homework and gender. *Gender and Education,* 5(2).

Hessari, R. and Hill, D. (1989) *Practical Ideas for Multicultural Learning and Teaching in the Primary Classroom.* London: Routledge.

Hill, D. (1990) *Something Old, Something New, Something Borrowed, Something Blue: Teacher Education, Schooling and the Radical Right in Britain and the USA.* London: Tufnell Press.

Hill, D. (1994) Cultural diversity and initial teacher education. In G. Verma and P. Pumfrey (eds) *Cultural Diversity and the Curriculum, vol. 4: Cross-Curricular Contexts, Themes and Dimensions in Primary Schools.* London: Falmer Press.

Hill, D. (1996) Reflection in teacher education. In K. Watson, C. Modgil and S. Modgil (eds) *Educational Dilemmas: Debate and Diversity, vol. 1: Teacher Education and Training.* London: Cassell.

Kelly, J. (1989) Class is still the central issue. *Communist Review,* 3, Spring.

Kelly, J. (1992) Postmodernism and feminism. *International Marxist Review,* 14, Winter.

Kelly, J. (1994) Feminism and postmodernism: a productive tension or an incompatible collusion? Paper given to the British Educational Research Association Annual Conference, Oxford.

La Fontaine, J. S. (1978) *Sex and Age as Principles of Social Differentiation.* London: Academic Press.

Lather, P. (1991) *Getting Smart: Feminist Research and Pedagogy With/In the Postmodern.* New York: Routledge.

Leicester, M. (1989) *Multicultural Education: From Theory to Practice.* Windsor: Nfer-Nelson.

Leicester, M. (1992) Antiracism versus the new multiculturalism: moving beyond the interminable debate. In J. Lynch, C. Modgil and S. Modgil (eds) *Cultural Diversity and the Schools, vol. 3: Equity or Excellence? Education and Cultural Reproduction.* London: Falmer Press.

Lynch, J., Modgil, C. and Modgil, S. (eds) (1992) *Cultural Diversity and the Schools, vol. 3: Equity or Excellence? Education and Cultural Reproduction.* London: Falmer Press.

Mama, A. (1992) Black women and the British state: race, class and gender analysis for the 1990s. In P. Braham *et al.* (eds) *Racism and Antiracism.* London: Sage.

Marshall, G., Rose, D., Newby, H. and Vogler, C. (1989) *Social Class in Modern Britain.* London: Unwin Hyman.

Marx, K. (1976) *Capital: A Critical Analysis of Capitalist Production, vol. 1* Harmondsworth: Penguin

Mason, D. (1994) On the dangers of disconnecting race and racism. *Sociology,* 28(4):845–58.

Mason, M. (1990) Special educational needs: just another label. In R. Rieser and M. Mason (eds) *Disability Equality in the Classroom: A Human Rights Issue.* London: Inner London Education Authority.

Mason, M. (1990) Integration v segregation. In Rieser and Mason (eds) *Disability Equality in the Classroom.*

Mason, M. and Rieser, R. (1990) The medical model and the social model of disability. In Rieser and Mason (eds) *Disability Equality in the Classroom.*

Measor, L. and Sikes, P. (1992) *Gender and Schools.* London: Cassell.

Miles, R. (1982) *Racism and Migrant Labour.* London: Routledge & Kegan Paul.

Modood, T. (1992) *Not Easy Being British: Colour, Culture and Citizenship.* London: Runnymede Trust and Trentham Books.

Modood, T. (1994) Political blackness and British Asians. *Sociology,* 28(4):858–76.

National Curriculum Council (1991) *Managing Economic and Industrial Understanding in Schools.* York: National Curriculum Council.

National Union of Teachers (1991) *Lesbians and Gays in Schools: An Issue for Every Teacher.* London: National Union of Teachers.

Redman, P. (1994) Shifting ground: rethinking sexuality education. In D. Epstein (ed.) *Challenging Lesbian and Gay Inequalities in Education.* Buckinghamshire: Open University Press.

Richardson, R. (1992) Preface to T. Modood *Not Easy Being British: Colour, Culture and Citizenship.* London: Runnymede Trust and Trentham Books.

Rieser, R. (1990) Disabled history or a history of the disabled. In Rieser and Mason (eds) *Disability Equality in the Classroom.*

Rieser, R. and Mason, M. (eds) (1990) *Disability Equality in the Classroom: A Human Rights Issue.* London: Inner London Education Authority.

Rogers, M. (1994) Growing up lesbian: the role of the school. In Epstein (ed.) *Challenging Lesbian and Gay Inequalities.*

Slee, R. (1993) The politics of integration – new sites for old practices? *Disability, Handicap Society,* 8(4).

Solity, J. E. (1991) Special needs: a discriminatory concept? *Educational Psychology in Practice,* 7(1):12–19.

Solity, J. E. (1995) Psychology, teachers and the early years. *International Journal of Early Years Education,* 3 (1):5–23.

Stanworth, M. (1983) *Gender and Schooling.* London: Hutchinson.

Tiger, L. and Fox, R. (1972) *The Imperial Animal.* London: Secker & Warburg.

Tomlinson, A. (ed.) (1995) *Gender, Sport and Leisure: Continuities and Challenges.* Brighton: Chelsea School Research Centre, University of Brighton.

Tomlinson, S. (1982) *A Sociology of Special Education.* London: Routledge & Kegan Paul.

Troyna, B. (1993) *Racism and Education.* Buckingham: Open University Press.

Walkerdine, V. (1981) Sex, power and pedagogy. *Screen Education,* 38.

Weber, M. (1968) *Economy and Society.* New York: Bedminster Press.

Wolpe, A. M. (1988) 'Experience' as analytical framework: does it account for girls' education? In Cole (ed.) *Bowles and Gintis Revisited.*

Young, R. E. (1984) Teaching equals indoctrination: the dominant epistemic practices of our schools. *British Journal of Education Studies,* 22(3):230–38.

CHAPTER 3

Putting principles into practice

Ros Bayley and Gillean Paterson

THE CONTEXT – THE TELEVISION SERIES AND THE PRESS

In this chapter we describe aspects of recent history and current practice at our school, which we believe might help to illuminate the area of equality in schools.

Towards the end of 1989 our school was approached by a television production team and we were asked to take part in a documentary series about primary education. After discussion among ourselves, and also with the producer and director, the staff agreed to participate. Although there were varying degrees of enthusiasm, there was a consensus that this was an important opportunity to take up. The two main reasons for the decision were these.

First, although education is such a profoundly formative, lengthy and common experience, there is remarkably little public discussion about the subject beyond the parroting of fairly stereotypical views along the lines of: 'there should be more discipline'; 'standards have fallen since my day' (my day can range from two years to seventy years ago); 'why don't they teach them tables?' and 'all they ever do is play'. Rarely do people have the chance to consider more deeply their own memories and experiences as children undergoing a varyingly rigid form of social control. Have they completely forgotten the pleasure and fun of discovery and learning, or the pain and misery of being powerless in the face of unfairness and adult severity?

If there was a chance to have a wider debate it would take place chiefly in the arena of the media where so many issues are reduced to oversimplified and polarized political platitudes. Popular culture abounds with examples of versions of other areas of work and life. Novels, TV series and drama illustrate the work of the medical and legal professions, the police, the fire service, the criminal world and the oil industry, among others. A huge amount of impressions and information are picked up from the fictionalized images seen on *Casualty, London's Burning* and *The Bill*, as well as from the realism of documentaries, newspaper reports and news bulletins. But what about similar images of the world of education? It is hard to think of examples, (with the honourable exception of *Grange Hill*), apart from the tempting and idealized glimpses of school life as portrayed in Australian TV soaps. There are numerous excellent education programmes but these seem to be viewed mostly by teachers and academics. Yet the experience of school directly touches all our lives, whether in our past as children, or in the present as parents. Why is such an important experience so undervalued by those in the adult world? We believed we could make a useful contribution to a much broader public debate by allowing the life of the school to be chronicled in a TV programme.

The second reason for our decision was that staff were angered and shocked by the Tory Campaign of 1988 onwards to abolish the Inner London Education Authority (ILEA). For the past two years thousands of Londoners – parents, teachers, pupils, youth workers, community workers, governors, politicians of all parties – had fought to maintain the service. The ILEA had huge popular support that was entirely ignored by the government. We felt that our school was fairly typical of so many London schools where real efforts were being made to recognize and try to reverse the inequalities and disadvantages caused by perceptions of ethnicity, gender, class, disability and sexuality. We had clear anti-racist and anti-sexist guidelines issued by the ILEA. There was in-service training (INSET) at all levels, in schools, locally and Londonwide. There were courses, conferences, specialist centres, networks and resources, at primary and secondary level, which supported development in the arts, literacy, maths, science, humanities and issues of urban education. All this, it was feared, would cease in April 1990 when the different London boroughs were to take over responsibility for education. We felt at the time – although in retrospect it may seem naive – that, by making a documentary about an inner city London school, we could place on record some lasting evidence to the value of the ILEA, whose existence the Tories seemed to want to obliterate from history.

This was the background to the decision to agree to allow the film crew into school. They spent the whole of 1990 filming material in classic 'fly-on-the-wall' style. The resulting six forty-minute programmes were transmitted over six weeks starting in mid-January 1991. The BBC2 series was entitled *Culloden – A Year in the Life of a Primary School*.

The series was well received and favourably reviewed in many papers, including the *Daily Mail* and the *Daily Telegraph*.[1] It seemed to have been successful in portraying the complexities of school life. It gave a realistic idea of how teachers often have to deal with a wide range of problems brought into school by children and parents, before they can continue with the relatively straightforward task of 'delivering the curriculum'. It succeeded in raising interest and causing discussion about strategies that can be used to sort out such problems. Having endured the embarrassment and discomfort of being watched by a camera for a year, the staff felt that our suffering had not been in vain. Many parents watched the series and enjoyed the experience of having a direct link with a television programme.

In the half-term of February 1991, a journalist from the *Mail on Sunday* came to the estate where the school is situated. She met a small group of racist parents who had always been very hostile towards the school on the grounds that we 'put the Pakis above the other kids'. She arranged for a right-wing educational psychologist to administer a reading test in a local community centre. About thirty children took the test. Some parents were under the impression that it was arranged by the school. Not all the children taking the tests attended the school. Two children were being assessed at the time by our educational psychologist so that they would receive extra provision for their special educational needs. The ages ranged from 4 to 11. At no time was the school consulted about the test, the results of which supposedly showed that most of the children were unable to read. Some weeks later we received a copy of the test results from a sympathizer working at the newspaper office. One 10-year-old who appeared as a non-reader on the score system used was currently reading *The Lion, the Witch and the Wardrobe* in class with understanding and enjoyment.

On the evidence thus gathered, the reporter published a front-page article in the *Mail on Sunday* alleging that although the school was held up as an example of good practice following the TV programme, it was in fact failing its working-class pupils by using 'trendy-lefty' methods which led to their being illiterate. Two days later, Kenneth Clarke, the then Education Secretary, announced that because of public concern an inspection of the school by Her Majesty's Inspectorate would take place in two weeks' time.

Despite being horrified by events, which included being besieged by reporters, we were not too daunted by the prospect of an HMI inspection. Previous dealings with HMI had caused us to see them as helpful colleagues. Although we were at the earliest stages of dealing with the implications of the newly arrived National Curriculum, we were making progress towards setting up systems. Like many other schools at the time we were in the process of developing policies to implement it. We had draft Science, Mathematics and English policies. We had a School Development plan arising from work done on two recent INSET days. Our London Reading Test results had been above the London average for the past five years. There were weaknesses in the school which we had identified and were working on, but we would not have agreed to being televised if we had felt that our children were underachieving or that the way that the school functioned was disadvantaging them. Such a programme would no doubt have been used for propaganda purposes by the radical Right. However, our confidence was seriously misplaced. The HMI report drew a picture of the school which was unrecognizable to those who worked there, or whose children attended it. Within six weeks the report was completed and leaked to the *Mail on Sunday* before the school governors had received a copy. During that time the press continued to search unscrupulously for information among parents and staff and there were further hostile articles published in the *Mail on Sunday*.[2]

The whole experience was traumatic for the staff and led sadly to the early retirement of the then headteacher. What sustained us was the extraordinary amount of support we received from the overwhelming majority of our parents, from many other teachers and colleagues in education, not just from London schools but from all over the country, and also from many members of the public who had watched the programmes and had read about the resulting controversy. All these people expressed their dismay at the way in which we had been scapegoated by a government intent on undermining certain educational ideas and principles which are completely at odds with their own divisive, elitist and punitive model of education.

The inspection by HMI might have had the effect of discrediting the efforts of staff at Culloden School to manage the school in an open and democratic way. The subsequent publicity and criticism could have changed the school irrevocably. However, the systems that were in place to involve pupils, staff, parents and governors in a wide range of decisions ensured continuing understanding of and commitment to the model of education being offered at Culloden.

THE SCHOOL'S PRINCIPLES

The philosophy of the school is based on a shared conviction, arrived at through observation and experience, that children have a very strong sense of natural justice, and also an innate desire to find out and learn about the world around them. As teachers, we have a responsibility to provide a safe environment, where children feel valued and respected. In such an environment, learning can only flourish. Equality is the keystone which supports the structure of the school from curriculum to learning experiences, to managing the school. This is hardly a controversial idea, but it is all too easy to claim as an educational principle, and all too often superficially applied. Real equality can only exist when power is not held by one group alone. In schools, this group is usually the adults/teachers, but everyone should have a voice. We as adults expect to be heard and we must also ensure that children have a voice.

What are the principles that underlie the promotion of equality in schools? We consider them to be fairness, trust, co-operation, communication and creativity. We try to apply them to all aspects and areas of school life, in the classroom, in the school as a whole and in the wider school community.

Most teachers agree that children learn better when they feel safe, when they are relaxed and free from anxieties. So it is a school's responsibility actively to create such an environment by building up a sense of trust and a certainty that issues, problems and injustices will be resolved fairly. At Culloden we use talking as the means to achieve this end. If something needs to be sorted out we talk about it, with all concerned, until a fair conclusion is reached. The issues which crop up most often requiring serious attention in this way are nearly always centred around equality and manifest themselves in general bullying behaviour: for example, when someone is taunted for being scruffily dressed, called names for being black, for living in a women's refuge, or for wearing hearing aids, or sometimes an incident such as stealing occurs.

CLASS MEETINGS

The classroom is where children spend most of their day, so for teachers this offers a valuable opportunity to model strategies for achieving equality, which children can use if and when they want to in their own lives, but which will be the framework within which fairness, trust, co-operation, communication and creativity can happen. One of the most important strategies is a system of class meetings. These take place between the teacher and her/his class. Some guidelines for good practice include:

- Regular meeting times are needed for communication, planning and discussion.
- Unplanned meetings can happen if an urgent need arises.
- A format which encourages all children to be actively involved should be developed.
- The teacher should be aware of and use a wide range of roles.
- Children can also develop a range of roles.
- Ideas can be brainstormed regularly to help children focus on the curriculum.

- The children and the teacher can establish the rules within which the class will operate.
- Work that is in process can be reflected upon and reviewed.
- Children are offered opportunities to develop their own interests and to work together on shared interests.

Regular meetings

Regular meeting times are needed for communication, planning and discussion. There are three regular meeting times each day – morning and afternoon registration and before hometime. The class gathers together on the carpet area of the room. Following registration, plans for the day's work will be discussed thoroughly and children given the chance to ask questions or make contributions.

This is a good opportunity for the teacher to make any special announcements, perhaps regarding visitors to school. This is a time when children can raise problems/issues which they would like sorting out.

The first afternoon meeting will settle the class, review the morning and set the afternoon off. The meeting before hometime will include a story and perhaps discussion and giving out information.

Unplanned meetings

Sometimes something happens which upsets a child or the whole class (perhaps a fight in the playground or an incident on the way to school). If left unresolved such an event can undermine all the positive things that are going on. As soon as the teacher recognizes this she should set up a class meeting to try to guide the group to resolve the problem and re-establish stability.

Active involvement of all children

A format should be developed which encourages all children to be actively involved. Forming a circle, signalling when you want a turn to speak, listening to the person who is speaking, asking for contributions from quiet children, valuing what each is saying to the other, asking children to interpret for others, writing down what is said and summing up are all important ingredients of a successful meeting.

Teacher's role

The teacher should be aware of and use a wide range of roles. Usually the teacher will start and finish the meeting. She may also act as listener, interpreter, leader, observer and recorder.

Children's role

Children can also develop a range of roles. The children benefit if all members of the class can gain experience of being: leader, recorder, observer, as well as listening and offering ideas. They will come to value such times together and see how important it is that everyone in the class group works together.

Sharing ideas

Ideas can be brainstormed regularly to help children focus on the curriculum. Well-structured meetings which focus on some aspect of the curriculum offer the teacher insight into the range of levels of skills and knowledge of the class. Well-focused discussion and questioning can advance the understanding of the children.

Class rules

The children and the teacher can establish the rules within which the class will operate. The teacher talks with the children about what things will make the classroom a safe and comfortable place to work. Guided by the teacher, the children can reach agreement on how to achieve them. They now have something which can be referred to if, for example, there is a spate of bad behaviour.

Work in progress

Work that is in process can be reflected upon and reviewed. Meetings that are specifically to share work place value on what the children do in their time at school and keep everyone in touch with each other. Children can learn a lot about each other simply by listening to accounts of events in their lives. Understanding can be advanced by children asking questions like 'I don't understand that bit, can you explain it?'

Interests and ideas

The meetings offer children opportunities to develop individual interests and to work together on shared ideas. When children talk, they often mention things which interest or concern them. Giving them time to explore those things which are special to them and helping them to plan, structure and monitor such projects is an invaluable aspect of their curriculum. A meeting is often the opportunity for their ideas to be spoken and listened to.

WHOLE SCHOOL MEETINGS

The system of class meetings can work beyond the classroom and into cross-year group meetings or whole school assemblies. The following is an example of how we worked with the whole school and a final agreement was negotiated.

While we were writing the school prospectus, we decided to draw up a school code of conduct as part of the statutory requirement for a behaviour policy. We held three large meetings for the infants, the lower juniors and the upper juniors. After an introductory discussion, we broke into groups of five or six children and adults. Each group produced some writing on ways in which they liked people to behave and on behaviour which they found unacceptable. The adults then took the pieces of shared writing and, having found a remarkable consistency in each piece, wrote a succinct redrafted version. This draft was shown to the children and a copy was sent to all parents, who were invited to offer comments or criticisms. Parents were very supportive of the suggested code and no one took the opportunity to dissent or disagree. We now have a Code of Conduct which all parents read and agree to before their child starts school. The governors recently decided to ask all new parents to sign an agreement in support of our Code of Conduct and also of our anti-racist statement.

A VOICE THROUGH WRITING

Our writing policy aims to develop children's skills as writers and to write for a range of purposes from as early as possible. One purpose is to write books which are to be read in the classroom. Children are encouraged to use their personal experiences if they wish, as well as to write fiction. This process can help both the writer and the reader in fundamental ways.

Here is an example. A Year 5 Somali girl had been in school for a year-and-a-half. Her behaviour was extremely hostile. She was verbally and physically aggressive and continually disruptive, but she had made excellent progress with English. She was unwilling to write about anything and finally, after much persuasion, agreed to write something about Somalia as part of a class geography theme. After a week's work she produced a first draft of a fascinating account of her life on her uncle's farm, the effect on her family of the emerging civil war and her arrival in England where her family was finally reunited. The book was finally published on the classroom computer and was widely read and popular with the rest of the class.

Two things happened as a result. First, her book gave the other children a clearer understanding and greater tolerance of her idiosyncratic ways. Second, her success as a writer increased her self-esteem and her behaviour became markedly less miserable and hostile. She had told her story and was heard.

STAFF AND DECISION-MAKING

We believe that all staff need to be involved in decision-making so that consensus can be reached and decisions put into practice. We take turns in chairing and minuting meetings, and drawing up agendas so that everyone is fully involved and also has opportunities to develop appropriate skills. We have different forums for meetings.

- Short pre-school meetings: daily.
- Head and deputy meetings: daily.
- Whole staff meetings: weekly.
- Year group class teacher meetings: weekly.
- Teachers of the deaf: weekly.

- Management team: weekly.
- Curriculum teams: half-termly.
- Curriculum co-ordinators: termly.
- Working parties: as necessary (e.g. equal opportunities, organizing celebrations, developing curriculum policies, clearing up the staffroom.
- Classroom meetings: as appropriate.

Good communication systems are essential, but we are continually aware of the danger of overloading the meetings timetable.

OUR SCHOOL AIM

Our school aim was arrived at during an INSET day when all the school staff contributed in a workshop session. It is reviewed annually and this enables new staff to be part of the process of change and development. In 1994 we decided to display the school's anti-racist statement alongside the school aim. When we have developed further equal opportunities statements, we shall also display them.

OUR SCHOOL AIM

Culloden School aims to provide a calm, safe, stimulating and challenging environment where children will:

1 learn to understand, respect and value their own and others' way of life.
2 develop the confidence, self-esteem and interest in learning which will enable them to think critically and independently.
3 have equal access to a broad and balanced curriculum in order to arrive at a high level of achievement.
4 prepare themselves to take an active part in our complex and diverse world.

CULLODEN SCHOOL ANTI-RACIST STATEMENT

Culloden School fully supports Tower Hamlets council's declared and active opposition to racism and all forms of discrimination on the grounds of colour, religion, ethnic or national origin.

We will support any individual or group subjected to racism

and will help them to seek assistance from the many voluntary and statutory agencies in the borough.

Most of the antiracist work done by staff happens in the school, using the curriculum and the issues raised in everyday life. We also try to work in the wider community. The following are two examples of ways in which the school tries to extend beyond the classroom to counter the racism which affects so many of our children.

1   We use our school budget to buy in a Home/School worker who spends 2.5 days a week working in school. Often she visits families as a result of children bringing problems to their class teacher, who then informs the Home/School worker. In partnership with other members of staff, including two Bengali-speaking colleagues, she has set up useful links with the housing office, the nearby community rights office, the local police and other community groups.

2   During the recent council by-election in Tower Hamlets, when a British National Party candidate stood locally, there was a campaign to persuade more women to register on the electoral roll, particularly since many women from minority ethnic communities are unaware of their rights as voters. We had posters publicising the campaign in every classroom, and staff talked to many mothers, explaining the campaign and putting them in touch with the organizers.

These are some examples of practical ways in which we have tried to tackle the issue of inequality. A school is a microcosm of the wider world and the principles of mutual understanding, mutual support and interdependence which we teach our children should stand them in good stead in their futures. It is vital that such work should continue to develop further.

There are many disturbing questions continually to be raised, particularly with the present government's policy to resell their educational dogma in this divided and fractured society.

• What purpose is served by using Standard Assessment Tasks to label children below average at 7, 11 and 14?
• What is the future for comprehensive education with growing pressure to move away from mixed ability teaching?

- What are the implications of increasing numbers of schools opting out?
- Why are more and more schools adopting school uniforms (nice little dresses for the girls and smart trousers for the boys)?
- Why do all advertisements in magazines and newspapers or in Department For Education documents have pictures of children in school uniform?
- How many women teachers are shown in the pictures in the Parents' Charter?
- How many Asian, black and other minority ethnic teachers are there in the profession?
- How many teachers of the deaf are themselves deaf?
- Should head teachers have so much power in the school?
- How many women head teachers are there in this country?
- Why are gay and lesbian teachers afraid to reveal their sexuality?
- What message is the Labour Party sending out when Tony Blair, leader of the Labour Party, sends his son to an elitist, Catholic, all boys school, which has opted out of local authority control to become directly maintained (and financially rewarded) by the government, and when Harriet Harman, a member of Labour's shadow cabinet, sends her son to a grammar school?
- How can working-class students have real access to higher education with the abolition of a fair system of grants?
- Why did the programme on Culloden provoke such a response from this government?

In conclusion, the practice at Culloden School is based on shared understanding which includes children and adults. We all feel the ethos of our school, know when it is under threat and are able to defend our principles. This is what we determined to do by striving to offer equality and democracy at Culloden School.

We have written on some aspects of equal opportunity practice in our school. This is not meant to be a comprehensive coverage of all areas of inequality and the way in which they can be countered in schools. As practising teachers it is very hard to find the time, space, objectivity and tranquillity to write more fully. We continue to be strongly committed to working as democratically as we can. It is essential to do what you can in a society like ours where many divisions have widened or remained the same rather than narrowed during the past years of Tory government.

NOTES

1   The *Daily Telegraph* (15 January 1991) commented:

> Numbers of our state schools could do with a vast dose of many of the ideals observed at multi-racial Culloden Primary in London's Tower Hamlets, one of the poorest inner city boroughs in the country ... [it] deserves some praise for drawing our attention to a setting that should be every schoolchild's right: fully staffed and caring.

The *Times Educational Supplement* (1 February 1991) concluded its review of the series with:

> The warmth of the reviews received by the first episodes of *Culloden* ('Ten out of ten', said the *Daily Mail*; 'Vivid vignettes from the educational front-line', said the *Evening Standard*) suggests that this series might establish a new popular reference point for discussing contemporary education. Television and cinematic stereotypes of teachers have in the past swung between a Mr Chips in gown and mortar board, to a beleaguered inner-city liberal, unable to control a class. In *Culloden* a serious alternative has been portrayed, with education taking to the prime-time stage in a convincing and entertaining form.

2   Sample headings include: 'Losing the battle of Culloden: a school renowned for caring fails its children' (*Mail on Sunday*, 3 March 1991) and a front-page headline, 'Failed on all counts' (*Mail on Sunday*, 14 April 1991). Radical right-wing educationalist John Marks joined in the attack on the school in his 'Reading the Riot Act' (*Times Educational Supplement*, 10 May 1991). In contrast, Ted Wragg and Robin Richardson respectively lampooned the attack on Culloden school and mounted a vigorous defence of the school in the *Times Educational Supplements* of 19 April and 26 April 1991. The school and its approach had become a *cause célèbre*.

SUGGESTIONS FOR FURTHER READING

Ashton Warner, S. (1980) *Teacher.* London: Virago.

Donaldson, M. (1990) *Children's Minds.* London: Fontana.

Maclure, S. (1990) *A History of Education in London 1870–1990.* Harmondsworth: Penguin.

Miller, A. (1983) *For Your Own Good.* New York: Farrar, Straus, Giroux.

Morrell, F. (1989) *Children of the Future, the Battle for Britain's Schools.* London: The Hogarth Press.

Neill, A. S. (1968) *Summerhill.* Harmondsworth: Penguin.

North, R. (1987) *Schools of Tomorrow.* Hartland: Green Books.

Russell, D. *The Tamarisk Tree*, vol. 1. London: Virago.

Waterland, L. (1994) *Not a Perfect Offering – A New School Year.* Stroud: Thimble Press.

CHAPTER 4

Equality and primary teacher education

Dave Hill, Mike Cole and Claudette Williams

INTRODUCTION

We argue in this chapter that all undergraduate and postgraduate 'teacher training'/teacher education courses should consider issues of social justice and therefore enable students actively to challenge racism, sexism, homophobia, discrimination against the disabled and the exploitation of the working class. At present, these issues in BEd/BA(QTS) and PGCE courses are very patchy, with some, like social class and sexuality, frequently untouched. Where a consideration of these issues does exist, such existence is being severely threatened by the Conservative nationalization of the teacher education curriculum (Hill, 1993, 1994a).

THE CONTEXT

Critical and egalitarian teacher education is under sustained attack. What is, in effect, the new National Curriculum for Initial Teacher Education (ITE) excludes, to a large extent, social, political and critical analysis of current education policy and the examination of alternatives.

91

Other measures such as the introduction of totally school-centred ITE and the reduction in funding for student teachers, are causing education departments in colleges and universities to contract. In some cases, colleges/universities are considering withdrawing from ITE altogether.

In this chapter, we begin by setting out some of the major characteristics of radical Right ideology on ITE. Next, we outline a recent history of changes/'reforms' in ITE. We discuss the effect of the Council for the Accreditation of Teacher Education (CATE) from its establishment in 1984 to its demise in 1995, and its replacement by the Teacher Training Agency (TTA). As case studies we look at some adaptations of government guidelines at the University of North London and elsewhere. We conclude by assessing three ideological and policy positions: first, liberal–progressive ideology (the dominant paradigm in Primary ITE through the 1970s and 1980s); second, what is claimed by some of its proponents to be the centre-left position;[1] and, third, the radical Left position. Rejecting liberal progressivism and the centre-left (the latter as suggested, for example, in recent Labour Party and Institute for Public Policy Research policy documents), we propose a series of principles which we believe should underlie policy-making. We also make proposals for a Core Curriculum for ITE and suggest some ways in which it might be better organized.

THE RADICAL RIGHT MODEL OF 'TEACHING TRAINING'

The legacy of Thatcherism in Britain remains, unfortunately, very much intact.[2] The Thatcherite revolution in education may be seen as an amalgam of the neo-liberal philosophy of Friedrich von Hayek, with its emphasis on the social morality of individual choice, competition, inequality and the free reign of the market,[3] and cultural restorationism (or neoconservatism) which stresses the importance of British (i.e. white, male, homophobic, able-bodied, ruling-class) culture, nation and 'race' (see Chapter 2).[4]

The radical Right believe that Primary Teacher Education should be scrapped, either totally or substantially and that 'training' (its proponents deliberately avoid the term 'education') should take place 'on the job' – in schools. This is to keep student teachers away from what they see as the trendy progressive egalitarian (the radical Right tend to conflate the two very different concepts of 'liberal progressivism' and 'egalitarianism') 'teacher trainers'. School-based training also accords with the notion that teaching does not need to be informed by theory, that all that is needed is a knowledge and love of one's subject (O'Hear, 1991). The radical Right believe that education should be about effective instruction in facts and national testing, to make sure that 'the facts' have been learned.

This model, favoured by the British government, can be criticized as an attempt to undermine critical thinking, to castigate theorizing and to deprofessionalize teachers. It can be seen as an exercise in ideological conformity (Cole, 1989; Hill, 1989, 1990, 1992, 1994a; Gilroy, 1992; Cole *et al.*, 1996). Its origins can be traced back to the late 1970s, with the then Labour Party Prime Minister James Callaghan's speech, which served notice on the teaching profession of changes to come. Areas which were to come under scrutiny were 'methods and aims of informal instruction, core curriculum of basic knowledge, national standards, the role of inspectors in maintenance of national standards, and relations between industry and education' (Callaghan, 1976).[5]

In the 1980s the exploitation of an existing tension between the establishment of academic content and knowledge on one hand and the acquisition of sets of skills on the other was heightened. The momentum and impact of the 1970s with its emphasis on 'teacher education' has been undermined by a government with an ideology which espouses the beliefs of a check-list of skill competencies. Here we would agree with Elliott that: 'Teaching cannot and should not be reduced to a series of atomistically specified, described skills, which are sold as a package in school market place' (Elliott, 1993:18).

More recently, the ideology prompted an attempt to introduce a 'Mum's Army' (of one-year trained, non-graduate Infant teachers) as sufficient preparation for the task of teaching. In 1984, the DES Circular 3/84 (DES, 1984) created the Council for the Accreditation of Teacher Education (CATE), with responsibility to scrutinize and accredit all Initial Teacher Training (ITT) institutions. Subject knowledge contained in Bachelor of Education (BEd) courses were extended to 50 per cent of the four-year BEd courses, thereby reducing space and time for theoretical ideas such as those deriving from sociology, psychology and philosophy.

The study of controversial issues and education theory was, in many institutions, reduced. The 1984 CATE criteria did, however, also provide space and legitimation, taken up in some institutions, for the development of courses in class, 'race' and gender, and also for the permeation of these issues (and of the issue of 'special needs') throughout the whole of the BEd and Postgraduate Certificate of Education (PGCE) courses (Hessari and Hill, 1989; Whitty, 1993; Hill, 1994a). (This space was to be considerably reduced, however, by the 1989 CATE Criteria (DES, 1989), and rendered virtually non-existent by the CATE Circular 14/93 (DFE, 1993) to which all Primary ITE courses had to conform by September 1995.)

In addition, the CATE criteria of 1989 introduced the requirement for 'recent and relevant' experience, by which staff involved in the professional preparation of student teachers were to return to the school classroom for an updating of experience for the equivalent of one term every five years. Circular 24/93 also increased the amount of 'Professional Curriculum' time requirement for the ITE courses, thereby further reducing time for 'Education' coursework (it is here that the theory is usually taught).

In order to meet these new 1989 criteria, institutions had already begun to revise their courses, and to make increased opportunities for more school-based experience. Although CATE presided over the reduction of education theory, courses could not, until the 1993 requirements, effectively jettison issues such as equal opportunities, the understanding of children's learning, and the need for students to be reflective and critically to evaluate their teaching. These issues had a persuasive hold on teacher educators. The 'education' of the teacher was still the fundamental part of ITE.

The tension between the transition from theory to practice, which the government attempted to exploit in validating their attack on ITE Institutions, had been at the centre of debates among the profession for a number of years. Institutions had acknowledged the difficulties which existed between the two central planks of students' education, that of theory and the move into practice. Kearney has argued that:

> For several years there has been a growing dissatisfaction with the theory to practice model which has developed in teacher education.... As a result, many institutes have effected fundamental changes to their courses, making both theoretical and practical element more clearly integrated and more directly relevant to the students' needs.
>
> (Kearney, 1994:13)

Developments in ITE courses had resulted in a mixture of subject knowledge, preparation for the classroom – both theoretical and practical – and on-the-job training. Preparation for life within the profession was seen to demand that students understood and made provision for children within a multi-cultural, multilingual learning environment. This emphasis in teacher education encouraged students actively to break with racist, sexist stereotypes and practices. The 'reflective teacher' in which the student (the novice) developed the capacity and confidence for independent thought helped emerging teachers to adopt a 'teacher-as-researcher' stance and constantly to view and review their practice and classroom management. The concept of 'the reflective teacher' is without a doubt one of the bedrocks on which teacher education over the previous twenty years had rested.

> Reflection has become one of the most popular issues in teacher education. The literature is replete with accounts of the reported success of reflective practitioners in changing and improving their own teaching ... of teacher education programs instilling reflective 'practices' in their students ... and of call for further reforms in pursuit of reflective stance in teaching.
> (Copeland *et al.*, 1993:347; see Hill, 1996a, for a critique of the concept of 'reflection')

By 1989 change which had taken place in teacher education was notably sufficient for the then Secretary of State for Education, Kenneth Clarke, to say that 'the academic content of teachers' training is now more rigorous, the professional content less theoretical and much more directly related to classroom practice' (DES, 1989a).

Yet continued claims regarding falling standards in schools, with the knock-on effect of inappropriate preparation for the classroom, continued to be popularized by the government, despite contrary claims by Her Majesty's Inspectorate of Education. Two HMI surveys of ITT and university training departments in 1987 and 1989 revealed that the training systems had considerable strengths and some weaknesses, but significant steps had been taken to improve training (DES, 1987, 1989a).

WHY CATE HAD TO GO

The demise of the Council for Accreditation of Teacher Education (CATE) should be seen as another step in undermining and weakening the professional content of teacher education. With the creation of self-accrediting universities and the government's emphasis on 'on-the-job training' and the possible return to a non-graduate teaching profession, much of CATE's function has been rendered obsolete. Like the demise of other independent and independent-minded institutions, such as the Inner London Education Authority, the University Grants Committee (set up in 1919 to buffer universities from central government interference and to protect their academic freedom), CATE had outlived its usefulness within the government's cost-cutting and conforming and deprofessionalization of teacher education (Hill, 1993, 1994a). The replacement authority, the Teacher Training Agency (TTA) has a mandate to oversee and fund the new arrangements concerning teacher 'training' and to provide quality assurance.

Some local developments

Under CATE's regulation, the University of North London (UNL) ran a four-year BEd honours programme, on which 43 per cent of students identified themselves as coming from a minority ethnic group and 82 per cent of whom were aged 21 years or over (University of North London, 1995).

The structure of the UNL BEd programme was similar to that of a number of programmes around the country, with the first year of the course concentrating on professional understanding, teaching through direct experience and providing the opportunity for students to reflect on and analyse practice with both tutors and school teachers. The second phase of the course, lasting eighteen months, allowed students to work alongside other degree students on BA programmes to develop appropriate subject pedagogical skills. On completion, students returned to the BEd programme, developing their understanding in the classroom. An assessed independent piece of work further helps students to apply their special subject knowledge to the pedagogical demands of the classroom. This is similar to the pattern of many BEd courses developed under the 1984 and 1989 CATE criteria, although a number retained the 'education', 'Professional Curriculum' and 'Academic Main Subject' parts of the degree running concurrently throughout the four years of the course.

The course team at UNL believes that the composition and destination of the studetns makes it imperative that they have a firm understanding of structural inequalities and how these impact and discriminate against specific groups in school. An education which disregards these fundamental issues would be doing a disservice not only to students, but to the school populations they are likely to teach as a whole.

Such considerations are applicable in all types of areas, and these intentions were built into many undergraduate and postgraduate ITE courses validated in the 1980s, regardless of the nature of their student intake or location. Some student intakes and locations, however, did make such concerns more pressing and salient.

PARTNERSHIP BETWEEN HIGHER EDUCATION AND SCHOOLS

CATE Circulars 3/84 and 24/89 outlined the responsibilities of training institutions to involve schools in planning and evaluating courses, in the selection of students, and in the supervision and assessment of students on school block practice. According to Mike Williams: 'By any standard this represents a fairly narrow definition of partnership but surprisingly these are the only mandatory obligations' (1993:3).

CATE Circular 14/93 (for Primary teacher education) (and Circular 9/92 for Secondary teacher education) have dramatically increased the amount of school-based undergraduate and postgraduate ITE courses. The basis on which partnership is to develop is very one-sided. Schools and local education authorities (LEAs) do not have a similar mandate to higher education institutes (HEIs). School-based teacher responsibilities for training are not reflected in the contractual hours of school staff. This one-sided partnership is lacking in resources at a time when schools are stretched by local financial management and required to cost their over-expenditure. At the same time, the government is insisting on the pursuit of competition, enterprise and individualism. It is therefore a contradiction in policy to expect schools and teachers to continue to interact on a basis of goodwill and underfunding. The former, in some areas, has become a largely redundant concept, with schools and HEIs scrabbling over Teacher Training Agency money, with HEIs facing widespread redundancies and loss of teaching expertise and research bases, and schools ill-equipped for and unused to some (though not by any means all) of the exigencies and demands of mentoring and supporting students on teaching practice.

School mentoring is the system by which school teachers guide, advise, support and grade student teachers in place of HEI lecturers. They or their schools are paid for this and there is some fairly minimal contact with HEI lecturers. HEI staff involvement in many schemes is limited to ascertaining that monitoring systems and relationships are functioning, and 'fire fighting' when things go wrong. (See Whiting *et al.*, 1996, for a detailed analysis of types of HEI–schools partnerships.)

The reality of Local Management of Schools (LMS) means that any school-based training will have to be locked into the budgetary constraints of the school, and will need to be seen to be beneficial to children and to the schools themselves, as well as to the student teachers and to the development of the profession as a whole. The pressure to deliver the National Curriculum has forced all schools to evaluate their relationships with training institutions.

An *Observer*/Cassell education survey carried out in 1993 about moving teacher training back into schools, revealed that

83 per cent of the one thousand politicians, local authority offi-
cers, parents and teachers surveyed rejected the idea that
'moving most teacher training back into schools will make better
teachers' (Nash, 1993). Of the thousand respondents 85 per cent
also believed that the government had a 'political or ideological
objective in limiting teacher training colleges ... with 79 per
cent believing this was a bad thing' (ibid.). Hill (1993),
Carrington and Tymms (1993), Blake and Hill (1995), and Hill
and Cole (1996c) report similar high levels of criticism of school-
centred 'teacher training' by headteachers, student teachers and
by the general public.

Other than increasing school-basing for college-based ITE
courses, the Conservative government has introduced three
types of school-based 'training' schemes, the Articled Teacher
(AT), the Licensed Teacher (LT), and the School-Centred Initial
Teacher Training (SCITT) schemes.

The Articled Teachers (AT) Scheme, a two-year postgraduate
course, was intended to attract graduates from other careers.
Students spent 80 per cent of their time in school and 20 per
cent in college. HMI has indicated that the scheme has been
successful in producing some quality teachers, even though the
cost was prohibitive (the training programme cost per student
was 30 per cent higher than the conventional cost for a student
on a conventional postgraduate course). HMI (and other) evalu-
ations of the scheme reveal that students felt that it negated the
need to step back from their school to think and talk to other
students in training (DES, 1991; Jacques, 1991). The AT
Scheme for Primary teachers ran for four years and came to an
end in June 1995 (that for secondary teachers was abandoned by
the government in 1992).

Criticisms of the AT scheme seem generic to those of school-
based schemes in general. The AT scheme at West Sussex
Institute of Higher Education, like that at UNL, found a number
of benefits, but shared some of the criticisms. Prime among these
were that, while Articled Teachers felt confident and well-
prepared for most aspects of classroom teaching, they felt they
had had an inadequate theoretical preparation. Furthermore,
while a number of school mentorship arrangements had worked
very satisfactorily, some mentors were ill-prepared for and did not
have sufficient time for supporting student teachers in difficulty.

The Licensed Teacher (LT) Scheme was much more controversial and continues to recruit nationally. Here recruits are unqualified teachers (required to have two years Higher Education or equivalent and to be at least 24 years of age), and are employed as teachers by schools. They received 'on-the-job' training. Teachers' unions objected to this non-graduate type of entry to teaching because it undermined and divided the profession (c.f. Cole, 1989; Hill, 1989).

There are a number of other problems with the scheme, some of which are highlighted by the experience of the UNL scheme. The University of North London worked with an LEA which recruited qualified teachers from the Caribbean, and subsequently found that they had to proceed via the Licensed Teacher route in order to obtain Qualified Teacher Status (QTS). This resulted in the need to devise a scheme which was wide enough to meet demands laid down in National Curriculum Council (NCC) guidelines for Licensed Teachers (NCC, 1991) and at the same time be unique enough to attempt to incorporate the teachers' existing skills and support them in their transition from one teaching environment to another.[6]

Equal opportunities was a major consideration in the UNL work with these Licensed Teachers, not only in how discrimination would impinge on their lives in the wider community, but how it would be manifested within the multicultural, multilingual community of inner city London schools. Difficulties arose in the selection of mentors and the allocation of classes. Licensed teachers with mentors who had less teaching experience than themselves and the presence of children who were demotivated and disrespectful presented many conflicts and contradictions which required the teachers to make a number of realignments. Because Licenses are attached to the teacher and the school, it meant that, for some teachers, poor and inappropriate initial placements were difficult to change.[7]

In this scheme the LEA was left with the responsibility of assessing and making recommendation to the DES (now the DFE) regarding the conferring of QTS. A major problem this created was that teacher educators/trainers had no opportunity to visit the teachers in school. HEI staff were dependent on the Licensed Teachers and their school mentors for relaying information and issues to which the teacher educators/trainers had to respond.

Many of the inherent limitations of the Licensed Teacher Scheme (see Hill, 1989; Cole, 1989; Barrett *et al.*, 1993) were not very apparent in the UNL experience outlined here, because of the unique status of the Caribbean teachers (already 'trained' and very experienced – albeit in a different national system). However, what was apparent was the need for these Licensed Teachers' experiences and training to be at graduate level or equivalent.

The Licensed Teacher Scheme fails to expose teachers to the two-year specialist subject, college-based study received by students on their BA (QTS) and BEd courses (and also received by students on PGCE courses in their first degrees). LT schemes also fail to introduce LTs to a variety of British school placements, their experience is limited to one school only. This is unacceptable given that teachers need to be orientated and inducted not only in life within one school, but into the profession as a whole. Another major objection is that Licensed Teachers are often paid considerably less than qualified teachers, consigning them to second-class status within the profession. In short, the Licensed Teacher Scheme undermines the strength of teacher education and is a disservice to children in schools and to the LTs themselves.

Some similar criticisms can be directed at School Centred Initial Teacher Training (SCITT), condemned in, for example, Pyke (1995) and criticized by OFSTED (1995a, b) in the first official evaluation. The SCITT scheme involves nine consortia of schools and six city technology colleges, both primary and secondary, to run their own 'teacher training', recruiting and training their own students. SCITT schemes are funded directly by the TTA and were instituted by the then Secretary of State for Education, John Patten, in 1993. Pyke reports on a forthcoming HMI Report which questions the effectiveness of SCITT, comparing it unfavourably with courses run by HEIs. Pyke's report quotes one Dean of Education (Graham Welch at Roehampton Institute of Higher Education) as observing that 'schools have found it an enormous amount of work. It's tied up a lot of senior staff for long periods of time. They have also found it difficult to balance the time required against the income; their costs are not covered. In our experience the teachers have put in far more work than they expected' (Pyke, 1995).

Partnership is necessary for bringing together various aspects of theory and practice, but its potential depends on the negotiation and delivery of a co-ordinated, well-documented and monitored series of experiences on campus and school (Norris, 1993:16). If it is to succeed, it has to be built on clear lines of communication and a recognition of the intellectual foundation of teaching, not just in curricular knowledge, but in the reflective and critical analysis of practice (Hill, 1991 and 1994a). Such analysis is seen as a foundation of effective teaching and of empowering student teachers to have an understanding of the society in which they teach and learn.

THE LIBERAL PROGRESSIVE MODEL

Prior to the ascendancy of the radical Right, the dominant paradigm in Britain was the liberal progressive one. Based on the philosophy of the Plowden Report (CACE, 1967), and championed by Labour governments and accepted as mainstream thinking in other parliamentary parties, it claimed to be child-centred and concerned with educating the whole child, so that the affective domain was equal in importance to the cognitive one. It stressed the worth of all children and their right to be active in the learning process. At first sight, this might seem to be an appropriate model for the new post-Conservative Britain. However, all was not what it seemed.

Debbie Epstein (1993), for one, has offered a trenchant critique of what liberal progressivism often meant in practice (see also Brehony, 1992; Sarup, 1983). Epstein is critical of the Plowden Report. She argues that its conceptualization of children as individuals rather than as members of groups (and the fact that social groups tend to be pathologized when they are mentioned) made it difficult to raise issues of power relations in primary schools. In addition, Plowden's deficit model of working-class children meant that efforts to promote equal opportunity 'focused on repairing the deficiencies of individual children rather than on structures and curriculum' (Epstein, 1993:92). Underpinning the Report, she reminds us, is the work of Piaget, who has suggested that children cannot 'decentre' (empathize with others) until they reach a 'mental age' of ten or eleven. In practice, this meant that 'teachers ... found it difficult to accept (or easy to reject) the idea that primary age children can handle concepts of racism and sexism' (ibid:91).

The Plowden Report, Epstein concludes, contains two contradictory views about the relationship between children and society. Society is treated both as something from which children must be protected and as an entity which they will enter at some further date and for which they therefore have to be moulded:

> Both these views were aspects of Plowden discourse which diminished the likelihood that primary teachers working within their framework would try to consider and challenge social inequalities with the children they teach – for if the school is regarded as a safe haven from the ills of society, why allow disruptive ideas about inequality to enter the classroom? Furthermore, while 'preparing' children to take their place in society (at some specified future date) might involve some ideas of liberal tolerance ... it also carries the implicit assumption that the 'nature' of society is fixed and that we can predict what kind of society children should be prepared for. Again, there is no compelling logic which says that predictions about a future society will not involve recognition of a need to combat inequalities but the notion does preclude the idea that children should be involved, in the here and now, in deconstruction of dominant ideologies.
>
> (Epstein, 1993:92–3)

In place of the Plowden/Piaget learning process set of perspectives, Epstein advocates a co-operative, democratic learning process, but in the mode of critical reflection, rather than Plowdenesque liberalism. She offers the work of Dunn, which shows that children are aware of the feelings of others as early as their second year of life and can therefore 'decentre' and are thus amenable to understanding issues of inequality. 'Child-centred' education *per se* is not the problem, she argues, and it is possible to reappropriate it and make it more 'political and oppositional' (Epstein, 1993:98).

We now turn to an outline of what a radical Left policy might mean in practice.

A RADICAL LEFT MODEL[8]

This model needs to be distinguished from Centre Left and 'Left in the Centre' policies suggested, for example, in recent Labour Party (1991; 1994) and Institute for Public Policy Research policy documents (Barber and Brighouse, 1992; IPPR, 1993).[9] Its defining features lie in its concept of equality as being 'egalitarian' rather than 'more efficiently meritocratic'. It is striving for significantly lower differentials in society (and in the outomes of schooling). This contrasts with the British Labour Party (centre-left) vision of high differentials between top and bottom strata, albeit in a more socially mobile meritocracy.

In addition a radical Left model stresses the development of teachers as critical, emancipatory, transformative intellectuals, who are democratic and active citizens and professionals committed to a morality of social justice. This is based on an interrogated and critical diversity of culture, class, 'race', sex and sexuality, special needs and disability, as part of a radical democratic egalitarian and anti-authoritarian political project (Giroux, 1988a, b; Hill, 1991, 1994).

It is concerned with democratic management and pedagogy within education (at classroom level as well as at school and college/HEI level), in opposition to the increasingly hierarchical, elitist and brutal systems of school, college and classroom management, which are in evidence not only in Britain, but in an increasing number of states worldwide.

It is concerned, finally, with a broader definition of 'standards' than narrowly defined and tested academic attainment. This involves an emphasis on collective and collaborative as well as individual responsibility.

A PRESCRIBED CORE CURRICULUM FOR INITIAL TEACHER EDUCATION

A prescribed core curriculum for ITE should include:

1   Classroom skills and competencies. All children need to attain excellence. In addition to a deep knowledge of core subjects, student teachers need to develop reflective skills on pupil/student learning, teaching and classroom management, and on stimulating all the children in their classes to learn. They also need to develop skills in monitoring the variety of standards referred to above, and in demanding/ facilitating the best from their pupils/students.

2   The skills to develop in children excellence in written and spoken standard English, in the context of full recognition of, and respect for dialect and accent, and the skills to facilitate the promotion of bilingualism and multilingualism, where appropriate.

3   Data on racism, sexism, social class inequality, homophobia, and oppression connected with disability and special needs. Many teachers and ITE students are not aware of the existence of such data or the impact of individual labelling, and of structural discriminations on the lives and education and life opportunities of the children in their classes, schools and society.

4   A holistic approach to social justice in the curriculum. 'Race', gender, social class, sexuality and disability and special needs should be considered as part of an overall understanding of social justice within teacher education courses. Inequalities in practice can be multi-dimensional and their effects can manifestly impact one upon the other. Inequalities and oppression can also be unidimensional – as, for example, with 'gay-bashing'.

5   Skills in dealing with verbal abuse, physical abuse and harassment related to social class, gender, 'race', sexuality or special needs and disability.

6   'Critical reflection' on competing approaches and ideologies of schooling and teacher education. This should include a consideration of anti-racism as well as multiculturalism and assimilationism, the concept of a classless society as well as meritocratic social mobility or elitist stratification and reproduction, anti-sexism as well as non-sexism. In addition, different models of special needs and disability and gay/lesbian/bisexual issues need to be addressed. (For an analysis of 'critical reflection', see Zeichner and Liston, 1987; Hill, 1991, 1992, 1994a and 1996.)

The above list is not exclusive. Furthermore, we recognize that however well educated and however critical and egalitarian student teachers and teachers might be, these qualities are of limited use if such teachers have limited classroom skills and competencies. What we are arguing for here is highly competent egalitarian teachers.

POLICY PROPOSALS FOR COURSE ENTRY, ORGANIZATION, LOCATION AND DURATION.[10]

A substantial higher education role should be retained with a closer delineation of which aspects of educating and training teachers are best done by schools and which by colleges. This should be based on experience of current schemes and research evidence, not on ministerial ideological agenda and/or prejudice.

Opposition must be expressed to total school-basing, to taking the education out of teacher education and training, to cheap-skate, quick-fire, non-graduate routes, to amputating the education components from BA (QTS)/BEd and PGCE courses. So the demand is for theory and practice together. This should not be the unpractised theory, lack of praxis, in many late 1980s/early 1990s BEd and PGCE courses, and certainly not the untheorized practice, untouched by critical theory, which is so obviously the intention of this government.

1 There should be easier entry to undergraduate ITE courses for those whose APEL (Alternative Prior Learning and Experience) is appropriate. However, while accepting different entry points into teacher education/training, all qualifying teachers should be graduates.

2 There should be a national system of sub-degree level certification for teacher assistants and helpers which should be an entitlement for those working a minimum number of hours with children in school (say 6 hours per week) and which should be mandatory for those working longer hours with children in school (say 25 hours per week). Such a graded system of certification should, after development, serve as the equivalent of the first year of a four-year BEd degree programme.

3 Articled Teacher type two-year PGCE courses should be extended, though with a 65/35 per cent school/college ratio rather than the 80/20 per cent ratio of the (now finished) Articled Teacher Scheme.

4 The Licensed Teaching Scheme should be abolished, with all teachers being educated into the profession to degree level on a theoretical as well as a practical basis.

5 The current balance should be maintained between HEI-

based and school-based work in four-year BA (QTS) courses established by CATE Circular 14/93 (i.e. 160 days of a 4-year (120-week) course). The 1989 CATE criteria (DES, 1989b) of 100 days in school on the then 4-year BEd course was too little and did not enable students adequately to interrelate theory and practice.

6 Primary PGCE courses, the most widely criticized of HEI-based courses, should be 60 weeks (or so) in length, half in school and half in HEI. This contrasts with the requirement in CATE Circular 14/93 that Primary PGCE student teachers should spend 20 weeks in HEI, and 18 weeks in school. Neither of these are long enough.

7 There should be a variety of different routes into ITE, but all should be subject to the same criteria as those set out above. Within this diversity there may be different patterns of school and HEI-based work. Totally school-based ITE such as School-Centred Initial Teacher Training (SCITT) should be abolished. Student teachers need to experience a variety of school styles, ethoses, problems and challenges.

8 School-based work in all ITE courses should be accompanied by rigorous and collaborative mentor training for school mentors.

9 There should be a General Teaching Council. This should be a representative body, one of whose functions should be to accredit teacher education courses. This would replace the Teacher Training Agency and incorporate aspects of its work.

10 Our proposals for Secondary PGCE courses are that they should be increased to 45 weeks in length, with half the term spent in school and half in HEI. CATE Circular 9/92 restricted the number of HEI-based days to 60 days for Secondary PGCE students (DFE, 1992). This is not enough. We suggest here approximately 112.5 days in school and the same in HEI.

CONCLUSION

Teacher educators from various other ideological and political perspectives may well agree with a number of the recommendations. What they may not agree with is the explicit emancipatory, critical and transformatory role of teacher educators, education, and schooling in the interests of social justice and equality. It is this role, and the role of teachers as intellectuals instead of mechanics, that is necessary for the development of a critical, active, interrogating, citizenry – thoughtful, questioning, perceptive as well as skilled – in the pursuit of a democratic, anti-authoritarian, socially responsible, socially just and equal society.

NOTES

1   How centre-left the 'New Labour' project is, in 1996, is open to dispute. See for example Hill and Cole 1996b, Cole 1997, as well as press comment throughout 1995 and 1996 in both tabloid and broadsheet newspapers and in, for example, *Tribune* and *New Statesman and Society*. 'New Labour' has clearly taken on board some aspects of neo-Thatchenism. While on a contemporary left–right spectrum, 'New Labour' Leadership and policy are (even if marginally) to the left of the Conservative Party, on a historical dimension there appears to be little continuity between the ideology and policies of 'Old Labour' and the pro-market 'New Labour'.

2   The following analysis draws heavily on Cole *et al.*, (1996).

3   Major advocates of this position with respect to teacher education are Sheila Lawlor (e.g. 1990), Stuart Sexton (e.g. 1987) and the 'think tanks', the Centre for Policy Studies (CPS) and Institute for Economic Affairs (IEA), with which Lawton and Sexton have been respectively involved.

4   Prominent exponents are the now defunct Hillgate Group (1989) and authors Anthony O'Hear (e.g. 1988, 1991), and Dennis O'Keeffe (e.g. 1990).

5   Any attributed irony can be dispelled by a variant of what Stuart Hall has referred to as 'the principal contradiction of social democracy in this period'. Labour has always been caught between the competing goals of improving working-class life chances and harnessing education to the economic and efficiency needs of the productive system. In conditions of recession, the educational experts, spokespersons, and educational press, sections of the profession, the media and other interest groups and organizations sided with the

Labour government and with the requirements of capitalism. (Hall, 1983:35–6; Cole, 1995; see also the discussion on Labour's dual repertoire in Chapter 5).

6   The teachers recruited were African and Indo-Caribbean, men and women, with between them five to twenty-three years' teaching experience. All had been educated and trained in a British colonial education system.

In terms of curriculum needs, the teachers were offered two In-Service courses from the UNL modular INSET (In-Service Education for Teachers) scheme. (In other schemes, such as the West Sussex Institute of Higher Education scheme, LTs slot into one weekly PGCE session as well as having tutorial support. What is common here is that LTs receive minimal HEI-based input). Initially at UNL, teachers pursued National Curriculum core subjects, but soon shifted to areas such as Intermediate Technology, Physical Education, Drama, Special Educational Needs and Early Years.

The initial cohort of Caribbean teachers all completed their courses, 'served' their two years Licence and have been granted Qualified Teacher Status (QTS).

7 Other kinds of personal circumstances also made initial adjustments difficult, such as finding suitable accommodation, placing their own children in appropriate schools, and illness.

8 Hill (1992) discusses three different models of radical Left discourse, and models of the teacher. These are summarized in Hill (1991, 1992).

9 The following analysis draws heavily on Hill (1991, 1994a, b; Hill and Cole, 1995a, b). Curricular proposals are further developed around the notion of 'critical reflection' in Hill (1996a). See note 1 concerning the label, centre-left.

10 These proposals are based on those in Hill (1994a).

REFERENCES

Barber, M. and Brighouse, T. (1992) *Partners in Change: Enhancing the Teaching Profession.* London: Institute for Public Policy Research (IPPR).

Barrett, E., Barton, L., Furlong, J., Galvin, C., Miles, S. and Whitty, G. (1993) *The Licensed Teacher Scheme: A Modes of Teacher Education Project.* London: London University Institute of Education.

Blake, D. and Hill, D. (1995) The newly qualified teacher in school. *Research Papers in Education*, 10(3) 309–39.

Brehony, K. (1992) What's left of progressive primary education? In A. Rattansi and D. Reeder (eds) *Rethinking Radical Education: Essays in Honour of Brian Simon.* London: Lawrence and Wishart.

Callaghan, J. (1976) Speech at Ruskin College. *Education*, 22 October.

Carrington, B. and Tymms, P. (1993) *For Primary Heads Mum's not the Word.* School of Education in University of Newcastle upon Tyne.

Central Advisory Council for Education (CACE) (1967) *Children and their Primary Schools (The Plowden Report).* London: HMSO.

Cole, M. (1989) Threat to Equality. *The Teacher*, 24 April.

Cole, M. (1992) Racism, history and educational policy: from the origins of the welfare state to the rise of the radical right. Unpublished PhD thesis, Dept of Sociology, University of Essex.

Cole, M. (1997) Equality and models of radical education. In D. Hill, M. Cole and S. Shan (eds) *Promoting Equality in Secondary Schools.* London: Cassell.

Cole, M. and Hill, D. (1995) Games of despair and rhetorics of resistance: postmodernism, education and reaction. *British Journal of Sociology of Education*, 16(2).

Cole, M. and Hill, D. (1996) Postmodernism, education and contemporary capitalism: a materialist critique. In O. Valente, A. Barrios, V. Teodoro and A. Gaspas (eds) *Teacher Training and Values Education.* Lisbon: Faculty of Science, Department of Education, University of Lisbon.

Cole, M., Hill, D., Pease, J. and Soudien, C. (1996) Critical transformative primary teacher education: some suggestions for the new South Africa. In J. Lynch, C. Modgil and S. Modgil (eds) *Education and Development: Tradition and Innovation, vol. 3: Innovations in Delivering Primary Education.* London: Cassell.

Copeland, W., Birmingham, C., De La Cruz, E. and Lewin, B. (1993) The reflective practitioner in teaching: towards a research agenda. *Teaching and Teacher Education*, 9(4).

Department for Education (DFE) (1992) *Initial Teaching Training (Secondary Phase) (Circular 9/92).* London: DFE.

Department for Education (DFE) (1993) *The Initial Training of Primary School Teachers: New Criteria for Course Approval (Circular 13/93).* London: DFE.

Department of Education and Science (DES) (1984) *Initial Teacher Training: Approval of Courses (Circular 3/84).* London: HMSO.

Department of Education and Science (DES) (1987) *Quality in Schools: The Initial Training of Teachers: an HMI Survey.* London: HMSO.

Department of Education and Science (DES) (1989a) *ITT in Universities in England, Northern Ireland and Wales: Education Observed, 7.* London: HMSO.

Department of Education and Science (DES) (1989b) *Initial Teacher Training: Approval of Courses (Circular 24/89).* London: DES.

Department of Education and Science (DES) (1991) *The Professional Training of Primary School Teachers: A Commentary on the Inspection of 20 Initial Teacher Training Courses.* London: DES.

Elliott, J. (1993) Three perspectives on coherence and continuity in teacher education. In J. Elliott (ed.) *Teacher Reconstructing Teacher Education.* Lewes: Falmer Press.

Epstein, D. (1993) *Changing Classroom Cultures: Anti-racism, Politics and Schools.* Stoke-on-Trent: Trentham Books.

Gilroy, D. (1992) The political rape of initial teacher education in England and Wales: a JET rebuttal. *Journal of Education for Teaching*, 18(1).

Giroux, H. (1988a) *Teachers as Intellectuals: Toward a Critical Pedagogy of Learning.* Granby, Massachusetts: Bergin and Harvey.

Giroux, H. (1988b) *Schooling and Democracy: Critical Pedagogy in the Modern Age.* London: Routledge.

Hall, S. (1983) The great moving right show. In S. Hall and P. Jacques (eds) *The Politics of Thatcherism.* London: Lawrence and Wishart.

Hall, S. and Jacques, P. (eds) (1983) *The Politics of Thatcherism.* London: Lawrence and Wishart.

Hatcher, R. (1994) Labour's Green Paper – modernising British education? *Socialist Teacher*, 54.

Hessari, R. and Hill, D. (1989) *Practical Approaches to Multicultural Learning and Teaching in Primary Schools.* London: Routledge.

Hill, D. (1989) *Charge of the Right Brigade: The Radical Right's Attack on Teacher Education.* Brighton: Institute for Education Policy Studies.

Hill, D. (1990) *Something Old, Something New, Something Borrowed, Something Blue: Teacher Education, Schooling and the Radical Right in Britain and the USA.* London: Tufnell Press.

Hill, D. (1991) *What's Left in Teacher Education: Teacher Education, the Radical Left, and Policy Proposals.* London: Tufnell Press.

Hill, D. (1992) What the radical right is doing to teacher education: a radical left critique. *Multicultural Teaching,* 10(3).

Hill, D. (1993) *What Teachers? School Basing and Critical Reflection in Teacher Education and Training.* Brighton: Institute for Education Policy Studies.

Hill, D. (1994a) Cultural diversity and initial teacher education. In G. Verma and P. Pumfrey (eds) *Cultural Diversity and the Curriculum, vol. 4, Cross-Curricular Contexts, Themes and Dimensions in Primary Schools.* London: Falmer Press.

Hill, D. (1994b) Teacher education, the radical right and the radical left. *Forum for the Promotion of 3–18 Comprehensive Education,* 37(3), Autumn.

Hill, D. (1994c) A radical left policy for teacher education. *Socialist Teacher,* 56.

Hill, D. (1996a) Critical reflection in initial teacher education. In K. Watson, C. Modgil and S Modgil (eds) *Educational Dilemmas: Debate and Diversity, vol. 1: Teacher Education and Training.* London: Cassell.

Hill, D. (1996b) Equality in primary schooling: the policy context, intentions and effects of the Conservative 'reforms'. Chapter 1 above.

Hill, D. and Cole, M. (1996a) Materialism and the postmodern fallacy: the case of education. In J. V. Fernandes (ed.) *Proceedings of the Second International Conference of Sociology of Education.* Lisbon: Gulbenkian Foundation.

Hill, D. and Cole, M. (1996b) *Radical Education and the Question of Equality.* London: Tufnell Pess.

Hill, D. and Cole, M. (1996c) Initial teacher education and the irrelevance of theory: mainstream thinking or ideological dogma? In K. Watson, C. Modgil and S. Modgil (eds) *Educational Dilemmas: Debate and Diversity, vol. 1: Teacher Education and Training.* London: Cassell.

Hillcole Group (1993) *Whose Teachers? A Radical Manifesto.* London: Tufnell Press.

Hillcole Group/Chitty, C. (ed.) (1991) *Changing the Future: Redprint for Education.* London: Tufnell Press.

Hillgate Group (1989) *Learning to Teach.* London: The Claridge Press.

Institute For Public Policy Research (IPPR) (1993) *Education: A Different Version. An Alternative White Paper.* London: IPPR.

Jacques, K. (1991) The articled teacher scheme. Paper delivered at BERA National Conference, Nottingham Polytechnic.

Kearney, C. (1994) *If It Ain't Broke, Why Fix It?* Unpublished.

Labour Party (1991) *Investing in Quality: Labour's Plan to Reform Teacher Education and Training.* London: The Labour Party.

Labour Party (1994) *Opening Doors to a Learning Society: A Policy Statement on Education.* London: The Labour Party.

Labour Party (1995) *Diverstiy and Excellence: A New Partnership for Schools.* London: Labour Party.

Lawlor, S. (1990) *Teachers Mistaught: Training in Theories or Education in Subjects.* London: Centre for Policy Studies.

Nash, S. (1993) Observer/Cassell survey. *Observer,* 5 September, p. 57.

National Curriculum Council (NCC) (1991) *The National Curriculum and Initial Training of Student, Articled and Licensed Teachers.* York: NCC.

National Foundation for Education Research (NFER) (1991) *Evaluation of the Articled Teachers scheme.* London: NFER.

Norris, R. (1993) Teacher education in the 1990s. Theory, practice and partnership. *Naptec Review,* 3(1).

Office for Standards in Education (OFSTED) (1995a) *School-Centred Initial Teacher Training 1993–1994.* London: HMSO.

Office for Standards in Education (OFSTED) (1995b) *News Release PN24/95 Mixed Beginnings for the New Teacher Training Scheme.* 15 August.

O'Hear, A. (1988) *Who Teaches the Teachers? A Contribution to Public Debate.* London: Social Affairs Unit.

O'Hear, A. (1991) Putting work before play in primary school. *Times Educational Supplement,* 10 October.

O'Keeffe, D. (1990) *The Wayward Elite.* London: The Adam Smith Institute.

Pyke, N. (1995) Inspectors cast doubt on in-school training. *Times Educational Supplement,* 10 March.

Sarup, M. (1983) *Marxism, Structuralism, Education.* Lewes: Falmer Press.

Sexton, S. (1987) *Our Schools: a Radical Policy.* London: Institute for Economic Affairs.

University of London (1995) Learning Support Unit statistics.

Welch, G. (1994) Teacher education. *Guardian,* 17 May.

Whitting, C., Whitty, G., Furlong, J., Miles, S. and Barton, L. (1996) *Partnership in Initial Teacher Education: A Topography: A Modes of Teacher Education Project.* London: London University Institute of Education.

Whitty, G. (1993) Education reform and teacher education in England in the 1990s. In P. Gilroy and M. Smith (eds) *International Analysis of Teacher Education.* Abingdon: Carfax Publishing Company.

Williams, M. (1993) Partnership with schools: the challenge for teacher education. *Naptec Review*, 3(1).

Zeichner, K. and Liston, D. (1987) Teaching student teachers to reflect. *Harvard Educational Review*, 5–7(1).

PART 2

FOUNDATION SUBJECTS KEY STAGES 1 AND 2: THE CORE SUBJECTS

CHAPTER 5

English

Derek Lovell

Classroom teachers in primary schools have always spent a good deal of time every week on language activities with the children in their class. Now that the final slimmed down post-Dearing English curriculum document has been published, they will have to work with an English National Curriculum which has been so battered and bashed by the ruling political ideology that it cannot even stand alongside the Cox Report (DES, 1989) in terms of consistency of approach. It is now even more essential that teachers who wish to address the issues of equality – class, gender, sexuality, race and ability – be resolved critically to reflect on the new English curriculum and clearly focus on a coherent pedagogy backed up by potent resources that will enable them to work on these issues all the time with the children in their class. This chapter intends:

- to explore issues relating to a pedagogy that will enable teachers to examine matters of equality consistently and persistently with specific regard to Key Stage 1 and 2 English (talking, listening, reading and writing).
- to make practical suggestions for strategies and materials that will enable teachers to use the New Orders for English to promote these issues of equality for the benefit of all children.

LANGUAGE AND LEARNING

If a school's drive to equality means anything it must reside not only in the hearts and minds of the teachers, let alone in their policy files, but in every working moment in the life of the class-room.

The model of learning from which a teacher operates has profound implications for how (s)he teaches children. The teacher who is concerned with equality of access/accessibility to the revised curriculum must now be aware of the importance of the social constructivist models of learning, developed by a number of social psychologists. Vygotsky's work is of vital importance in this respect. His insights have steadily gained influence since his work first appeared in the West in the early 1960s. Unlike Piaget (whose work also has children depicted as meaning-makers and interacting with the environment), he placed language at the heart of the process by which children learned to think. It is through verbalizing aloud and interacting with others, for example, that young children develop their thinking. Later children develop an inner voice to reformulate their thinking into new schemata but all the time need to be interacting with others. This view heralds a shift from the Plowden-inspired progressive primary schools of the 1960s and 1970s which typically focused on personal discovery and a wide-ranging choice of activities. Tizard and Hughes (1984) recognized the importance of Vygotsky's position in their research into nurseries where they saw the vital importance for young children to interact with adults rather than range freely over a wide range of activities without social interaction with an adult (this was how Piaget was being interpreted in the settings at which Tizard and Hughes looked).

For teachers faced with a class of children of differing abilities, social class, gender, sexuality and race Vygotsky's work gave further support to the importance of the quality of the interac-tion and communication of adults with the children (Vygotsky, 1981). He stressed that the cultural development of children's learning was enhanced through this interaction. Indeed, the role of adults and children themselves to push thinking forward through interaction with each other is another critical insight made by Vygotsky. In his concept of 'the zone of proximal development' a fundamental principle is that children need to be helped into a new dimension of thinking by others before they are able to go it alone.

Bruner's work too tracks along the same lines. He is concerned to find out why children sometimes find learning so difficult in school. He asserts that a child actively selects, keeps and transforms information to an internalized system of representation by which (s)he understands the world (1966). Bruner places great emphasis on the importance of language in this process for it is through social interactions with other children and adults that the child actively makes meaning of the world. An important factor in his work is the notion of 'scaffolding' which he describes as 'the steps taken to reduce the degrees of freedom in carrying out some task so that the child can concentrate on the difficult skill she is in the process of acquiring' (Bruner, 1978:19). An adult or child can provide cognitive support that will enable the child to cope with a new idea and through a combination of that support and interaction with language move the thinking of that child onwards.

Yet the limitations of these social psychological analyses lies in their underemphasis of the socially divisive and diverse nature of the society in which we live and the effect that these divisions will have on the cultural meanings which children bring into the classroom and continue to reshape. Analyses of the social and cultural dimension in the form of the interplay between a child's identity and the learning stance, for example, have begun to be explored (see Pollard, 1990). This is to be welcomed for teachers need to be clearer about what strategies help all children to develop their learning as well as focus on the critical need to empower all children to learn more effectively by reflecting on the cultural context of the learning.

LANGUAGE, ENGLISH AND THE LEARNING PROCESS

Consider then these observations on the teaching/learning processes. The child's first language is critically important for her intellectual development. All teachers must provide widespread opportunities for the child to interact with teachers in the most appropriate language as often as possible. For bilingual children interactions between children and between adults and children in the mother tongue becomes an important learning strategy for promoting intellectual development as well as cultural identity.

The management of adults in the classroom is vital. Clearly a shared view of how the child learns through language must be understood by all adults who work with children. 'Scaffolding learning' demands a detailed awareness on the part of staff and takes account of where the child's conceptual learning lies. It demands that a whole staff (teaching and non-teaching) share common assumptions about language which are concomitant with equal opportunities policy statements. Schools need to commit all staff to examining how all children use language by virtue of being human and how teachers can approach their work in the classroom for the benefit of the children rather than setting up individual pedagogical approaches which deny constructivist insights. Peel and Bell (1994) have stressed the importance of teachers (and by implication classroom assistants) considering the language implications of all their sessions, not just in terms of what language work will be covered but also in terms of:

- the language with which the activity will be introduced and presented to the children;
- the language skills that the children will need to have in order to carry out the activity successfully;
- the language and literacy skills that the teacher will formally address or draw attention to in offering guidelines for the activity;
- the literacy and language factors which will feature in the criteria for the formative assessment

Certainly the 1992 Language In the National Curriculum (LINC) materials are useful for staff in-service sessions to help them arrive at a consensus of a constructivist approach to language in the primary school.

It is almost a truism that schools concerned with promoting an egalitarian curriculum have stressed the importance of collaborative learning. Many would agree with the sentiments expressed in *Education in a Multiethnic Society* (ILEA, 1984):

The important role of collaboration of children's educational development is now widely acknowledged in primary schools. Confidence, social awareness, the capacity to reason and communicate are all demanded and given the chance to develop in situations where learning is co-operative. When children work together on specific learning tasks, they learn to take new sorts of responsibility for their own learning. ... It is through collaboration that the possibilities for day-to-day learning across cultures and ethnic groups becomes so evident. Children can learn from each other and teachers can learn from the children – as well as vice versa.

(ILEA, 1984:50–51)

Yet eleven years on the reality is far from this; the ORACLE project set up under the direction of Galton to examine the effectiveness of group work in classrooms has demonstrated that children do not like group work. They are not sure what they are supposed to achieve. The interactions between teachers and children, for example, tend to be short in length and routinely organizational and low level in form because teachers tended to spend the bulk of their time interacting with individuals rather than with groups. (Galton, 1987; Mortimer *et al.*, 1988). Conversely, both Galton and Mortimer stress the importance of high levels of questioning and the need to engage in activities with children which allow a maximum of sustained interaction (e.g. Gipps, 1994).

The message is clear. Teachers need to interact with challenging questioning on activities that have powerful meanings for the children. The social context of the learning gives the activity power but to push thinking on lies in the quality of the teaching which also makes the difference.

SPEAKING, LISTENING AND EQUALITY

The Programmes of Study for Speaking and Listening at Key Stage 1 and Key Stage 2 in the National Curriculum (DFE 1995) make it quite clear that teachers have the discretion to build on what language the children bring to school while at the same time inducting them into the forms and uses of Standard English:

Pupils should be introduced with *appropriate* sensitivity to the importance of standard English.... Pupils should be given opportunities to consider *their own speech.*

(DFE, 1995:5)

Pupils' appreciation and use of standard English should be developed by involvement with others.... They should be given opportunities to ... investigate how language varies according to the context and purpose and between standard and dialect forms.

(DFE, 1995:12)

It is now entirely legitimate to build on the personal, cultural and class-specific identities of the children. *Did I Hear You Write?* (Rosen, 1989) gives a stunning list of the components of a young person's culture that (s)he brings into school. Rosen's experience as a popular poet with mainly working-class children in culturally pluralistic schools makes his work a powerful resource which the National Oracy Project have incorporated into their materials. Here is part of the list:

Courtships, marriage, weddings, divorces. Alternatives like single
    parenting, gay relationships.
Holidaying.
Outings.
Slangs, dialects, ingroup jargons and new words.
Family sagas, stories.
Street spectacles and events, as seen or participated in.
Superstitions and charms.
Oaths and secrets, about secret illicit deeds, for instance.
Street cries, market traders, bus conductors.
Local legends, myths, urban folk stories.
It's not fair: wrong-doers, cheats, conmen, cruel people.
Gender-determined activities – questioning this.
Attitudes to change – could things be better for me/my cultural
    group/my family?
Authority and control: attitudes to it – parental/school/outside.
Goings on in the attitudes to institutions I belong in, like school,
    workplace, blocks of flats, family.

(Rosen, 1989:18–19)

The idea of the list is for teachers to prompt talk on any number of these elements with questions like 'What do you do when?' or 'What do you say when?' 'Has your father/mother ever?, and by so doing the contexts for group discussions become accessible and grounds for the teacher to interact to prompt the discussion into important new areas of challenge, while at the same time celebrating the cultural and class-specific context of the talk. It also acknowledges the rich linguistic interactions of the home so clearly researched in the work of Tizard and Hughes (1984).

Siraj-Blatchford (1994) also asserts the importance of the cultural analysis view of English for the early years in overcoming prejudice and racism and in promoting the multilingual classroom. She maintains:

- that society is dynamic and ever changing and so is language.
- that diversity in language, such as accents, does not threaten standard forms of English.
- that all children have a right to learn standard English for future empowerment in the workplace and for public writing because it is the language of power in our society.
- that talking and listening skills are crucial.

(Siraj-Blatchford, 1994:43)

In her opinion, the cultural analysis view of language is the model of language that is needed to promote an anti-racist classroom. Mother tongue teaching and support materials help to promote a positive climate and she urges educators to reflect critically on three areas:

- the attitudes of educators towards the home languages;
- the extent and quality of anti-racist training (particularly linguistic racism;
- the procedures, records and assessments available to measure a child's competence in her home language and English.

Siraj-Blatchford calls for teachers and classroom assistants to learn words and phrases of the children's languages in order to promote security, value to the first language and respect for the community. It is also important to recognize that English as a second language should not only be identified with South Asian Communities. If we use Cole's (1993) useful nomenclature of 'Asian, black and other minority ethnic' as an all-embracing term to describe minority ethnic groups in Britain, then we must recognize that many African-Caribbean families are bilingual and that other communities such as Jewish, Polish, Turkish, Greek or Lithuanian also have multilingual traditions.

One powerful way of putting the talk into context is through telling stories. In the context of the strong link between language and learning, Wells's (1987) assertion (quoted by Howe and Johnson, 1992:3) is apposite: 'Our natural response to an abstract idea is to find some anecdote – or story – to make it concrete. Stories are the bridge of abstraction.' Howe and

Johnson's (1992) work for the National Oracy Project on story-telling is a powerful resource and contains a number of interesting case studies which give practical guidance for the teacher. It is also a vehicle for 'redistributing the conversational initiative'. Talking and listening are affected by class, ethnicity, gender, peer group pressure, and the balance of power between those communicating, but the teacher can address these issues through children telling stories. A key starting-point for the teacher is the question 'In whose interest is the story told?'. The traditional stereotypical fairy stories which portray girls and women in a repressed role can be retold from a different perspective or the same story can be told in several languages. Stories can be taken from many cultures or from traditional communities. Teachers can and should give children many opportunities to work on retelling stories which they already know, have heard from the teacher or a professional storyteller or which they have invented from a picture book or a series of artefacts. In this way they are able to reevaluate their thinking by appropriating new ideas and forms in their own terms. It is, therefore, welcome that the Programmes of Study for Speaking and Listening for both Key Stages 1 and 2 do specifically mention drama, for this is another powerful medium to extend and develop talk for equality.

> Pupils should be encouraged to participate in drama activities, improvisation and performances of varying kinds, using language appropriate to a role or situation.
>
> (DFE, 1995:4)

> Pupils should be given opportunities to participate in a wide range of drama activities, including improvisation, role-play ... In responding to drama, they should be encouraged to evaluate their own and others' contributions.
>
> (DFE, 1995:11)

There is little recognition here of the use of drama as a learning medium and its power to allow children to reevaluate and transform meanings. Merely doing a play about an issue in which meanings are reproduced for an evaluated performance does not give children access to potential new meanings and devalues the important role that the teacher must play in helping the children to reexamine conventional attitudes and values to class, race, gender and sexuality.

The works of radical theatre practitioners such as Boal (1976, 1994) and drama teachers such as Heathcote (see her collected writings, edited by Johnson and O'Neill, 1984), Bolton (1980, 1984), O'Neill and Lambert (1982), Davies (1983), Neelands (1984, 1990) in the field of drama in education have suggested to teachers the ways and means to create dramatic fictions in which real issues and experiences can be explored. Using a range of strategies which enable the whole class group to call upon theatrical conventions and forms (the use of symbols, tension, role play, etc.) the group can try out different power relationships, linguistic registers, gender/race roles within the safety net of the created dramatic fiction. New meanings can even be put on traditional tales without altering any words through the exploration of the spaces in the tale. The key question 'In whose interest is this story told?' can be explored jointly by the children and the teacher with the teacher doing the controlling from within the drama. In this way even young children can become empowered to explore roles both close to and far removed from their own lives within the confines of the 'real' experienced fiction and try out new linguistic registers. With the teacher in role working alongside the children they can question, accept new challenges, make decisions, reexamine stereotypes with the setting of the drama. As Morgan and Saxton (1987) have put it, there is the play for the children and the play for the teacher in any session. Through the use of specific strategic interventions the teacher has the opportunity to deepen the children's mastery of language, even change their thinking by having the chance to reflect upon what they are doing and saying within the drama and to carry those developmental points into discussions afterwards.[10]

A Year 1 class were suddenly confronted by a male owner of a wildlife park who wanted to get rid of half the animals. In the course of the drama the children's deep anger was channelled into their decision to take the animals away and set up their own park where they all had a say in how it should be run.

A Year 3 class working on the story of Rumpelstiltskin rehearsed ways of speaking to a king by acting out imagined conversations in the village before they went to the palace to seek the return of the miller's daughter.

A Year 6 class explored corruption in local government by analysing the conversations that took place between some councillors and a group of planners of a proposed leisure complex in out-of-the-way venues (e.g. pubs and car parks). Working with two teachers in role the group came to realize that the decision-makers were mainly male but that the potential users of the centre were likely to be mostly female. In this way they revealed the distinctive way in which power and money were interlinked for self-interest, even though the councillors appeared to be serving the interests of the community.

READING AND ISSUES OF EQUALITY

The complexity of the reading process and its holistic nature is recognized in the Programmes of Study for Reading at Key Stages 1 and 2. All teachers concerned with tackling equality issues must retain the importance of the social and cultural dimensions of the reading process within a whole language approach and that every aspect of classroom practice must reflect this.

With the welcome dropping of the canon of texts in Key Stages 1 and 2, schools are now able to select their texts on criteria which enable equality issues to be addressed. The diversity of cultural and social identities represented in Britain should be reflected in the reading texts available in the classroom, from inexperienced readers to the more demanding texts, as well as texts which are bilingual, texts which deal specifically with gender issues, texts which show local dialects being used, texts which deal with physical and mental disability, texts which are non-fiction as well as fiction. A good use of staff development time would be to draw up more detailed selection criteria for each of these categories to ensure that a whole school approach can be developed. In short, every school should have a set of core texts available to all children in all classes, which are selected as much for the social and cultural meanings that they portray as for literary worth. We must acknowledge that while the majority of these texts are books, we must not overlook other sources of printed materials (magazines, comics, instruction booklets, etc.).

To this end, resource agencies such as the Centre For Language in Primary Education, based in London, provide up-to-date core book lists – as do the Signal publications and *Books To*

Break Barriers (Gutteridge *et al.*, 1992). Journals such as *Books For Keeps, Language Matters* and *Language and Learning* provide critical reviews of the latest books and catalogues. Letterbox Library provides lists of non-sexist and multicultural texts. It is important to have a strong link with a local bookseller who is knowledgeable about a full range of texts available but, failing this, large booksellers such as Morleys (based in Leeds and London) and small independent organizations such as Letterbox Library and New Beacon Books are a necessary part of that important network which can help schools to provide the wide range of texts vital to meet the needs of all groups of children.

There is no doubt that there has been much work done in the areas of race and gender to make teachers aware of texts for every type of reading experience (see Gutteridge *et al.*, 1992; Minns, 1991). However, texts relating, for example, to gay and lesbian issues for primary aged children are limited to fleeting references in the latest teenage sex information books.

Brigid Smith's work on getting children with special needs to write their own reading material through the intervention of scribes/listeners (trained helpers/volunteers) is an important contribution to the way that teachers can improve literacy standards. In her important book *Through Writing to Reading* (1994) she is clear that learning to read is most effective when learners use their own linguistic resources in a supporting and enabling situation. Her thoroughly documented approach gives the teacher a valuable handbook for enabling all groups of children whose self-esteem and linguistic confidence has taken a battering to write and then read their own reading materials and thereby create in themselves enough confidence and competence in reading so that they can take on other texts. Of course, it is again critical that the helpers have adequate training, not just in organizational procedures but in the underpinning philosophy of the holistic/social constructivist approach. Scaffolding strategies like the deployment of adults to work with children are a key element in the drive towards an equal access curriculum and schools must look beyond the classroom to involve family members in the process. Many schools do have home–school reading schemes and meetings with parents, but teachers have only gradually become aware of how the child's culture outside the school affects the child's ability to acquire literacy skills (see Brice Heath, 1983; Minns, 1990).

The challenge for all teachers is to create more open dialogues with parents which allow teachers to engage in what parents say about their child's reading life outside school and to extend and develop what is already being done. Boroughs such as Hackney and Tower Hamlets have now begun to extend the practice of the well-tried model of starting from where people are beyond the sense of this in terms of children's learning to that of the lives and experiences of parents. Engaging in this reflective activity with parents from different ethnic and social class backgrounds demands more attention to detail in interactions with parents. Hancock's (1994) practical advice includes the avoidance of professional language that could make parents feel excluded, confirming what is already happening in the home to support the child and the provision of interpreter support for parents who lack confidence in English. Now that the new Code Of Practice on the identification and assessment of special educational needs (DFE, 1994) is being implemented, teachers are becoming more adept at liaising with parents to discuss the Individual Educational Programme for the children. This practice needs to be more informed, focused and sensitized to the cultural and social identities of the parents in discussions about literacy matters.

In the classroom there has been a marked development in collaborative reading strategies and in the recognition by teachers that matching meaningful texts to groups of children enables them to reach an emotional understanding of the text which they can relate to their own social experience. Yet with the development of these book discussion packs or literature circles we must be clear that careful prompting by the teacher for close interrogation of the text is needed to move the children's thinking and perceptions further on. Certainly the approach lends itself to support all children, particularly if the packs can be made up of books from a core book list which is based on equal access criteria and allows children with special needs to focus with peer group and adult help on the meaning of texts rather than on word recognition and graphic skills. The necessity of these interrogative skills cannot be underestimated. Rosen's words have a powerful ring to them:

In a society where it is possible for there to be miscarriages of justice like the Birmingham 6, swindles like Robert Maxwell or for millionaires to sack miners, and the stroke of a pen to turn away asylum seekers ... in a society like that we are in desperate need for millions of people with the ability to interrogate texts – where texts mean every form of discourse from the teenage magazine to the politician's speech, the benefit entitlement form, or 'Hamlet'... What I'm talking about is a widening and a deepening of that interrogation which can only come if we are given a wide and deep range of texts, where we can learn how to cross-reference from fiction to fiction, from TV to poetry from one text to another that directly contradicts it.

(Rosen, 1992:18–19)

Reading in the primary school must give children the opportunity to compare and contrast views and opinions across the cultures and the classes and it is in the reading activities that teachers must allow children the chance to work through what they feel and think about the different meanings with which they are dealing. Texts cannot compensate for injustices in society but the skills to interrogate and interpret them are critically important in an unequal society.

WRITING AND EQUALITY

Current dominant models of the teaching of writing (National Writing Project, 1989; Graves, 1983) are encapsulated in the Key Stage 1 and 2 Programmes of Study. The new document speaks about planning, drafting, revising, proofreading and presenting (National Curriculum, 1995:15), about writing for different purposes and audiences (ibid.:9, 15). Building on the children's own experiences is also there in phrases such as:

Pupils should be given opportunities to write in response to a variety of stimuli, including ... classroom activities and personal experience.

(Ibid.:9)

They should write in response to a wide range of stimuli ... their interests and experiences, and the activities of the classroom.

(Ibid.:15)

But what also clearly underpins the Programmes of Study is the view that children should rapidly come to accept that there are big differences between how most children speak and how they write. Even at Key Stage 1 the grammatical conventions of Standard English are expected to be worked on and forms of what Perera calls 'non chronological writing' (1984) – lists, captions, records, notices, invitations, instructions – are given prominence (ibid.:9). By the end of Key Stage 2 children are expected to be given opportunities to learn about:

> discourse structure ... phrase, clause and sentence structure ...
> words – components including stem, prefix, suffix, inflection ...
> the use of the full range of punctuation marks.
>
> (Ibid.:24)

The concern here lies not in the wish to give all children access to the language of the powerful (what Standard English is) in an unequal society, but that teachers must not push out the cultural and social specificness of the writing with its feeling and emotional response (i.e. the ingredients which make it My Voice, in their drive to have children inducted into Standard English (i.e. Our Voice) which quickly becomes The Voice. Writing is acknowledged as a way of coming to terms with personal experience and for many children they should be encouraged to document their experiences in their own terms. Too little account is taken of the literary importance of colloquialisms and dialects and the rhythms and rhymes of speech in the writings of novice writers as a way of 'nudging' (Tannen's term) their way into other more conventional types of writing (see Smith, 1994; Perera, 1984; Tannen, 1985; Rosen, 1989). All these writers recognize that for many groups of children whose cultural milieu does not use Standard English as the dominant mode of discourse (e.g. children from working-class communities, or whose parents speak another language at home) have distinct literary advantages precisely because their spontaneous contextualized conversations have more in common with imaginative literature than with typical school language. For example, Tannen's conclusion (1985) is that literary language builds on and perfects conversation because like conversation it depends for its effect on interpersonal involvement.

> Rachel (aged 11) wrote very quickly, simply and powerfully about her unhappiness in the class.
>
> Why do the boys have to take the mickey out of me?
> They always make me feel bad
> It's not fair
> I hate all the boys
> I do not want to be near any of the boys.
> They always do it to me now
> Boys are the worst for making people bad.
> It's funny they never take the mickey out of the boys.
> It's true.
> I know most people go through this but just because they have been through it
> Does not make you feel any better.
> People always tell me they know how I feel. They don't know
> How I feel. They don't. It is
> impossible for them to know.

The powerful direct bitter voice (with its repetition of sounds and words, its recurrent figure of speech – 'taking the mickey', its heavy personal involvement) tells us how it is in a literary way. But this piece, written in response to a request from the girl's headteacher, is also conscious of the audience and the need to write in a school type Standard English language ('does not' rather than doesn't). Working-class girls who have to put up with comments from boys are only one group of children needing to express themselves in their own terms. The need to access children to Standard English cannot come at the expense of the worth of their literary voices. Indeed teachers need to become more aware of the literary worth of children's writing and tap into that rich vein of childhood experience. (See the work of Armstrong, 1983, 1989, who has analysed children's writing in this way.)

We have already stressed the importance of adults in the classroom and their use as scribes for children who find that the orthographic features of the writing process get in the way of what they want to say should be extended throughout the primary phase. Most schools can easily produce wordprocessed and bound books, which is a way of creating a range of texts which express points of views difficult to find in children's books (e.g. experiences related to one-parent families, living with unemployment, being disabled, girls taking the lead). Their own texts can be set alongside conventional texts and children and teachers can engage in the important skills related to text inter-rogation mentioned earlier.

REFERENCES

Language, English and the learning process

Bourne, J. (ed.) (1994) *Thinking Through Primary Practice*. London: Routledge with The Open University.

Bruner, J. (1966) *Towards a Theory For Instruction*. Cambridge, MA: Harvard University Press.

Bruner, J. (1978) The role of dialogue in language acquisition. In A. Sinclair, R. Jarvella, and W. J. M. Levelt (eds) *The Child's Conception of Language*. New York: Springer-Verlag.

Cole, M. (1993) 'Black and ethnic minority' or 'Asian, black and other minority ethnic': a further note on nomenclature. *Sociology*, 27(4):671–3.

Department For Education (DFE) (1994) *Code Of Practice on the Identification and Assessment of Special Educational Needs*. London: HMSO.

Department For Education (DFE) (1995) *The National Curriculum*. London: HMSO.

Department of Education and Science (DES) (1989) *The Cox Report*. London: HMSO.

Galton, M. (1987) An ORACLE chronicle: a decade of classroom research. *Teaching and Teacher Education*, 3(4).

Gipp, C. (1994) What we know about effective teaching. In J. Bourne (ed.) *Thinking Through*.

ILEA (1984) *Education in a Multiethnic Society: The Primary School*. London: ILEA publications.

LINC (1992) *Language in the National Curriculum: Materials for Professional Development*. Unpublished.

Mortimer, P., Sammons, P., Stoll, L., Lewis, D. and Ecob, R. (1988) *School Matters: The Junior Years*. London: Open Books.

Peel, R. and Bell, M. (1994) *The Primary Language Leader's Book*. London: David Fulton.

Pollard, A. (1990) Towards a sociology of learning in primary schools. *British Journal of Sociology of Education*. II(3).

Siraj-Blatchford, I. (1994) *The Early Years: Laying the Foundations for Racial Equality*. Stoke-on-Trent: Trentham Books.

Tizard, B. and Hughes, M. (1984) *Young Children Learning.* London: Fontana.

Vygotsky, L. S. (1978) *Mind In Society: The Development of Higher Psychological Processes.* London: Harvard University Press.

Vygotsky, L. S. (1981) The genesis of higher mental functions. In J. Wertsch (ed.) *The Concept of Activity in Soviet Psychology.* Annask, New York: Sharpe.

Speaking, listening and equality

Many of the books listed in this section contain practical ideas which can be used by teachers for use in the classroom and are recommended for staff libraries.

Boal, A. (1976) *Theatre Of The Oppressed.* London: Pluto Press.

Boal, A. (1994) *The Rainbow Of Desires.* London: Routledge.

Bolton, G. (1980) *Towards A Theory Of Drama In Education.* London: Longman.

Bolton, G. (1984) *Drama As Education.* Harlow: Longman.

Davies, G. (1983) *Primary Practical Drama.* London: Heinemann Educational Books.

Howe, A. and Johnson, J. (1992) *Common Bonds: Storytelling in the Classroom.* London: Hodder and Stoughton. This book is part of the National Oracy Project output and contains many practical suggestions.

Johnson, L. and O'Neill, C. (eds) (1984) *Dorothy Heathcote: Collected Writings on Education and Drama.* London: Hutchinson. The best way for the teacher to be introduced to the seminal work of Heathcote. Her dense, idiosyncratic style does not make this an easy read but her work needs understanding.

Morgan, N. and Saxton, J. (1987) *Teaching Drama: A Mind of Many Wonders.* London: Hutchinson. More difficult to use but still has many good ideas for teachers to interact with their children in a reflective manner.

Neelands, J. (1984) *Making Sense of Drama.* Oxford: Heinemann.

Neelands, J. (1990) *Structuring Drama Work.* Cambridge: Cambridge University Press. This book has many suggestions for strategies to be used in the class with the teacher-in-role.

O'Neill, C. and Lambert, A. (1982) *Drama Structures: A Practical Handbook for Teachers.* London: Hutchinson. Another excellent source book with many practical ideas.

Rosen, M. (1989) *Did I Hear You Write?* London: Andre Deutsch.

This book contains many examples of how children's 'voices'/interests need to find their way more into the classroom so that their writing and literary skills can flourish.

Reading and issues of equality

The following books and articles deal with practical issues on developing issues as readers and contain extremely useful bibliographies of academic and children's books relating to issues of equality.

Barrs, M. and Pidgeon, S. (eds) (1993) *Reading the Difference: Gender and Reading in the Primary School.* London: Centre for Language in Primary Education. Published by the important Centre For Language in Primary Education, Webber Row, London SE1 8QW, this is a good source book for teacher INSET work. It has a first-rate bibliography of children's books.

Barr, M. and Thomas, A. (eds) (1989) *The Reading Book.* London: Centre For Language In Primary Education. A very practical source book which deals with equality issues. It has many useful addresses of specialist book suppliers.

Gutteridge, T. (ed.) (1992) *Books To Break Barriers.* Oxford: Oxford Developmental Education Centre. This bibliography contains reviews (not always complimentary) on many multicultural books and has an extensive list of names and addresses of specialist bookshops and organizations which supply useful reading materials. It includes the addresses of New Beacon Books and Letterbox Library.

Handcock, R. (1994) Professional language, literacy and parents. *Language Matters* 1993/1994, no. 3, pp. 16–19.

Heath, Shirley Brice (1983) *Way With Words: Language, Life and Work in Communities and Classrooms.* Cambridge: Cambridge University Press. An important American study which highlights the importance of understanding how cultural meanings in the home translate into the classroom.

Minns, H. (1990) *Read It To Me Now.* London: Virago.

Minns, H. (1991) *Language, Literacy and Gender.* London: Hodder and Stoughton.

Rosen, M. (1992) Books and schools: books in schools. The Patrick Hardy Lecture, November.

Smith, B. (1994) *Through Writing to Reading.* London: Routledge. The book outlines a whole approach to detailing how the stories that children tell can be transcribed and then used to help them to read. A whole language approach with many case studies.

Writing and issues of equality

Armstrong, M. (1983) The story of studies. An enquiry into childhood narrative thought. *Curriculum* 4:5–13.
Armstrong, M. (1989) Another way of looking. *Forum* 33(1).
Graves, D. (1983) *Writing: Teachers and Children at Work.* London: Heinemann.
National Writing Project (1990) *Ways Of Looking: Issues Arising from the National Writing Project.* London: Nelson.
National Writing Project (1990) *What are Writers Made Of?: Issues of Gender and Writing.* London: Nelson.
Perera, K. (1984) *Children's Reading and Writing.* Oxford: Blackwell.
Tannen, D. (1985) Relative focus on involvement in oral and written discourse. In D. Olson, N. Torrance, and A. Hildyard (eds) *Literacy, Language and Learning.* Cambridge: Cambridge University Press.

CHAPTER 6

Mathematics

Sharanjeet Shan

What kind of educational theory has been used to render the National Mathematics Curriculum free of making connections with 'real-life' investigations, let alone any global connections, is not clear. It is only by embedding the real-life investigations into a socio-economic context that issues of equality: gender, 'race', class, sexuality and ability can be explored. Getting rid of such a contextual basis for teaching and learning can only mean a return to the neutrality myth within the Mathematics Curriculum (Gill and Levidow, 1987). In the first report on the Mathematics Curriculum, devised under the Education Reform Act, in a section on 'Ethnic and Cultural Diversity' (DFE, 1989), there is a reference to 'some black youngsters being disorientated and disadvantaged because of their culture and language [sic]'. When we consider that the vast majority of 'ethnic minority' children have been born and brought up in Britain, it serves to expose the ignorance and bigotry of the policy-makers.

There is little or no understanding in any of the official National Curriculum documentation of the most exciting developments worldwide in the national and international organizations of mathematics education. Very little thought has been given to the Cockcroft report (1982) or *Better Mathematics* (DES, 1987). These two documents emphasized the importance of constructivist approaches to the learning of mathematics (Orton, 1987/1992). There have been further developments in mathematics education, politicizing and democratizing both the content and the process of learning mathematics. Yet very little acknowledgement has been made of the work of any of the progressive theorists in the construction of the national mathematics curriculum. Mathematics has been set into a social and cultural context by eminent mathematicians of our time such as Alan Bishop (England), Chandler Davis (America), Paules Gerdes (Mozambique), Leoni Burton (England) and Munir Fasheh (Jordan) to name but a few. National Curriculum English documents make for deceiving reading at first glance. They are methodical, systematic, including an elaborate non-statutory guidance. While initially one may see glimpses of Bruner's theory of instruction (Lawton, 1978), a closer examination reveals that the nature of instruction and intervention will not be decided by the teacher. It will be controlled and directed by the end of key stage outcomes and league tables.

The educational theory is perhaps that of Gagne – teachers need only concern themselves with the facilitation of learning, not deciding upon the nature of it. Upon careful examination, the difficulties are revealed. There is a predetermined orientation set by the Standard Assessment Tasks. The pressure placed by league tables and 'rich' parents to influence the quality of teaching and learning will make it impossible to meet Bruner's demand that if information is to be used effectively, it must be translated into the learner's way of attempting to solve a problem. His argument for pluralism and enlightened opportunism in the materials and methods of instruction is likely to be lost or seriously impeded.

However, this chapter is about hope, not despair and aims to give teachers practical ideas to energize the mathematics curriculum with empowering methodology, context and content. Teachers must convert these into worksheets or lesson plans based on their own ideas as well as the level of understanding and attainment at which their pupils are working. There are few ready-made resources – teachers will need to be willing, innovative and committed to transform their existing teaching and learning styles to those emphasized in this chapter. The list of resources at the end of the chapter will give them further reference points.

In the final analysis, it is not only educational and employment opportunities that have a major role to play in enhancing the life chances of pupils. Mathematics for equality and justice will engage pupils and teachers in order for them to become partners in a struggle for demanding and gaining equal opportunities.

The 1988 and the 1993 education legislation encompasses the basic rights of all children to education, regardless of their background: 'Broad and balanced education which meets the needs of all the children regardless of race, class, gender' (Education Reform Act, 1988). There are few who would disagree with this notion of equality enshrined in law. It seems to be in line with the Rights of the Child as adopted by the United Nations on 25 November 1959. For the National Curriculum delivery to operate from such a fundamental premise requires that teachers understand the starting-point of all the pupils in their classes. 'Equal entitlement' can only be met by equalizing opportunities, which in turn can only be created if the learning environment is free of 'race', culture, ability, sexuality, class and gender bias in its organization and management. In such a motivating and challenging environment, the teacher makes genuine attempts to take cognizance of the diverse life experiences which are one of the most important resources available in a multicultural society. The word culture is used here to denote subcultures not only based in ethnicity but on other social characteristics such as social class.

Sadly, much too often teachers of mathematics believe multiculturalism to be congruent with equal opportunities. A token dip into the history of mathematics or cultural expressions such as Rangoli patterns is seen as equalizing opportunities. While it is important to redress the balance of contribution to the knowledge of mathematics, celebration of difference must not mean its perpetuation and promotion of segregation. If a teaching and learning environment fails to increase life chances of all the pupils – irrespective of specific needs, class, gender, sexual orientation and disability – by raising standards of the quality of teaching and learning, it cannot be regarded as equal or effective.

In addition to securing high grades in an examination, mathematics is a most powerful tool for understanding how the wealth creation in the world works, how land is distributed, why women are often trapped on the lowest rung of the economic ladder and why one half of humanity lives below the bread line. Mathematics can also be used to operate competently and humanely in the real world.

Teaching approaches and learning targets need to be clear to the teacher and the pupil. What is being taught and what is the role of a particular piece of learning? When assessing, are we assessing mathematics and its application or language learning or mechanical learning which is dependent upon memory and the ability to regurgitate that learning. Pupils learn within a very controlled environment where different forms of power define the limitations of teacher intervention:

- the power of the teacher;
- the power of mathematics as a subject;
- the power of the context;
- the power of the organization.

Teachers need to examine the total dimension of the power of their professionalism within the context of classroom practice.

THE POWER OF THE TEACHER

There are several ways in which a teacher of mathematics influences her/his pupils. The teacher's understanding of the pupil's perceived and received view of mathematics learning can often clash with her interpretation of her own delivery. The delivery should depend on the teacher's knowledge of the pupil, of mathematics, of how children learn and use mathematical language, of the place of mathematics education in the curriculum and the ability to interest and motivate children. Sadly, often, it emanates from a desire to comply with the statutory orders alone. Equal opportunities can simply mean ensuring good quality teaching whether or not it matches good quality learning: 'the cruel delusion of teachers who mistake the reflection of their own mental processes on the brain of an intuitional pupil for personal mental action on the pupil' (Tahta, 1972).

The teacher's confidence in dealing with new and challenging situations is of fundamental importance if she is to use mathematics for promoting less anachronistic and more informed attitudes in her pupils to the world around them. It is easy to recall many personal experiences of 'switching on' and 'switching off' which came from doing, seeing, hearing, reading, watching and feeling something that killed, sparked or sustained interest and enthusiasm. Much too often, mathematics learning is a formal, impersonal, mechanical and a didactic activity.

The teacher's own explanation of 'what is mathematics?' and 'how is it learnt?' would influence the selection of teaching and learning styles, as well as resources. An awareness of some fundamental influences, operating in a mathematics classroom is a good starting-point when deciding upon the nature of provision in the name of equal opportunities.

- Who decides upon the nature of groupings?
- Who decides which tests to use for ranking pupils in order of ability?
- Who decides when and how to intervene?
- Who makes the decisions about the choice of the content?
- Who chooses the presentation style?
- Are the assessment techniques a whole school development?
- Who selects the context?
- Who influences teacher/pupil or pupil/pupil relationships?

If teachers of mathematics seek to achieve creativity, group cohesion, expressiveness, extroversion and collaboration and to develop thinking and discussion skills, they need to understand the power that they wield in a classroom. They need to know their pupils well, for they influence many aspects of a pupil's personality such as the intellectual self, the physical self, the emotional self, the sexual self, the political self, the thinking self. This does not simply mean knowing the pupil's cultural background or what different languages are spoken. More importantly a teacher needs to know clearly:

- How do children make meanings in a mathematics classroom?
- What kind of pre-school knowledge of emerging mathematical concepts do they bring to school?
- What is the level of their communicative competence?
- How do they see a mathematics lesson?
- How do pupils view themselves as opposed to teachers clas-

sifying them into categories such as Sikh, Asian, black, Caribbean, ableless, able, Punjabi-speaking.
- Accents: 'well-spoken', formal or casual mode of speech. If a pupil's accent reflects her/his class, is there discrimination as a result from the teacher or from other pupils?

THE POWER OF MATHEMATICS AS A SUBJECT

Teachers need to engage in a debate on curriculum construction.

- Who selects the knowledge?
- Who defines the skills needed?
- Do the values of the pupil and the teacher conflict?

Figure 6.1 illustrates one way of making connections between those who make decisions about what to include and what to exclude when constructing curriculum syllabi. Teachers might like to engage in an activity to brainstorm and compile a different syllabus, appropriate to the experience, needs and aspirations of their pupils. This is not to suggest that each child should have a different syllabus: simply to understand and then to narrow the gap between pupils' lived experiences and school expectations. It would help a teacher to understand the pupils better.

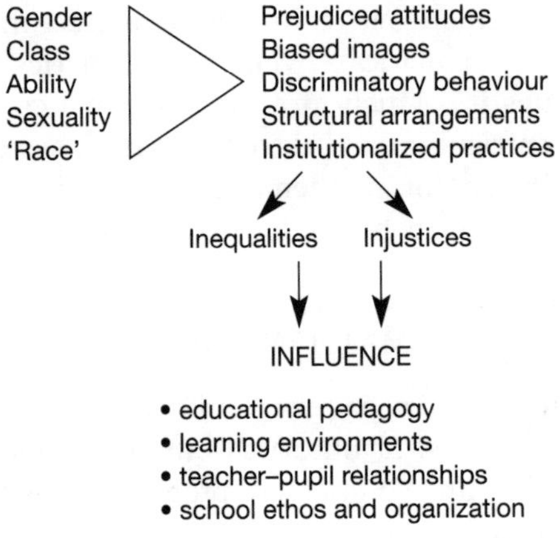

Figure 6.1   Construction of knowledge

As a subject, mathematics is very powerful in terms of raising questions and doubts of competence. It is used institutionally to set pupils apart from each other – generally being considered to be a measure of 'intelligence', both by the teacher and by the pupils. Teachers have to ask questions and challenge assumptions, if they wish to create a learning environment which will motivate, initiate and create equal access and equalize opportunities.

- Are there different logic systems in different cultures?
- Do the learner and the teacher share an understanding of the 'power' of mathematics in everyday life?
- Why do such a large number of pupils feel threatened and disempowered rather than enabled and inspired to become problem-solvers and independent thinkers?
- Could 'independent' thinking mean becoming selfish – as opposed to collaborative and co-operative?

The nature and definition of mathematics itself can be problematic for many. Teachers of mathematics in primary classrooms will need to understand the basic nature of the subject: how it is constructed; how it is defined; and how it is learnt. Let us take a brief look at the notion of abstract and concrete mathematics. In classroom situations, they are two sides of the same coin called mathematics and yet many mathematicians would not include the concretization of mathematics as a part of mathematics itself in order to protect the 'purity and neutrality' of mathematics – whose mathematics is it anyway and who defines it? Which form of mathematics has a higher status in the curriculum and the examination system? Can the following definition of mathematics be applied both to the abstract form and the concrete form? Who decides?

MATHEMATICS

The ability to recognize patterns and to see relationships that exist between related or unrelated bits of knowledge. It is a language used to find solutions to problems. It is therefore as powerful a language for communication as the spoken word itself.

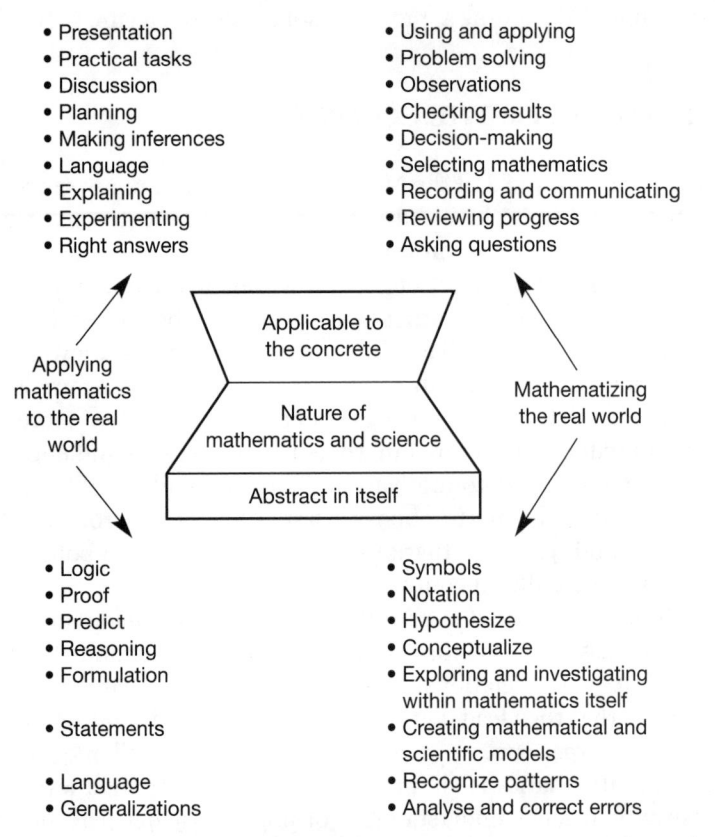

- Presentation
- Practical tasks
- Discussion
- Planning
- Making inferences
- Language
- Explaining
- Experimenting
- Right answers

- Using and applying
- Problem solving
- Observations
- Checking results
- Decision-making
- Selecting mathematics
- Recording and communicating
- Reviewing progress
- Asking questions

Applying mathematics to the real world

Applicable to the concrete

Nature of mathematics and science

Mathematizing the real world

Abstract in itself

- Logic
- Proof
- Predict
- Reasoning
- Formulation

- Statements

- Language
- Generalizations

- Symbols
- Notation
- Hypothesize
- Conceptualize
- Exploring and investigating within mathematics itself
- Creating mathematical and scientific models
- Recognize patterns
- Analyse and correct errors

Figure 6.2 A way of connecting abstract and concrete mathematics

Abstract mathematics can be a solitary activity and may be able to exist without solving any real problems from a vibrating and dynamic, social, political, economic, dead and alive, cultural and religious, sad and happy world. Many 'pure and neutral' mathematicians develop their ideas behind closed doors without any reference to the real world and leave them either to gather dust on shelves or restrict the debate to a few academics. Fortunately many Primary Mathematics Schemes make connections in pupil-friendly contexts and experiences as opposed to pages and pages of 'sums'. Concrete mathematics is commonly a group activity and cannot have a shape or form without locating and constructing solutions in abstract models. Concrete mathematics is about contextualized reflective knowledge, about evaluating and criticizing while finding appropriate solutions (see Figure 6.2).

THE POWER OF THE CONTEXT

At Key Stages 1 and 2 of the National Curriculum, many schools are beginning to be involved with their local industry, particularly in relation to environmental projects. As an incidental benefit, real and practical opportunities for using and applying mathematics emerge. At other times pupils can be provided with examples from the familiar. They can add on broader knowledge about their surroundings in a mathematics lesson, in a purposeful and planned, meaningful and coherent manner. Any content that will reduce anxiety in a mathematics classroom and engage a pupil can only lead to motivation. Shan and Bailey (1991) give a variety of problems to choose from. They range from local, national and global situations set within a socio-political, economic and cultural context (see Figure 6.3).

In order to construct such investigations/problem-solving in a primary classroom – so that pupils will begin to be confident and talk about gender relations, kinds of food that they eat, kinds of life styles that they lead, without demeaning and devaluing their individual experiences – a teacher needs to be well prepared. Such a mathematics is simple yet complex. A very high level of sensitivity, teacher understanding of pupils, teacher perception of their feelings, attitudes and beliefs is a basic requirement. The use of mathematics and real-life relevant issues enhances critical perception of the world and raises awareness of equality and justice. Recognizing, understanding and using real-life problems as opportunities for seeking solutions is a powerful way to move towards participation in a multicultural society, while at the same time learning to make sense of economic and political construction about their lives. The choice of 'real-life contexts' is up to the teacher – she could choose from a range rather than restrict herself to shoe sizes, heights, cars on the road and vegetables in the local greengrocers.

A large number of investigative problems for teaching the Four Rules of Number – Multiplication, Division, Addition and Subtraction – at Key Stage 1 can be constructed around

---

Volume and Surface Area

Q. Women in some countries have to carry water for miles. Sometimes they use water containers made out of cylinders. If a cylinder has diameter of 80cms height 1m, what is the volume of water? Use the lengths first in centimetres and then in metres.

Calculate your water requirement for a day at home.

Q. A well in Ethiopia is 50ft deep and has a radius of 5ft. The depth of water is 20ft. What is the volume of water? Calculate the area of the walls of the well. If the sides of bricks measure 12" by 5", how many bricks will be needed to build the walls?

Population Explosion

Q. Use an atlas or Whitaker's Almanac to find information:
Look up 'land area' and 'population' for a number of countries.
Calculate the ratio of people per square mile.
Example: France: land area – 130,165 sq. miles
population – 54 million
density of people per sq. mile = 415

Q. Choose 20 countries from all parts of the world. Work out the number of people per sq. mile for each country. Write a few comments about your results. Do countries usually labelled 'POOR' always have high density of people? If this is not the case, what other reason might there be for their poverty?

Percentages/calculator sums

Q. Under apartheid, the population of South Africa was divided into four separate and officially separately classified groups:
African: 24,103,458
Coloured: 2,830,301
Indian: 890,292
White: 4,818,679

Make sure you can say these numbers in millions and thousands etc. Then calculate the total percentage of various populations.

Present this information on a pie chart

Figure 6.3   Challenging racism through classroom mathematics
Source: Shan and Bailey (1991:167).

Figure 6.4. In any discussion of diet, pupils' awareness can be raised regarding the unfair and stereotyped reporting of the eating habits of people, particularly those of the working classes and from the North of England.

Milk, whole	5 pints	£1.05	Apples	28 (1 each day)	£2.79
Milk, skimmed	16 pints	£3.20	Oranges	28 (each day)	£3.36
Cheese, Edam	5oz	32p	Dried fruit (raisins)	1½ lb	82p
Cheese, Cheddar	5oz	29p	Bread, wholemeal	7 large loaves	£3.22
Beefburgers	10	99p	Muffins	4	34p
Pork chops	4 medium	£2.82	Flour, white	1 small pack	22p
Bacon (lean)	¾ lb	£1.70	Flour, wholemeal	1 small pack	22p
Chicken, whole	1 small	£2.15	Doughnuts	4	52p
Chicken, breast	5oz.	75p	Biscuits, digestive	2 packets	52p
Sausages, beef	1½ lb	£1.09	Cornflakes	500g pack	58p
Mackerel, tinned	1½ lb	£1.60	Muesli	340g pack	47p
Fish fingers	6	30p	Spaghetti, wholemeal	1lb	22p
Pilchards	2 cans	50p	Pudding rice	1 small packet	49p
Eggs	1 dozen	87p	Semolina	1lb	36p
Butter	250g	48p	Red kidney beans, dry	200g	30p
Margarine, sunflower	700g	78p	Tea	8oz	£1.20
Vegetable oil	½ litre	40p	Instant coffee	1 small jar	£1.19
Sugar	1 kilo	46p	Squash	½ large bottle	32p
Potatoes	11lb	£1.21	Canned drinks	2	64p
Green veg, fresh	1¾ lb	32p	Wine	1 bottle	£2
Root veg	3lb	45p	Beer	2 pints	£1.39
Frozen peas	1lb	44p	Ice cream	½ litre	49p
Tomatoes, fresh	¾ kg	67p	Chocolate	1 med bar	£1.35
Lettuce	1 medium	20p	Toffees	1 packet	59p
Cucumber	1 medium	45p	Crisps	6 packets	47p
Baked beans	3 × 440g tins	48p			
				TOTAL	£48.04

Figure 6.4   Shopping list for a healthy diet
Source: *Guardian* (1986) 18 October, as illustrated in Shan and Bailey (1991).

With Key Stage 2 pupils, in addition to understanding graphical representation of data, the link between class, poor health of infants and higher rate of mortality and consequently higher birth rate can be explored (see Figure 6.5). Data can be provided by the teacher to illustrate the imbalance of economic power as created by the multinationals. *My Name is Today* (Morley and Lovel, 1986) provides examples around which very young children can discuss pertinent issues such as child health, poverty, education and employment around the world.

Such subject matter needs to be handled from a strong information base in case a teacher ends up creating more stereotypes, rather than demolishing them. It would be important for teachers to read *Pedagogy of the Oppressed* (Freire, 1985) if they believe in the liberating power of education and in engaging in a shared learning process with their pupils.

The educational practice in a mathematics classroom where

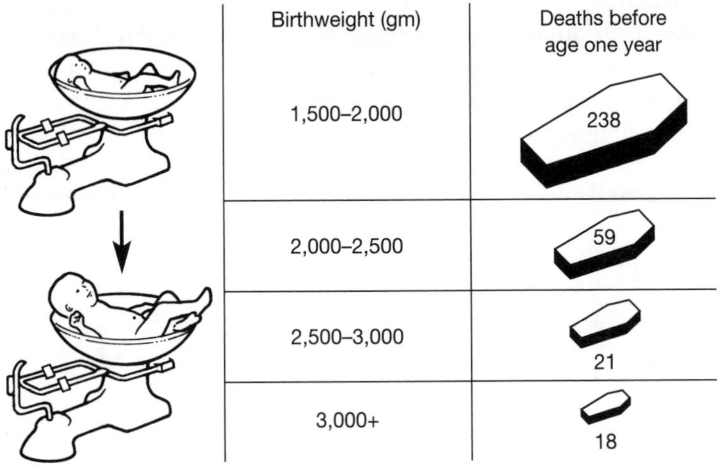

Birthweight (gm)	Deaths before age one year
1,500–2,000	238
2,000–2,500	59
2,500–3,000	21
3,000+	18

Figure 6.5   Birthweight and mortality
Source: from a study in New Delhi, India.

pupils seek to reflect critically on the so-called 'reality' with the teacher acting as a facilitator, would encourage pupils to learn to make informed choices. Such a critical stance to learning removes the limitations in a prescribed curriculum and allows pupils to develop a sharp focus on issues of interrelatedness and interdependence of human beings, of systems and of cultures and experiences.

Such a classroom will promote a wide variety of contextualized representations of mathematical knowledge, values and skills, from all over the world. Examples of costs to human life can be collected from the marketplace and mega multinationals; from cash crop fields and weapons of war; from famine and flooding, to name but a few. Hundreds of examples can be found in *Multiple Factors: Classroom Mathematics for Equality and Justice* (Shan and Bailey, 1991). Any curriculum of mathematics is admirably suited to exploring a whole range of the magic of mathematics. Different mathematics educators have come up with different names.

Ethnomathematics

Teachers should explore the mathematics of farmers, fishermen and crafts folk. An exciting range of decorative art, ranging from the ornamentation of plaited mats and baskets to paintings on house walls and sand drawings is put together in *Lusona – Geometrical Recreations of Africa* (Gerdes, 1991). Lusona is the word for sand drawings from Angola. These refer to fables, games, riddles, animals, birds, etc. (see Figure 6.6).

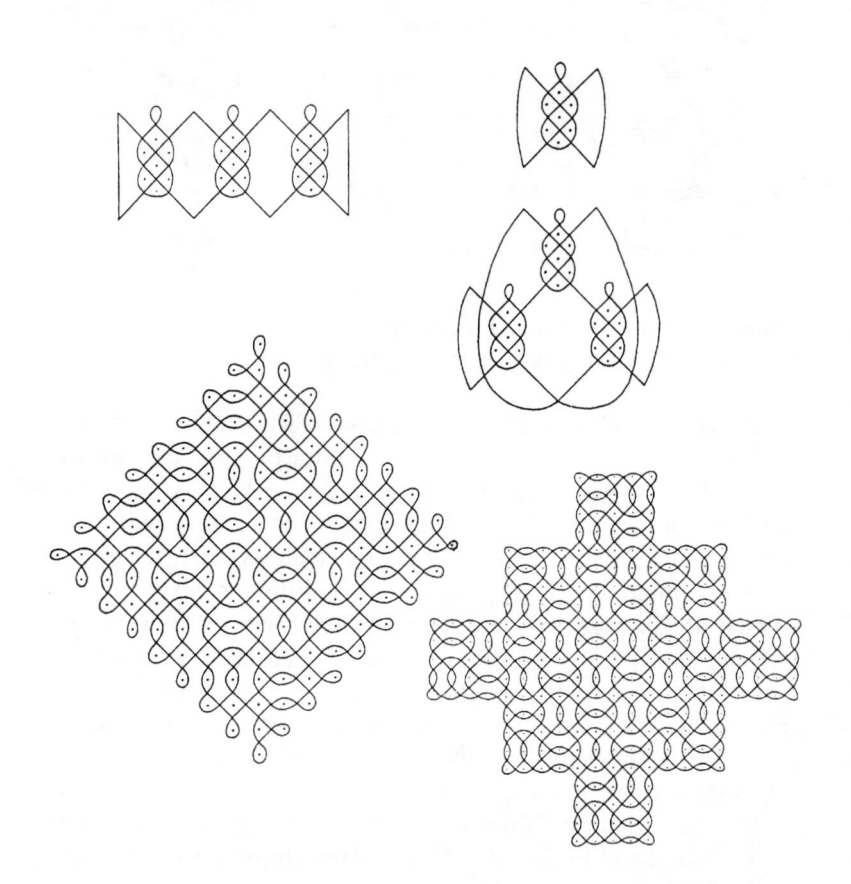

Figure 6.6   A glimpse of myriad sand drawings which can contribute to the knowledge of mathematical constructions. These line drawings are composed out of one closed line. The first set represents three birds flying together. Make up your own – remember – only one closed line.
Source: Gerdes (1991).

Multicultural mathematics

Shan and Bailey (1991) have gathered together hundreds of examples of cultural contributions from around the world: embroidery, architectural patterns, geometry in Islam, kite mathematics, games ancient and new, history of mathematics, different ways of doing multiplication and division, mathematics in the work place, and much more (see Figure 6.7).

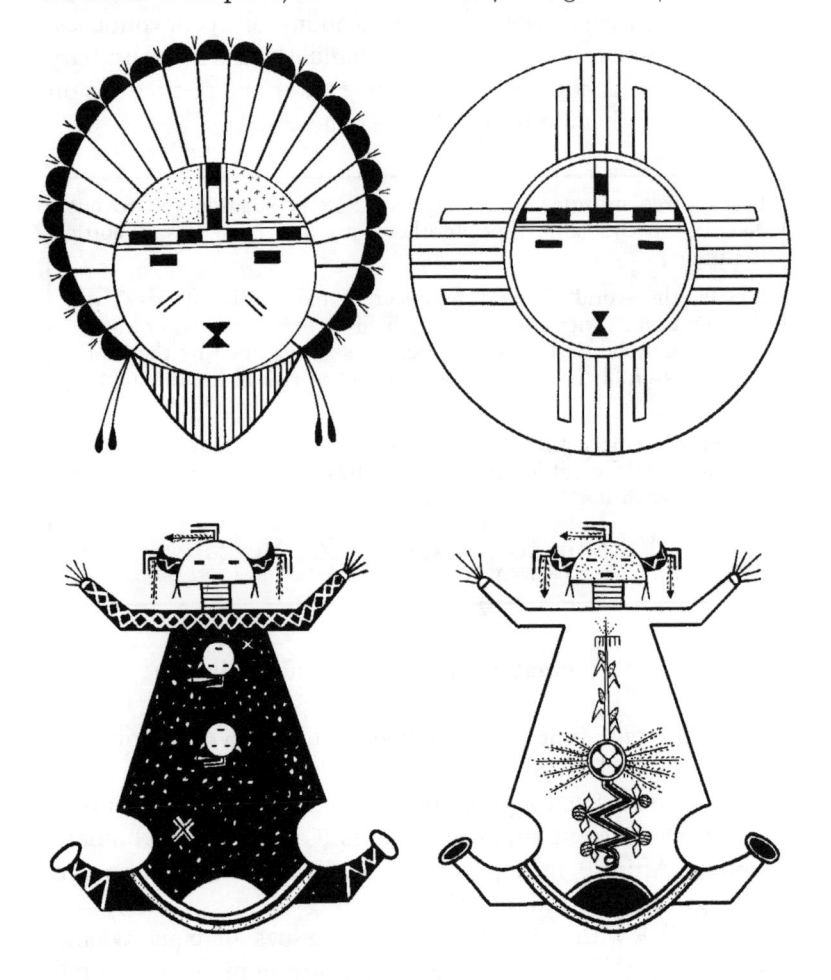

Figure 6.7   Indian designs
Source: Villasenor, J. and Villasenor, D. (1983) *Indian Designs*. Colchester: Jonathan Press.

Mathematics for equality and justice

There is no shortage of examples which illustrate the positioning of women and children in the poverty trap worldwide. The issue of bottle feeding connects directly to the control of the baby milk market by men for the benefit of owners of multinationals. The anti-Nestlé campaign is a well-known example (see Figure 6.8). The control of the contraceptives market by men directly influences the population growth in economically poor countries. Such adult issues may be difficult to handle by the lower primary age range – it is possible for them to explore the restrictions on their own mothers in terms of career choices.

Every three minutes, Nestlé spends £18 persuading you to buy Nescafé. In the same time another baby dies from unsafe bottle feeding.

Nestlé, the world's largest producer of baby milk, floods Third World hospitals with enough free baby milk to ensure that newborns are routinely bottle fed. This practice is condemned by the World Health Assembly because it places babies at risk of life-threatening infections.

Breastmilk is free and safe – but companies know that unless they get babies on the bottle, they don't do business. **We can't let them get away with it.**

Wake up to the facts. Not Nescafé.
Baby Milk Action (BMAC) 6 Regent Terrace, Cambridge, CB2 1AA

Figure 6.8   Mathematics for equality and justice

Arguments rage among mathematicians as to the origin of mathematical ideas. See for example: *The Crest of the Peacock* (Joseph, 1991). Such a panorama of mathematical happenings from many different times and places (Greek, Hindu, Roman, Egyptian, African) in appropriate, pupil-friendly language can challenge, interest and motivate.

In parallel with all other learning, issues of equality and justice have to be understood as a continuum on the spiral curriculum, from nursery to A level and beyond. A thematic approach which makes cross-curricular connections, as well as promoting co-operative, collaborative ways of working, is the

best method. Environment education, particularly the built environment around the experience of the pupils, is an important
cross-curricular dimension for teachers to consider in the twentieth century and beyond.

**Compare and contrast a 7-year-old's life in an inner city school
in England to that of a South African child in a township**.
(Write to SJSR: Director – Mathematics Centre for Primary
Teachers. PO Box 117, Auckland Park, Johannesburg, RSA.)

**Make links with schools in South Africa as well as construct-
ing problem-solving activities as a means to raise awareness
and empathy.**

Consider issues such as:

- Water/electric supply
- Distances from home to school
- Modes of transport
- Playground games
- School buildings
- Cost and supply of books and stationery
- Size of classes
- Employment types of both mothers and fathers

Oxfam produces several role-play packages around themes such
as water and trade to support understanding of gender and class-
related issues. Some organizations such as the Centre for World
Development Education produce videos, tapes, slides and
computer materials. *Water Game,* based on the daily use and
supply of water, is highly engaging for 10- and 11-year-olds.

> This is a simulation in which the user goes to a country cottage
> with no running water and has to estimate the water needs of the
> humans, animals and crops. The user takes on the role of the
> water-carrier, to fetch water from the lakes or wells or river with
> suitable events such as pollution, dried up river or broken pumps
> cluttering up the path from time to time. Decisions are taken by
> the pupils, during which they discuss quantities of water, dangers
> of water shortages, hazards of pollution etc.
>
> (CWDE, quote from the catalogue, 1993)

Water is a fascinating topic for young children. The different
areas connect to many levels of National Curriculum
Mathematics and the children will connect to it in many different daily experiences (see Figure 6.9).

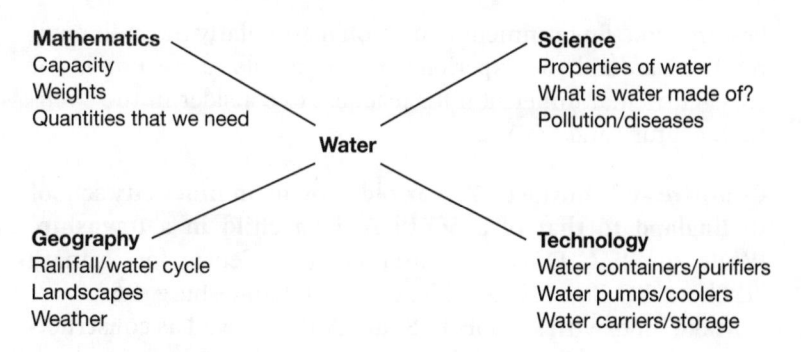

Figure 6.9   Water

Titles listed under Mathematics in the water topic web are components of the National Curriculum Mathematics at Key Stage 1. An example on water is shown in Figure 6.10 (Shan and Bailey, 1991).

Estimation

Q. Using the figures below giving average water usage, estimate the amount of water a household uses in a week? In a year?

Bath	90 litres	Shower	27 litres
Toilet	9 litres	Wash face, hands	9 litres
Drink	1 litre	Wash teeth	1 litre
Wash clothes	118 litres per load	Sprinkler	9 litres per minute

(The average U.K. household amount is 1301 litres per day.)

Q. It is much harder to calculate how much water is used on your behalf by the people who provide some of the basic services.

Estimate

a. How much water is used in making the newspapers that you have in your house, if 1,200 litres are needed for one Sunday newspaper?

b. How much water is used to provide for your weekly transport if each gallon of petrol uses about 60 litres of water in the refining process. Note that buses and trains require less fuel per passenger – roughly one quarter.

Figure 6.10   Water
Source: Shan and Bailey (1991).

Teachers may feel that exploring such approaches is made diffi-cult by a lack of resources. However, with a measure of commitment and awareness, materials can be compiled from many different sources: travelling, shops, catalogues, news-papers. Oxfam, Friends of the Earth, Christian Aid, Greenlight publications, Traidcraft and Education Development Centres all produce and market attractive teacher and pupil packages of case studies, linked into the National Curriculum.

Examples in ths chapter can be used as guidelines by teachers to review their existing teaching and learning styles – content and process – and provide stimulus for developing their practice in new dimensions. While exploring new ways of doing math-ematics, they will make connections between 'race', gender and class experiences. Whether they are teachers or nursery age chil-dren or infants, juniors or middle school, teachers cannot/do not take a neutral position. The teaching and learning styles preferred and promoted are a product of the teacher's own learn-ing, values and attitudes. Children notice a wide variety of race and gender characteristics, social class and cultural backgrounds about each other and place them in the same order of import-ance as reflected by their home as well as their learning environment. For example, those teachers or carers, who believe that in the early years children are not aware of each other's colour, shape or size, and therefore cannot discriminate, need to be asked a very basic question:

> If young children do not notice each other's colour or any other descriptors, why do we then insist that Colours, Shapes and Sizes are the three key areas for exploration and development in the nursery curriculum?

Can we really say that as children learn to recognize the differences in many other colours, they cannot distinguish between black, white, brown and the shades in between? Or that they do not notice the degree of privilege experienced by different classes of people in the shape of cars, clothes, houses, etc. Or the differences between the kind of toys that they play with? Pupils whose teachers claim to 'treat all pupils equally' would learn that they are disregarding the differences and unique qualities of their pupils as individuals, denying them the right to grow, learn and develop their strengths.

Milner (1975) documents the psychological repercussions of the damage done, when children's experiences are not acknowledged. It is a carefully documented study of black and white children, responding to experiences of 'race' over a period of ten years. Well-meaning token inputs on issues of equality and justice within a school's programme may do more harm than good. Teaching very young children about the notion of giving on special occasions such as the Harvest festival and Christmas or Diwali is simply relieving them of the responsibility of understanding how power positions work in an interdependent world. Children often have elderly relatives. They should be asking:

- How and why do many old people in a prosperous society like Britain end their days in difficult and degrading conditions?
- Why are there so many homeless in inner cities – why are they on the increase?
- How many people get into debt to provide 'gifts' for their loved ones?

On such occasions, real thanksgiving could involve an understanding of how their own lifestyles are not only connected to

Setting the Scene

Divide the class into four countries – India, Brazil, Philippines and Kenya.

Explain that these are poorer countries of the world, but that they produce things that we need, for example, cotton, coffee, pineapples, bananas.

They sell these products to buy things that they need and want, for example, medicines, machinery.

Playing the Game – an Explanation

The children are going to play a game in which they have to pretend that they live in a community in another country (India, Kenya, Philippines or Brazil). They want to improve their community by getting things for it.

In this game they will be pretending to grow and make things, sell them and buy other things. To make and grow they will have to cut out and colour shapes. These they will exchange for tokens/counters which act as money. The tokens will be used to purchase things they want, but cannot grow or make.

Starter Activity

At this stage turn their attention to the playing board that each group has before it. To start the game they will have to make food for every group member – that means cutting and colouring the shapes they can see on the plate.

Hand out food templates to each group. Encourage careful production – perhaps using the analogy of farmers who have to take care if their crop is to survive. Each group cuts and colours food for each member. The food is then put on the plate on the group's board.

Before moving on to Level One, put up the Big Buy Board in a prominent place.

Figure 6.11 Marketplace international trade game

Figure 6.12   Marketplace international trade game

those in 'poor' parts of the world where most of the consumable commodities are grown and developed – but that their lifestyles are made possible because most of the world is 'made' to stay poor. Children and teachers can conclude their findings by making changes such as taking a pledge to explore alternative methods of trade and check out how one's own part in exploitation could be reduced (see Figures 6.11 and 6.12).

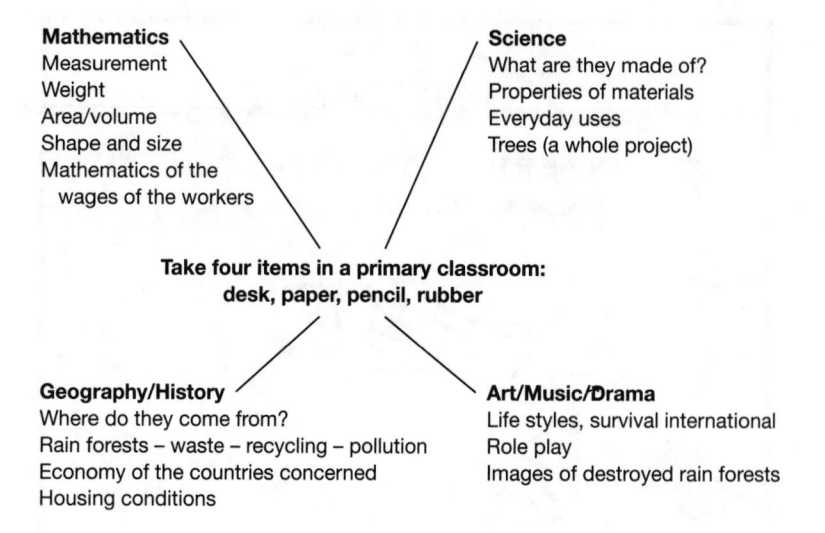

Mathematics
Measurement
Weight
Area/volume
Shape and size
Mathematics of the
    wages of the workers

Science
What are they made of?
Properties of materials
Everyday uses
Trees (a whole project)

**Take four items in a primary classroom:
desk, paper, pencil, rubber**

Geography/History
Where do they come from?
Rain forests – waste – recycling – pollution
Economy of the countries concerned
Housing conditions

Art/Music/Drama
Life styles, survival international
Role play
Images of destroyed rain forests

Figure 6.13   Mathematics and cross-curricular connections

Another example of making cross-curricular connections is shown in Figure 6.13.

Mathematics and language

An aspect that is often ignored across the world is the power and influence of language as used in a mathematics classroom and in a school as an organization. It is often underemphasized. Pupils speak many different languages and dialects. In a mathematics classroom, ordinary words can have different meanings.

The delivery of all mathematical concepts requires an elaborate visual imagery – shapes, symbols, equations, modelling of problems in diagrammatic form, etc. Explanations that accompany such imagery often make use of complex, precise and sophisticated mathematical language. Many words used in a mathematical context have precise meanings as opposed to a broad interpretation when used as everyday language. Line, average, round, mean, corner, side, surface are examples. For pupils whose vocabulary is not well developed or very advanced, does this imply that a low-level learning could result from not being able to describe in many words complex visual imagery? Does retention and understanding relate directly to the verbal imagery? Where does this leave pupils for whom English is a second language or those who come from linguistically poor homes or those who are slow learners? Important questions have been asked by Strevens (Shan and Bailey, 1991):

- Do learner and teacher share the same language?
- Do they share the same logic systems?

A question that teachers need to ask is: How much and what level of vocabulary do I use in my explanations and deliberations during my teaching? How much of what I say do pupils understand? For example, in addition to the usual everyday language which will be used during explanations, words required to introduce properties of shape and space to 6- and 7-year-olds may possibly include the following:

> IN OUT SIDE UP DOWN DRAW BELOW
> STRAIGHT LINE BEND VERTICAL TRIANGLE RIGHT
> LEFT OPPOSITE PARALLEL ANGLE BELOW ABOVE
> BEHIND SHORT LONG EXTEND EQUAL SAME
> DIFFERENT MEASURE DEGREE HOLD RULER
> LENGTH DEPTH CORNER NEAT PROTRACTOR
> CORRECT RECTANGLE TRAPEZIUM ISOSCELES
> EQUILATERAL DIAMOND RHOMBUS PARALLELOGRAM

Teachers can help pupils if they prepare a vocabulary sheet on any of the concepts before delivering their lesson. 'Fractions' and 'long division' have particular difficulty for most primary school children. Definitions of flat and solid shapes often cause confusion. Perhaps an analysis of the language used will help teachers to make helpful feedback and comments to pupils who continually get stuck. 'Equivalence' must be the most difficult concept to teach and provides an interesting example of how language used in a mathematics classroom can be misunderstood until one puts it into context.

For example: Are all these equal quantities?
Does 100 cents in one Rand = 100 cents in one Dollar?
Does 100 pence in one Pound = 100 new pence in one Rupee?
Does one South African cent equal one American cent?
Would they weigh the same? Would they look the same?
These questions can only be answered sensibly when something needs to be paid for.

Another example can be found in the teacher's own preference for a particular way of saying a mathematical expression, causing distress and confusion among pupils, such as during the teaching of fractions.

How many ways can you say: 4 into 3?

*3 divided by 4   *3 fourths   *3 shared between 4
*1 quarter of 3
*3 out of 4   *3 over 4   *$^3/_4$ and so on.

THE POWER OF THE ORGANIZATION

Staff development and some focused ongoing action–research is an essential prerequisite to instigating a shared understanding of the mathematical concepts used in promoting, equalizing and empowering opportunities. The school as an organization needs to understand and remain aware of how knowledge is constructed, its role in the selection of 'appropriate' learning materials and the making of appropriately contextualized learning environments. There must be a conscientious and shared understanding of the various influences on pupil lives, particularly language. In the case of pupils of Asian backgrounds (referred to as emergent bilinguals), it is quite possible that they come to school with a passive vocabulary of English while having a high level of communicative competence in their mother tongue or vice versa. Similarly, there is a huge misunderstanding of the language/s of pupils of Caribbean/African backgrounds. This is explored further in Chapter 7. Schools cannot afford to ignore this vital element of a child's development. Before planning schemes of work strictly in accordance with the statutory documents, questions must be asked:

1 How is knowledge constructed within the planning and development of the curriculum?
2 Is mathematics in a league of its own or is it delivered as an integrated area of learning, making connections with geography, science, technology, music, etc.
3 Where do pupils feature in the decision-making process in a school?

- black, emergent bilingual pupils?
- poor, working-class pupils?
- shy boys and girls?
- disturbed and confused pupils of divorced parents?
- competitive vs. co-operative pupils?
- pupils distressed by the experience of learning?
- what does the school assess?

To conclude, while teachers focus on formal abstract mathematics, keen to ensure attainment and competence in their pupils, they may overlook the fact that equalizing opportunities can only be achieved if pupils' received view of mathematics is enhanced. Language, presentation and context, as well as the process of delivery, all play an equal part. Relevant, real-life, problem-solving, mathematics focuses on demystification, empowerment and democratization. Far from being 'free and neutral', mathematics is a very powerful area of the curriculum in which to ignore or promote education for empowerment. Equalizing opportunities does not mean token celebrations of cultural differences. It can only work if all pupils are treated as separate but equal individuals. Through differentiated learning and critical perspectives, they can learn to become evaluators of their world and to make informed choices. It is a challenging, most interesting and rewarding task to work with pupils in a mathematics lesson so that they grow up to be participants in their own emancipation.

RESOURCES

The following are some of the best resource material available for promoting problem-solving, investigative work in mathematics from a constructivist approach.

Leoni Burton's books (see References) are a must for all Primary teachers.

Mathematics Programmes of Study: Inset for Key Stages 1 and 2 (1993). Written and developed by the Shell Centre in Nottingham for the National Curriculum Council. Despite the Dearing Review, the INSET activities in this pack are first rate.

Mathematics in the Primary Curriculum. Available from the

Open University only as it is a professional course for teachers; a primary profile module prepared by Hilary Claire for the course team – however the pack is extremely useful by itself even if you are not doing a course with the Open University. Buckingham: Open University.

Prime: Children, Mathematics and Learning. Eight inset units for primary teachers, produced by the National Curriculum Council. New York: Simon and Schuster.

Multiple Factors: Classroom Mathematics for Equality and Justice (Shan and Bailey, 1991). Seven chapters of examples for use in the classroom, with little or no theoretical background required, only a willingness to try out the ideas. Stoke-on-Trent: Trentham Books.

The following associations produce excellent materials, teacher's books, posters, puzzles, charts, etc., for support in a mathematics classroom.

Association of Teachers of Mathematics, 7 Shaftesbury Street, Derby DE23 8YB.

Mathematics Association, 259 London Road, Leicester LE2 3BE.

The following are organizations good sources for reference material. Addresses can be found in the local telephone directory or the library.

Friends of the Earth
Traidcraft
Christian Aid
Oxfam

Development Education Centres: many cities have their own development education centres. The one in Birmingham, located in Selly Oak, is particularly good as its materials span a whole range of national and international contexts.

REFERENCES

Bishop, A. J. (1979) Visualising and mathematics in a pre-technological culture. *Education Studies in Mathematics* 10:135–46.

Bishop, A. J. (1988) *Mathematics Enculturation*. Lancaster: Kluwer.

Boole, M. (1972) *A Boolean Anthology. Selected Writings of Mary Boole on Mathematical Education* (1832–1916). Compiled by

D. G. Tahta. Derby: Association of Mathematics Teachers.

Burton, L. (1986) *Girls into Maths Can Go.* Milton Keynes: Open University Press.

Burton, L. (1994) *Children Learning Mathematics: Patterns and Relationships.* New York: Simon and Schuster.

Burton, L. (ed.) (1990) *Gender and Mathematics Education: An International Perspective.* London: Cassell.

Burton, L. (1984) *Thinking Things Through: Problem Solving in Mathematics.* Oxford: Basil Blackwell.

Cockcroft, W. H. (1982) *Mathematics Counts* (Report of the Committee of Inquiry into the Teaching of Mathematics in schools). London: HMSO.

Davis, A. and Pettitt, D. (1994) *Developing Understanding in Primary Mathematics.* London: Falmer Press.

Department of Education and Science (DES) (1987) *Better Mathematics.* London: HMSO.

Department of Education and Science (DES) (1989) *The National Curriculum: From Policy to Practice.* London: HMSO.

DFE (1989) *The Maths Report.* London: HMSO.

Freire, P. (1985) *Pedagogy of the Oppressed.* Harmondsworth: Penguin.

Gerdes, P. (1988a) On possible uses of traditional Angolan sand drawings in the mathematics classroom. *Educational Studies in Mathematics,* 19(1).

Gerdes, P. (1988b) Find the missing figures. A series of geometric problems inspired by traditional Tchokwe sand drawings (Angola) and Tamil threshold designs (India). *Mathematics Teaching,* 124.

Gerdes, P. (1991) *Lusona: Geometrical Recreations of Africa.* Mozambique: African Mathematical Union.

Gill, D. and Levidow, L. (1987) *Anti-racist Science Teaching.* London: Free Association Books.

Harris, P. (1991) *Mathematics in a Cultural Context: Aboriginal Perspectives on Space, Time and Money.* Australia: Deakin University.

Joseph, George (1991) *The Crest of the Peacock: Non-European Roots of Mathematics.* London: I.B. Tauris.

Lawton, D. (1978) *Class, Culture and the Curriculum.* London: Routledge and Kegan Paul.

The Mathematics Association (1992) *Maths Talk.* Cheltenham: Stanley Thornes.

The Mathematics Association (1987) *Sharing Mathematics with Parents.* Cheltenham: Stanley Thornes.

Mellin-Olsen, S. (1993) *The Politics of Mathematics Education.* Lancaster: Kluwer.

Milner, D. (1975) *Children and Race.* Harmondsworth: Penguin.

Morley, D. and Lovel, H. (1986) *My Name is Today.* London and Basingstoke: Macmillan Publishers.

Orton, A. (1987/1992) *Learning Mathematics: Issues, Theory and Classroom Practice.* London: Cassell.

Shan, S. and Bailey, P. (1991) *Multiple Factors: Classroom Mathematics for Equality and Justice.* Stoke-on-Trent: Trentham Books.

CHAPTER 7

Science

Sharanjeet Shan

This chapter is about science education in a primary classroom. The intention is not to leave teachers feeling that they need to become 'scientists' in order to understand how their pupils may construct scientific knowledge and the dangers inherent in it if that construction goes unchecked. The intention is to show teachers that science is a very powerful subject through which to address inequalities and that they have an enormous range of resources available to them. In the last section, a range of tangible examples are given – these will help both to increase the teacher's knowledge of science and to help children to increase their powers of rationalizing the world around them.

Science as commonly taught in our schools is intensely 'culture specific', around the model of 'Western high-tech', specifically developed for Western-style mechanization and a society which is dependent on creating and maintaining class differentials. The chapter deals briefly with how inequalities are justified using 'science' as a lever to explain away class differences, gender inequities and distorted 'race' constructions. Children as young as three understand differences in colour, poverty and gender and prefer to be associated with more positive role models (Milner, 1975). Primary school teachers use topics such as 'My home', 'Ourselves' and 'My family' in order to allow young pupils to be aware of the variety of facets of their immediate environments. This is therefore the most important stage of a child's development at which to prevent the creation of stereotypes, particularly behaviour patterns and myths about males and females, black and white, rich and poor. The way that we respond to our environment is not written in our genes; it is a consequence of our own received experiences.

Science, nature and human beings are connected: ozone layer depletion; the global greenhouse effect; increased use of drugs by humans, creation of deserts as a result of agribusiness all are direct consequences of capitalist greed and science which continues to reject the notion of sustainability. Animal extinction will also mean our extinction. The factors which take away the land, clean air and water from the animals are the same factors which will destroy life's vital elements for humans. Teachers need to create resources in a classroom which expose children to the reality of the consequences of capitalist science.

BIOLOGICAL REDUCTIONISM AND SCIENCE: THE CONNECTION

Throughout the eighteenth and the nineteenth centuries, many of the distortions of scientific theories were used to place black people, women and peoples of lower social classes in inferior positions of the hierarchy of human beings (Rose *et al.*, 1984). The authors put forward a powerful discourse on the role that biological determinism played in legitimizing inequalities around gender, class and race and how claims were made in the name of 'science' which were anything but science. ' "Science" is the ultimate legitimator of bourgeois ideology. To oppose "science", to prefer values to facts, is to transgress not merely against a human law but against a law of nature' (Rose *et al.*, 1984:65).

Behaviour scientists of the eighteenth and nineteenth centuries went to great lengths to try to prove that the size of the brain was an indicator of the intellectual capability of a human being (Young, 1971) and that the behaviour and educational performance was linked to this – a very dangerous hypothesis indeed. They believed that a society's ills were the result of the behaviour of certain individuals rather than the society itself. Evidence was sought in scientific explanations. The pseudo-science of measuring skulls of blacks and women – craniometry – was promoted by Samuel George Morton who collected 1,000 skulls in order to establish the ranking of races by measuring their size (Gould, 1981). Paul Broca, who is credited with being the father of anthropology and was also the founder of the East India Company, went to great lengths to formulate, contest and publish his views on differences in brain size being related to superior and inferior intelligence.

Arthur Jenson (1969) in the USA and Eysenck (1971) in the UK used the same theories to underpin their claims on IQ and achievement among blacks and poor working classes. Maria Montessori, the great educationist, while dismissing Paul Broca's work on women, condoned and used his conclusions on young children, measuring her pupils' heads to determine who were the better learners (Montessori, 1913).

Fortunately, many scientists have a clear understanding of their social responsibility. Professor Stephen Jay Gould explodes the myth of the significance of the size of brains of male and female/black and white – the 'science' of phrenology – in *The Mismeasure of Man* (1984). This book should be compulsory study for every science teacher. In a detailed study of Paul Broca's obsession with measuring skulls and brains of blacks and women as well as other Europeans, Gould scrutinizes the data for any scientific basis and finally discredits it:

> Despite thousands of published pages, we do not know – as if it mattered at all – whether blacks on average have larger or smaller brains than whites. Investigators have gotten nowhere, not because there are no answers, but because the answers are so difficult to get and because the a priori convictions are so clear and controlling. Self-interest, for whatever reasons has been the wellspring of opinion on this heady issue from the start.
>
> (Gould, 1984)

Gould's chapter on Cyril Burt, 'The Real Error of Sir Cyril Burt', is a testimony to the incredible power and influence of so-called 'scientists'. Burt's fabricated findings (Hearnshaw, 1979) of fifty identical twins brought up in different social classes and yet displaying very high correlation between IQ scores led to the designing of mental tests, later to be made respectable in the form of 'eleven-plus' tests in the UK. Many generations of working-class children were denied access to higher education because 'Burt had a Eugenic vision of saving Britain by finding and educating its few people of eminent talent – 80% were branded unfit for higher education by reason of low innate intellectual ability' (Gould, 1984). The Hadow Report (1926, 1931) on education defined children's development in terms of Burt's favoured terms of 'innate, general, cognitive' ability. It is imperative that science teachers understand the misconstruction of 'intelligence' and the powerful effect of such abuse in society.

While the issue of 'race' has been openly challenged, the more subtle prejudices of class and gender (though not so subtle to those who experience abject poverty and sexual discrimination), continue to be woven into right-wing education, employment and health policies and practices in twentieth-century British politics. For example, in some countries, the sexuality of women is controlled by scientists who develop drugs for the pharmaceutical companies who pay for their research. In *More than the Parts: Biology and Politics* (Birke and Silvertown, 1984) look at the direct, everyday effects of scientific research on the behaviour of post-menopausal women. In a chapter titled 'Women, hormones and biological determinism' she cites the examples of hormone replacement therapy (HRT) and tranquillizers. Without denying the absolue benefit for some, she argues systematically about the larger constructions and legitimization of the control of sexuality as in population politics.

> the discovery of the various, different hormones has greatly facilitated the proliferation of such ideas as suggestions of a hormonal basis for a variety of behaviours, including aggression, sexual preference, a predisposition to being a victim of violence, being good at typing, attempting suicide and many more.... If say, someone produced a hypothesis that the rather low number of women in engineering was due to female hormones, then there is not much point in bemoaning the fact and discussing alternative forms of technical education.
>
> (Birke and Silvertown, 1984:48)

It is not difficult to understand why 'science' should be used in this way. The image of science as pure, neutral, value-free and reliable has undoubtedly been powerful. Definitions of science are convincing in making it sound as an objective body of knowledge. Yet it is inaccessible to most of our pupils whose lives are lived in a value-laden, political, social, economic and cultural context.

THE NATURE OF SCIENCE

In order to reject and never to allow again such hideous crimes as apartheid, colonialism and slavery, it is important for teachers and pupils of science to understand that it is in the interpretation of the nature of science that racist and sexist ideology were born and used to perpetuate and justify white, male supremacy and racism. The term 'science' implies a precise discipline and a hegemonic canon of objective knowledge.

In our schools science is a high status subject, alongside English and mathematics, claiming a major share of the school timetable. This status has been acquired by the popular belief that science has an empirical method of research, scientific knowledge progresses by induction, knowledge derived from facts of experience which are acquired by observation and experimentation. By careful observations in experiments, singular statements can pass on to universal statements such as hypotheses and theories. Scientific methods of controlled experiments and the process of reasoning and inference lead from the particular to the general, thus resulting in general principles of systematic laws of science (Francis Bacon, 1500). Laws give rise to 'indisputable' facts which are used in further explanations of unknown phenomena. Using this process of science, progress is seen as being made through new discoveries and new theories.

The most direct challenge to Bacon's methodology in science came from Sir Karl Popper in *Logic of Scientific Discovery* (1934). He argued vehemently against the proposition that science progresses by induction and his work on the logic of scientific discovery, identified as the 'hypothetico-deductive method', underpins most of school science. Popper argued that a hypothesis is not merely derived from observations, but also through a more imaginative and creative process which cannot be objective as it must depend upon previous knowledge and theoretical understanding of the observations. There is no written statement as to how many observations have to be made. As theories can be fallible, observations too can be fallible. For a hypothesis to be scientific, it must be logically falsifiable. Falsification of a theory is the moment at which science grows. And therein lies another problem – if an observation of a prediction from a theory indicates that a theory is falsifiable, how could one 'prove' that the observation itself was not false (Aicken, 1984).

Kuhn, another modern philosopher on science, in *The Structure of Scientific Revolutions* (1972), places his theories in the historical context for the development of physics in the Western world and comes up with the revolutionary nature of scientific progress. The structure of 'theories' is called a paradigm by Kuhn. A revolution occurs when one set of paradigms is replaced by another, after a number of different explanations. It is within an existing paradigm that scientific communities work and take their cue to proceed forward with appropriate ideas for that time and space. At another time, that paradigm may be falsified by another set of theories. Scientists are often not critical of the paradigm within which they are working. New discovery begins, according to Kuhn, by an awareness of the anomaly which is at first resisted. As more and more individual scientists are converted to the new paradigm, it is adopted while the old one is discarded. Kuhn believes that the aims of seeking scientific knowledge depend upon what is appropriate for the individual and the community in which a scientist is placed. In other words, research is context specific. In this sense, Kuhn is valuable in that he begins to open up the kind of questions that concern us when looking at 'race', racism, sexism and the scientific connections. It is also in this notion that we understand how science has progressed in the West. Scientific knowledge consists of those concepts which a community of scientists accepts. Its progress is therefore defined by the set of social and political notions dominant at the time. The research agenda is also controlled and dictated by the funders:

> Nature 'answers' only the questions that get asked and pursued long enough to lead to results that enter the public domain. Whether or not they get asked, how far they get pursued, are matters for a given society, its educational system, its patronage system, and its funding bodies.
>
> (Robert Young in Gill and Levidow, 1987:19)

Followers of Popper however, believe as he did, that there is a single, timeless, universal criterion with reference to which the relative merits of rival theories are to be assessed. Truth, rationality and hence science are thus seen to be absolute. Proponents of this claim would advocate that science is culturally neutral and hence school science should not be mixed with any notions of culture or politics. This is ideally suited to the ideological position currently dominant in the UK, that knowledge is ideologically neutral.

However, since the 1980s there has appeared a burgeoning groundswell of critique of this scientific world view. In Western societies these voices are those of feminist academics, of environmentalists and of the young themselves. Epistemological questions are being raised about the possibility of a feminist science and its different characteristics. The media continue to promote traditional images of science and scientists. But there is so much noise emerging critical of the results of so-called scientific 'progress', particularly in relation to the environment, ethical issues in health and the practices of agribusiness as well as the ubiquitous context of modern warfare, that we find professorial roles in British universities specifically designated to promote the 'public understanding of science'. Yet as Ruth Bleier writes:

> ... while feminists within science and without have been dissenting from and criticizing the many damaging and self-defeating features of science (the absolutism, authoritarianism, determinist thinking, cause–effect simplifications, androcentrism, ethnocentrism, pretensions to objectivity and neutrality), the elephant has not even flicked its trunk or noticeably glanced in our direction, let alone rolled over and given up.
>
> (Bleier, 1986)

In confronting and contesting science, feminist academic scientists are questioning its epistemological validity and its practices and attempting to reconstruct a feminist science different from the Western, modernist Enlightenment-constrained model (Harding, 1985, 1991; Keller, 1985; Bleier, 1986). From the environmental camp comes even more radical and passionate critique of reductionist science. This, science's monopoly on the world view,

> results in fourfold violence – violence against the subject of knowledge, the object of knowledge, and beneficiary of knowledge, and

against knowledge itself . ... The multidimensional ecological crisis all over the world is an eloquent testimony to the violence that reductionist science perpetrates on nature.

(Shiva in Nandy, 1988)

From these feminist and ecological critiques are arising important pedagogical implications and classroom applications are being addressed (Kelly, 1984; Whatley in Bleier, 1986; Rosser, 1986; Clay in Baker *et al.*, 1996). Of particular interest are the developing models of multiple literacies, in spite of present national science education policies, as science educators talk about scientific literacy and ecological literacy as new pedagogical models for the new century. The relationship between science and nature is a hugely contested one at the moment. A yet further and interesting debate, caused by the introduction of National Curriculum Science, centres around the idea of primary teachers 'doing nature' and not 'science'.

WHAT DOES 'NATURE' MEAN AND DOES IT DIFFER FROM 'SCIENCE'?

Nature was and continues to be a very feminine word. It is something to be conquered, controlled, manipulated and even altered for the pursuit of comfort, convenience and cure of ailments for the human kind – the sole pupose of 'mother nature'. This is a simple and broad generalization of the wide interpretations of the concept of 'nature' which may exist. Primary teachers can reject this distorted and misdirected interpretation. Nature can never be controlled. It is not 'mother earth' who is in danger. It is human beings who are running scared having denied for so long the power of 'mother nature'. Steve Van Matre's book *Earth Education: A New Beginning* is worth reading. He sounds very angry at times but pupils will be thrilled by the programme of magical learning adventures.

Teachers wishing to retain the teaching of natural science and to develop an argument in favour of 'science for people' paradigm, need to ask three crucial questions:

- Why are most philosophical discussions and theories constructed around the Western model of science?

- Why did science progress in the particular way that it did during the sixteenth and seventeenth centuries?
- Why are these developments not linked with other civilizations?

This lack of linking may suggest to school pupils that the ancient civilizations of China, India and the Arab world did not carry out any scientific investigations. Yet, at a time which predates Stonehenge, the Chinese made and used ploughs, studied astronomy and were skilled in the art of paper-making. Colonialism and slavery led to the blocking and obscuring of scientific developments in Asia and Africa – often they were banned by English law. One such example is the practice of small pox vaccination: 'Vaccination against smallpox had been practised over the entire length and breadth of the continent until it was banned by the English in the early 19th century' (Goonatilake, 1984).

The answers to these three questions are related to the other great invention of Europe – capitalism – which began its expansionist policies soon after its conception and was historically accompanied by enslavement of almost two-thirds of humanity and of its own domestic working classes in the capitalist economies.

SCIENCE AND BIAS

Before we look at some practical ideas and strategies for primary classrooms, we need to understand exactly how biases are communicated during teaching and learning. Within a school setting, broadly speaking, bias is communicated to pupils in three ways:

1 By giving an ethnocentric view of science.
2 By not encouraging a critical appraisal of world events using the skills of science.
3 By a lack of awareness of the hidden curriculum.

By and large, most pupils, across both phases of education, receive a narrow experience of science (Gill and Levidow, 1987). The pedagogy as well as the content of science often creates mysterious notions irrelevant to real life, thus alienating most girls (Whyte, 1986). Steven Rose, in a talk to ILEA teachers, explained the reductionist nature of science as it is taught in British schools:

> It goes deeper than changing the racist stereotypes which fill the text books and which assume the inevitable supremacy of white civilisation – we have to find a way of replacing the reductionism of western science by a holistic science that understands that you cannot reduce wholes to simply component parts thereof.... We do not understand the existential distress of our society by finding chemicals that change moods – we have to understand the problem where it arises, that is in the social order.
>
> (Rose, 1985)

Children's Learning in Science (CLIS) and Science Progress and Concept Exploration (SPACE) support a constructivist view of learning and have been successful in promoting the following:

- that the learner's prior knowledge and the learning environment influence the learning outcomes directly.
- that children construct meanings during the process of learning.
- that within the construction of meaning, patterns can be noticed which are a direct result of the shared language, culture and the environment.

Details of the projects can be obtained from the Association for Science Education.

An issue that concerns primary teachers in Britain is that many pupils come to school with only a very basic level of English vocabulary. As with mathematics, connections must be made and understood between everyday language and specific language words required to explain 'scientific' investigations. For pupils with a limited English vocabulary, a science investigation can seem like a hurdle and not an enjoyable experience. For emergent bilingual/multilingual pupils (pupils who have more than one language being spoken and read at home), there are particular difficulties while reporting on observations and results of experiments. An excellent book and a must for every science teacher is *Language of Science – Science Report for Teachers* (1988). There is little produced on infant children and language issues but the ideas contained in the APU report apply equally to infants. Appleton (1989) has postulated a learning model for science which is helpful to teachers of emergent bilinguals teaching science, particularly infants. It combines 'generative learning theory' and Piaget's notion of assimilation, disequilibrium and accommodation. The model has a significant bearing on the teacher's and the learner's use of language.

Step 1	Learning situation is approached by the learner with a set of existing ideas.
Step 2	Learner selects particular aspects of the new encounter based on previous knowledge and experience.
Step 3	Learner tries to make sense and assimilate the new event or task.
Step 4	If there is an incomplete fit of the existing idea, a state of disequilibrium occurs. If the new learning and past experiences satisfy each other, those memories increase in status, resulting in reinforcement of previous learning.
Step 5	If the disequilibrium continues, if the explanations being given are superficial, in order to gain an understanding, the learner will acquire erroneous ideas.
Step 6	From the state of conceptual conflict, the following outcomes are likely:

- Restructuring of new ideas – a state of equilibrium is established.
- Ideas are learnt without understanding.
- A high degree of frustration is experienced. In the case of emergent bilinguals or pupils with difficulties in learning, the state of disequilibrium may give rise to dissatisfaction with school. May lead further to a feeling of failure and possible 'getting into trouble'.

Teachers who are conscientiously constructing programmes for emergent bilinguals to take account of their previous learning and vocabulary restrictions will find that this may also apply to pupils from poor socio-economic backgrounds. Therefore the kind of support which is provided for an emergent bilingual should also be made available to other pupils whose learning in science is being disadvantaged because of vocabulary limitations.

STRATEGIES FOR SCIENCE CLASSROOM PRACTICE IN A PRIMARY SCHOOL

The position of primary teachers in Britain has shifted dramatically. Many have had to become specialists, although the curriculum which they followed at teacher training college would have been more general. Within National Curriculum Science, this has meant that primary teachers have been forced to make a giant leap from 'doing nature' in the pre-National Curriculum days to schemes of work planned for achieving specific National Curriculum attainment targets. This transformation has tested their ingenuity for in most cases new resources and professional development have been limited. In anticipation of the national inspections most schools have spent some time formulating 'equal opportunities' policies (Runnymede Trust, 1994). Critical, holistic perspectives on equalizing opportunities and access in Science, indeed in any area of the Curriculum, are being developed. Before writing schemes of work which will promote equality and challenge pupils holistically, teachers need to be critically reflective on their own understanding about the world, scientific concepts and the socio-cultural nature of those concepts.

Teachers of science need to consider the implications if they are to use science for promoting a better understanding of how inequality and injustice is a created phenomenon, so that pupils can engage in finding fairer solutions. This can be achieved by:

- removing bias in images and content of textbooks, schemes and other resources and replacing it with positive images from around the world;
- placing science in the local community;
- placing science in the national and global context of the commodities;
- using science in children's stories.

Removing bias in resources

Content presented to the pupils must eliminate stereotypical, incorrect 'scientific' classifications of human beings (Gould, 1984). There is only one 'race' – the human 'race'. Colour and physical features are only relevant in the context of 'continuous variation' in the study of genetics. The images chosen must be such that all children can relate to them. This does not mean that in every topic and in every concept all of the disadvantages can be considered. They key is not to let opportunities slip when they present themselves.

With the help of a critically knowledgeable and ideologically aware teacher, the science classroom is the ideal place for children to begin to discard bankrupt theories and make better informed choices. Key Stage 1 pupils are often provided with an environment for learning science which forces them to see a very wide range of activities as scientific. While learning to mix bread dough, growing cress seeds, or learning the parts of the body and what they do, the children can be referred to their daily life at home with parents/carers. Very early on, differences can be emphasized as the necessary diversity which 'mother nature' has created to make us more interesting and adaptable to different environments. In Chapter 6, on mathematics, I talked about the three most common activities in which we engage young children: the learning of shapes, colours and sizes. Using stories and music, this kind of opportunity can also be used to inculcate pride in different likes and dislikes, abilities and temperaments, such as shy children or those who like working in groups rather than as individuals. By making more explicit connections and providing a wider range of experiences science can be endorsed as an empowering tool to use later in life.

Older primary school children, in a reassuring caring environment, can explore the reasons why choices made for the kind of research in science throughout the nineteenth and the twentieth centuries reflected a dominating desire to subjugate and exploit. Internalizing their experiences and through influences such as the media, children are formulating their beliefs about heredity and intelligence, comparing private and state school provision and internalizing the roles of mothers and women generally. Racist and sexist stereotypes are assimilated at a very young age. The general concept of different 'races' is an accepted myth in British society, used in everyday conversation, books and official documents. People are often asked to which 'race' do they belong. In the past, it was common practice to be asked to place oneself within a social class category on an official document. Other terms such as 'race relations', 'ethnic minority' and 'commonwealth citizens' put non-white people into a separate category and continually give credence to the now descredited 'scientific' theories. Primary teachers can use the topic of Genetics and Variation to endorse the law: 'it is intended that the curriculum should reflect the culturally diverse society to which pupils belong and of which they will become adult members' (DES Circular 5/89).

Consideration should be given to whether the context promotes only poor, poverty stricken images of Asia and Africa in the form of 'Third World'. This term has no credibility and produces a strong and powerful hierarchical position for the northern hemisphere. Asia, Africa and South America are the sources of much of our daily food supplies, medicines and materials yet they are mentioned only in the context of poverty and famine.

Take the example of the African Mapingo Tree which supplies wood for clarinets for the world's orchestras. Pupils may not be able to go to Africa to see, feel and observe the Mapingo tree but there are trees all around them. Figure 7.1 shows a topic web of suggestions mainly suitable for infant pupils. Stretch it as long as the interest remains both for teacher and pupil. Key Stage 1 pupils will understand a simplified version of photosynthesis and the fact that no one can survive if there were no trees. The mention of the Mapingo tree is incidental and an example of the destructive and greedy nature of human beings. Get other examples from children.

Older pupils can improve research and study skills by looking for information on rainforests and what is happening to the atmosphere as a result of cutting down acres of rainforest; 10- and 11-year-olds can:

- write to the local Urban Forestry Commission and find out about the responsibilities of a local council regarding the landscape and the environment. They can invite someone to come and talk about the protection of trees, particularly when water, gas and electric cables are laid.
- write to the Department of the Environment and ask relevant questions on tree planting, the Clean Air Act, carbon-dioxide emissions, creation of local parks, etc.
- find out about British Conservation Volunteers and join them.
- join the local branch of the Royal Society for the Protection of Birds (RSPB).

Consider developments from Chinese science and Islamic science (Goonatilake, 1984). Newton said: 'Whatever I have learnt, I have done so by standing on the shoulders of giants.'

How many pupils/teachers would know that the success of the steam engine was at least as much due to the invention of a black slave – the lubricating cup – the Real McCoy? (Sertima, 1986). Who invented the traffic lights? How many would know about the scientist behind the 'Raman effect' and that the scientist Raman was a Nobel Prize winner?

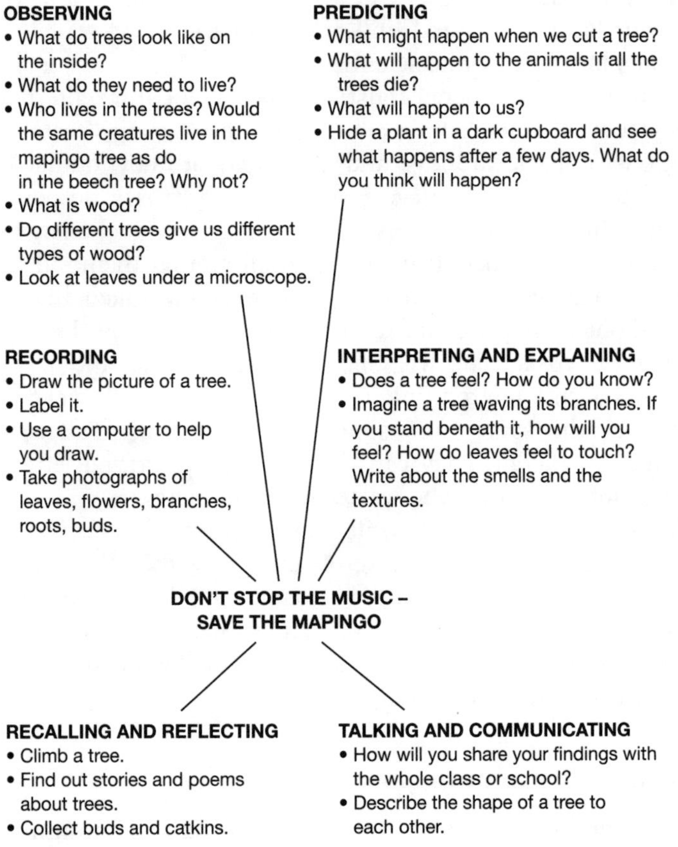

OBSERVING
- What do trees look like on the inside?
- What do they need to live?
- Who lives in the trees? Would the same creatures live in the mapingo tree as do in the beech tree? Why not?
- What is wood?
- Do different trees give us different types of wood?
- Look at leaves under a microscope.

PREDICTING
- What might happen when we cut a tree?
- What will happen to the animals if all the trees die?
- What will happen to us?
- Hide a plant in a dark cupboard and see what happens after a few days. What do you think will happen?

RECORDING
- Draw the picture of a tree.
- Label it.
- Use a computer to help you draw.
- Take photographs of leaves, flowers, branches, roots, buds.

INTERPRETING AND EXPLAINING
- Does a tree feel? How do you know?
- Imagine a tree waving its branches. If you stand beneath it, how will you feel? How do leaves feel to touch? Write about the smells and the textures.

**DON'T STOP THE MUSIC –
SAVE THE MAPINGO**

RECALLING AND REFLECTING
- Climb a tree.
- Find out stories and poems about trees.
- Collect buds and catkins.

TALKING AND COMMUNICATING
- How will you share your findings with the whole class or school?
- Describe the shape of a tree to each other.

Figure 7.1   Save the Mapingo tree
Source: ASE (1990)

In teaching history and contemporary science, inform pupils of achievements of all scientists – not only dead, white, male, middle-class scientists. There are many examples from around the world which could be included in any curriculum: Abdul Abbas who won the Nobel prize for research on particle physics; Dr Manku for his research on Evening Primrose Oil; Vandana Shiva, a nuclear physicist turned environmentalist whose 'feminine principle' now forms the basis of much of the environmental science all over the world – to name but a few. Write to your local library and find out about the living – male and female, black and white scientists.

Topics such as energy must now be taught from alternative perspectives giving pupils a true picture of energy costs. The notions of 'backwardness' and 'primitive' are now outdated in the face of energy shortage worldwide. There is little point in telling children that there is a shortage of fossil fuel energy and that they must turn off lights when all around them, all night and often all day, lights are on everywhere. How much difference would one light switch make? They should be involved in calculating the costs. The worksheets in Figures 7.2 and 7.3 will encourage children to think of the true costs of fossil fuel energy while at the same time appreciating the use of alternative sources of energy. They can then engage in writing letters to owners of corporates who waste the most energy.

An excellent pack which will help any primary teacher to liven up the teaching and learning of 'Energy' within the National Curriculum has been produced by Sandwell Education Authority (Assi *et al.*, 1992). It looks at many different ways in which communities the world over use solar and windpower in an interesting and pupil-friendly manner.

Placing science in the local community

If teachers and children live within a diverse community, in reltion to class or culture, the opportunities to draw on a multiplicity of examples of everyday life are tremendous and must not be missed. A few hours' research in any large city library should prove to be fruitful.

- The science of cooking, preserving food. How did great-grandmother preserve food in the absence of fridges and tin cans?

- Different ways of making 'bread' with or without yeast; the science of baking, roasting, frying, steaming.
- An appreciation of how different fruits and vegetables come from different parts of the world – a trip to the local green-grocer.
- Making candles, wine, family and fun science.
- Designing ways to keep warm and to keep cool – skin colour. How does it protect?
- Variety of ways for cleaning teeth.
- Did your grandmother make soap? How did she do it? Where did she learn science?
- Herbal remedies for coughs and colds, cuts and bruises, heart attacks. Collect ideas from health food shops, parents, chemists. Who taught them?
- Herbs and plants from the rainforest – write to Friends of the Earth.
- Measure and compare the use of water by different members of the family and also for different purposes. Put a display together. Get all teachers and children in school to take part. Write to local industry and ask how much water is used for cooling systems in different operations including the computer industry.

Placing science in the national and global context of the commodities

- Consider a project on paper and wood.
- Research on the 'Chipko movement of India'.
- Astronomy – science of the stars: how do Aboriginals find their way home without a compass or a map?
- Women, the original agriculturists – debate.
- Find out the amount of water is takes to make a can of beans.
- Calculate the total energy it takes to make a beefburger.
- The science of tea growing, making and drinking around different practices.
- Coffee and chocolate – the journey from a bean to a cup – what happens in between?
- Science of the textiles – silk, cotton, jute, linen, leather, etc.

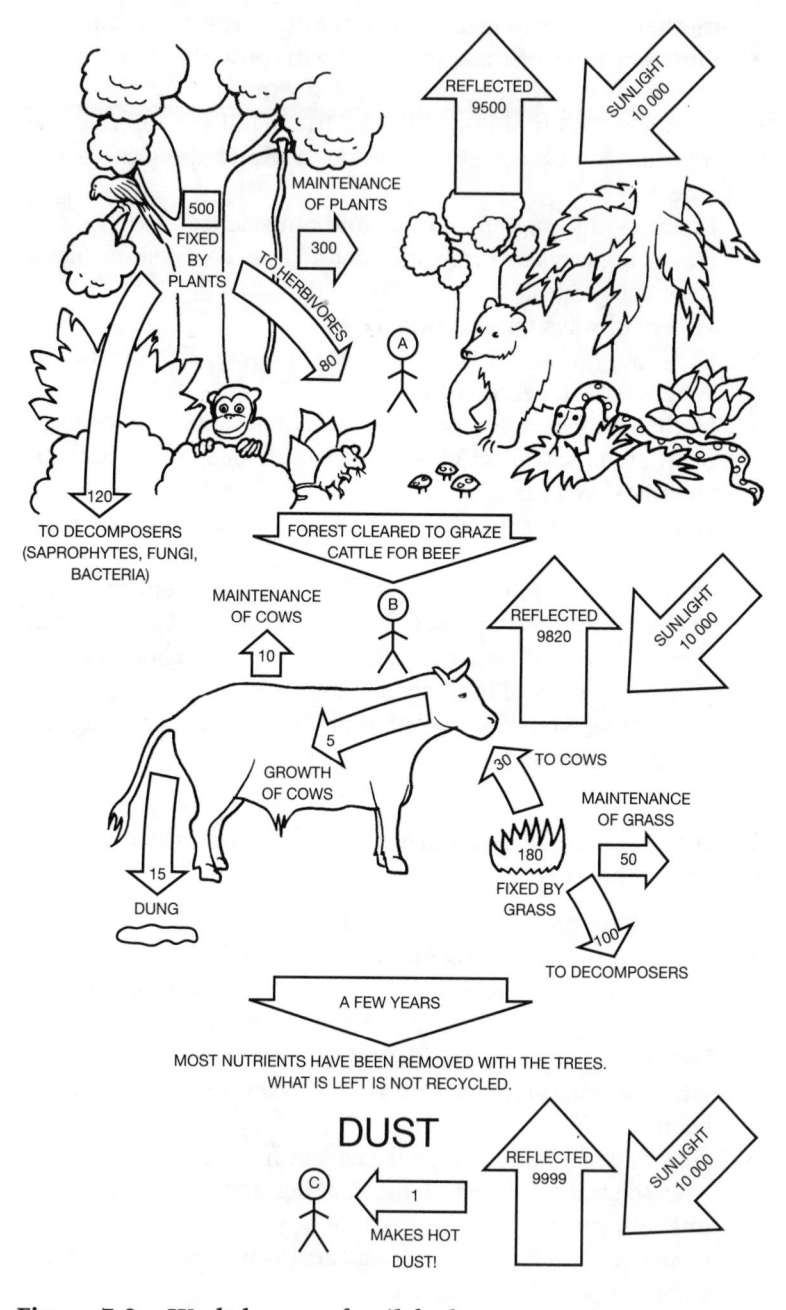

Figure 7.2   Worksheet on fossil fuel energy

WORK IN GROUPS OF 3.
DISCUSSION SECTION:

Q:1. Look at the diagram.

IMAGINE:

One of you standing in the middle of the forest. A.
One of you standing in the middle of the field. B.
One of you standing in the middle of the desert. C.

Each person describes in detail to the other members of the group what they can see in their immediate environment, taking into account the rich variety of animals and plants.

Q:2. Decide where you think this piece of land might be.

Q:3. Intervention of human beings has led to the three stages that you see in the diagram. Decide in your groups, after discussion, what you think might have happened.

Q;4. What do the numbers and the arrows tell us?

WRITTEN SECTION.

Q:5. Where does the energy come from?

Q:6. Copy and complete the following table:

	FOREST	*FIELD*	*DESERT*
SUNLIGHT ENERGY			
REFLECTED ENERGY			
AVAILABLE ENERGY ENERGY USED FOR MAINTENANCE OF PLANTS			
ENERGY FIXED BY THE PLANTS			
ENERGY TO HERBIVORES			
ENERGY TO DECOMPOSERS			

Figure 7.3 Worksheet on fossil fuel energy

- Where does milk come from? What happens to the calves?
- Water cycle – water and photosynthesis, the basis of all life.
- Ask a high school teacher to visit and share teaching and learning.

181

- Where do we get our bananas, coffee, pineapples, peaches, flowers from? Compare the schooling, health, employment and nutrition of the children in plantations with pupils of your own class, emphasizing the connections between their lives – the children in the plantations are poor so that the rest of the world can consume the commodities at affordable prices.
- Make contact with Traidcraft, Oxfam, Christian Aid and develop links with schools in Brazil, Kenya, India, South Africa and the Philippines. Write to embassies of these countries.
- Why is the Mapingo tree dying in Kenya?
- Trace the energy path and calculate the energy cycle in a rainforest.
- Organize a trip to the Alternative Technology Centre in Wales or ask someone to come, bring a display and talk about the work of the Centre.

Using science in children's stories

Children's stories around animals, plants and pollution are a valuable and safe way in which to explore feelings, attitudes, beliefs and values. Teachers can easily and comfortably provide scientific activities around stories chosen carefully for their content which also reflect life in a diverse society. The stories can cover the totality of a young life experience.

If available, pupils' photographs of themselves as babies can be immensely useful and may be explored well by teachers. Children's drawings based on real-life images will reflect the true image rather than the one they are so often forced to choose because of negative self-esteem. Parents can be asked to give a demonstration on the management of different types of hair and hairstyles.

Stories can be chosen for awareness raising, appreciating music and instruments from around the world. Stories around a variety of food and festivals in different communities can be included.

Stories must also be chosen for promoting a healthier and objective view on the lives of animals, not simply a romantic notion of the friendliness of wild animals – this is far removed from reality. Greenlight publications produce Active Learning packs designed for use with the National Curriculum. They are an invaluable resource for primary schools planning to engage in cross-curricular work, including science, mathematics, environment education, the arts and geography. The packs include: A Rainforest Child; A Mountain Child; An Arctic Child; Forest Matters.

Through an appropriate intervention with such resources teachers can explore:

- describing and communicating observations;
- identifying similarities and differences;
- observing the use of senses;
- noticing patterns in groups of people and the variation;
- an acute awareness of environmental science.

However, teachers prepared to develop this approach, will need to be sharply focused in the strategies required to achieve an effective process of teaching and learning styles and willing to instigate these before starting science for equality and justice. Such strategies include:

- appropriate intervention;
- interesting, engaging and wide-ranging presentation;
- organizing appropriate, clearly targeted and differentiated activities;
- arranging groupings which encourage collaborative learning and thoughtful interaction;
- sympathetic knowledge of pupils' capabilities, backgrounds, languages;
- creating an effective as well as a safe learning environment for challenging stereotypes;
- choosing learning experiences which enhance and extend the children's interests;
- involving children and other adults in planning and sometimes delivering.

CONCLUSION

To summarize, I would like to hope that the teachers feel sufficiently motivated and stimulated to compile ideas for teacher delivery using any of the prompts in this chapter. It is well worth finding out more about the Association for Science Education (ASE) and subscribing to the *Primary Journal*. Generally the resources from the ASE are of excellent quality. The Association has also produced two books on 'race', science and education.

The Development Education Centre is another treasure trove of ideas, activities, conferences, swap shops and projects. The Centre brings teachers together on various projects and has produced several excellent resource packs around science at primary level for a multicultural society.

To conclude, there is only one race, the human race. Science should promote growth and development in all our pupils. It should never be used to support prejudice of any kind, at any level. Every teacher of science must engage actively in the debate and can make a difference.

ACKNOWLEDGEMENT

I would like to thank Katrina Miller for her very helpful comments on this chapter.

RESOURCES

A large number of organizations have now begun to produce teacher packs. This is not an exhaustive list but includes those which I have found particularly useful.

Association for Science Education, College Lane, Hatfield, Hertfordshire AL10 9AA
Centre for Alternative Technology, Llwyngwern Quarry, Machynlleth, Powys SY20 9AZ
Centre for Global Education, University of York, Heslington, York YO1 5DD
Centre for World Development Education, Regent's College Inner Circle, Regent's Park, London NW1 4NS
Development Education Centre, Gillett Centre, 998 Bristol Road, Selly Oak, Birmingham B29 6LE
Early SATIS Project (SATIS – Science and Technology in Society), Barclays Venture Centre, University of Warwick Science Park,

Sir Williams Lyons Road, Coventry CV4 7EZ
Earth Education, Ufton Court Centre, Green Lane, Nervet, Berkshire RG7 4HD
Friends of the Earth, 26–28 Underwood Street, London N1 7JQ
Greenlight Publications, Ty Bryn, Coomb Gardens, Llangynog, Carmarthen, Dyfed SA33 5AY
Tidy Britain Group, The Pier, Wigan, Lancashire WN3 4EX
World Wildlife Fund for Nature, Panda House, Weyside Park, Godalming, Surrey GU7 1XR

REFERENCES

Aicken, F. (1984) *The Nature of Science*, London: Heinemann.
Appleton, K. (1989) A learning model for science education. *Research in Science Education*, 19.
Assessment of Performance Unit (1988) Language of Science – Science Report for Teachers. Hatfield: ASE.
Assi, P., Chapman, R., Harrison, S., Riggon, P. (1992) *An Introduction to Energy.* Sandwell: Sandwell Education Authority.
Association for Science Education (ASE) (1990) *The National Curriculum: Making it Work for the Primary School.* Hatfield: ASE.
Barker, M. (1981) *The New Racism.* London: Junction Books.
Bertell, R. (1985) *No Immediate Danger: Diagnosis for a Radioactive Earth.* London: The Women's Press.
Birke, L. and Silvertown, J. (1984) *More than the Parts: Biology and Politics.* London: Pluto Press.
Bleier, R. (1986) *Feminist Approaches to Science.* New York: Pergamon Press.
Chorover, S. (1979) *From Genesis to Genocide.* Cambridge, MA: MIT Press.
Clay, J. (1996) Scientific literacy: Whose science? Whose Literacy? In D. Baker, J. Clay and C. Fox (eds) *Challenging Ways of Knowing in English, Maths and Science.* London: Falmer Press.
Department of Education and Science (DES) (1989) *Circular 5/89.* London: HMSO.
Eysenck, H. J. (1971) *Race, Intelligence and Education.* London: Temple Smith.
Gill, D. and Levidow, L. (1987) *Anti-racist Science Teaching.* London: Free Association Books.
Gould, S. J. (1984) *The Mismeasure of Man.* Harmondsworth: Penguin.

Goonatilake, S. (1984) *Aborted Discovery.* London: Zed Books.

Harding, S. (1985) *The Science Question in Feminism.* New York: Cornell University Press.

Harding, S. (1991) *Whose Science? Whose Knowledge? Thinking from Women's Lives.* Milton Keynes: Open University Press.

Hearnshaw, L. S. (1979) *Cyril Burt Psychologist.* London: Hodder and Stoughton.

Keller, E. F. (1985) *Reflections on Gender and Science.* New Haven: Yale University Press.

Kuhn, T. (1972) *The Structure of Scientific Revolution.* Chicago: University of Chicago Press.

Jensen, A. R. (1969) How much can we boost I.Q. and scholastic achievement?. *Harvard Educational Review,* 39.

Language of Science – Science Report for Teachers (1988). Assessment of Performance Unit.

Milner, D. (1975) *Children and Race.* Harmondsworth: Penguin.

Montessori, M. (1913) *Pedagogical Anthropology.* New York: F. A. Stokes Company.

Nandy, A. (ed.) (1988) *Science, Hegemony and Violence: A Requiem for Modernity.* Oxford: Oxford University Press.

Rose, S., Kamin, J. and Lewontin, R. C. (1984) *Not in Our Genes – Biology, Ideology and Human Nature.* Harmondsworth: Pelican.

Rosser, S.V. (1986) *Teaching Science and Health from a Feminist Perspective: A Practical Guide.* New York: Pergamon Press.

Runnymede Trust (1994) *The First Fifty: OFSTED Inspections Report.* London: Runnymede Trust.

Stanton, W. (1960) *The Leopard's Spots: Scientific Attitudes towards Race in America 1815–1859.* Chicago: University of Chicago Press.

Van Matre, S. (1990) *Earth Education: A New Beginning.* Warrenville, Illinois: The Institute for Earth Education.

Whyte, J. (1986) *Girls into Science and Technology.* London: Routledge.

Young, R. M. (1971) *Mind, Brain and Adaptation in the Nineteenth Century.* Oxford: Oxford University Press.

PART 3

FOUNDATION SUBJECTS KEY STAGES 1 AND 2: THE NON-CORE SUBJECTS

CHAPTER 8

Design and Technology

Sharanjeet Shan and Margaret Cox

Technology is the one subject in the National Curriculum that is directly concerned with generating ideas, making and doing. In emphasising the importance of practical capability, and providing opportunities for pupils to develop their powers to innovate, to make decisions, to create new solutions, it can play a unique role.

(National Curriculum Council, 1989)

There has never been a more urgent need in human history to create and innovate human-friendly solutions to the many problems, complications and consequences that technological advances and impacts have created worldwide. This is a good time for teachers to be engaging in the debate and finding answers. Yet there is not a single statement in the Programmes of Study for Key Stages 1 and 2 in the new National Curriculum document for Design and Technology, part of the original Technology curriculum, which will encourage them to examine the attitudes and values imparted during lessons. Because of the removal of specific examples to 'slim down' the National Curriculum orders, the consequences of technological innovations for the environment are not mentioned, specifically at Key Stages 1 and 2, nor the influence on employment patterns and on people's daily lives. Teachers can either take a conformist stance and teach technology, setting it into a 'high-tech' context, or they can broaden the

189

curriculum by acknowledging the social, political, environmental, health and employment consequences of all technological inventions and use their knowledge to instil awareness and responsibility in their pupils. Design and technology lessons can provide the foundations for developing 'independent thinking', considering the negative as well as the positive impacts technology has had on human life. It is too easy to collude with technological developments rather than assessing their impact on our lives and our planet, some of which is irreversible.

What needs to be understood is the blockage which is imposed on children's imagination as a by-product of so much being 'solved' by technology, particularly consumer products which children use and throw away, almost on a daily basis: school bags, watches, trainers, pencils and pens, paper, toys and games. Calculators are another good example. While few adults can deny their usefulness, there are some basic arithmetic concepts that pupils need to understand in order to advance mathematical thinking skills. Calculators on watches and pencil cases may discourage the development of basic numeracy skills in many school children. It is important to lay the foundations of challenging technological developments at a primary school level. Young children may not understand the impact of technology on the agricultural industry leading to the erosion of soils throughout Asia, Africa and Latin America; or how millions of women worldwide are trapped in low-paid, hazardous and dangerous jobs in the electronics industry, but they can understand the role of the trees in paper and pencil-making. The children can begin to appreciate that there is a need for a variety of housing for different weather conditions and cultural practices and that not everyone needs or wants a centrally heated, semi-detached house with a kitchen full of modern appliances.

Victor Papanek's book *Design for the Real World* (1974) provides a good foundation for every primary school teacher. Foundations can be laid to guide children into appreciation of humane and fundamental values in relation to people, places and to nature. Another excellent resource for ideas which can be adapted for use in both Key Stages 1 and 2 is *World-Active: Facts and Puzzles about our World* (Manley, 1992). There are games and puzzles from around the world which can be made from sticks and stones, pebbles and scrap paper, cardboard boxes and empty cartons, in a design and technology lesson, of course, which will help pupils 'investigate, disassemble and evaluate simple products' (DFE, 1995) for many different cultural contexts.

The Primary School in a Changing World (Button, 1979) provides useful pointers for primary school teachers to use in reconsidering their aims and objectives (see Figure 8.1 and Table 8.1).

A question of images

- How does a child begin to learn about the world?

Figure 8.1   A question of images
Source: Button (1979)

Table 8.1   Aims and objectives
Source: Button (1979).

Aims	Objectives
Knowledge To increase children's knowledge and understanding of the world and the interdependence of its peoples.	For children to explore their own and other cultures and recognize diversity in society. To find out about economic, cultural and ecological interdependence. To understand the inequalities within and between countries and why they exist.
Skills To stimulate enquiry and to develop an appreciation of the rapidly changing world through observation and experience.	To enable children to assimilate and evaluate information and attitudes from all sources. To increase children's ability to form and communicate opinions. To make children aware of the value of the contribution they make within their community.
Attitudes To develop a greater awareness of the values of all people; to recognize and overcome prejudice and stereotyping; to appreciate an ability to influence the future.	To encourage children to become more aware of their own responsibilities to one another and to the local and wider community. To foster a greater respect for the positive aspects of their own and other cultures. To develop empathy with and sensitivity to the experiences and rights of others, both locally and globally. To encourage children to become aware of and to question their own attitudes.

- What are the strongest influences in building up a picture?
- What distortions and confusions are created?

What should the primary school be doing to equip children for life in the changing world? The list of aims and objectives in Table 8.1 may help you reconsider your own. They may seem rather remote and abstract, but nevertheless they should provide some signposts through the day-to-day concerns of teaching with a global perspective.

Table 8.1 can be used to build on the Design and Technology primary curriculum attainment targets for designing and making. For example, for children to explore their own and other cultures to learn to 'recognise the simple features of familiar products', they should be encouraged to bring in simple items used by the family to reflect their own cultural background to build on 'their experiences of using materials, techniques and products to help generate ideas'. A good use of IT here is to help pupils develop skills in selecting useful and relevant information about different cultures and the global community. (Cox, 1996)

There is an evergrowing demand on scientists and technologists to find new solutions to make human lives last longer and be lived more comfortably. Medical innovations have saved the lives of men, women and children in peace and war zones across the world, assisted by better and faster transport and communications methods. There are obvious benefits to be gained from technology: some have made life more pleasurable (washing machines, cookers, fridges); some have improved health care (kidney machines, ESG monitors, eye operations); some have speeded up services (computers, fax machines, telephones, E-mail). Some have helped extend the skills and competencies of people handicapped with physical and mental disabilities. However, technological inventions are not restricted solely to enhancing human lives. The same technology that saves lives in an accident or a bomb explosion, develops and makes the weapons that caused the emergency – the destruction during a war, the poverty trap in economically poor nations – thus fragmenting human existence. Consequences of technological disasters are not confined to national boundaries; sulphur emission from Europe is producing acid rain in Asia, gradually eroding one of the seven wonders of the world, the Taj Mahal in India (McCormick, 1985). The Chernobyl nuclear plant accident in

Russia caused heavy damage to farms in the English Lake District. Teachers should be aware of the many consequences of modern technology.

From saving lives, technology has 'progressed' to creating lives. The latest debate around the ethics of artificial insemination, surrogate mothers and the use of aborted foetuses to save lives has challenged definitions such as 'parent' and 'genetic inheritance'. In the name of 'freedom of choice', technology defines and controls the totality of our existence. Maintenance of the technological revolution has been at the expense of necessary human processes such as collaboration, co-operation and participation. Technology controls and dominates, creating a dependency culture. Those that stand outside the culture will run the risk of becoming permanently excluded, unskilled, ill-informed, and therefore unemployed (see Figures 8.2 and 8.3).

Until the 1980s at the level of the national economy, technocrats and economists did not acknowledge that it is impossible to continue to aspire towards continued unlimited growth from limited resources (Schumacher, 1975). A declaration made by the then Trade and Industry Secretary, Kenneth Baker, in 1982 that 'the message is automate or liquidate' (Baker, 1982) set the agenda for changing our social, economic and political lives. Technology and information technology have radically changed telecommunications, offices, information and management systems, transport facilities, supermarkets, gas and electricity supplies and classrooms – all in the name of giving consumers more choice.

In the face of such developments, many pressure groups have mushroomed, looking for an alternative lifestyle. Ethical consumerism is yet in its infancy but questions have begun to be asked:

- Why and how do we make choices as consumers?
- What and who influences our choices?
- What criteria should we use when making choices regarding our food, clothes and houses?
- What is the connection between consumerism of the West and poverty of the planet?
- What should we do so that modern technological society does not remove all choices from future generations in the process of safeguarding them? (See George, 1992.)

Some answers for the world of tomorrow lie in Schumacher's

PROGRESS

A technical revolution
This piece of technology knocked 200 minutes off the time it took to transport 100 people from London to New York. It has sonic boom. It costs $40,000,000.

Figure 8.2   Concorde

Another technological revolution
This piece of technology knocked 14 hours off the time it took to transport a day's supply of clean water for a village from the well. It has no sonic boom. It costs $42.

Figure 8.3   Water carrier

Small is Beautiful (1976) and McRobie's *Small is Possible* (1981) in challenging the definitions of 'efficiency, growth and progress'. It may be neither practical nor advisable to give up our cars, fridges, computers and washing machines, but they need to be produced using more environmentally friendly and safe processes. This would inevitably mean higher prices but at a fraction of the cost of repairing the damaged environment (Jackson, 1990).

Although 'many nations around the world are adopting new approaches – replanting deforested areas, conserving energy ... an era of unprecedented global cooperation and commitment is essential ... given the scope and complexity of the challenges before us' (Barney, 1982).

Despite the intentions of the United Nations Conference on Environment and Development ('the Earth Summit') in Rio, 1992, 'sustainability' may not yet have become a buzz word in the private or public arena, but it will have to be one of the key concepts of the twenty-first century – to be explored and developed in the classroom by those preparing the intellects and minds of tomorrow's consumers and producers.

DESIGN AND TECHNOLOGY AND EQUAL OPPORTUNITIES

The National Curriculum for Design and Technology provides very little guidance for equalizing opportunities. It states clearly that 'appropriate provision should be made for all pupils'. There follows a list of clear directions for teachers to take for special needs pupils (Design and Technology in the National Curriculum, HMSO, 1995). However, there is no mention of the Design and Technology Curriculum being a vehicle for understanding how gender, 'race' and class connections establish inequalities and injustices in a society. One of the easiest and simplest exercises that a primary teacher can do with young children is to collect information on the kinds of toys that boys and girls play with, the manner in which these toys are marketed, the times and the manner in which they are advertised on television, their cost and affordability. A large display can be made on 'Our favourite toys' and pupils can be moved towards evaluating the play value; expensive does not always mean interesting and/or enjoyable.

There is a clear focus on 'designing and making' in the new National Curriculum. Teachers should endeavour to explore local museums and/or look out for old toys in antique shops. Young children should be provided with opportunities to explain their imaginary world, particularly with cardboard boxes and various dressing-up techniques. The value and attitudes of the teacher towards technology will be reflected in choice of materials and topics. Care should be taken to select a broad spectrum of ideas for designing and making in order that all pupils can identify and value themselves, both in the content and the process.

From the many dimensions of equal opportunities, this chapter now considers four influences which may be considered in design and technology teaching in the primary classroom in order to contextualize and enhance learning:

- Human consequences of 'Western high-tech'
- Rediscovery of the 'feminine principle' in human interaction to combat violent and aggressive technologies (Shiva, 1982, 1990, 1991)

- Intermediate technology for developing countries (Schumacher, 1975)
- Ancient science and technology

HUMAN CONSEQUENCES OF 'WESTERN HIGH-TECH'

The values embedded in 'Western high-tech' conflict with some of the more traditional, appropriate, people-friendly technologies of Asia and Africa. It is crucial to consider the speed at which Western technology is replacing appropriate and optimum technology in Asia and Africa, with the resultant exploitation of natural resources and creation of a dependency culture implicit in such developments. The following examples will assist teachers of design and technology in broadening the context of teaching and learning, thus giving pupils an opportunity to develop ideas in favour of the solutions which they create and indeed may prefer. Of course, success depends upon the enthusiasm and knowledge of the teacher.

Cars in the twenty-first century

Presented in an attractive, challenging style, this topic could capture every pupil's attention, regardless of background. Gender issues, in particular around advertising can be an opportunity for girls to voice their opinions and to design alternative adverts. It can be an excellent topic around which societal, environmental, cultural, political, economic, emotional, health and gender aspects of pupils' lives can be constructed. Pupils of all ages (5–11) can engage in designing and making models of people-friendly cars move and alternative, more environmentally friendly modes of transport. Even when using cardboard, wood and paper, their imaginations can be stimulated to becoming aware of the car industry in general; properties and availability of materials; the issue of recycling; crowded cities and pollution. The following ideas will fit easily into all aspects of the Programmes of Study for Key Stages 1 and 2, providing opportunities to develop design and technology capability. Catalogues from car showrooms will provide comparisons for 'products and applications'; 'quality';

'materials and components'. Resources are easily available at next to no cost for this topic.

- Shape, size, capacity: what are cars a symbol of, apart from means of transport? Historical changes and developments? Who are the decision-makers? Are they in touch with the needs of a variety of people? What is their motivation?
- Materials: rubber/metal/glass – where do they come from? working and living conditions of employees.
- Manufacture: what is the key influence? EEC regulations, major companies? Profit? Comfort? Care of the planet? Economy? If the car industry is one of the largest employers in the UK, what will be the consequences of reduced demand?
- Investigate contexts: can cars be made to suit the needs of the planet?
- Energy consumption: which petrol? What is the difference? Alternative fuel? Do a display on alternative fuels.
- Road construction: distances covered. Will it ever be enough? Forecast: Roads and traffic in 2020?
- Carbon monoxide and dioxide poisoning: read Timberlake and Thomas's *When the Bough Breaks* (1990).
- Advertising: techniques, image, lifestyle, role-play, sexism. Put together a varied display on car advertising – discuss the common images? Ask children to write about their feelings.
- Design a car for a disabled person, easier access, modified power-assisted controls.

When the Bough Breaks (Timberlake and Thomas, 1990) is essential reading for teachers of science and technology. If the following scares you, then think of the reality in ten years' time for the children concerned:

> Infants have a larger surface area in relation to their weight, so that they have higher metabolic rates. They process calories and oxygen faster than adults ... resting children younger than three ... take in twice as much pollution per unit of body weight ... they have little body fat, so pollutants circulate longer throughout the body ... kidneys, livers, blood brain barriers are not fully developed ... they cannot process the 'pollutants' the way adults can ... poorer children are often smaller and thinner and have an even larger surface area in relation to weight than do 'normal' children ... most vulnerable are children still in the womb.
>
> (Timberlake and Thomas, 1990)

It is often easy to forget who is responsible for carbon monoxide poisoning – it is not visible as are many other pollutants. Blame can easily be placed on the 'overpopulated third world' – nothing could be further from the truth. The USA already emits a higher amount of carbon monoxide into the atmosphere per capita (Sharma, 1993) than the reduction agreed at Rio.

An extension to this topic can be to use IT to help the pupils design on screen, using Draw, Paint Brush or another graphics package, alternative types of transport which cause less damage to the environment, such as trains, bicycles and electric-powered buses. If the school has access to the INTERNET, up to date information about the latest types of such transport can be obtained through the World Wide Web.

A food technology project

A critical look by teachers and pupils alike would reveal that this basic need for staying alive has been harnessed by the multi-nationals and agricultural industries to make slaves of all of us – individuals, societies, nations alike. There are laws, reports, acts, guidelines, healthy eating programmes – a whole industry. Yet the latest victims of Western high-tech food production are 12-year-olds in Britain who eat so many sausages and burgers that they may well be on their way to developing arteriosclerosis. Evidence of the damage such large-scale automated food production can cause is obvious from the widespread contamination of eggs with salmonella, the use of hormones in cattle and the disastrous spread of BSE to humans in the form of CJD (Creutzfeldt-Jakob Disease).

In National Curriculum terms there is a lot in this project to practise design and making; to evaluate products and applications; to examine health and quality issues and to select appropriate materials and tools.

- Packaging: convenience foods – how do they control our eating habits? What happened to an 'old-fashioned' balanced diet? For children as young as 6 years old, it should be possible to do a survey of the number and type of packaged/convenience foods used in any one week at home.
- Processing: food value taken out, monetary value added. Who benefits? Write to Heinz, Birds Eye, Iceland, etc. to get

Write down common sense answers to the following:
• What is fibre?
• Is fibre found in:

a) plants?

b) animals?

• Is fibre good for you? Briefly explain the answer.
• Write down the names of 5 foods from your everyday diet that contain fibre.
• Collect some pictures of breakfast cereals that claim to prevent constipation. Look at the labels carefully.

a) What is constipation?

b) What is bran?

c) How can constipation be prevented?

d) How do animals prevent constipation?

Figure 8.4   Fibre in the diet

information on processing. Which foods have to be processed before we could eat them? Which foods are processed for convenience?

• Heart disease, cancer and obesity: are there any links to food?
• Traditional Asian and African diets: why may they be leading the way to health?
• Where has all the fibre gone? Why is fibre important? (See Figure 8.4.)
• Sugar and tooth decay?

A project on farms can cover science as well as design and technology criteria. Pupils can be provided with opportunities to bring in different types of food they eat and to consider how it is produced. Plan with the pupils the design of a farm using cardboard, glue, sellotape, etc. and include in the design the following topics:

- What kind of food should we be producing?
- Beef on the back of the milk industry: how do we treat our animals? Vegetarianism – is it just a fad or are there any real benefits to animals and humans?
- Free range or factory farming? Who benefits? With Key Stage 1 pupils, use puppets or cartoons to raise awareness of respect for animals and why and how they are equally important in the large scheme of the natural world. With Key Stage 2 pupils, read *The Egg Machine* (Shan and Bailey, 1990).
- Health food industry: why do we pay more for natural, unprocessed food? Read *The Food Scandal* (Walker and Cannon, 1984)
- Additives (E numbers) have been shown to aggravate asthma and allergies – who suffers most?
- Pesticides: a necessary evil or a *Circle of Poison* (Shapiro and Weir, 1981)?

An energy project

In the framework of a primary school, as pupils learn to 'design and make' and 'evaluate', they should be taught to consider their work critically, connecting it to the broader concerns. Several schools plan and develop design and technology lessons in a cross-curricular mode and in the context of the many celebrations to encompass the experiences and traditional practices of a diverse school community. This can be extended to designing and exploring ideas beyond pupil experience of the familiar and the modern, to look at the past and other countries, such as follows:

- Design containers for keeping food cool in a hot climate – without using fossil fuel energy. Put cold water in an earthenware pot and place it next to water in a glass jug.

Measure the temperature every ten minutes for an hour. This can be done using either a traditional thermometer or temperature sensors connected to your class computers and plotted on the screen. Draw a graph for both. What do you notice?

- Design an insulating jacket for the glass jug and then repeat the experiment.
- How can we keep cool without using fossil fuels? Watch a David Attenborough programme on animals in a desert. What do the animals and plants do to keep cool in temperatures of 120°F and what do they do about their water supply? Can we try some of their ways?
- How did the poor Victorians keep warm if they couldn't afford coal?
- Energy: pupils in general have a low opinion and poor understanding of appropriate forms of energy. The teacher has a key role to help pupils understand that a lot of fossil fuel energy has to be spent to provide usable energy sources, such as gas and electricity (see Clarke, 1978). Howard Odum's ideas (1978) are also a good basis for understanding the connections between the stability of world economics and the health of ecosystems.
- Design a human waste disposal mechanism when water supply is limited.
- What kinds of energy inputs are needed for the production of a tin of beans?
- Use a computer-based modelling activity such as Energy Expert (1993) to enable children to model heat lost and gained from homes in different cultures and climates.
- Use Energy Expert to model how less active old people and disabled people can keep warm.
- Compare the amount of energy used by a variety of farming appliances from the East and West, and discuss the impact on the local community, social as well as economic.
- Make a model windmill and study alternate sources of energy – visit the Alternative Technology Centre in Wales.

REDISCOVERY OF THE 'FEMININE PRINCIPLE' IN HUMAN INTERACTION TO COMBAT VIOLENT AND AGGRESSIVE TECHNOLOGIES

Vandana Shiva is a leading nuclear physicist who abandoned an 'exciting' career in India's nuclear energy programme 'in favour of nature against further artifice and destruction'. She is highly critical of agricultural and reproductive technologies and is a proponent of the 'feminine' principle which advocates that there is a clear and undeniable relationship between women, food chains and forests. In her two beautiful and very readable books, *Staying Alive* (1990) and *The Violence of the Green Revolution* (1991), she establishes and defines the links between the oppression of women, capitalism and ecological crisis. She describes many movements in India, particularly the role that women are beginning to play in sustainable development, reversing the ravages caused by aggressive exploitation of nature, using a human alternative to the contemporary science and technological paradigms (see Figure 8.5).

> Design puppets, papier mâché flowers and leaves and dress a tree. Hold a tree-dressing ceremony for parents. Write to the local conservation volunteers.

In *The Violence of the Green Revolution* Shiva systematically explores the destruction of valuable genetic diversity in wheat and rice varieties as a result of the narrow genetic base which led to large-scale monocultural production in India. This in turn created vulnerability and a threat to the diverse indigenous agriculture. The tragedy that followed as a result of this narrow vision, systematic destruction of the natural pest control phenomenon, spread of diseases, increased use of violent and poisonous pesticides, must serve as a lesson for all generations to come. Large areas of forest and many different crops were replaced by just two varieties. The control of nature through the 'miracle' use of chemicals and seeds became a nightmare for all. Landowners and landworkers alike were affected (Alvares, 1986; Shiva and Bandyopadhay, 1982).

According to Shiva, women were the world's original food producers and continue to be central to food production, pack-

Figure 8.5   The Chipko movement to protect trees in India

aging and processing systems throughout the world. Young children would do well to study the key, significant role of women in agriculture when humans made a transition from hunter-gatherers to farmers. The paradigm of male dominance gave way to interdependence of the sexes through co-operation and collaboration.

The world-wide destruction of the feminine knowledge of agriculture, which evolved over four to five-thousand years, by a handful of white, male scientists in less than two decades has not merely violated women as experts; since their expertise in agriculture has been related to modelling agriculture on nature's methods of renewability, its destruction has gone hand in hand with the ecological destruction of nature's processes and the economic destruction of poorer people in rural areas.

(Shiva, 1990:105)

Commenting on water technology and the recent famines in Africa and India, Shiva says:

The cause of the water crisis and the failure of solutions both arise from reductionist science and maldevelopment working against the logic of the water cycle, and hence violating the integrity of water flows which allows rivers, streams and wells to regenerate themselves. The arrogance of these anti-nature and anti-women development programmes lies in their belief that they create water and have the power to 'augment' it. They fail to recognise that humans, like all living things, are participants in the water cycle and can survive sustainability only through that participation.

(Shiva, 1990:182)

INTERMEDIATE TECHNOLOGY FOR DEVELOPING COUNTRIES

In Schumacher's *Small is Beautiful* (1975) and McRobie's *Small is Possible* (1981), Western high-tech is challenged on the concept of intermediate technology for developing countries. There is a direct relationship between the large-scale greed and profit-motivated Western high-tech in the 'developed industrialised' world, and the creation and maintenance of poverty in the 'developing' world.

Key Stage 2 pupils can be provided with the opportunity to do a major topic on Textiles from around the world, particularly natural materials such as silk, linen, cotton and wool. This can be accompanied by incidental learning about the lifestyles of the workers for these different industries. Investigate whether the standards of living, housing and wages match the value that a particular textile is accorded in the world market.

For many industrialists, there is only one motive for exporting technology to 'developing' nations, the motive of profit and creating dependence, not interdependence. The victims are the poor people, especially women and children. Answers located in

Western 'high-tech' have led to the ozone hole in the stratosphere. While a large majority of school children in India and Africa remain underfed, their counterparts in Tanzania and South Africa dare not play outside unless they own hats for protection against the ultra-violet rays of the sun.

According to Schumacher, scientists and technologists need to produce methods and equipment for industry and agriculture, which are:

- cheap enough to be accessible to virtually everyone;
- suitable for small-scale application;
- compatible with human need for creativity.

If these three conditions are satisfied in the production of any technological appliances, it is possible to create:

- a non-violent technology;
- a sustainable future, costs, employment, incomes;
- freedom for human beings to achieve true independence through co-operative, collaborative means of production.

Applying such principles to industry and agriculture, it is possible for the workers to share in the: ownership of the means of production; ownership of political and economic power; and ownership of land. Landowners and company directors, mostly men, may argue about the damage that small, independent communities can also deliver to the environment. Their short-sightedness ignores the fact that smaller communities do not own the land nor belong to unions nor have the means of production and therefore have little or no say in the policies and plans. They conveniently forget that the damage done is very small scale and it is caused through lack of knowledge; what is needed is education and not control by those who consider the whole of the universe to be their quarry.

If taken as the basis of all future developments Schumacher's concept would create:

- holistic application of scientific knowledge to industry and agriculture;
- harmony with the natural environment instead of its ever-growing erosion;
- an understanding of the needless, frenzied and aggressive control of world markets and their unsustainability.

There has been an increase in the understanding that capital-intensive farming systems are ill-suited for wholesale export to the 'developing' countries. Developing economies are beginning to show the way to the developed world, that technology is not the anchorage of the human 'race'; it is the humans who must make and control informed choices in farming, transport, education, health and employment.

Within the 'Knowledge and Understanding' part of the National Curriculum at Key Stage 2, it is incumbent upon teachers to develop a view of 'Quality':

> h) to distinguish between how well a product has been made and how well it has been designed;
> i) to consider the effectiveness of a product, including the extent to which it meets a clear need, is fit for purpose, and uses resources appropriately.
>
> (DFE, 1995)

Planning for such an objective and its interpretation can range from bland, 'pure and neutral, scientific' to:

- What is the 'quality' of life of men and women trapped in low-paid, unhealthy, boring, menial conveyer-belt occupations?
- What is 'quality' in the context of our green environment?
- How much of the earth's precious raw materials have been exhausted in the process?
- What is the 'quality' of life of the creatures who share the planet with us?
- Do commodity markets and stockbrokers ever consider either the extent to which the products that they trade are exploiting and damaging the environment or the ethics of building profits by exploiting human beings?

The teacher in a primary classroom is the enabler of ideas, thoughts and beliefs and must ensure that the National Curriculum that she delivers will not be a 'monstrous simplification of reality which pretends to answer all questions' (Schumacher, 1974) leading to further estrangement. An alternative view is that:

> We cannot live on the human level without ideas, upon them depends what we do. Living is nothing more or less than doing one thing instead of another. Education is to live a life which is something above meaningless tragedy or inward disgrace.
>
> (Ortega y Gasset, quoted in Schumacher, 1974)

ANCIENT SCIENCE AND TECHNOLOGY

This last selection introduces briefly the possibilities that await a teacher who is willing to invest some time in research. It is primarily aimed at the teacher wanting to increase her knowledge base. The popular view learnt and taught by teachers and teacher-educators is that European culture, including science and technology, is strongly influenced by the classical civilizations of Rome and Greece. However, in science and technology, the works of many Arab scholars have been translated from Arabic into Latin and are much sought after by the West (al-Hassan and Hill, 1986). Such scholars and scientists include al-Farabi, al-Ghazali and al-Farghani, little known to most teachers educated in the Western tradition. Their influence on scientific and philosophical thought is well documented (al-Hassan and Hill, 1986). In early medieval India, more technological products were exported than imported. *The History of Science and Technology in India* (1981) reveals the interchange of knowledge and thought in technology between the Moghul rulers and the wider population of India. Prior to this, the sciences of India, in particular mathematics and medicine, were well known to the Moghuls. Six centuries of Moghul rule, from the beginning of the thirteenth century to the end of the eighteenth century, saw many significant developments in technology and science.

A teacher's own knowledge must be balanced and broad before she can impart a fair view of technological developments to her pupils. In pre-medieval India techniques had been developed for smelting and extraction of metals such as copper, silver, gold, iron and their alloys. *Aspects of Ancient Indian Technology* (Bhardwaj, 1979) reveals the rich heritage of India unearthed in the many archaeological sites which he studied, using modern scientific methodology. (Particularly fascinating is the 'chemical analysis of glass beads from Rajghat (600–200 BC)', an archaeological site in North-east India.) Colouring agents obtained from metal oxides were widely used. Silver coins dating as far back as 400 BC provide evidence of Indian gold and silver metallurgy.

In skill and inventiveness during most of the period AD500 to 1500, the Near East was superior to the West.... For nearly all branches of technology the best products available to the West were those of the Near East.... Technologically, the West had little to bring to the East. The Technological movement was in the other direction.

(Singer, quoted in al-Hassan and Hill, 1986)

How the transfer of ideas and techniques took place during the following centuries is discussed by al-Hassan and Hill (1986). This can have a direct interest for classroom practice since many words in the European languages, particularly Spanish, Italian and English, reflect this transfer.

To find out more about the rich heritage of India, if you have access to the World Wide Web on the INTERNET in your school, you can use a Search Engine (an automatic information seeker) such as ALTA-VISTA, with the key words 'India, history and heritage' and obtain up to 100,000 screens of information. For example at the site (http://WWW.wcmc.org.lit./igcmc/main.html), presenting a biodiversity profile of India, pupils can get information on Forests and Species diversity.

Task:
In English, pupils would find it interesting to explore the origin of words such as: muslin, taffeta, alcohol, alkali, ream, sugar, sherbet, saffron, shampoo, etc. A whole world of evidence and influence concerning the contributions of ancient cultures to modern-day living is connected with such words.

Topics such as 'homes, buildings, bridges, canals' are popular themes around which to plan the teaching of national Curriculum Design and Technology. Older primary pupils can be given interesting opportunities to demolish myths about 'backwardness, mudhuts, primitive' connected with homes in other cultures and countries by considering:

- building technology;
- irrigation technology;
- textile technology;
- paper technology;
- food technology;
- silver, gold and other metals;
- soaps, pigments, perfumes, inks, dyes;

Building technology

Homes in hot countries

Homes in countries like Saudi Arabia often have huge spaces with tall towers in the middle. These have a purpose. They are used to create cooling currents throughout the day, without using any fossil fuel energy.

Task:
Design a tall thin tower with vents facing the prevailing wind. How would you know what is happening to the air currents?
(Key Stage 2: Use information sources to help in their designing, clarify their ideas, develop criteria for their designs and suggest ways forward).

Building materials through the ages and in different climates

Stone, baked and unbaked bricks, clay, hardwood, limestone, mud.

Task:
Study the effect of temperature and rainfall on different materials. The Lake District is a good subject for comprehensive study in the use of a variety of building materials.

Irrigation technology

Throughout the world, there are well-developed canal systems around great rivers:

- Wells, springs and streams are used for irrigation as well as domestic use.
- Ingenious methods for irrigation exist where there is restricted rainfall.
- Crops are grown where rivers flood, such as in the Nile valley, where a rich fertilizing sediment is left behind.
- Dykes and dams, known from AD 960 in Iran.
- Impact of modern technology on appropriate technological practices.

Textile technology

Task:
Natural materials – how do they grow? It is probably a more theoretical topic as in an English climate it will be difficult to grow
cotton or keep silk worms unless the special conditions required can
be created. However, pupils of any age can study the effect of heat
and cold on these materials.

While the Western technology of the fifteenth and sixteenth
centuries focused on military inventions, the textile industry grew
and flourished in Asia, supplying the second most important need
of human beings. Words such as taffeta, gingham, muslin, mohair
have come into the English language from Asian influence. The
fine woollen shawls, silk garments, cotton industry of the East
were all envied at one time or another by the West. Indeed,
Mahatma Gandhi came to the Lancashire cotton mills to attempt
to stop the practice of buying raw cotton from India and then
selling it back to Indian producers at an inflated rate after dyeing
and refinement.

Paper technology

Task:
Make paper and use it for writing. Most companies that sell
scientific equipment and materials will also sell paper-making kits.

When the Chinese first made paper in AD 105 from mulberry
bark, no one could have imagined that the paper industry would
become one of the largest destroyers of rain forests. The cultural
revolution that was created is linked very closely with the
creation of schools and universities as centres of learning.

Food technology

Water mills, stones, clay ovens, husking and pounding appliances, milling techniques, water wheels, pressing and crushing
processes were all in existence in Asia and Africa during the fourth
century AD (al-Hassan and Hill, 1986) and make fascinating study.

Silver, gold and other metals

Silver and gold coins have been excavated during the discovery of the ancient Indian city of Mohinjodaro (City of Coventry Minority Support Service produces informative and attractive packs.) Other ancient cities, dating as far back as 400 BC, give evidence of the extraction processes involved. Chemical and metallurgic technological processes were devised to refine metals and shape them into ornaments and tools.

Soaps, pigments, perfumes, inks and dyes

Task:
Make soap and ink, perfumes and dyes from flowers and leaves – a major topic.

Both at Key Stages 1 and 2, most of the criteria for 'Making Skills' and 'Knowledge and Understanding' from the National Curriculum Design and Technology can be satisfied around a well-planned topic on making soap.

• Write to Traidcraft and Body Shop. How do they make soap?
• Write to Intermediate Technology Publications, 9 King Street, London WC2E 8HW for a booklet: *Small Scale Soap Making: A Handbook*, by Peter Donkor.

In many parts of Asia and Africa, ancient methods are still used to produce such luxuries as soap and perfumes. There are ordinary household chores for many women and men – the same skills being passed on from parents to children as they were many centuries ago. Indeed, in today's world, such methods are being revived in the name of fair trade and ethical consumerism. The negative images of 'appropriate' technology have begun to be the positive answers for tomorrow's world.

To conclude, this chapter has been just a glimpse of the landscape of design and technology. Based on the principles of equality and justice, design and technology teaching and learning in a primary classroom cannot be considered in a passive, 'pure and neutral' mode of delivery. At primary school level, until the skills have been acquired, it is not easy for young children to make connections and understand such complex ideas as 'Small is Beautiful' or 'paradigm of subservience created by technological traps'.

It is to be hoped that in a classroom which actively and interestingly promotes enquiry-driven learning around simple games, home-made toys, making candles and soap; pressing flowers and making displays, dyeing clothes, a satisfaction will emerge which might outlast the temporary fascination of computer games, and expensive toys. Principles of equality and justice will require a lot of very hard work to shift children's thinking from high-tech to appropriate-tech. Many of the ideas presented in this chapter can form the basis of schemes of work to ensure that our pupils will receive a wide range of experiences and also have enormous fun. At the same time it is hoped that they will learn to understand and use these experiences wisely and appropriately to seek out and develop people- and planet-friendly solutions.

REFERENCES

al-Hassan, A. and Hill, R. (1986) *Islamic Technology: An Illustrated History*. Cambridge: Cambridge University Press.

Alvares, C. (1986) The great gene robbery. *Illustrated Weekly of India*, March.

Baker, K. (1982) Speech to the Royal Society of Arts. 10 May.

Barney, G. O. (1982) *The Global 2000 Report to the President. Entering the Twenty-first Century*. Harmondsworth: Penguin.

Bhardwaj, H. C. (1979) *Aspects of Ancient Indian Technology*. Delhi: Motilal Banarsidas.

Button, J. (1989) *The Primary School in a Changing World*. Centre for World Development Education.

Clarke, W. (1978) It takes energy to get energy. In L. D. Moll, and G. Coe (eds) *Stepping Stones: Appropriate Technology and Beyond*. London. Marion Boyars.

Cox, M. J. (1996) Using multi-media and the INTERNET in education. Proceedings of the 10th National Conference on Computer Assisted Instruction, Ministry of Education, Taiwan, pp. 49–63.

Cox, M. J. Webb, M., Booth, B. and Robbins, P. A. J. (1993) *Energy Expert*. The Modus Project, 1 St James Road, Harpenden, Hertfordshire.

DFE (1995) *Design and Technology in the National Curriculum.* London: HMSO.

Donkor, P. (1986) *Small Scale Soap Making: A Handbook.* London: Intermediate Technology Publications.

George, S. (1992) *The Debt Boomerang: How Third World Debt Harms Us All.* London: Pluto Press.

Jackson, B. (1990) *Poverty and the Planet: A Question of Survival.* London: World Development Movement.

Jaggi, O. P. (1981) *Science and Technology in Medieval India*: vol. 7. Delhi: Atma Ram and Sons.

McCormick, J. (1985) *Acid Earth: The Global Threat of Acid Pollution.* London: Earthscan Publications.

McRobie, G. (1981) *Small is Possible.* London: Jonathan Cape.

Manley, D. (1992) *World-Active: Facts and Puzzles about our World.* London: Piccolo Books.

Mitra, A. (1992) Down to earth: the class that failed. *Down to Earth*, 15 July.

National Curriculum Council (1989) *Technology: A Consultation Document.* London: HMSO.

Odum, H. D. (1978) Energy, ecology and economic. In L. D. Moll and G. Coe (eds) *Stepping Stones: Appropriate Technology and Beyond.* London: Marion Boyars.

Papanek, V. (1974) *Design for the Real World.* Boulder: Paladin Press.

Porritt, J. (1984) *Seeing Green.* Oxford: Basil Blackwell.

Schumacher, E. F. (1974) *Small is Beautiful.* London: Abacus.

Shan, S. and Bailey, P. (1990) *The Egg Machine.* Stoke-on-Trent: Trentham Books.

Shapiro, M. and Weir, D. (1981) *Circle of Poison: Pesticides and People in a Hungry World.* London: Food First – Institute for Food and Development Policy.

Sharma, R. (1993) USA may soften its stand on global warming. *Down to Earth*, 30 April.

Shiva, V. and Bandyopadhyay, J. (1982) Political economy of technological polarisation. *Economic and Political Weekly*, 17 (45).

Shiva, V. (1990) *Staying Alive: Women, Ecology and Development.* London: Zed Books.

Shiva, V. (1991) *The Violence of the Green Revolution.* London: Zed Books.

Timberlake, L. and Thomas, L. (1990) *When the Bough Breaks: Our children, Our Environment.* London: Earthscan Publications.

Walker, C. and Cannon, G. (1984) *The Food Scandal.* London: Century.

CHAPTER 9

History

Lina Patel

INTRODUCTION

History in the primary classroom provides many varied and
exciting opportunities for children to explore their own histories
and that of people in the wider communities. In this chapter, I
would like to explore the range of possibilities, issues and
approaches that can enhance children's understanding of the
world they live in and examine how issues of class, gender and
race can be developed and integrated. Within this debate an
understanding of issues of disability, sexual orientation and
bilingualism needs to be examined. Most articles on teaching
history render these issues invisible. The Dearing Report (1994)
has greatly reduced the content of the History Programme of
Study and this is reflected in the revised History Curriculum
(DES, 1995). However, little has changed in relation to incorpor-
ating a wider perspective that takes into account race, gender
and class factors. If anything, there is more emphasis on British
history, the underlying message being that Britain has existed in
isolation to the rest of the world and therefore we do not need to
address issues of the empire, colonialism and imperialism. The
emphasis on British history does make reference to the lives of
men, women and children at different levels of society, but

unless this is examined in relation to the theme of education for citizenship, there is little discussion of issues of oppression or why working-class history and women's history has often remained hidden.

History for schools has been a much debated subject with questions of whose histories and what content and processes are valued in multiracial, multicultural Britain. Although the National Curriculum remains predominantly Eurocentric, teachers can ensure that issues of race, gender and class are considered. It is important to draw on children's direct and indirect experiences of their environment, and by valuing their cultural and social background, their self-esteem and confidence can be enhanced. Children need to understand how, during this century, globalization, greater interdependence, the expansion of multinationals and technological and social changes in general, have had immense impact on all our lives in a short period of time. This century also marks a period of two world wars, where women, black people (I use black to mean people from African, Caribbean and South Asian background), people from the colonies and young men from all sections of society fought for Britain. The Second World War provides a context in which to investigate the struggles against fascism, both then and in the contemporary period. For children to understand present-day society, they need to understand the past in order to think about the future. A people without knowledge of their history is like a tree without roots: 'Black people cannot make sense of the present and look to the future without fear until they understand their past' (Plentie, 1989). This is indeed also true of women, of working-class people, of disabled people and of gays and lesbians.

WHAT IS HISTORY, WHOSE HISTORY?

History is concerned with human motivations, with the beliefs and points of view of people in the past and present together with becoming aware of what happened and questioning why. A knowledge of the past contributes to the personal development of both teachers and pupils. Children studying history should examine how different societies have developed and interacted over a period of time and the effect of this on people. Learning about the past provides children with an opportunity to develop their own social concepts about humanity which can be applied to their understanding of the present day.

Collingwood gives a definition of history as being 'a kind of research or inquiry ... it belongs to what we call the sciences: that is, the forms of thought whereby we ask questions and try to answer them' (1983:9). He goes on to say that each science differs from another in that each tries to find out different things and that history tries to find out about past actions of human beings. This raises the controversial issue in Britain in relation to whose past are we talking about: 'History proceeds by the interpretation of evidence.' This again raises further questions as to whose evidence, what evidence, and how is it to be interpreted?

The teaching of history has raised many complex questions and the debates around history and the National Curriculum reflect this, but it has also been controversial because for the first time the Curriculum content has been legislated. The premise of the National Curriculum has been Anglocentric and presented from a very specific perspective, that of the Tory party. As Geoff Whitty suggests, 'neo-conservative rhetorics of legitimation are evident in the very emphasis on "National" in the National Curriculum'. He goes on to argue that 'attempts to construct a particular sense of national identity, together with a prescribed epistemology to secure adherence to one particular way of reading history, were evident in the debate surrounding the work of the history curriculum working group' (1992:295). The Conservative government has insisted on determining the content, methods and the processes of history teaching. Mrs Thatcher told the then Education Secretary, John MacGregor, 'to take a tougher line than Mr Baker and to insist on more British and less world history, a more chronological approach and greater emphasis on facts rather than on skills and understanding' (*Observer*, 20 August 1989).

There are a number of questions that need to be raised from such a statement; for instance, the assumption that the UK is one nation. This obscures the fact that there were several national pasts and that these still exist today, those of the Welsh, Scottish and Northern Irish. Although within the National

Curriculum there has been an emphasis on teaching British history this has often meant the teaching of English history, for instance learning about English queens and kings. As Hugh Kearney argues, 'British history, it would appear, is in essence English history. "We" look back to the Tudors, for example, and forget that Scotland had no Tudor dynasty' (1994:49). In the revised history curriculum, Study Unit 2 has been changed and is now called Life in Tudor Times instead of Tudor and Stuart Times. However, there is recognition of the limitations of a narrow perspective. These are outlined in detail in the section on implementing Key Stage 2, Study Unit 7, which states that 'pupils should be given the opportunities to study: aspects of the histories of England, Ireland, Scotland and Wales: where appropriate, the history of Britain should be set in its European and world context' (DES, 1995:4). Study Unit 7 was added when the National Curriculum was revised, retaining the Eurocentric nature of the history curriculum.

The debate as to whether the recent past is 'history' has also been an issue. The then Secretary of State for Education, Kenneth Clarke, made the decision that the recent past does not constitute history and that therefore much of the work around oral history would not be seen to be valid. However, the history curriculum does include approaches that indicate a change of mind. For example, oral history is mentioned as part of developing key elements and these skills could be developed within a study unit on Britain since the 1930s and study of the local area. If teachers take into account children's experiences, which are reflected in the prescribed curriculum content along with appropriate teaching methods, it seems that history can be made more lively and be an exciting subject. Many approaches, such as oral history, thinking about bias or thinking about multiple perspectives, have made visible the histories of women, black people and working-class people. Anti-sexist and anti-racist approaches have also raised such issues to show that it is not enough to look only at the culture of a people. Discrimination needs to be challenged and history needs to show how people have fought for justice and their rights: the right to strike, gay rights, votes for women, independence from British rule, civil rights for black people in the USA and the rights of disabled people.

Eric Hobsbawm believes that recent past does constitute

history. In *Age of Extremes* (1994) he includes events of the recent past as a valid part of history and gives a view of the history in which he grew up. He argues: 'I think it is now possible to see the Short Twentieth Century from 1914 to the end of the Soviet era in some historical perspective' (1994:iv). However, the book concentrates mainly on the developed world and the capitalist countries, with little analysis of the developments and histories of the 'third world'. Yet our view of history is influenced by our cultures, race, gender and class, political thinking and beliefs, all of which are reflected in what we believe to be the role of history in our society and schools. Collingwood argues that 'history is "for" human self-knowledge. It is generally thought to be of importance to a man that he should know himself.... The value of history, then, is that it teaches us what man has done and thus what man is' (1983:10). So what have we done? What are we? Who are 'we'?

In asking, 'Why should black history be taught in schools?' Debbie Plentie (1989) reflects that it was a painful process of rediscovering her heritage and reclaiming her black identity: 'Now I know something about the diverse accomplishments of the black races around the globe. I know that for every white inventor, writer or leader of note, there has been a black equivalent, even if their achievements have not been documented in the white annals of history. I know that one of the main reasons for the abolition of slavery was the ceaseless resistance of slaves'.

WHY HISTORY IN THE PRIMARY SCHOOL?

History has gained its rightful place as one of the foundation subjects. Prior to the National Curriculum, one effect of Piagetian theory, that most children at primary school are unable to think in the abstract, meant that the teaching of history was patchy because it was felt that the concepts were too complex and difficult for children in this age range. Short and Carrington (1992) have also shown that Piagetian theory had similar implications regarding issues of race. They cite research by Jeffcoate (1979) which, 'not only highlights the existence of racism in the very young, but shows that such children are well aware of its taboo status' (254). It is not so much that the concepts are too difficult but how they might be broken down to make sense to the children. As Bruner has argued 'any idea can be represented honestly and usefully in the thought forms of children of school age' (1966).

How, for example, can we encourage children to think about world issues and begin to think about the empire? Using objects and artefacts is one approach which can be used as a starting-point to explore these complex issues; for instance, a 'tea pot' can be used to encourage children in a Year 2 class to make close observational drawing. This gets them to think about recording events which enable us to find out about the past and also leads to discussions of where tea comes from, has it always come from there, who picks the tea and how do we get the tea? Closer to home, the discussions about who makes the tea and how is it made are easy questions for children. Such discussions will inevitably raise issues of race, class and gender.

HISTORY AND THE THREE ACTS

The Sex Discrimination Act 1975, Race Relations Act 1976, Education Act 1988 – in particular the National Curriculum – all need to be implemented to ensure that issues of discrimination and oppression are addressed when planning and teaching history. Since the 1975 and 1976 Acts were passed, it has been against the law to discriminate on grounds of sex and race in: employment and training, education, housing, and the provision of goods, facilities and services. Andrew Dorn points out that, 'with reference to sections relating specifically to education in the Race Relations Act, section 71 places a duty on local authorities to "make appropriate arrangements" with a view to securing that their various functions are carried out with due regard to the need to "eliminate discrimination and promote equality of opportunity and good relations between persons of different racial groups"' (1985:16).

How can race, gender and class be integrated into the teaching of history? Issues of race and racism, of sexism and class bias need to be discussed and understood through the curriculum and everyday experiences. When teaching, for instance, about the Victorians, we need to ask questions about what were the experiences and position of black people, women and working-class people in society. The study unit on the Victorian period enables children to explore working conditions for children and adults in Britain and in the colonies for example, the Match Girls' strike, the Tolpuddle Martyrs and the experiences of slaves in the colonies (Aylett, 1985). An understanding of the British Empire will begin to show and explain the black presence in Britain today and contextualize why the Race Relations Act was passed. *The Peopling of London* (Merriman, 1993) gives a wealth of information regarding the lives and histories of London communities.

Issues of race, gender and class can be raised by examining children's own personal experiences within taught topics and themes: for example, a topic on the history of childhood with a focus on the playground or a local study with a focus on schools then and now, opens up the debate on bullying, racism, sexism, homophobia and general harassment, raising questions such as how children feel about the playground and play time? What changes do they want to see and what do they like and dislike?

Whole class discussions and collaborative activities enable children to understand the reasons why others are racist or sexist and they can begin to empathize with other pupils' experiences. *Can I Stay in Today, Miss?* (Ross and Ryan, 1990) gives a range of strategies and approaches to the playground topic which could be extended to examine the similarities and differences in the past and around the world. This can be developed through stories such as *Nowhere to Play* (Kurusa, 1981). It is important that issues in the playground are not ignored; a great deal of bullying occurs during this time, and it has even led to murder. The book *Murder in the Playground* (Macdonald *et al.*, 1989) was written as a result of the death of Alla Uddin. The authors show the importance of having clear anti-racist policies that are worked through and implemented in order to create a safe and secure environment for children. A clear understanding of policy-making helps to plan for effective whole school and classroom practice; *Race and Gender* (Arnot (ed.), 1985) gives an overview of education policy-making and the different views of understanding education policies.

Other themes or topics that can be developed include how people have fought for equal rights/civil rights to ensure that we all have the right to work, vote, live and be educated, regardless of status, class, gender or race.

RACE, GENDER AND CLASS

Over the past three decades there has been much debate, research and development in relation to race and gender, but little work has been done around issues of class. Yet social class remains an important factor in determining pupils' achievement and confidence. As David Gillborn argues: 'Individually, social class background was found to explain more of the variance than either ethnic group or gender' (1990:129). He goes on to confirm what many parents have felt for a long time, 'that a "good" or "bad" school can have a greater influence upon examination results than membership of a particular ethnic group' (1990: 140). Individual schools and teachers influence the achievement of the pupils and it seems that appropriate pedagogical styles and curriculum content can enhance their identity, self-confidence and self-image.

The debate and work developed around equal opportunities has attempted to understand issues of race, gender and class and how these issues interact. As Harriet Bradley states:

> Class, race and gender need to be considered, I would argue, as three separate but interacting dynamics. Phizacklea's study suggests how these dynamics work in one particular context. In any given social structure, class, gender and race interact together in complex ways. The foundations produced by this interaction are the foundation of the social hierarchies and inequalities character-istic of contemporary social formations.
>
> (Bradley, 1992:55)

Any programme for race, gender and class equality needs to give pupils a sense of who they are, their identity, by acknowledging their histories and daily experiences and ensuring that oppor-tunities are available to all pupils. The complexity of the interacting and changing factors of race, gender and class need to be understood and seen within the context of pupils evolving and sometimes struggling to shape their identity and self-image. Indeed as Bradley shows, class structures have been fragmented through the interaction of class with gender and ethnic divi-sions. She argues 'All this does not mean that a sense of class is lost; just that for some individuals it is weakened and that, for most of us, a wider range of identities is on offer than was the case in the 1930s (1992:54). History enables children to have a sense of their past and through interactions with others, children can develop their own identity or identities. Through appropriate lesson content pupils should be given opportunities to extrapolate ways of challenging bias, racism, sexism and class domination.

Although these three structural issues have separate histories it is also important not to compartmentalize them; within this debate due consideration needs to be given to issues of bilingualism, special needs, sexual orientation and disability. For example, when teaching a topic on the family the diverse range of family structures needs to be considered. Many children will be brought up in a single-family unit, or an extended family, or within a gay or lesbian relationship. Families will speak different languages, have different traditions, some will have moved around the country or will have settled in Britain from either the ex-colonies or as refugees. Not all families will have the same access to resources in their communities in relation to housing, employment or leisure facilities. Where families have special needs in terms of disabilities, the resources available to them will depend on where they live and their class background. It should be pointed out that in the past fifteen years the gap between wealth and poverty in Britain has grown. Indeed, teachers need to be sensitive when teaching about the family. One lesbian parent realized that her daughter did not want to go to school because she had to talk and write about her family. It is important that children should know there is a supportive and safe atmosphere and environment in the classroom where they may feel confident in raising issues without being ridiculed or humiliated.

WAYS OF TEACHING HISTORY

The pedagogy and methodology of teaching social studies, history and geography has been developed since the 1970s. Within the field of history, a focus on collaborative approaches was prominent, where children were encouraged to investigate and challenge the past through primary and secondary sources. Oral history was one such approach. The work of both Vygotsky and Bruner is important as they have addressed how children learn in an interactive manner. What is exciting about Vygotsky's work is the core role he outlines for formal education, not just for individual development but for human development. Vygotsky's zone of proximal development suggests that a child's developmental level can be assessed by examining what the child can do unaided. Of far greater importance is the difference between what the child can do with the help of a teacher and what s/he can do unaided. This shows the next point of the child's development and is far more illuminating than an assessment only of what can or cannot be done. It seems difficult to test what children can understand when history has not been implemented or researched on any large scale. However, many schools from nursery classroom onwards are developing the necessary historical concepts, skills, attitudes and values in order for children to develop and build on these through the primary school.

Although an impressive range of resources was developed during the 1980s, many have not been republished; it is important to ensure that these resources are rescued and new ones developed. This chapter gives a few examples of structure and content and it is hoped that teachers can develop their own resources and structures from this.

The most powerful way of teaching and learning history is through an investigative and questioning approach that is interactive and practical. Appropriate concepts and skills should be developed through the use of a range of evidence and sources that enable children to interpret, understand, question and be critical about the material being used. Children can begin to think like historians when they understand concepts of change and continuity, cause and effect, and develop a sense of empathy. For the primary classroom, in general, the history curriculum does highlight this approach, but for Key Stage 2 there is an emphasis on learning facts chronologically. However, if the purpose of history is to empower the children to understand themselves and the society they live in, then we need to continue to develop an investigative and questioning approach.

The understanding of historical concepts and skills should be addressed frequently in order that progress is sustained. In history, as in other curriculum areas, there are specific concepts and skills that children need to develop. *Social Studies in the Primary School* (ILEA, 1980) lists the main concepts to enable teachers to plan effectively. These are useful when planning history or humanities and include:

- Distribution of power and authority
- Division of labour
- Social control
- Conflict
- Interdependence
- Co-operation
- Tradition
- Social change

Change is an important concept in history. It needs to include not only social change, but also political, economic and industrial change. Children need to have an understanding of what causes change and the consequences of these changes and to look for evidence of continuity and similarities and differences. This enables them to see history as a process and not just a body of facts and content. The main skills that should be covered in history include:

- learning to detect bias, propaganda and prejudiced attitudes;
- thinking about different perspectives;
- a sense of empathy;
- concern and appreciation for evidence and being critical about the evidence;
- interpreting the past through a range of different sources (for example, personal experiences, written evidence, visual materials, artefacts, buildings, museums and oral history);
- understanding chronology and sequencing;
- asking historical questions.

Learning through such approaches will enable children to work collaboratively, to understand chronology and the passing of time ('ancient', 'modern', 'BC', 'AD', 'century' and 'decade') and terms which define different periods, for example, 'Ancient Egypt', 'Victorian'.

Teachers need to use a range of different sources to develop

225

historical concepts and skills, including the use of historical language and an awareness of the role of language. Because history is practical and interactive, bilingual children and children with special needs will develop their understanding. A range of approaches can be used to enable children to question evidence and think about interpretations.

- A group of children can examine some source material.
- A group of children can be encouraged to devise ten questions from which they can research and question the reliability of the evidence.
- A child can write a description of an object and another child can draw from the description.

  This will also raise issues of how reliable the written evidence is and how it is interpreted.

- A child asks another child ten questions about a mystery object and will soon realize not to ask questions that give a yes and no reply.
- Children unpack a lost suitcase or shopping bag and record what evidence is certain and what is speculative.

  The children are thinking like detectives, like historians.

As a part of the process of developing skills in using different sources, children can also engage in questioning complex ideas and issues. Learning through the use of visual materials (for example, photographs and pictures) is an effective means which enables all pupils to contribute their ideas and opinions. An appropriate choice of sources and evidence will raise questions of whose past and history we are dealing with. Children are amazed when presented with images and evidence that are not stereotypical, for example, of the developing world, women fighting for equality, black people in professional jobs or working-class people presenting their views on television. However, they are also very perceptive when asked to analyse these images and their ability to do so should not be underestimated (see Merriman, 1993).

Learning about the past through objects and artefacts begins to give children an insight into how we find out about the past. *Learning from Objects* (Durbin *et al.*, 1990) presents more ways of using objects to make history come alive.

Learning through oral history gives an insight of the past which would otherwise be difficult to obtain and acknowledges the history of women, black people and working-class people. As Joan Blyth points out: 'Oral history may be interpreted as the evidence gained about the past from the spoken word, originally one person telling another about his [sic] past. This handing on of tradition and information in story form has taken place from time immemorial as story-telling' (1988:40).

Learning from written sources is also important: using books, archive records, maps, newspapers, letters, diaries and inventories. The careful selection of books, for example, involves a critical appraisal of the quality of the information and the nature of the illustrations. Does the text indicate that there may be more than one point of view? Do the illustrations or photographs present an unbiased image to the reader?

HOW BEST TO IMPLEMENT HISTORY IN THE INFANT CLASSROOM

Many teachers in infant classrooms are committed to a topic approach to teaching history, such as 'myself', 'my family' and 'my local environment'. Through a systematic approach, teachers can lay the foundations of developing historical skills that enable children to think critically and investigate and examine events through a range of sources. Indeed there are many publications that deal with the implementation of the history curriculum, but what is still lacking is an equal opportunities approach in terms of the content and process. In the early years classroom, children can begin to think about perspective, empathy, bias and interpretations. This can be developed through the use of stories, written evidence, pictures, videos, films, objects, local museums, oral history and the local environment.

One of the themes outlined in the National Curriculum History for Early Years is examining the 'lives of different kinds of famous men and women'. This can be developed as part of a broader topic or through stories and does not have to remain eurocentric if experiences of people around the world are highlighted. Brief histories of the lives of some famous men and women are outlined below together with a range of questions that can be asked. These include Mary Seacole, Harriet Tubman, Rosa Parks, Martin Luther King and Rabindranath Tagore.

Mary Seacole

Mary Seacole was born in Kingston, Jamaica, in 1805 and died in 1881. She learnt many of the skills of traditional natural cures from her mother. She helped British doctors to cure the sick when cholera hit Jamaica in 1850 and later travelled to Panama, Cuba and the USA, selling her medicines and nursing soldiers and sailors. In 1854, when many of the soldiers she knew had been sent to fight in the Crimean war, Mary travelled to England to offer her services as a nurse to the British Army. She was turned down because she was black, but she used her own money to go to Crimea and set up a hostel to nurse and feed wounded and dying soldiers (see Collicott and Sanders, 1991).

The story of Mary Seacole can be developed to include more detail. From this children need to begin to think about questions in relation to her experience and to empathize.

- Where is Jamaica?
- What kind of medicine did she give to the soldiers?
- Why could she not get work?
- How would she have felt?
- Where did she travel to?
- What was the name of the nurse working at the same time?
- Why is Mary Seacole not as famous as Florence Nightingale?
- How long did the Crimean war last?
- What might the soldiers have thought of Mary?

Apart from raising these questions, children can plot her journey and ascertain how she travelled.

Harriet Tubman

Harriet Tubman was born a slave in Maryland, USA, about 1826. She grew up to hate slavery and began to fight against it. In 1849, after her sisters had been sold and taken away to another plantation, Harriet escaped from slavery and made the long journey on foot to Pennsylvania, sheltering in the homes of people who helped runaway slaves. Once Harriet reached Canada, she was free from her owners and helped other slaves to freedom.

During the American Civil War she served as a secret agent and nurse for the Northern States. She was given a grand military funeral when she died in 1913.

Rosa Parks

On 1 December 1955 Rosa Parks, a dressmaker in a department store in Montgomery, Alabama, was going home on a city bus. She sat towards the front of the section for blacks. When a number of white passengers boarded the crowded bus, the black passengers were ordered to give up their seats by the bus conductor. Rosa refused to move. Because she broke the law she was arrested, but eventually released. People in her community thought this was unfair and organized a one-day boycott of the city buses, which was a success. However, the law remained the same. This led to a longer boycott and the case was eventually taken to court on 13 November 1956, where it was decided that everyone should have an equal right to sit on the bus.

Martin Luther King

Martin Luther King was a civil rights fighter. He was born in 1929 and died in 1968. He was the most famous campaigner for civil rights that the USA has ever seen. His work in the 1960s in the southern states of the USA led to the issues surrounding black segregation being brought more to the forefront than ever before. His murder shocked the world and made him a true martyr to the cause of equality. He is perhaps best known for his oratory, for example, his famous speech in which he had a dream of all people being equal.

Rabindranath Tagore

Tagore was born in Bengal in 1861 and died in 1941. Hailed by Mahatma Gandhi as 'the Great Teacher' and known by his followers as 'the sun of India', Tagore was a novelist, philosopher, playwright, educator and musician. He was also an outstanding poet. His most celebrated collection of lyrics is *'Gitanjali'* ('song offerings') (1912). In 1913 he won the Nobel Prize for literature.

The theme of women leaders in South Asia can also be developed, for example: Sirimavo Bandaranayake, Prime Minister of Sri Lanka; Indira Gandhi, Prime Minister of India; Benazir Bhutto, Prime Minister of Pakistan; Begum Khaleda Zia, Prime Minister of Bangladesh. For further information about women leaders refer to *Women in India and Pakistan* (Visram, 1992).

Past events

Another theme that needs to be taught across the key stage is about past events of different types. Teachers could focus on a diverse range of collective struggles, events and celebrations. Within the theme of childhood, pictures and photographs can be used to investigate people's experiences then and now, for example: the Match Girls' strike; children working in the mines; the struggles of children in Soweto, South Africa, to abolish apartheid. Children also need to have some sense of recent struggles, for example, the miners' strike, the fight against racism, the fight for gay rights, rights for disabled people and the fight against the poll tax.

At Key Stage 1 children also need to be taught about changes in their lives and those of their family or adults around them and about aspects of the life of people in the past. For this area, topics on 'Ourselves', 'My family' and 'My home' are appropriate.

A TOPIC ON 'OURSELVES'

Topics on 'Ourselves' should remain a central concern for teachers in the early years classroom. Children need to be given the opportunity to explore their own identity, their image and their self-confidence, as well as changes in their lives. This means exploring some of the following questions:

- Who am I?
- Where do I live?

- Where did my parents/grandparents live?
- What is important to me?
- How have I changed?
- Where do I belong?

From these questions children can begin to see who their significant others are and to broaden their understanding of the world they live in, from the local to the national and international.

Visual images are powerful and enable children and teachers to raise issues through some of the following strategies: children's own drawings of themselves and each other; the development of their own poster, using images and photos of who they are. This might entail images of what and who is important to them; where they live; whether they have always lived there. Such posters serve as an art-biography and from them children have a structure to write about themselves. They can also develop their own photo books about their cultural roots and histories and use books such as *Uzma's Photo Album* (Morris and Larson, 1989) as a starting-point. Within a multi-cultural classroom some of the following aspects should emerge: language; family roots and history; religion; significance of family names; cultural diversity within the classroom and community and a sense of belonging. Many of these themes need to be developed with the support of parents and adults, with children inviting parents to come into the classroom to answer questions which they have formulated.

HOW BEST TO IMPLEMENT THE STUDY UNITS IN THE JUNIOR CLASSROOM

Teaching the units at Key Stage 2 needs a structured framework that indicates when and how each unit will be taught. Each unit needs an identified focus, for example, a topic on the Victorians could be titled 'Who were the Victorians?' or 'How did the Victorians live?'. Consideration of equal opportunities would mean taking into account a world perspective which incorporates and recognizes the diverse nature of communities and varying pedagogical styles. Here children could explore the lives of a merchant, working-class people or a slave family during the Victorian period. This would lead to investigating the British empire and the place of the three families during this time. Adopting varying pedagogical styles gives children a sense of the period that shows the function of the empire while working collaboratively sharpens their understanding. At Key Stage 2 there are six study units which have to be taught:

1 Romans, Anglo-Saxons and Vikings in Britain.
2 Life in Tudor times.
3a Victorian Britain or 3b Britain since the 1930s.
4 Ancient Greece
5 Local history
6 A past European society – one from the following list: Ancient Egypt; Mesopotamia; the Indus Valley; the Maya; Benin; the Aztecs.
7 Across the key stage, pupils should be given opportunities to study:
   (a) aspects of the past in outline and in depth;
   (b) aspects of the histories of England, Ireland, Scotland and Wales; where appropriate, the history of Britain should be set in its European and world context;
   (c) history from a variety of perspectives – political; economic, technological and scientific; social; religious; cultural and aesthetic.

The first five study units remain Eurocentric in nature, but it is possible to incorporate issues of equality, especially if the seventh study unit is taken into consideration. Below I examine the study of Ancient Egypt, the local study and the Victorians.

Ancient Egypt

A topic on Ancient Egypt needs to encourage children to think about what perceptions they have of Ancient Egypt and some of the reasons for them. The theme of planning 'a journey to Egypt' can give a context and starts with children finding out information they need for the journey. The main sources that they will learn from will be written evidence, photos and pictures. The selection of appropriate sources can be used to raise concepts of power/authority and beliefs/values in relation to issues of bias, interpretations and perspective. The hierarchy of Egyptian society can provide children with a clear example of power and authority, for example, the pyramid form where the pharaohs are at the top, then the scribes and then the slaves. There are also great opportunities for class discussions regarding the discovery of the tombs. There are possibilities for drama relating to intruders and those being intruded upon. Children can empathize and develop an awareness that there is always more than one point of view. Children should consider not only how to make a pyramid, but receive encouragement to think about formulating their own questions. They might investigate some of the following:

• *Where is Egypt?*
What do they need to enable them to go to Egypt?
What do they need to find out before they go to Egypt?
Where is Egypt?
How will they get there?
Where will they go once in Egypt?
What was life like in Ancient Egypt?
What is life like now?

• *About the Egyptians*
What view is given in books written this century about who the Ancient Egyptians were?
How long ago did they live?
What was life like for people in different aspects of society?
Who were the rulers?
Did everyone have the same rights?
What role did women play in that society?
What else was happening in the world?

• *Examining the evidence*
What primary evidence still exists today (tombs, pyramids, temples)?
Who built the pyramids, tombs and temples?
What does this primary evidence tell us about the way people in different sections of society lived, worked and what they believed in?
Why was some of the evidence destroyed?
What issues are there in relation to who discovered the evidence? Why is this? Was Carter right to disturb the tomb of

Tutankhamun? Did he respect the beliefs of the Ancient Egyptians?
What secondary evidence is there?
From whose perspective is it written?

• *Issues of conservation*
How are the ancient sites, temples and tombs affected by the weather, pollution and tourism?
What are the pros and cons of tourism?

A topic on London – our local community

Many adults are surprised to learn that London has a long history of people settling in the city – from the Romans in the first century, the Huguenot refugees during the seventeenth century, settlers from the Caribbean and Indian sub-continent, to refugees from Turkey, Ethiopia, Eritrea and Somalia. If a history of Britain is to be given, then recognition has to be made of the different community groups that have settled and continue to settle here. Communities and groups of people continue to struggle against oppression and discrimination. This might involve, for instance, people fighting for the right to form and belong to trade unions; unions beginning to set up better working conditions in factories during the industrial revolution; women campaigning for the right to vote; the fight against poverty and the creation of the welfare state. In recent times black people, women, gay people and disabled people have fought and continue to fight for equal rights and for recognition of their identities as individuals and communities. *Peopling of London* (Merriman, 1993) and *Refugees – We Left Because We Had To* (Rutter, 1991) are useful and informative resources.

A local study based on a walk

Studying about the past through the local environment enables children to have a sense of place and understand the present by examining the past. Direct experience of bringing about change in their local area should enable them to be part of shaping the future. Children get excited, even when taken on a walk they have done hundreds of times. They begin to notice buildings, people, shops, signs and other things they have not focused on before. It raises their awareness of their local area and the different communities. This curiosity should lead them on to asking questions such as: What has changed? How do we know? Who makes decisions? Do we have any say? What do we feel about our local area? An example of one 'walk' is set out below.

King's Cross to Holloway Road – London

The walk can be done a number of times. It could be used as a starting-point in order to get the children to think about the areas by posing a range of questions. The work can be focused on the theme of then, now and the future. The walk is from King's Cross Station to Holloway Road and sections of the walk would be used. The main concepts to examine might be: change/cause and consequences; division of labour. The issues raised from this study would be those of class, race and gender.

Teachers could devise questions similar to those outlined below to think through the issues and areas to be investigated or given to children to research.

- *Then*

What was there before the King's Cross area was built?

Why was it built? Who built it?

Who lived in and around King's Cross?

How did this change the landscape and what opportunities did this open up for people in Camden? How did it affect people's lives?

Why did some people leave the area and others move in?

Which jobs were not required? Which jobs were created? What did they get paid?

To what parts of the country did the trains go? Could everyone afford to use them?

- *Now*

What has changed? What are the reasons for this change? What are the effects of these changes?

What evidence is still there of the past?

Who runs and owns the stations, railway tracks and trains today?

Who works at King's Cross station? What do the people working at the station get paid?

Who decides what they get paid?

Who uses the trains? Is it still the best form of transport?

Who lives in and around the station?

What contributions have different community groups made to the local area?

How are people in the area affected? What attracts people to move into the area?

What are the effects of pollution on people working and living in the area? What can be done?

A topic on Regent's Canal

Within this study children could explore a range of concepts, for example, conflict, change, power and authority, similarities and differences. This topic can be developed in its own right or canals can be included in topics such as Victorians, water or homes. It is possible to include this theme in many parts of the country where children can see the evidence or visit the canals, since many large industrial towns did or do have canals running through them. During the period between 1760 and 1840 a network of over 6,400 kilometres of canal were built across Britain. Children should examine the similarities and differences between canals and rivers and why the need arose to build canals. Canals developed on a large scale, first to link major rivers and then to link factories and towns during the industrial revolution. Canals were used to transport raw materials needed by the factories from around the country such as coal and iron. Other types of raw materials such as cotton, sugar cane and coffee were transported to the factories from the colonies and the finished manufactured products were again transported by the canals all over Britain and also to much of the world which provided the raw materials in the first place.

This work should enable pupils to think about the impact of industrialization and what made it possible to buy or gain cheap raw materials from the colonies.

When looking at the canals children need to investigate issues of conflict such as the struggle between the use of the canal and the railway and the cause and consequences brought about by these changes. Questions relating to change will raise issues such as is all change about progress? Who loses out and who benefits? Children could develop some of these points and think about issues of power and authority by investigating the following questions, or teachers could use the questions to devise activities:

- When and why were the canals built?
- Why were the canals built by private companies?
- Who worked on building the canals?
- Why were the locks and bridges built as narrow as possible?
- What were they used for?
- How did they transport the goods and raw materials?
- Where did the raw material come from?
- What made it possible to get cheap raw materials from these countries?
- Why did Regent's Canal have such a short working life?
- What factors were taken into account when King's Cross station was built so near the canal?
- Who plans what is to be built for the city, then and now?
- What are the canals used for today?
- Who and what lives in and around the canals?
- Who is responsible for the upkeep of the canals?

Children should be able to see that much of the land in London was privately owned so, unlike Paris or New York, there was little planning or state money used to develop the city over the last two centuries.

A topic on Victorians

There are many aspects that can be developed when teaching this topic, including the impact of industrialization on the landscape, working-class people and the economy and Britain's involvement in the colonies which supported and spearheaded the industrial revolution. Concepts that could be developed include: social change; interdependence; power and authority; division of labour.

The local area

Using the local area as a starting-point, children's awareness can be raised with respect to the evidence that still exists about the

Victorian period; for instance, the architecture, the street furniture, transport. From this, a number of themes can be explored, for example, that of change where children compare and contrast maps from different periods and formulate their own questions for investigation or exchange these with another group. From the work on maps, children should begin to realize that the landscape changed quite significantly during the Victorian period and will be encouraged to think about and ask questions such as why did things change? What made it possible to build and expand the factories, mansions and railways? As Rozina Visram argues: 'Profits from the Empire transformed Britain's physical landscape. Witness the manor houses and estates built by the sugar barons and the nabobs' (1994:58). Indeed, it was not just the landscape in Britain that changed, but also in the colonies. 'Britain developed trade and industries in her colonies to suit her economic needs and to benefit British trade and manufacture. For instance, acres of farming land in northern India were turned into poppy fields' (Visram, 1994:58).

The industrial revolution had many positive outcomes, including a thriving economy, but in the process many people suffered – in Britain it was the working classes and in the Caribbean it was the slaves taken by force from Africa. 'The wealth gained from the profits of the slave trade and slavery was another important factor in the growth of Britain as the first Industrial nation' (Visram, 1994:57).

Looking closely at a Victorian household would enable children to investigate how people lived, ranging from the roles and hierarchy of the people in the house; the servants, the chimney sweeps and the owners. Many became rich or richer with the profits from the colonies and were able to buy larger houses. By examining photographs of factory buildings, manor houses, images of children and people in the factories and by reading source materials of different people's experiences, children should be able to empathize and understand what life was like. For instance, the conditions of factory workers would lead on to addressing issues of their rights (or lack of them), living and working conditions and the struggles that led to the passing of the Factory Acts to ensure better conditions. Many of the slave owners lived a prosperous life, owning houses in Britain and the colonies, while the enslaved people endured humiliating living and working conditions, having lost their families, language and culture. However, the slaves fought against this and so did many white people.

The use of a flow diagram or a large class frieze/display helps children to make these links. Some of the questions highlighted on the frieze could be:

- Where did the raw material come from (for instance sugar)?
- How much did it cost? What did the workers get paid? What rights did they have?
- How were the goods transported from the country of origin to the factories in this country?
- What happened to it here?
- Who worked in the factory and under what conditions?
- How much were they paid?

Cotton

Another focus that links the colonies to development during the Victorian period is cotton. The use of objects (for instance, a spool from a Lancashire textile mill) enables children to explore the following questions: What is the object? What was it used for? Children can be asked to think of ten questions about the object. They can research their questions and explore some of the following questions:

- Where did the raw material come from that was used in the factories during the industrial revolution?
- What made it possible to get cotton from India and North America?
- What was the raw cotton used for?
- Where was it sold?
- Who did it benefit?

Children should realize that raw cotton from India benefited the Lancashire and Manchester manufacturers. In the mean time the Indian tax payer lost out and village industry was destroyed in India. A movement led by Gandhi of non-cooperation encouraged women to take up home spinning in order to gain back their economic base. As Rozina Visram points, 'women publicly burned their costly saris and adopted the coarse white homespun cloth (khadi), ... Khadi became a badge of equality and a nationalist 'uniform' (Visram, 1992:24). This was followed by successful picketing of foreign cloth shops by the women, but as the government lost revenue this was declared illegal. Although women were being imprisoned, ill treated and generally abused, they were not deterred and stood firm against injustice. This illustrates the fight against the colonial power and the resistance of the people, especially women. Children can examine the situation from a number of perspectives and investigative issues of power and authority and dispel stereotypes of women being passive.

Through the teaching of multiple histories and multiple perspectives children will be empowered to understand the world they live in and play a part in changing it for the better. The National Curriculum has defined what is legitimate knowledge, but teachers can still develop a perspective that incorporates issues of race, gender and class; within this approach the range of people's experiences from the personal to the political can be examined. Unless the foundations are laid in the primary school the future generation will be at a disadvantage. As Gillborn argues: 'Schools and teachers are not powerless: they retain the ability to affect their pupil's progress and achievement drastically' (1990:141).

ACKNOWLEDGEMENT

I would like to thank Jill Williams for her comments on an earlier draft of this chapter.

REFERENCES

Aldrich, R. (1991) *History in the National Curriculum*. London: Kogan Press Institute of Education.

Arnot, M. (ed.) (1985) *Race and Gender*. Oxford: Open University/Pergamon.

Aylett, J. P. (1985) *In Search of History*. London: Hodder and Stoughton.

Blyth, J. (1988) *History 5 to 9*. London: Hodder and Stoughton.

Bradley, H. (1992) Changes social divisions: class, gender and race. In Bocock, R. (ed.) *Social and Cultural Forms of*

Modernity. London: Polity Press and The Open University.

Bruner, J. S. (1966) *Towards a Theory of Instruction*. Cambridge, MA: Belknap Press.

Bruner, J. S. (1986) *Actual Minds, Possible Worlds*. Cambridge, MA: Harvard University Press.

Collicott, S. and Sanders, B. (1991) *Mary Seacole*. London: Ginn.

Collingwood, R. (1983) *The Idea of History*. Oxford: Oxford University Press.

Department of Education and Science (DES) (1995) *History in the National Curriculum*. London: DES.

Donaldson, M. (1978) *Children's Minds*. Glasgow: Fontana/Collins.

Dorn, A. (1985) Education and the Race Relations Act. In M. Arnot (ed.) *Race and Gender*. Oxford: Open University.

Durbin, G., Morris, S. and Wilkinson, S. (1990) *A Teacher's Guide to Learning from Objects*. London: English Heritage.

Gillborn, D. (1990) *'Race', Ethnicity and Education*. London: Unwin Hyman Ltd.

Hobsbawm, E. (1994) *Age of Extremes*. London: Michael Joseph.

ILEA (1980) *Social Studies in the Primary School*. London: ILEA.

Jeffcoate, R. (1979) A multi-curricular curriculum: beyond the orthodoxy. *Trends in Education*, 4(4).

Kearney, H. (1994) Four nations or one? In Bourdillon, H. (ed.) *Teaching History*. London: Routledge.

Kurusa (1981) *Nowhere to Play*. London: A. & C. Black.

Macdonald, I. (1989) *Murder in the Playground: The Burnage Report*. London: Longsight Press.

Merriman, N. (1993) *The Peopling of London*. London: Museum of London.

Morris, A. and Larson, H. (1989) *Uzma's Photo Album*. London: A. & C. Black.

Morris, M. (1992) *Using Portraits*. Colchester: English Heritage.

Plentie, D. L. (1989) Why should black history be taught in schools? *The Voice*, 14 February.

Ross, A. (1988) *Bright Ideas, Environmental Studies*. London: Scholastic.

Ross, C. and Ryan, A. (1990) *Can I Stay in Today, Miss! Improving the School Playground*. Stoke-on-Trent: Trentham Books.

Rutter, J. (1991) *Refugees – We Left Because We Had To*. London: The Refugee Council.

Short, G. and Carrington, B. (1992) Towards an anti-racist initiative. In Gill, D., Major, B. and Blair, M. (eds) *Racism and Education*. London: Sage/Open University.

Visram, R. (1992) *Women in India and Pakistan*. Cambridge: Cambridge University Press.

Visram, R. (1994) British history: whose history? Black perspectives on British history. In Bourdillon, H. (ed.) *Teaching History*. London: Routledge/Open University.

Vygotsky, L. S. (1962) *Thought and Language*. Cambridge, MA: MIT Press.

Whitty, G. (1992) Education, economy and national culture. In Bocock, R. and Thompson, K. (eds) *Social and Cultural Forms of Modernity*. London: Open University/Polity Press.

Wright, C. (1990) Early education: multiracial primary school classrooms. In Gill, D., Mayor, B. and Blair, M. (eds) *Racism and Education*. London: Sage/Open University.

CHAPTER 10

Geography

Jackie Barnes, Fiona Bellett and Gianna Knowles

Geography has an important role to play in the promotion of equality. Long discussed in primary terms as a humanity and often overlooked in favour of history, it has, in recent years, risen to the status of a science (see DFE 1991, 1995). Both the Dearing and pre-Dearing National Curricula place emphasis on the scientific side of geography; publications such as the *Times Educational Supplement* discuss the subject in a new light; primary schools are devoting more time to geography and with this new status within primary education comes a greater chance to use the subject to promote equality. One of the aims of this chapter is to examine to what extent geography is an elitist subject and how equality issues can be included within the geography curriculum and taught to primary age children.

The National Curriculum has brought geography to greater prominence, but how can we ensure that there is full access for all. In this chapter we shall explore how, through good practice, it may be possible that equality and equal access to the curriculum for pupils can be achieved. However, before reclaiming geography for all, it is first important to examine what the geography aspect of the National Curriculum is actually asking us to teach.

EQUAL ACCESS FOR ALL?

Smith and Noble (1994) found that all of the reforms and funding policies which the government has introduced over the past fifteen years have 'failed to remove barriers to learning'. The National Curriculum, it was claimed, would offer more choices to all children, but does this really happen? And is it possible for this to happen through a curriculum designed by a radical capitalist government? As Peet states in *Radical Geography* (1977:1), 'inequality and poverty are functional components of capitalist production'. Therefore any curriculum designed by a capitalist government will be careful to ensure that the education system perpetuates these inequalities. There are many examples within the geography aspect of the National Curriculum that demonstrate this to be the case. Quite simply, for example, geography, with its new more scientific approach requires sometimes costly apparatus resources, fieldwork and visits to locations outside the local area. Can all schools provide this?

Peet states: 'the normal operation of capitalism necessarily produces a more-or-less permanent underclass of unemployed and, therefore, poor people' (1977:3). This is important to consider since schools seeking to provide equality for all must ensure equality of provision. Those disadvantaged by finance must still be able to take full advantage of the opportunities offered to the children who can afford them. Some children depend entirely on school trips or journeys to venture beyond their local environment and visit other areas. Many children who live in economically deprived areas, whether in cities or rural communities, exist in a triangle which consists of home, school and the local shop or supermarket. Lack of money is a major factor in these children's geographically restricted lives, but there are other issues too. In the cities, fear of attack and their parents' own timidity mean that their world often consists of three or four streets. In rural communities where there is a lack of public transport, children whose parents do not own a car might rarely or never leave their immediate environment. If financially impoverished city children have never visited the countryside, then some children from rural backgrounds have never or rarely visited the city – even their nearest local town, perhaps only a few miles away. Both groups, urban and rural, grow up polarized and with some misinformed beliefs about the other. Many children who grow up in these impoverished communities are at risk, not only in terms of the material goods and travel that they miss out on, but also because of the mind set or local introspective culture in which they grow up. For many, 'the most significant connections are formed by the people who the individual knows – the friends and relatives of [their] social network.... Background institutions and information networks together form the social resources available to an individual' (Peet, 1977:117). It is also the case that because of this local culture the 'acceptance' of their impoverished status, *vis-à-vis* other classes in society, may be passed on from one generation to the next via the 'environment of opportunities and services into which each individual is implanted at birth (ibid.:112).

In small communities, including those in cities, many of the children's parents will have grown up in the area and grandparents, aunts, uncles and cousins may all live close by. This has the advantage of the support network of the extended family, but it can also reinforce a restrictive local mind set. If the extended family lives nearby this is yet another reason not to travel out of a given area. It becomes the case that, because of familiarity with the local environment and local culture and fear of unknown places, people will not or cannot leave the areas they grew up in, sometimes enduring considerable hardship to remain. Even when there may be better housing or potentially better jobs in a different place, many people choose to stay with what they know.

One of the authors of this chapter recently worked in a primary school of 350 children in a rural village in the Midlands. She was surprised by how narrow were the parents' expectations for their children. Education was not generally seen as a process which might provide a way of broadening the children's horizons. It was seen more as a holding shop, something children do until they are sixteen. The secondary school to which the children transfer is in a nearby village, some four miles away. The children are bussed there in a fleet of coaches and symbolically have to cross a river which frequently floods and becomes impassable during the winter. The anxiety of some parents when sending their first child to the secondary school was palpable; they may as well be going to school on a different continent. Parents who were only too happy to come to the primary school refused to set foot in the secondary school. This may be because it is difficult to reach without a car, but also has something to do with their fear of the foreign. Indeed, one mother who was upset about reports of her son's bad behaviour and lack of academic motivation at the secondary school came back to the primary school, rather than travel to the appropriate school, to shout the odds at the teachers. Although this mother had done little but complain about the primary school she still intended to send her youngest son there, rather than to the next local primary school. The journey would be no different for the child and parent, but it would mean going outside familiar territory, even though the mother felt that the known primary school did not do the best for her sons.

The Year 5 and 6 children from this school were taken to a local museum; 50 per cent of the funds for the trip came out of school funds. The museum is on the site of a recently closed-down mine. On the drive through the small mining town – now famed for its cut-price supermarket – one child pointed to the town's clocktower monument, all of ten metres high, and shouted excitedly, 'Look! Look! It's Big Ben.' To such children, from both cities and rural communities, a visit to a museum or a farm are opportunities for broadening their outlook which no school can ignore. A week at a fieldwork centre may easily be the only holiday they ever have and their only long journey.

Certainly there are as many social as geographical benefits in taking children on school trips, since it is part of every curriculum area to show children choice and to empower them to take their lives in the directions which they wish. If you know nothing of life expect a small council flat on an impoverished housing estate, urban or rural, the amount of choices you feel you have in adult life are limited. It is because of this that the study of non-local place in the UK is a valuable part of a child's education and should be available to all.

Fieldwork, beginning in the school grounds and leading out to more distant places, is central to geography:

> Fieldwork permits study in depth. Learning in the field can thus encourage a concentration and persistence in pupils which is diffi-

cult to achieve in school ... in effect field study can make a unique contribution to pupil motivation ... and enhanced motivation can be harnessed towards more effective learning.

(Hargreaves, 1983)

Unfortunately, the opportunities for fieldwork are too often dependent on financial constraints. School journey grants are now no longer available. Where schools have a large proportion of children entitled to free school meals, there is very little money available for contributions towards the cost of travel. Therefore the school must finance the cost of all such trips. This only becomes possible if there is an equal commitment from the school's governing body, which has to set aside money from the delegated budget to allow all children to participate in residential fieldwork studies. The issue of equality across the curriculum is put to the test here. Which other curriculum areas will be denied resource to finance this commitment? Cuts are being made in school budgets each year, yet the costs of residential field trips are increasing annually. For how long can a school give a commitment to finance this type of education for those children who cannot afford the cost themselves?

In predominantly middle-class areas, with very few children entitled to free school meals, most parents are able to meet whatever costs are asked, ensuring that their children take full advantage of all the necessary learning experiences. The school may then have the resources to subsidize those few children whose families are unable to pay. The National Curriculum was intended to offer more choices to all children, but how can those children benefit who are not in a position to take advantage of the choices.

Fund-raising events can be used to top up the money available for school trips and fieldwork studies. However, inequalities become only too apparent here. Schools where the majority of families are not suffering financially are often able to raise lots of money. Other schools where the great number of children are living below the poverty line are unable to obtain such financial support. It is one thing to invest in the future of education when immediate needs are being catered for, but quite another to invest in the future when living on the bread line.

In the rural Midlands school already mentioned, all the Year 6 children are given the opportunity to spend three or four days camping in Derbyshire. The school has managed to keep down the cost of the trip by raising the money to buy the camping equipment and spending the trip doing walking activities, rather than increase the cost by entry fees into museums, for example. Parents are allowed to pay by instalments. The local church also helps with the price of the trip. The teachers do all the cooking, which means no canteen prices.

Some schools cannot even rely on this amount of help with raising money and providing trips. One example of this is an inner city primary school which was trying to raise money for the older children to participate in a two-day residential field trip. The school collected old coats for a winter coat sale. The children and their families could either buy a coat for ten pence or they could swap the coat they were wearing for a bigger one. Approximately two hundred coats were either swapped or bought. Although the school was trying to raise money for the school journey, a far greater need became evident. This did not happen at a 'ragged school' of the nineteenth century, it happened in an inner city school in the 1990s.

Resourcing schools is not the only issue to come out of the National Curriculum with reference to equal access. The overall impact of recent government policy on schooling has been vast and the very nature of teaching today can promote inequality. Language and geography are irretrievably linked and both are deeply affected by recent pressures placed on schools. Increased class sizes have made it more difficult for whole class discussions to take place. In a class with hearing and non-hearing children, for instance, it is essential that all children can sit in such a way as to see the faces of the whole group. Numbers permitting, the class can sit in a circle on a carpeted area, thus allowing the non-hearing children to see everyone's lips and participate in the discussion. With increased class size, geography work, with its emphasis on questioning and enquiry which all children should share, will suffer. Questioning and enquiry are vital to all areas of geography. Talking is important in order to gain comprehension and learning. Issues of language, bilingualism and provision for special educational needs are as apparent when teaching geography as they are within any other subject; provision within the National Curriculum is in many ways inadequate.

Clearly, lack of money in schools, large classes and a curriculum overloaded with subject content put teachers under pressure to teach and assess in a certain way. External pressures from inspectors, the Office for Standards in Education (OFSTED) and the media have meant that, from a child's point of view, school is a less pleasant place to be. Often the subjects and the way they are being taught have little to do with the children's personal experiences.

To ignore the child's experiences is to lose a strong motivational force. Such experiences can provide starting-points from which to move onward and outward in educationally valuable directions. Far too often, children have to 'fit into school' rather than the school accommodating them. The Geography National Curriculum cannot be taught with fair access for all until the actual structure of society has been changed. There will always be great difficulty in obtaining 'true' equality of educational opportunity. Issues of inequality, including 'race', gender, disability and social class, affect how geography is taught. Is the content of the Geography National Curriculum geared to promoting such equality?

A FAIR CURRICULUM

The content of the Geography National Curriculum raises some issues about equality. When groups of children become conscious of having similar values and interests, different from other groups, then social class, gender, 'race' and disability issues arise. Those with money, health, good surroundings and confidence in their place in Britain are at an advantage. Children are aware of their differences at an early age. Does the study of place (i.e. comparing and contrasting localities) within the Geography National Curriculum reinforce these divisions, with its emphasis on comparison? The study of place must be approached carefully if stereotypes and prejudices are not to be reinforced. It is all too easy to describe some areas in negative terms when comparing, for example, housing, employment, leisure and lifestyles. This holds true whether studying a locality abroad or a region in Britain. 'Different', not 'worse than', should be the key emphasis, but does the National Curriculum address this? 'World citizenship' is not mentioned in the guidelines. The Dearing Report (DFE, 1994) offers little in the way of equality footnotes, as compared with the Non-Statutory Guidelines previously used by teachers alongside the National Curriculum. A contrast of regions in Britain is perhaps not the fairest way to discuss the varied cultures and ways of living/existing today. Such issues as racism can ideally be addressed during a study of place, but equally they can be ignored. Prejudice and stereotypes are easy to transmit unconsciously and even easier to ignore when mentioned by children. In all 'white' or 'all-employed' areas of the country, a study of an inner city may seem daunting to many teachers. Reinforcing ideas already fostered by the media must, however, be countered. Even reception age children have perceptions of what life is like in the countryside/city/by the coast. It is easy to overemphasize the positive/negative sides of an area and reinforce their ideas (i.e. living in the countryside is healthy and everyone owns a horse; inner city life is poverty stricken and ethnic communities cannot mix). The study of place and comparisons need to be readdressed within the National Curriculum.

As already mentioned, many issues relating to language arise within the geography curriculum, such as bilingual access and special educational needs. Is the curriculum fair and balanced if, for example, those with disabilities are not catered for? Is fieldwork easily accessible to all children?

Environmental issues are mentioned throughout the National Curriculum geography document. In the statutory Programmes of Study children are asked to look at issues concerning the environment. At Key Stage 1 infant children are asked to express views on the attractive and unattractive features of a given environment, to study how that environment is changing and how the quality of that environment can be sustained and improved (Programme of Study 6a, b and c). At Key Stage 2 these ideas are developed under the environmental change aspect of the Programme of Study (10a and b).

On the face of it, doing work on the environment may seem an area of the geography curriculum which children from all backgrounds can approach equally. Most districts, if not schools, have an environmental problem that can be discussed. Litter in the playground is one example. In studying the environment no expensive or additional equipment is needed. However, closer examination of the issues which will be raised when exploring the environment and environmental damage will show that the degree to which one can be environmentally friendly depends how much one can afford. For example, in the course of talking about damage to the environment children will learn that cars cause a lot of problems. The exhaust fumes from cars pollute the atmosphere causing harm to plants, animals and people. Cleaner cars do less damage. The newer the car the less pollution it will cause; it may even have a catalytic converter. It is unlikely that the parents of children from financially impoverished backgrounds will be able to afford new cars, particularly with the added extra of catalytic converters. They may also be unable to afford to maintain their cars adequately to ensure they are as clean as possible.

In studying environmental issues, children will learn that the pesticides and fertilizers put on the crops to ensure maximum yields also cause damage. Nitrates from fertilizers are leaked into rivers, causing pollution; pesticides sprayed on to crops escape into the atmosphere, causing harm to many living species. However, using these agents to raise crops also keeps the price of food down. Organic food is more expensive than non-organically produced foodstuffs. Industry causes immense damage to the environment, but also employs people.

Exploration of environmental issues in other countries also highlights questions of equality. Many children are aware of the damage being caused by the destruction of the rain forests. Teachers can point out that in many cases the forests are being destroyed to raise money to pay to the West. Countries which are in debt to the West use products gained from destroying the forests to pay off these debts. The forests are cut down for timber and for the mineral wealth beneath them. They are destroyed to rear cattle for beef to sell to the West. Much of this large-scale destruction of the environment is organized and managed at a state level. The financial success of large companies and the political success of various governments go hand in hand; this applies across the world. In Britain the Conservative government privatized the electricity and gas industry, virtually shutting down the still-nationalized mining industry and endorsing the building of more nuclear power stations. Nuclear power does not require coal and therefore the need by the 'government for the coal-mining industry virtually disappeared. It goes without saying that the environmental impact of nuclear power, including the dumping of radioactive waste is a greater environmental hazard than burning coal. Truly environmentally friendly ways of generating energy such as wind and wave power are just not good moneyspinners for governments.

Even in studying the environment and environmental issues, it is clear that there is not equal access for all children. However, with careful thought, the teacher can redress this imbalance to a degree. It is possible to raise children's awareness about environmental issues, although not all children will feel that they are able to make as much impact as they would wish to limit the damage. However, they will all be able to recognize the inequality that exists between the environmental damage acceptable in the West and that caused in developing countries, often directly or indirectly by the West.

Schools can help children to feel more empowered by giving them support in cleaning up the environment. In areas with no recycling centre, schools can provide bins to collect cans, paper and glass. Such provisions may not be available to everyone because of vandalism, for example, setting fire to the paper. If it is difficult for children to become directly involved in improving their immediate environment outside the school they can be encouraged to act responsibly within school, for example, by keeping the playground free of litter and by redesigning it – perhaps with seating areas and trees. Children can also look at improving the environment within the school and check whether the stock is free of CFCs. These may seem small measures, but for children who may have very little control over their lives, they may be extremely empowering. Schools may be concerned that to invest money in improving the playground would be a waste of time because of vandalism. However, in schools where these measures have been tried, not only have the children felt empowered but also the local community, and vandalism has not occurred.

There also exists in the geography aspect of the National Curriculum gender and sexuality inequality. Geography is, traditionally a masculinist subject and has traditionally studied the relationship between home and work. In the Programme of Study children are expected to undertake fieldwork activities in the locality of the school (Key Stage 1, PoS 3b). At Key Stage 2, this extends to detailed work on describing the locality – its relation to other places and transport networks (KS2, PoS 5 A–E).

Unless approached carefully, it is possible to fall into traditional ways of exploring these areas/topics. For example, children may look at a series of maps depicting a particular locality over a period of years. The maps will show how the settlement patterns have changed and developed, where houses and new roads have been built and where shops are. These findings then tend to be reported in a descriptive rather than analytical way – that is the children describe what they see rather than analysing it. Often what they are describing is a locality built by male architects to produce the most functional way of housing a workforce and transporting them to the workplace. As stated by Gillian Rose, geography may be called masculinist since 'while claiming to be exhaustive, [it] forgets about women's existence and concerns itself with the position of men' (1993:3). Left to women, localities may have developed in a very different way; shops, playgrounds, green areas, as a small example, would be far more accessible than they often are. Pushchair and wheelchair access would be a consideration. If geography is masculinist in that it takes little or no account of female designs and aspirations, it may be the case that masculine also means heterosexual. Those who are not heterosexual may also wish to design and make judgements about their locality in non-traditional ways. Therefore, in dealing with these areas of the Programmes of Study in school, it is necessary to ensure that the children ask not only 'why is this place like this?', but also 'does this place have to be like this?'. They should consider how it could be best designed to accommodate everyone's wants and needs'.

The content of the National Curriculum raises issues which cannot be ignored. Does the Geography Curriculum have too much room for bias and teachers' personal interpretations? Dearing has removed many of the restrictions on free thinking which previously constrained teachers within the 1991 National Curriculum, but perhaps geography is one area which needed more direction to ensure a curriculum that could be interpreted in such a way as to promote issues of equality.

PLANNING FOR EQUALITY

The following section provides sample plans for a geography topic. They are intended to give a structure for offering a differentiated curriculum which attempts to work towards eliminating inequality of educational opportunity by acknowledging and highlighting the existence of social inequalities. Although only examples, they show how geography in the National Curriculum can be approached to ensure that some of the inherent pitfalls can be overcome.

A topic on the local area (Key Stage 1)

The aims are:

* to promote active learning, children taking key roles and empathizing about what it might be like living in a different place;
* to encourage children to ask geographical questions and question fairness, particularly through using seven key questions (see Figure 10.1):
  Where is this place?
  What is this place like?
  Why is this place as it is?
  How is this place connected to other places?
  How is this place changing?
  What is it like to be in this place?
  How is the place similar to, or different from, another place?
* to challenge stereotypes of other people and places and encourage empathy;
* to encourage concern for the quality of the environment by looking at possible threats to the environment and both local and global.

The plan demonstrates how commitment to improving the environment and consideration of how far one's own actions can lead to environmental improvements can be explored and how geography can:

* make links with work in other curricular areas such as English, maths, history and science;
* be enjoyable and fun, with the children understanding the purpose of the work;

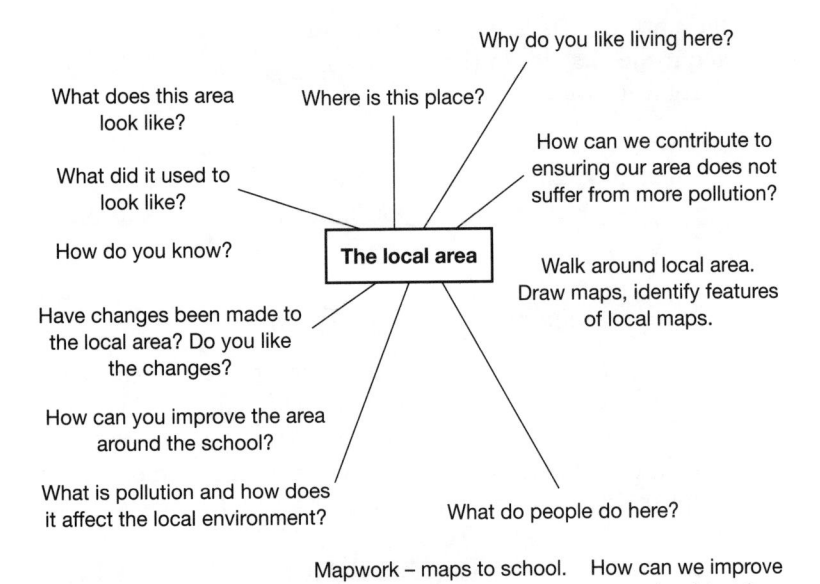

Figure 10.1   Topic web on the local area (Key Stage 1)

- have activities that are differentiated and allow for pupils to work co-operatively with each other;
- provide opportunities for pupils to take decisions about and responsibility for their own learning.

Within this topic the children can investigate the locality of the school and the history of the local area. In using some of the ideas from the above topic web as starting-points, the children's work will focus on:

- Finding out about physical and human features of the present local area. Fieldwork map-making and plans will be undertaken.
- Exploring proposed changes for the local area by interviewing local people and reading up-to-date information about the changes.
- Placing the local area in its wider geographical context, using maps/globes.

- Presenting a display including word-processed descriptions about the changes in the local area.
- Becoming aware of gender issues.

History work will include looking at the local area within its historical context and investigating the changes that have taken place over the years by drawing on a range of sources of information.

A topic on transport (Key Stages 1 and 2)

The subject of transport gives ideal opportunities to discuss many equality issues (e.g. pollution, ecology, changes in the local environment, communities and commuters). This theme also enables children to think about how a community can empower itself and be involved in decision-making about issues such as local transport. See Figure 10.2.

In using some of the ideas from the topic web the children's work will focus on:

- Exploring the background to proposals to build, for example, a new river crossing, a new bus route, etc. (Geography PoS 3d, 3e, 5a, 5d, 9b, 9c).
- Designing a questionnaire and computer database to gather local opinion about the issue and undertaking fieldwork at the local shops to collect the data. (Geography 2a, 2b and 3b, IT, 2B, 2C. Handling Data 1a and 1b).
- Making decisions about how to present and interpret the data and drawing some preliminary conclusion about the impact of the new development on the local environment (Mathematics Handling Data 2c, IT 2a and 2b).
- Preparing a report with recommendations to submit, for example, to the local action group (Mathematics Handling Data 2a and 2c, Geography 3d, 5e and 9b).

Topic on a locality in Africa: Nigeria (Key Stage 2)

All children should have access to learning about the richness of African culture. Choosing Nigeria as your foreign locality to study in Key Stage 2 has many benefits, not least the chance to raise equality issues such as world citizenship, rich and poor

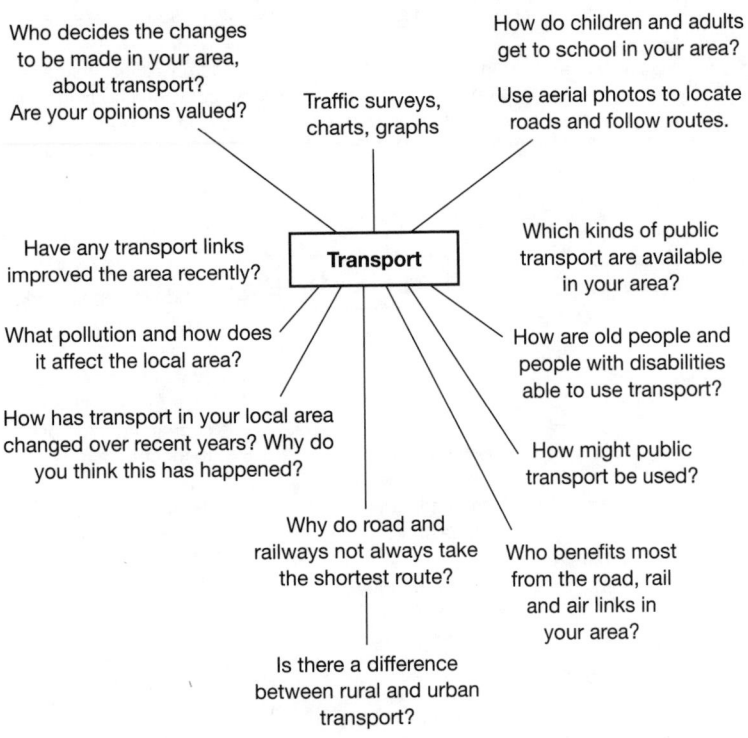

How does traffic affect
your life and other people's lives?

Who decides the changes
to be made in your area,
about transport?
Are your opinions valued?

How do children and adults
get to school in your area?

Traffic surveys,
charts, graphs

Use aerial photos to locate
roads and follow routes.

Have any transport links
improved the area recently?

Transport

Which kinds of public
transport are available
in your area?

What pollution and how does
it affect the local area?

How are old people and
people with disabilities
able to use transport?

How has transport in your local area
changed over recent years? Why do
you think this has happened?

How might public
transport be used?

Why do road and
railways not always take
the shortest route?

Who benefits most
from the road, rail
and air links in
your area?

Is there a difference
between rural and urban
transport?

Figure 10.2   Topic web on transport (Key Stage 2)

around the world and racism. Nigeria is also a good topic
because it can be taught with Benin, part of KS2 History (Core
Study Unit History of a non-European Society and 'The Tudors';
both topics cover the same time period). Empire, slavery and so-
called 'Third World' countries can be discussed. It is also a
perfect topic for introducing equality issues in general.

When we have taught this topic it has proved to be an amazing
springboard for discussion, art and language work. Children
talked about how they perceived Africa and then we examined
what it is really like. They discussed why they thought of it in
such limited ways and media issues were introduced. We looked
at how the media treated local issues; the topic had only just

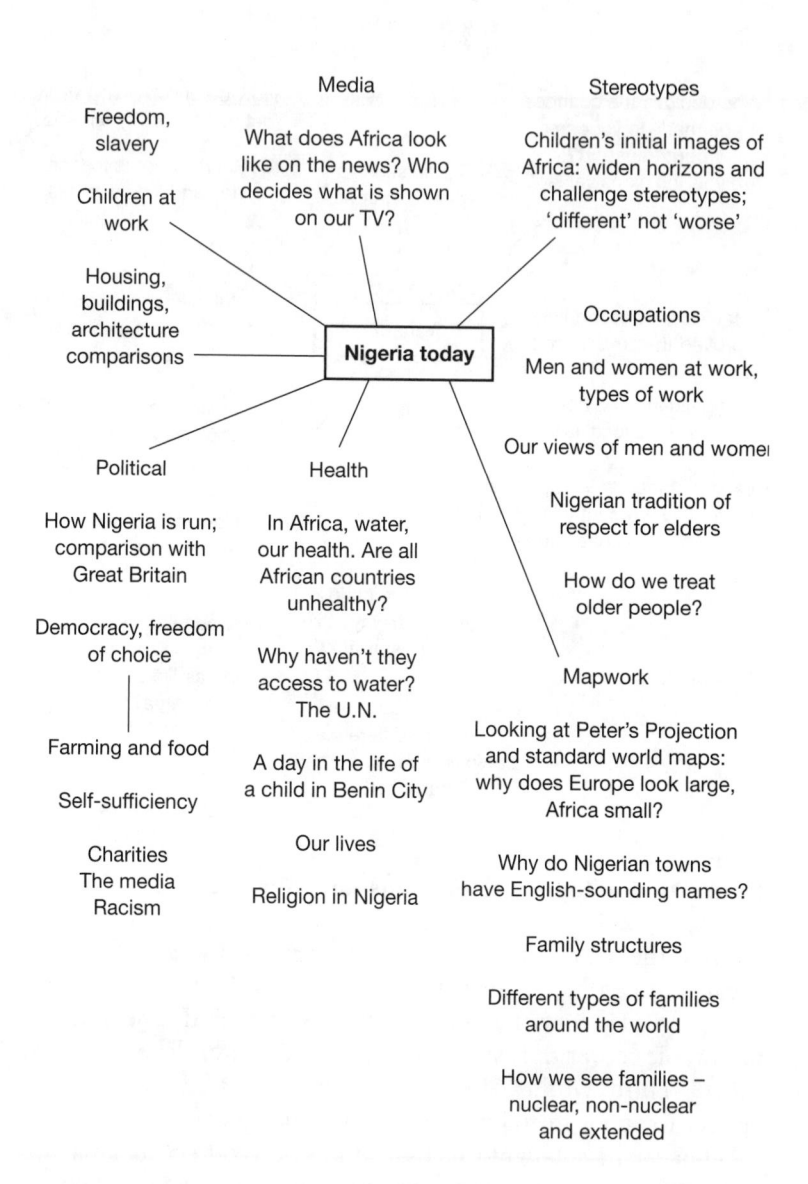

Media

What does Africa look like on the news? Who decides what is shown on our TV?

Freedom, slavery

Children at work

Housing, buildings, architecture comparisons

Stereotypes

Children's initial images of Africa: widen horizons and challenge stereotypes; 'different' not 'worse'

Nigeria today

Occupations

Men and women at work, types of work

Our views of men and women

Nigerian tradition of respect for elders

How do we treat older people?

Political

How Nigeria is run; comparison with Great Britain

Democracy, freedom of choice

Farming and food

Self-sufficiency

Charities
The media
Racism

Health

In Africa, water, our health. Are all African countries unhealthy?

Why haven't they access to water? The U.N.

A day in the life of a child in Benin City

Our lives

Religion in Nigeria

Mapwork

Looking at Peter's Projection and standard world maps: why does Europe look large, Africa small?

Why do Nigerian towns have English-sounding names?

Family structures

Different types of families around the world

How we see families – nuclear, non-nuclear and extended

Figure 10.3   Topic web on Nigeria today (Key Stage 2)

been started and a Pandora's box of thoughts had already been opened. We spent a lot of time exploring African folk tales and a lot of excellent language work was produced. The topic can lead in many directions. Figure 10.3 illustrates how some ideas on equality issues may be included.

USEFUL ADDRESSES

Centre for Global Education, University of York, Heslington, York YO1 5DD.
Commonwealth Institute, Kensington High Street, London W8 6NQ.
The Geographical Association, 342 Fulwood Road, Sheffield S10 3BP.
Oxfam, 27a Banbury Road, Oxford, OX2 7DZ.
World Wide Fund for Nature, Panda House, Weyside Park, Catteshall Lane, Surrey, GU7 1XR.

REFERENCES

Department For Education (DfE) (1991) *Geography in the National Curriculum: Non-Statutory Guidance for Teachers.* London: HMSO.
Department for Education (DfE) (1994) *Final Report on the National Curriculum and its Assessment: the Government's Response* (the Dearing Report). London: HMSO.
Department For Education (DfE) (1995) *Key Stages 1 and 2: Geography, the New Requirements.* London: HMSO.
ILEA (1983) *Learning Out of School: The Hargreaves Report.* London: ILEA.
Peet, R. (1977) *Radical Geography.* London: Methuen.
Rose, G. (1993) *Feminism and Geography.* London: Polity Press.
Smith, T. and Noble, M. (1994) *Education Divides: Poverty and Schooling in the 1990s.* London: CPAG.

CHAPTER 11

Music

Rod Paton

INTRODUCTION

This chapter aims:

- to demonstrate how issues of equality are central to the process of music education;
- to suggest some ways in which the classroom teacher can address issues of equality while fulfilling the statutory demands of the National Curriculum at Key Stages 1 and 2;
- to contribute to the debate on music and equality;
- to offer some practical ideas for classroom activity.

The Department for Education document *Music in the National Curriculum*, revised by Dearing and published in January 1995, is referred to throughout this chapter as MINC (1995).

Issues of equality may seem less relevant to the abstract world of music than in curriculum areas such as history or religious education where the ideological framework can be more readily identified. But musical texts are in every way as socially and culturally engaged as any other type of activity, although this is a notion which musical purists often find difficult to accept. There is a tradition of autonomy in musical learning which entertains the view that musical forms are products of individual expressive impulses and therefore have no direct relevance to ideology or social issues. This traditional view of musical forms renders its structural messages accessible only to specialists and neglects, or even denies, its social meanings. One of the results of this viewpoint has been a brand of elitism which regards the classical canon as superior to other forms of music and thus seeks to protect its own territory by blinding the non-specialist with musical science. For this reason, many primary school teachers without a specialized musical training feel overawed or disadvantaged when it comes to music. And yet a specialized training in music may produce a kind of musician and musicality which carries its own problems. Much specialized training fosters a belief that there is a correct way of doing things which may well be true within the relatively narrow field of classical performance, with its dependence on notation and the lionization of the composer, but specialized training can also force the musician into a mould too narrow for personal needs or social usefulness. (How many children, for example, 'put to the piano' at an early age, abandon it in their teens on discovering that it is a socially isolating and narrowly focused pursuit?) The enculturation that accompanies a formal musical training supports the kind of belief that, for example, the ability to play the piano is of prime importance to the would-be music teacher and yet many would argue, myself included, that the piano can be a major obstacle to musical learning, especially in the primary school. The piano stands as a symbol of highly specialized individual skill, whereas the principal aim of music education, especially at this early stage of a child's development, is to develop a sense of collective identity through musical activity.

The non-specialist music teacher in the primary school may well be overawed by the skills of trained musicians and easily forget that musical ability is a birthright shared by all, a 'common tongue' (Small, 1987). Instead of looking outwards to the lionized geniuses of the past, why not look inwards into the rich diversity of the musical present with its hordes of buskers, street musicians, playground games (see Opie, 1985), local musicians in pubs, church halls, summer fairs and so many more occasions and venues in which music lives? Everyone hums and sings by nature: the difficulty is in doing it without self-judgement (if Winnie the Pooh can do it ...) and almost any object can become a musical instrument simply by tapping it or shaking it or waving it. The prime musical instruments we carry with us are our bodies and voices. Music is all around us and within us: it is not only for 'experts'.

Thankfully, the advent of fresh debate surrounding music as social discourse (see, for example, Attali, 1977; Shepherd, 1977; Vulliamy and Lee, 1982; Small, 1987) is beginning to widen perspectives on musical meaning and lend fresh impetus to the cultural transformations which music both signifies and heralds. As musical debate and practice is made more accessible to the non-specialist, so music's power to influence human thought and behaviour is coming to be more widely recognized. Within the school system, music can be seen to embrace, in keeping with the other arts, issues of 'race', class, gender, sexuality and ethnicity. Furthermore, in the area of disability, we may find models of learning which, though growing from the pragmatic demands of the special needs classroom, assist us in redefining and reshaping our approaches to general class teaching. It is worth considering that we all have special needs when it comes to music.

PUSH-BUTTON MUSIC

We live in a musical period which Jacques Attali (1977) has called 'repeating'. By this, he is referring to the unprecedented distribution of musical experience through a seemingly infinite range of social and media outlets – radio, television, supermarkets, airports, lifts, telephones, streets, railway stations, waiting rooms, living rooms, recital rooms, churches, chapels, crematoriums, in-car entertainment and, of course, schools. This extraordinary level of access ensures that we are potentially or actually bombarded by organized noise while working, resting, travelling, even sleeping, and supplying as well as creating this demand for push-button music is an industry supported by 'a higher level of spending than we lavish on food, drink or keeping warm' (Attali, 1977:3). If I were to choose one experience which perfectly characterizes this post-modern musical culture, it would be listening to Gregorian Chant in stereo on the car radio while stuck in a traffic jam on the M25. This level of access to recorded music also ensures that identical experiences are available with push-button ease to all members of society – all levels of social class, all cultural groups, all members of the various minority ethnic communities, all age groups and people with a variety of physical and learning disability, giving rise most surely to an increasing commonality of cultural encounter.

MUSIC IN SCHOOL AND SOCIETY

Given this general cultural backdrop, how does music as practised in schools measure up to the experience of music in society? Schools, after all, reflect as well as influence social patterning. The seemingly abstract forms of music are profoundly linked with the patterns of feeling which permeate social groups and this needs to be taken into account in the way that we operate a music curriculum. If the purpose of music in schools is, broadly speaking, to educate the feelings (see Witkin, 1974), the first step for a sensitive teacher should be to ensure that the feelings of young children are engaged in the learning process: without feeling, there is no meaning. As Keith Swanwick (1980:39) puts it: 'Music is one mode of understanding the world and our experience of it, it is a *way of knowing the affective* and knowing *through* feeling.'

MINC (1995) makes quite explicit the need for flexibility of approach in dealing with children with special educational needs. Furthermore, within the Programmes of Study at each Key Stage, the demands of a culturally and ideologically diverse community are also acknowledged. Thus, in referring to repertoire for Performing and Listening, the teacher is required to select works 'from different times and cultures' (ibid.:2) and under the parallel heading for Key Stage 2, we find more explicit, non-statutory examples 'from the European "classical" tradition; folk and popular music; the countries and regions of the British Isles; cultures across the world.' (ibid.:4).

This, of course, means all kinds of music and is a vast improvement on the previous sets of non-statutory guidelines which were almost exclusively Eurocentric. For example, the only musicians mentioned by name in the listening section (Attainment Target 2) of the former document at Key Stage 1 were drawn exclusively from the classical canon – Tchaikovsky, Saint-Saëns, Haydn, and so on, the argument for this being that children should be made aware of their cultural heritage. Such positioning was misleading since non-specialist teachers, looking for specific guidelines, may well assume that this cultural narrowness and Eurocentricity was not merely intended (which it was, and, in some circles, still is) but statutory (which it never was). This perspective on musical culture arising from the previous document seemed to be fixated with the products of a predominantly white, suburban middle class. Yet for most children (and their parents) cultural heritage is more likely to be articulated through popular music while, for others, feelings are more aroused by say, reggae or Indian film music than by Bach or Beethoven. To cite a handful of German or Russian composers as representatives of our national musical expression is unrepresentative as well as misleading (if not irresponsible). Even, for example, Elgar's explicitly English characteristics appeal only to those particular social groups that patronize concert music or 'The Proms'. The argument that the classical canon is superior by virtue of its complexities, would be an argument for its exclusion from the curriculum at early Key Stages.

There is much to support the notion that music of the classical tradition is drawn into the curriculum largely because many teachers themselves share the aspiring middle-class values which are ritualized by the contexts of performance and production of this particular genre (see Small, 1987, Chapter 2). We cannot expect pupils from different social and ethnic groups to share these values any more than we can expect children with special needs to understand the finer points of sonata and fugue. This is not to prescribe or proscribe any particular musical genre, but to encourage teachers to be aware and acknowledge that music does have social meanings which need to be taken into account when choosing repertoire.

This is all of relevance to Attainment Target 2 (Listening and Appraising). But what about the even greater challenges of Attainment Target 1 (Composing and Performing)? The notion of composing needs very careful definition if it is to embrace what the average child at these early Key Stages can be expected to achieve and what the non-specialist teacher can be expected to deliver. Composing is often thought of as an act of genius and within the framework of European culture the image of the solitary, male, inspired artist, hunched over his working desk notating a complex orchestral score is largely historically accurate. But the act of composition has been opened up considerably within the educational field through the pioneering efforts of leading music educators and musicians whose influence on the development of the National Curriculum has ensured that Composing and Performing (AT1) are given twice the weighting of Listening and Appraising (AT2). Furthermore, composing has been redefined, collectivized and harnessed with dance, art, drama and creative writing as an activity which can be embraced by all ages, all classes, all ethnic groups, by both sexes and by disabled people. The implications of this underline many of the practical suggestions contained in this chapter. It would be unthinkable to run an art session in a primary school in which the children did not get paint on their fingers; or a dance lesson comprised entirely of watching videos of ballet. Children are as capable of experimenting and improvising with sound as they are of playing around with shapes and colours. Experimenting with the shapes and structures of sound within flexible structures is no more and no less than an act of composition.

Many schools do achieve a high standard of musical activity working within styles which reflect the emotional needs and social contexts of the communities in which these schools thrive and grow. This needs, from teachers, breadth of imagination in the interpretation of the statutory orders (which are sufficiently broad to admit this) and, from managers and governors, flexibility, tolerance and a willingness to permit experiment. But most of all, it requires a willingness to listen to children, to facilitate rather than to prescribe and to learn through teaching. From my own experience of in-service training, I also believe strongly that the surest way to achieve results is for teachers themselves to make time available (twenty minutes per week would suffice) to get together themselves to improvise as a group in exactly the same manner as pupils. A short weekly 'jam session' such as this will surely result in a vibrant and constantly evolving musical environment which is responsive to all abilities, all social classes and all ethnic groups. Music has enormous bonding potential if approached from this non-partisan, collective angle.

DELIVERING THE GOODS

Although we find the NC orders a division of ATs into AT1 (Performing and Composing) and AT2 (Listening and Appraising) it is also clearly intended that these targets are to be achieved through integrated teaching: 'activities that bring together requirements from both Performing and Composing and Listening and Appraising wherever possible' (MINC, 1995: 2). It is tempting perhaps to imagine that playing CDs of classical war horses to children as they file into assembly or entertaining them with amusing anecdotes about the lives of composers and performers is in some way fulfilling the requirements of AT2. But most teachers, recognizing the limited usefulness of this, would endorse models which engage the children's own creative energy. For example, a Year 2 class could work on a project based upon animals over, say, six weeks. They could improvise short percussion pieces which depict the movements or characterization of a variety of creatures. As the project developed they could then perform their work in assembly, live, to the rest of the school. They would spend some time appraising their own music in the light of its performance and only at this point in the process be introduced to recorded examples of other music which depicts similar images (e.g. *The Carnival of the Animals* by Saint-Saëns). Children will be more open to listening to music once their own imaginations are engaged and their curiosity prompted by the demands of doing it themselves.

Another method of integrated work might involve 'borrowing' material from familiar pieces. An example would be a project run a few years ago with a group of Key Stage 2 pupils in a West Sussex Primary School. Without informing them of the source of the material, the children were introduced to some simple rhythms and melodic shapes based directly on the theme for 'Ghostbusters' which was current in the pop charts at that time. In groups of five or six, the children were encouraged to improvise and eventually structure short pieces based upon these ideas. This resulted in five contrasted compositions, each lasting approximately two minutes. Only at the end of the project (which spread itself over five lessons) were the children introduced to the source of the material, music with which they were naturally very familiar and into which they were now being offered fresh insight.

Such an approach is focused upon the child's own musical world. There is less danger of imposing an alien aesthetic upon the work: recorded examples of music are inevitably coloured by the particular cultural frame of reference in which they have been produced and any inherent meanings in the music (that is, meaning contained in the structure and shape of the musical sounds, regardless of their social context) will be initially swamped by its cultural fingerprinting. For example, many children (and adults) find the music of Mozart heavy with delineated (culture-specific) and associative meanings, hardly surprising considering that the composer's major patrons were the established church and the aristocracy. This largely accounts for its eighteenth-century grace, seeming predictability and aristocratic flavour. Influenced by this associative flavour children may well miss the wit and invention inherent in the music. But, having once attempted to improvise or compose music themselves, in whatever style, there is a far greater chance of an authentic musical response to the music of other places and other times, including Mozart's. Jimmy Knapp, the Rail Union leader, recently admitted being moved to tears on his discovery of Mozart, having had the unique opportunity to witness a performance of the D minor Piano Concerto in Salzburg, where it was composed and even using the composer's own piano. Here, context and occasion opened up a window of feeling previously closed.

MUSIC FOR PUPILS WITH SPECIAL EDUCATIONAL NEEDS OR 'IT'S BETTER THAN BAA BAA BLACK SHEEP!'

Music has a vital role to play in the education of children with special needs. Where learning disability interferes with the child's cognitive performance, the affective nature of music can sometimes produce surprising, even exceptional responses. This has been recognized for some time now in the field of Music Therapy where much valuable and innovative work has centred upon techniques which directly involve the pupil or client in music improvisation. The classroom teacher will need to explore and experiment with a range of improvised activities tailored to the pupils' needs, which will extend to vision, touch and movement as well as aural stimuli.

In this area, combined arts come into their own. And it must be remembered that the healing and therapeutic powers of music have been recognized since the earliest times. As long ago as the third century BC, Pythagoras was using music to relieve stress and calm the soul. There is today a wealth of interest in the ways in which music improvisation with groups and individuals can open up whole channels of communication and affective discourse. The patterns of music seem to reflect and create patterns of feeling and this unique property makes it especially valuable when working with pupils who are emotionally disturbed or closed in. The pioneering work of Alvin (1975), Nordoff and Robbins (1971) and Wisbey (1980), to name only a few, point the way to novel functions of music as well as techniques which can serve as valuable models for general work in special schools.

The quotation at the head of this section comes from a 14-year-old with moderate learning disabilities at a special school during a multi-media arts project. An imaginary undersea environment had been created in the corner of the hall using gym apparatus from which were suspended all manner of objects, many of which were capable of making musical sounds (tubes of metal, brake drums, bunches of shells, wood blocks, wind chimes, etc.) The children were encouraged to play with these sounds while the teacher sang or chanted long notes using different vowel formations (overtone singing). Before long, the children were also singing in the same manner while simultaneously accompanying themselves with the 'floating' instruments. The result was a 'sea' of texture. 'It's better than Baa Baa Black Sheep' points to this pupil's previous diet of nursery rhymes, demonstrating the danger of believing, mistakenly, that merely because a 14-year-old has a mental age of five she/he automatically possesses a feeling age of five. Music is the language of feeling and crosses barriers of age as well as ability.

In cases of physical disability which exist independently of learning problems, musical performance, while presenting some problems, offers enormous potential for all children provided that teachers are prepared to adapt the musical environment along with the physical environment. As in all areas of disability, the essential principles are access and autonomy. In music, we can address these problems through imaginative instrumental work and by adapting musical structures.

First, in improving access to instruments teachers may need to use straps to attach beaters to hands or foot pedals to feet. Stringed instruments may need to be laid out on tables and played by unconventional means. I have found battery-operated mini-fans ideal replacements for conventional bows or plucking, and the sounds produced are unique and expressive. And it may be more worthwhile to invest in a single large (but really large) drum which can be laid on the floor surrounded by four or five players rather than five smaller drums which are difficult for disabled hands to hold.

Electronic keyboards which operate on the MIDI system (Musical Instrument Digital Interface, the industry standard for instruments which are compatible with computer technology) can be invaluable and, in combination with sampling and sequencing programmes and QWERTY (i.e. typewriter rather than musical) keyboards, can facilitate valuable compositional work. The research of Phil Ellis and Rosemary Dowsett (Ellis and Dowsett, 1987) has highlighted how the resources of micro-electronics can open up a completely new world of composing and improvising for children and adults with disabilities, the principles and practice of which have been further emphasized by David Collins, who also states, quite accurately: 'We all ... carry with us our own sets of special needs, a fact which I hope remains at the background of anything we plan or do' (Collins, 1992).

Secondly, musical structure itself may also need to be adapted to accommodate special needs. Improvisation is central to this process, plus a willingness to accept unusual or surprising results. Certain aesthetic criteria may need to be jettisoned en route to success. An example of this is a session with a small group of KS2 children with cerebral palsy, one of whom was intent on performing the *EastEnders* theme tune on keyboard. He had a clear idea of the sequence of notes of the tune but, naturally, could only execute these at a very slow pace. By regarding this as a perfectly legitimate reworking of the original (rather than a travesty) it became possible to construct an original piece with this theme at its core, each note providing the anchor for lots of decorative improvisation by others in the group. The combined effect sounded not unlike a piece of Indonesian gamelan music and all agreed that the end result was far more interesting than the original. Such parallels with the musical idioms of other cultures and their usefulness in music with disability has been explored by Sanger and Kippen (1987); but it must be obvious that any genre in which improvisation plays a central role is going to be of use in adaptive musical acts and this means almost any music outside of the Western European classical tradition. This principle of adaptation is central to work with disability, and demonstrates not merely an accommodation to special needs but an enhancement of musical models which would work equally well with the non-disabled.

My final example homes in on the area of musical perception and furnishes further evidence of how the limitations which disabilities impose can be turned to advantage. A child with multiple disability (partially deaf, severely limited vision, learning problems and cerebral palsy) is participating in a music session combining movement with voicework. During the singing, she reaches out and holds the throat of the facilitator as he sings and then proceeds to imitate the chanting while grasping the voice box. I now encourage this technique in all voicework sessions since it greatly enhances the capacity to feel the sounds and, of course, also assists in bonding between participants. It is well known that the deaf feel sounds through movement and through other body areas, and to introduce techniques which use these faculties (which we all share) can only strengthen musical listening and perception.

In summary, then, it can be seen that by redefining what we might understand as 'musical', reassessing our sense of aesthetic discipline, raising our awareness of alternative musical acts and being willing to listen, observe and absorb what the disabled have to offer us, children with a variety of disabilities can stand equal to others in all essentials of the music curriculum. We are not talking here of equality in terms of levels of skill but equality in terms of level of imagination and aesthetic response.

MUSIC AND GENDER

It may seem strange in the present climate of opinion to reflect that until relatively recently many of Europe's leading orchestras excluded women from their ranks. But this is less surprising given the historical context of Western European classical music in which women have been (and still are) largely denied the key roles of composers, conductors and directors. Indeed, such was the determination of the early church (the major patron of music) to keep women out of the Vatican choir that young boys were castrated in order to make it possible for them to continue singing the high (angelic?) parts after puberty. This tradition of castrato singing (the last survivor of which died as recently as 1927) was the strongest influence on the *bel canto* style which dominated the early history of opera and which still permeates present-day attitudes to what constitutes 'correct' singing tone. Little wonder, given its genesis, that boys are nervous and reluctant to sing in their teens. Whatever other principles are involved, this demonstrates how an aspect of musical style can become inextricably linked with an aspect of social tradition. Much the same situation exists in Asian music, especially in Indian classical music and also in Qowali (Muslim) singing which is exclusively a male preserve. The absence of this strict gender division in African music reflects the different types of hierarchies which pertain in African communities.

Given the history of male dominance in the art music of Western Europe, it is unsurprising that in the lists of suggested examples for listening and appraising (AT2) at Key Stages 1 and 2, we find no women's names at all. Even at KS3 the only window of opportunity is contained in the suggestion to 'listen to and discuss music sung and played during the years 1939–1945'. Presumably, this would include Vera Lynn, that perfect role model for the girl who wants to grow up as a supportive female keeping the home fires burning while her man is off defending the realm.

If the role of women in music is to be addressed properly, within the National Curriculum, teachers will need to draw upon a less discriminatory range of examples than those given in the document. This may well mean a willingness to explore the music of women composers or to draw upon traditions which have not denied women centrality, particularly the field of popular music. The only popular musicians mentioned in the given examples are, predictably, Lennon and McCartney. But what about someone of the calibre and quality of Madonna? Herein, of course, lies the problem: a great deal of popular music is about sex and while many teachers may regard a lot of material as unsuitable for younger children, there is no denying that media coverage ensures far greater exposure to this material up to the age of twelve than to any of the composers suggested in the National Curriculum. This is not to prescribe the one or to proscribe the other, but merely to urge an honest assessment of what kind of musical culture our children are actually being exposed to, what role women play in this culture and then to allow this pragmatic awareness to influence our teaching.

Running alongside the social history of music is the development of musical form itself and it is here that we may find some clues regarding the links between music and social meaning. The music of the classical canon, at least from around 1600 to the present century, is dominated by the principles of tonality (I can already hear the yawns of non-specialists ... but read on!). For most people, tonality is taken for granted, the details of its structures as inaccessible to them as the laws of particle physics. Yet, like physics, the structures of tonal music are evident and comprehensible at a non-cognitive level of feeling even though they are inexplicable (for example, every child can distinguish a 'bum' chord introduced into the National Anthem.) In short, tonality is based upon a hierarchical arrangement of chords and keys, the functions of which create patterns of tension and resolution. These patterns are felt directly by listeners and create particular and infinitely varied affective responses. Interestingly, resolution in tonal music of the classical tradition (e.g. the final chord of a symphony or a concerto) is always to the tonic triad, a three-note chord which excludes a fourth note (ubiquitous in the blues) known to musicians as the flattened seventh. Not only is this flattened seventh excluded from resolutions, but there is often considerable drama in the process by which it and its associated structural properties is negated. Even more significantly, the labelling of these musical processes are often gender laden (as in 'feminine cadence'), giving us some clues to the link between musical structures and socio-sexual patterning. It is not difficult to see within the hierarchical functions of tonality and the associated banishment of the flattened seventh an analogue to a social and religious framework dominated by a male trinity and a system of industrial and class layering largely governed by men.

Traditionally, musicologists have steered clear of this kind of thinking, preferring to regard musical meaning as autonomous, not culture bound but the relatively new and emergent area of feminist musicology has found it necessary to challenge and open up this narrow focus, illuminating, in the process, the social meanings inherent in musical form. (See, for example, Susan Mclary, *Feminine Endings*, 1991.) Whether or not we accept this symbolic interpretation of musical form, there can be no doubt that, historically, the musical world of the establishment (by which I mean the music of concert halls, opera houses and recital rooms) is largely controlled by men. Women feature more prominently as opera singers (where the heroines they depict are quite likely to be 'fallen' women, like Carmen) or as concert soloists – pianists, harpists (almost exclusive to women), violinists and cellists where, in an age of marketing they are increasingly prone to sexual commodification. In addressing this situation, teachers are faced with a number of tasks:

- to draw attention to the particular historical patterns which have discriminated against women in music;
- to encourage girls to compose and direct performances on equal terms with boys;
- to encourage forms of music-making, such as group improvisation, which reflect collective responsibility and sexual equality;
- to focus upon women artists who are successful in producing quality music while providing role models (popular singers from Ella Fitzgerald to Gloria Estefan);
- to become aware of functions of music in which women and men have always been equal (e.g. music therapy and healing);
- to encourage music-making in styles which are not necessarily tonally based – not difficult since European classical music is virtually the only tradition which has employed functional tonality as a central feature of its style.

MUSIC, CLASS AND 'RACE' – POPULAR AND ETHNIC STYLES

What constitutes a musical culture? A quick glance through the CD racks of the local record store reveals a plethora of labels the diversity of which can be baffling, if not staggering. But this is only music as commodity. In the shadows are innumerable sub-cultures and independent labels and all the unrecorded 'gigs' of local rock bands and jazz trios – poorly paid or unpaid but therefore music which is genuinely responding to cultural needs at grassroots level. At the opposite end of the spectrum is the massive resource of the music industry with its twin pillars of heavily subsidized 'serious' music on the one hand, paid for by a public purse but listened to by a relative minority of that public, and, on the other hand, the world of highly marketable and commoditized popular music, where a group like Pink Floyd can gross in excess of £125,000,000 in the course of a single world tour.

There are also complex issues at stake in the identification of classical music with the notion of cultural heritage, a situation which also distorts values in the art world. It has always seemed to me a curious fact that large amounts of taxpayers' money are consumed annually by institutions such as Covent Garden, the products of which are inaccessible both financially and culturally to a majority of the population. Yet, somehow, this is tolerated, due to a set of principles which holds that the health of a nation is, in some way, measured by its capacity to produce, among other things, good opera. During a conference on the arts in education at the Further Education Staff College in 1977, I put this question to the then Minister for the Arts: 'Given a climate of financial restraint in education, and given Kodaly's dictum that the work of the village music teacher is more significant to the musical health of the nation than that of the Director of the National Opera, which job should be the first to go?'

Predictably, perhaps, the reply came that, during a recent visit to Hungary, he had seen some of the outstanding work in primary schools (for which Hungary is famous), but that he had also witnessed some shoddy operatic performances in Budapest: as if this furnished proof that the Hungarian model was faulty. Yet maybe a balance of priorities which develops localized community excellence at the expense of less-than-glittering metropolitan extravaganzas is about right. And we may just be approaching a period where the majority will become impatient with the diversion of increasingly scarce resources to forms of culture presently enjoyed by an elite.

Culture is not static; that much is certain. And knowledge is not a 'body', wrapped up like a consumerist item to be bought and devoured. Culture and knowledge are organic processes involving people, and musical culture involves musical people, which means everybody. Children share in the development of musical culture and their particular cultural environment both assists in the development of their identity and is created by them as they search for identity. We talk of ethnic music or world music as if they were particular genres: but all music inhabits an ethnic frame and music belongs to the world. Of course, these are commodity labels developed for marketing purposes to distinguish music of the African or Indian continents, or the relatively unknown folk music of Eastern Europe perhaps. The world has been opened up and we are free to plunder and maybe even to desecrate the music of other cultures. For all their ideological correctness, many ethnomusicologists still insist upon notating musics whose sole previous function may have been to guide spirits during a sacred ceremony; the notation killing this function as surely as the knife of the biologist kills the fish on the dissecting table.

If we are not to destroy musical experience in the pursuit of musical knowledge it is essential to respect the cultural integrity of music which inevitably means acknowledging its roots in community and society and the identities of those whose sense of themselves is being articulated and constantly renewed through their music. And these people, these children are not separate in any way from us. We, as teachers also belong to this constantly developing organic process called culture – we are learning through teaching – growing with our children.

In a multicultural society a whole variety of musical strands will be finding their way into schools. The feeling of each of these strands can be identified as style (reggae, bhangra, blues, rock, garage music, indie-pop, house, hip-hop, etc.). But the school itself provides a kind of alchemical vessel, a container in which these various elements can mix and boil and occasionally produce a strand of gold. There is no prescription beyond somehow tapping into the collective spirit of our children. For the non-specialist class teacher this may be less of a problem than for the music specialist whose training may well have concentrated so much time and energy on the grasp of a single genre. The teacher needs to be a kind of musical sponge, capable of soaking up the spontaneous musical energy of children and assisting in shaping it into a renewed collective experience.

There are two major issues involved in the use of popular and ethnic styles in the classroom; one is concerned with ideology and the other is largely technical. The ideological issue is relevant to AT2 (Listening and Appraising) and raises the whole question of the appraisal and judgement of music and how we test musical knowledge. In the past, much of what passed for music education was often centred on learning and testing facts about the music rather than direct involvement with the musical act itself. If we try to judge popular music according to the kind of principles developed for the appraisal of classical forms we can fall into some deep ideological water. As Graham Vulliamy and Ed Lee put it: 'This can result in a distortion of the nature of popular music because of the imposition of inappropriate musical concepts and terminology derived from the totally different ("classical") tradition of music.' Vulliamy and Lee (1987:1).

So, since most of our procedures for appraisal and testing have been developed in relation to a particular, Eurocentric tradition, applying these to popular or minority ethnic styles is very likely to be alien to the spirit and meaning of those musics. The style of classical music grows out of a tradition of intellectual rationalism (a viewpoint unpopular with traditional musicologists) and this renders it readily accessible to rational appraisal. But try (as I have) discussing or appraising pop, rock or minority ethnic styles in a similar fashion and one quickly drowns in a sea of irrelevance.

The technical issues involved in the use of ethnic and popular music in the classroom are much more easily resolved and books and materials such as that quoted from above which offer practical advice and guidance are increasingly common. Performing and Composing is at the heart of school music within the National Curriculum. This provides a unique opportunity for shared musical experience. As mentioned earlier, most music is composed through improvisation and improvisation does not have to be culture specific. Given the opportunities to work within frameworks which are not idiomatically prescribed (i.e. not in any particular style or genre, but simply an idea) children are capable of producing their own pieces which will reflect their own specific cultural roots. But where children are being required to perform already composed pieces, then it is important to ensure that it is music which the children can be reasonably expected to own. This means respecting both the child's own cultural background and the cultural framework of the school within which teachers and children operate and ideally feel kindred.

In some extreme cases, music, by its very presence, or at least in certain forms, may be felt to be an undesirable element in the curriculum altogether. Recent research by Halstead (1994) has raised the problems presented by the diversity of attitudes to music in some Muslim communities and the necessity for a sensitive and responsible approach by teachers to the historical opposition to certain types of music within Islam. Some styles are inherently undesirable for use in classrooms (I am thinking here of types of black American rap which responds directly to violence, poverty and racism with music and language which is obscene, racist, misogynistic and anti-semitic). But, for the most part, allowing pupils a degree of autonomy, facilitating their musical development without imposing an alien aesthetic will fulfil the commitments to the curriculum while preserving the authenticity and integrity of the musical act.

SOUND IDEAS

Many, if not most of the techniques available to teachers for promoting listening, performing and composing skills are adaptable for use within a wide variety of contexts. The usefulness of a music project lies in its generative qualities, its flexibility and its breadth of applications. Such a project needs to be clearly framed without being overly prescriptive, a holding form which pupils and teachers can use with imagination and invention and which can be the vessel for a wide variety of expressive activity. The following suggestions are not specifically aimed at any particular type of group but it is to be hoped that the ideas will be taken up and used with freedom of imagination and a sense of adventure. They include: circles, empowerment, sharing, counting, chanting and drumming.

Circles

A circle automatically suggests equality. But what kind of musical patterns can come from circles?

1   Send a squeeze around the circle. Send a word around the circle. Send two words around the circle (one in each direction). See what happens when they cross. Now send a small percussion instrument around the circle (in silence). Repeat this exercise with each pupil playing a single sound on the instrument. Repeat again with closed eyes. Send two or three or four instruments around the circle with each pupil playing one or more sounds on each. Build up a piece in this way.

2   Using a bell, or a triangle, present this to one pupil in the circle and ask him/her to play a single note and say out loud their name and favourite colour before the bell stops ringing. They can then pass the bell on to someone of their choosing in the circle for a repeat of the same and so on. Try not to rush this exercise.

3   Everyone stands in a circle. One at a time, make a movement or body shape which the rest of the group can imitate. Go around the circle again, making a sound which goes with each movement in turn. Repeat each movement/sound at least six times. Now choose two or three movement/sounds and repeat them over and over to create a layered ostinato pattern with the pupils divided into two or three groups but still in a circle formation. (An ostinato is a short rhythmic idea or musical phrase which repeats over and over.) Every so often, call out 'all change' which is the signal for the groups to swap their patterns.

Empowerment

Allow your pupils to feel what it is to be in control of their own music.

1   Still in a circle, everyone drums on their knees. Make a sign to stop. Silence. Repeat the same idea but allow your pupils to control the stopping and starting (the sound and silence) with a variety of signs. Whoever stops the drumming can be

acknowledged with a Sound Wave in which the rest of the group wiggle their fingers and ululate ('diddle-diddle-diddle-diddle ...').

2   The same as (1) but instead of making a sign to stop, make a vocal sound like HO or HOO or HA or HEY. Everyone in the circle then imitates this calling sound and gives the caller a sound wave before continuing with the process.

3   Place some instruments in the middle of the circle and invite one child at a time to choose one and play a sound on it which expresses how they feel. Combine these sounds/feelings in groups of two, three, four or five.

4   Divide the pupils into two, three or four groups. Each group improvises ostinato patterns using a mixture of bodies, voices and instruments. One at a time, single pupils can stand in front of the groups and conduct, bringing the different patterns in and out, combining them in different ways and indicating loud and soft.

Sharing

Do you know where your pupils are coming from (musically)? Do they know where you are coming from?

1   Still in a circle, ask everyone to close their eyes and think of their favourite tune. After a count of three, everyone begins humming their tune simultaneously. Repeat the exercise with open eyes. Everyone looks around the circle while thinking of their tune. When they make eye contact with someone else, they go to the centre of the circle and swap tunes. Repeat many times on many occasions. This is one way of building up a repertoire of tunes that belongs entirely to the group.

2   Still using favourite tunes or improvised ostinatos the pupils move slowly around the room, swapping and sharing their tunes or patterns at will.

3   Divide the pupils into three or four groups. Each group devises (through improvisation) a sound pattern made up of individual, interlocking ostinatos. When each group is ready, they play their sound patterns one at a time to the rest of the class. Once all the groups have performed, group one begins

playing again and group two is instructed to listen very carefully. Each player in group two identifies a pattern in group one which she/he then begins to play, changing it slightly in the process. As group two picks up in volume, group one fades out, leaving group two performing a paraphrase of group one's improvisation. The process is then repeated until each group has copied and developed the material devised by group one, whereupon, the whole class can improvise together. Start all over again with group two playing their own original patterns for the other groups to paraphrase.

Counting

Time is the basic element of music. It is all about counting.

1 Sitting in a circle, everyone chants *one-two* over and over until a steady tempo has been achieved. Repeat the exercise but leave out a *one* or a *two* from time to time and see what happens.

2 Everyone chants either a *one* or a *two* (but not both) in sequence. Every so often, hop forwards onto a *one* or backwards on to a *two*. (In this form, this counting exercise is identical to the first exercise in John Stevens's excellent workshop manual, *Search and Reflect*, 1987.)

3 Increase the counts to three or four with each pupil chanting one count in sequence. Reintroduce the 'hopping' idea.

4 Substitute vocal sounds like 'Doo' or 'Dap' or 'Beep' or 'Bap' for the counting.

5 Every so often, pupils can hold on to one of these sounds to make a long note before continuing with the sequence. The piece could end when everyone is holding on to a long note together.

6 All count to six over and over again. Clap on *one*. Clap on *two*. Clap on *one* and *three*. Clap on *one* and *four*. Alternate between these. Let the pupils choose where to clap. Use percussion instruments instead of claps. Clap or play the instruments without the counting. Make up a piece on this basis.

Chanting

Much, if not all the music of particular cultures grows out of language.

1 Choose four short phrases in any language. Your pupils can supply these. Chant the phrases over and over until they turn into tunes. (This should happen spontaneously). Then allow each pupil to choose (silently) one of the chants. After a count of three everyone chants together, moving around the room until they have teamed up with others chanting on the same text. Repeat with a variety of texts.

2 A variation of this involves supplying each pupil with a work card on which is printed a text for chanting. (Try to ensure an even number of cards for each text.) For example:

   • Work Card 1 – *All the rivers run into the sea.*
   • Work Card 2 – *You never miss the water 'til the well runs dry.*
   • Work Card 3 – *Water, water everywhere.*
   • Work Card 4 – *It's raining, it's pouring.*

   With eyes closed, or blindfolded, the pupils move slowly around the hall chanting their own text and listening out for others chanting the same. Team up into groups accordingly, as before.

3 The chanting can now be transferred to instruments resulting in three or four contrasting pieces based upon the texts.

4 Chants can be built up using a call and response technique. For example:

Teacher: *don't*	Pupils: DON'T (4×)
don't care …	DON'T CARE (2×)
don't care, didn't care…	DON'T CARE, DIDN'T CARE (2×)

   Don't care, didn't care, don't care was wild …
   The whole of this text goes:
   Don't care didn't care, don't care was wild,
   Don't care stole plum and pear, like any beggar's child.

   Don't care was made to care, don't care was hung,
   Don't care was put in a pot, and boiled 'til he was done!

5 In a circle again, everybody thinks of an action associated

with physical work (e.g. sawing, chopping wood, digging, hoovering). Everybody moves together, making up a chant to fit with the movement. For a variation, everyone makes the same movement and the teacher sets up a call and response chant to go with it. (*Day-o ... DAY O/Day-day-do ... DAY-DAY-DO*, etc.)

6   Here is an easily remembered lyric:

Oh what a lot, oh what a lot, oh what of lot of fun (3×)
Oh what a lot, oh what a lot of fun fun fun!

This can be chanted with movement. Each pupil walks in time to the chant, in a straight line but all in different directions. Change direction on each line. Chant on the spot ... fun (space) – fun (space) – it's fun (space) – fun (space) – without moving, and then begin the whole lyric/movement again, each starting individually as they choose. This can form the basis of a collective improvisation, playing freely with the suggested melodies within the chant, adding percussion instruments when appropriate.

Drumming

The essential, unifying and grounding activity.

1   On laps, or desks, or even drums (if you can get enough together), set up a 2 + 2 pattern (two left hand strokes followed by two right hand strokes) using the hands (more immediate and less noisy than beaters). If the children experience co-ordination problems with this, try chanting *Beep-beep, Bap-bap* at the same time. This may help to keep the hands in time.
2   Repeat the exercise, leaving out occasional beats. Repeat, leaving out more and more beats until total silence is achieved. Repeat again, making up lots of different patterns.
3   Start with lots of different patterns and see if everyone can end up on the same pattern.
4   Sit in a circle and pass drumming patterns around in any direction. Three adjacent pupils in the circle drum their patterns; when the fourth starts drumming the first drops out. Repeat this process all the way around the circle.

5   Here are some more drumming patterns to chant and play:

Billy doo dap doo da/Billy doo dap doo da/ etc.
*Taka tak/Taka tak/Taa – /Taka tak/Taka tak/Taka tak/ Taa –
/* etc.
Bap – Bap – Shaka tak tak – / Bap – Bap – Shaka tak tak – / etc.

6   Everyone begins drumming together. If necessary, the teacher can keep time by beating out the pulse on a pair of claves. The pupils drop out one at a time, in any order, until one is left drumming solo. After about ten seconds, everyone joins in again and the process is repeated until everyone has played a solo.

SUMMARY

Within the constraints of this book it would be impossible to present a full range of practical activities which could be immediately put into practice in the classroom. Furthermore, music, by its very nature, makes special demands on the teacher: the real essence of the subject can never be conveyed in print, only through practical demonstration can anything authentic be absorbed. It is my hope that the suggested publications listed at the end of the chapter will give the teacher an idea of the kinds of approach which reflect the principles outlined above. In summary these are:

- respecting the cultural and class backgrounds of our pupils;
- avoiding the imposition of an alien aesthetic;
- being aware of those aspects of our musical traditions which militate against equality (such as the predominance of male influence in the classical music world);
- understanding that musical quality resides not in levels of skill but in levels of imagination (this is of particular relevance to groups with special educational needs);
- placing the emphasis on techniques which serve the development of the individual expressive imagination but also,
- facilitating a kind of music making which promotes the collective imagination (e.g. group improvisation), thus placing emphasis on commonality of feeling.

MINC 1995 does provide wide scope for interpretation. Where, for example, it states that 'Pupils should be given opportunities to ... listen to, and develop understanding of music from different times and places, applying knowledge to their own work' this is in full recognition of the diversity of cultural needs that exist in British schools. It is very much up to the individual teacher to decide, through sensitive awareness of pupils' needs and cultural backgrounds, what choices to make in respect of style, form, complexity and meaning in music. It will also mean using teaching techniques which either draw upon the widest possible range of styles or, as in the case of many improvisational forms, avoid cultural fingerprinting altogether. The resources list at the end of this chapter will, hopefully demonstrate the kinds of materials that are available.

A final example might be instructive. MINC 1995 states that 'pupils should be taught to ... refine and record their compositions using notation(s), where appropriate'. Recent research (Mills, 1994) (admittedly based upon the original orders but essentially about the same point), has shown that this area (the employment of notation) was one in which teachers were tending to fall down. Yet this failure was based upon a narrow interpretation of 'notation' – many non-specialist teachers not being aware that traditional staff notation (five lines, clefs and black dots, etc.), which develops out of and reflects the European classical tradition, is only one of a whole range of possibilities and that children will often devise their own diverse and imaginative methods of notating their work. Another study (Lawson *et al.*, 1994) demonstrates a similar reluctance to address the problems of notation as well as difficulties with the choice of repertoire for Listening and Appraising.

Yet this study also reflects my own experience of working in a wide variety of educational and community contexts, which reveals that teachers are more than willing to try new methods, especially when they are not unduly prescriptive and provided that they attempt, in the words of Chris Small (1987), 'to give back to the people the music that belongs to them'. Given that the revised, 'slimmed down' version of the National Curriculum is less prescriptive and more manageable, the outlook for a music education which responds to the needs of all children is very positive indeed.

RESOURCES

This list, far from being exhaustive, is intended to demonstrate the kinds of teaching materials which reflect the principles outlined above. The major resource for music is to be found in live and recorded performances.

Addison, R. (1987) *Bright Ideas: Music*. Leamington Spa: Scholastic.

Bean, J. and Oldfield, D. (1991) *A Pied Piper*. Cambridge: Cambridge University Press. Specific to Special Needs children.

Binns, P. and Chacksfield, M. (1983) *Sound Ideas*. Oxford: Oxford University Press. Various titles aimed at music making in a variety of styles.

Bird, W. and Barrett, E. (1988) *Music All the Time*. London: Chester. Of particular use to the non-specialist.

Black, A. & C. (publishers), *Mango Spice, Phantasmagoria, Sing for Your Life, The Singing Sack, Tinder Box*, etc. An invaluable resource of songs in all styles and from many cultural and ethnic sources.

Burnett, M. (1980) *Pop Music Topic Book*. Oxford: Oxford University Press. Useful projects for AT2.

Catherall, E. (1989) *Exploring Sound*. Hove: Wayland.

Chambers, Iain (1985) *Urban Rhythms*. London: Macmillan.

Clarke, S. (1980) *Jah Music*. London: Heinemann.

Davies, L. (1985) *Sound Waves: Practical Ideas for Children's Music Making*. London: Bell and Hyman.

Dunbar-Hall, P. and Hodge, G. (1991) *A Guide to Rock and Pop*. London: Science Press.

Farrell, G. (1990) *Indian Music in Education*. Cambridge: Cambridge University Press.

Floyd, L. (1980) *Indian Music*. Oxford: Oxford University Press.

Frith, S. (1978) *The Sociology of Rock*. London: Constable.

Gilbert, J. (1991) *Topic Anthology*. Oxford: Oxford University Press.

Glover, J. and Ward, S. (eds) (1993) *Teaching Music in the Primary School*. London: Cassell. An invaluable, up-to-date, entirely practical general introduction to Key Stages 1 and 2.

Griffin, Clive (1985) *Music Matters*. London: Dryad Press. A variety of titles and a wide cultural reference in this series.

Holdstock, J. (1986) *Earwiggo up, Earwiggo down: Pitch Games*. Tadcaster: Ray Lovely Music. Excellent material for pupils with special educational needs.

Jennings, S. (ed.) (1975) *Creative Therapy*. London: Pitman.

McNicol, R. (1993) *Sound Inventions*. Oxford: Oxford

University Press. Although aimed at older children, the approach in this book is wide-reaching and valuable to all age-ranges.

Nettl B., Capwell, C. and Wong, I. K. F. (eds) (1992) *Excursions in World Music*. Englewood Cliffs, New Jersey: Prentice-Hall.

Paynter, J. (1982) *All Kinds of Music*. Cambridge: Cambridge Educational. A diverse set of ideas and resources covering a wide range of styles and cultures.

Paynter, J. (1992) *Sound and Structure*. Cambridge: Cambridge University Press.

Paynter, J. and Aston, P. (1970) *Sound and Silence*. Cambridge: Cambridge University Press. A seminal book of creative classroom projects. More relevant than ever twenty-five years after publication.

Pepper, Dolly (1982) *High Low*. London: A. & C. Black. Useful project work.

Pugh, Aelwyn (1991) *Women in Music*. Cambridge: Cambridge University Press. A simple history of the role of women in music from Hildegard of Bingen to the present day. Sets the record straight.

Robbins, C. (1980) *Music for the Hearing Impaired*. London: Magnamusic-Baton.

Ross, M. (1978) *The Creative Arts*. London: Heinemann.

Salaman, W. (1983) *Living School Music*. Cambridge: Cambridge University Press.

Schulberg, C. H. (1981) *The Music Therapy Source Book*. New York: Human Sciences Press.

Shepherd, J. (1977) *Whose Music? A Sociology of Musical Styles*. London: Routledge.

Shepherd, M. (1989) *Music is Childsplay: Shared Learning Activities*. Harlow: Longman.

Small, C. (1987) *Music of the Common Tongue*. London: Calder.

Stevens, J. (1987) *Search and Reflect*. London: Community Music. Invaluable improvisation handbook.

Storms, G. (1981) *Handbook of Music Games*. London: Hutchinson.

Streeter, E. (1993) *Making Music with the Young Child with Special Educational Needs*. London: Jessica Kingsley Publications.

Swanwick, K. (1988) *Music, Mind and Education*. London: Routledge.

Vulliamy, G. and Lee, E. (1982) *Popular Music: A Teacher's Guide*. London: Routledge.

Vulliamy, G. and Lee, E. (eds) (1987) *Pop, Rock and Ethnic Music in Schools*. Cambridge: Cambridge Educational.

Wakeley, G. (1984) *Adventures in Music for the Very Young*. London: Schott.
Ward Lock Educational (1985) *Musical Starting Points with Young Children*. London: Ward Lock.

REFERENCES

Alvin, J. (1975) *Music Therapy*. London: John Clare Books.
Attali, J. (1977) *Noise: The Political Economy of Music*. Manchester: Manchester University Press.
Collins, D. (1992) Creativity and special needs: A suggested framework for technology Applications. *British Journal of Music Education*, 9:103–10.
Ellis, P. and Dowsett, R. (1987) Microelectronics and special Education. *British Journal of Music Education*, 4(1):17–25.
Halstead, J. M. (1994) Muslim attidues to music in schools. *British Journal of Music Education*, 11:143–56.
Lawson, D., Plummeridge, C. and Swanwick, K. (1994) Music and the National Curriculum in primary schools. *British Journal of Music Education*, 11:8–14.
Mclary, S. (1991) *Feminine Endings*, Minneapolis: University of Minnesota Press.
Mills, J. (1994) Music in the National Curriculum: The first Year. *British Journal of Music Education*, 11:191–6.
Nordoff, P. and Robbins, C. (1971) *Therapy in Music for Handicapped Children*. London: Victor Gollancz.
Opie, I. (1985) *The Singing Game*. Oxford: Oxford University Press.
Sanger, A. and Kippen, J. (1987) Applied ethnomusicology. *British Journal of Music Education*, 4(1):5–16.
Shepherd, J. (1977) *Whose Music? A Sociology of Musical Styles*. London: Routledge.
Small, C. (1987) Introduction. In John Stevens, *Search and Reflect*. London: Community Music.
Swanwick, K. (1979) *A Basis for Music Education*. Windsor: NFER-Nelson.
Swanwick, K. (1980) *A Basis for Music Education*. Windsor: NFER Publishing Company.
Vulliamy, G. and Lee, E. (1982) *Pop, Rock and Ethnic Music in Schools*. Cambridge: Cambridge Educational.
Wisbey, A. S. (1980) *Learning Through Music*. London: MTP Press.
Witkin, R. (1974) *The Intelligence of Feeling*. London: Heinemann.

CHAPTER 12

Art

Janet Sang and Jenny Ellwood

The prospect of art becoming a statutory part of the curriculum was heralded by many professionals in the late 1980s as an opportunity both for security and for reform. In its early stages of development, debate was fuelled by this prospect and there was considerable challenging of the status quo and some engagement in equality issues. The current situation is not so encouraging. Although the entitlement to an art education survives, its status is threatened by increased requirements for core subject provision. Rewriting of the recommendations of the Art Working Party's report (DES, 1990) and subsequent revision after the Dearing Report (DFE, 1994a), have considerably diluted any explicit attempts to radicalize the art curriculum.

This chapter attempts both a critique and an appreciation of the National Curriculum for Art. It recognizes that this curriculum must, by its very function, be underpinned by ideologies which support rather than challenge the status quo. It sets out, briefly, to identify these informing ideologies and the notions of art that they promote, so that they can be recognized and addressed. This chapter is also an appreciation, in that it points to that structure and content of the National Curriculum which bears witness to the early attempts at reform, and the opportunities it provides for equality education. This is followed by a discussion of examples of practice which have taken up some of these opportunities. This discussion does not attempt to cover all aspects of equality, but to provide some material for reflective practitioners interested in developing their own practice. These discussions are accompanied by a checklist for positive practice.

What does an entitlement to art education consist of? The ideological context in which the National Curriculum was devised is one in which several models of 'art' compete, conflict, coexist, or elide. The romantic notion of art and artists is very pervasive in mainstream culture. This notion characterizes the artist as distinct, eccentric, individualistic, holding special powers, and by implication white and male. It also positions the activity of art on the margins rather than at the centre of cultural production.

The view of children's art which is derived from the theories of developmental psychology makes a rather uncomfortable bedfellow. Developmental accounts have been particularly persistent in initial teacher education in Britain and in North America (see, for example, Gardner, 1980, 1990). Since there has been such an emphasis in primary art education on the production of art by children, such accounts may appear to provide a rationale for the consideration of children's work in the context of their intellectual development, rather than in the context of expectations and assumptions about art production in an adult world. Critics of such accounts, however, have pointed to their tendency to universalize and to mask individual and cultural differences (Atkinson, 1991, 1993). Although developmental accounts appear to liberate children's art from adult models, they may in fact be reinforcing and promoting particular dominant conventions, disguised as natural development (Wolf and Perry, 1988).

A third aspect of the current ideological context of the National Curriculum is produced by the tendency of a market economy to commodify art. Art products are packaged and presented with accompanying biographies and histories which shape and set their value. One result is that art as a subject is conceptualized as object based rather than relation based. Art products are less likely to be considered in terms of their social production and function.

This is the context in which the content and shape of the National Curriculum has been constructed. Assumptions about the romantic artist undermine the very notion of entitlement. They privilege individualism against collaboration and they imply a connection between success as an artist, being white and masculinity. Implicit acceptance of developmental accounts masks the elision of normal with Western and tends to underrate the significance of the curriculum in determining the direction of 'development'. This is a fundamental problem in relation to all equality issues, but is probably easiest to identify in relation to gender and ethnicity. An emphasis on objects rather than their human and social context militates against children's engagement in learning and reinforces an established canon.

REREADING THE NATIONAL CURRICULUM FOR ART

How do these notions of art operate within the National Curriculum for Art? They operate largely as subtexts and the silences and gaps in the content serve to support them. The revised Orders (DFE, 1995), operational from September 1995, are the briefest version yet. The Programmes of Study are without examples which might serve to provide positive illustrations and there is no new Non-Statutory Guidance in which provision for minority groups, for example, might be explicated. The Orders have a very simple structure, with a list of common requirements which refer to some equality issues and have implications for others. This list is followed by a double-page spread describing the Programme of Study for each Key Stage. Each Programme of Study has a section describing general requirements for the subject in this Key Stage, followed by a list of the teaching requirements for two Attainment Targets: Investigating and Making, and Knowledge and Understanding; the teaching requirements are accompanied by a list of required 'opportunities'.

What are the silences? The original Working Party (DES, 1990) did engage in a debate about the content of what has now become Attainment Target 2: Knowledge and Understanding, its potential role in establishing the canon, and the danger of uncritically establishing a gender-biased and Eurocentric curriculum. The new emphasis in the art curriculum on using the work of artists was said to be the aspect of the National Curriculum which caused teachers the most concern (Clement, 1994:9–21). The Draft Proposals for Art (DFE, 1994b:ii) interpreted this 'concern' as 'confusion' caused by the examples of art and artists used in the 1992 Orders. This interpretation was used as a justification for expunging all examples of particular art and artists and *Art in the National Curriculum* (DFE, 1995) is cleansed of all references to artists whose work might have represented a challenge to the status quo. The absence of mention of any male artists appears to silence accusations of gender bias. The addition of 'and non-Western' whenever Western cultures or traditions are mentioned appears to counter accusations of Eurocentricism. It is claimed in the SCAA Draft Proposals (DFE, 1994:i) that 'greater flexibility' of the Programmes of Study allows the special needs of pupils to be met.

Despite the attempt to present its content in apparently neutral terms, the introduction of AT2: Knowledge and Understanding represents an opportunity in primary education. A legacy, and perhaps a misunderstanding, of the 'Child Art' movement, was a tendency to try to protect children's art production from cultural influences. This tendency was supported by developmental accounts which emphasized the difference between the ways in which children as opposed to adults described the world in visual terms. The legacy was a mistrust of, or at least an uncertainty about, using art produced by adults in the classroom. The requirements of AT2 demand a change in this tendency. They set out purposes which represent opportunities for change and for equality education.

What are these opportunities? The first is in the choice of material for study. For KS1, there is a clear invitation to 'identify in the school and the locality the work of artists, craftspeople and designers' (DFE, 1995:3). This is an opportunity to establish, from the start of formal education, an understanding of art which incorporates visual material from a wide range of sources, as opposed to any narrow interpretation of fine art. In KS2, the requirement is more demanding, requiring attention to 'the materials and methods used by artists, craftspeople and designers' (DFE, 1995:5). Second, this strand firmly makes the connection between the products and their producers, supporting an approach which acknowledges and explores the human context of the designing, making, use and reception of art. For both Key Stages, the opportunity which must be offered, to 'apply knowledge to their own work', needs to be recognized as a very positive requirement. This invites children to use visual means to explore their relation to the cultural production of others.

There is a further strand, which begins in KS1 with the response to and description of art, craft and design. In KS2, not only is the requirement that a vocabulary to describe and express opinions about art is developed, but that children should be taught to 'use knowledge to support views'. This knowledge requires them to 'recognise ways in which works of art, craft and design reflect the time and place in which they were made' (DFE, 1995:5). What is offered here is an invitation to emphasize context and function and to engage in critical debate. Considering the ideological subtexts of the National Curriculum described in the first section of this chapter, we would like to suggest that what is needed in this context is to encourage children in an interrogatory approach to the content and production of art. This is what is necessary if both the opportunities art offers as an issue-based education and the challenges that equality issues pose for the art curriculum are to be recognized and faced.

The next section in this chapter takes up these opportunities in turn, illustrating and discussing ways in which they have been explored in particular examples of professional practice.

MAKING THE MOST OF THE NATIONAL CURRICULUM FOR ART

Choosing material to study

A positive reading of the National Curriculum suggests that a range of art, craft and design is appropriate material for study. There is also a requirement that this includes non-Western art (DFE, 1995:2,4). This is a strong invitation not to consider exclusively 'gallery' or fine art and is important since it supports the practice of beginning, in KS1, with a critical appreciation of the cultural products which children and their communities use. It is an invitation to examine and appreciate the artistic practices which people engage in as part of their everyday lives – for example, the designing, arranging and decorating of their living spaces, their gardens, their appearance, their food. And it is an invitation critically to consider the cultural products with and through which they live their lives – their toys, their bags, their lunchboxes, their bikes, as well as the books and television programmes they choose and the pictures they hang on their walls.

In this way, diversity can be celebrated and a start made in understanding the functions of art and the ways in which people can use art to organize a response to the world and to act upon and shape the world. This is an important aspect of under-standing, particularly if the processes of investigating and making in AT1 are to be meaningful. When children make their own art work, an understanding that this is a medium in which they can organize, communicate and act is essentially an empowering understanding.

Such a beginning provides a context for the introduction of more art which might be beyond their everyday experience. Particular forms of fine art have become much more visible. The last few years have witnessed an explosion in the publication of reproductions, particularly of paintings, in many forms, includ-ing on T-shirts and tablemats. The increasing commodification of art, promoted by the marketing of particular gallery exhibi-tions and of gallery art in general has resulted in a proliferation of images in circulation. When the Interim Report of the Working Party (DES, 1990) and the Statutory Orders and Non-Statutory Guidance (DES, 1992) were published, schools were brought into the market as purchasers of reproductions of paint-ings in a big way.

In some ways this has been very helpful for teachers trying to integrate the demands of AT2 with their practice. Because the Working Party (DES, 1990) did engage in debate about the signif-icance of the examples of art and artists used, a number of Asian, black and other minority ethnic British artists and women artists, for example, have had their work more widely reproduced than previously.

However, the availability of images does not guarantee their accessibility. A positive reading of the National Curriculum suggests, as we have seen, that it acknowledges that making art is a human function and that for art to be understood it needs to be seen in a social context.

Making material accessible

How can these works be used in the classroom? What kind of approach would make access meaningful? We know that providing positive images, for example, by including work by women artists, is not enough to challenge young people's perceptions. However, the suggestion in the National Curriculum, to start in KS1 by considering a range of art, craft and design in the locality (DFE, 1995:3), is a helpful one, since it facilitates not only a geographical context, but also the prospect of a human and social one. An example of a school introducing children to the work of a local painter in this way was documented on the BBC programme for KS2 children, *Artshow*, in 1992. The artist brought her young baby into school and set up a working area; children were able to see and talk to her about the particular circumstances of her working life as an artist and as a mother, the way she organized her life, as well as their responses to her drawings and paintings and their concerns about their own.

This kind of contextual approach provides a framework in which to address equality issues, in this case associated with gender. It might also provide a lens through which to view and consider examples of gallery art by women artists. As children progress into KS2, the use of secondary sources, such as the reproductions described above, becomes more feasible, and issues can be revisited in the context of the study of particular artists, using historical and biographical data with the images themselves. The requirement that 'pupils should be taught to recognise ways in which works of art, craft and design reflect the time and place in which they were made' (DFE, 1995:5) supports such contextualization. This is an important opportunity to address, for example, the work of artists such as Chila Burman and Sonia Boyce who challenge dominant ideas by cross-culturally exploring and exploding their gendered identity.

Working with artists in schools

The opportunities offered by contact with practising artists are very potent. Contact between artists and schools has increased and a tradition has developed of involvement, particularly based in community art groups, in equal opportunity issues. An

extremely useful guide, the result of a research project for the
National Foundation for Educational Research, offers careful
advice and suggests strategies for setting up artists-in-schools
projects (Sharp and Dust, 1990). An example, from an East
London primary school, describes how the involvement of a
local photographer contributed to the school's anti-racist work
by producing positive images of people from different local
communities (Sharp and Dust, 1990:128–9). The photographer
engaged several 8-year-old children in making photographs
which they considered best represented their own lives. These
were then made into a tape-slide presentation for which they
made a soundtrack. The children had the advantage of
discussing with a professional artist their judgements about
content and artistic form, and in doing so became more knowledgeable and respectful of each other's identities. In addition, a
valuable multicultural teaching resource was produced.

In a similar project sponsored by Portsmouth City Arts, the
results form an exhibition, 'Take a Look through Our Eyes'
(1993 and 1995) which is available for hire. Judy Harrison, who
co-ordinated and took part in two parts of the project, worked
with two poets – Ketaki Kushari Dyson (part one) and Fiona
Sampson (part two). In the most recent project, a small group of
6-year-olds were selected to represent the diversity of ethnicity
and family group in the communities using an infant and junior
school. These children were equipped with a camera.

> The idea was to reach out from the individual children, to their
> families and into their communities. The schools invited the fami-
> lies in, and we ran poetry and photography workshops. What we
> aimed to do was to produce a piece of work, featuring poetry and
> photography produced by the children and their families, which
> showed the positive side of living in a multi-ethnic and multi-
> cultural community.
>
> The workshops included using the cameras in the locality and
> some families took them home to use. Bringing the families into the
> school was really important. Sometimes, whole families came. It
> established connections which might not have been there before.
> And having the children and adults working together, giving them
> equal status, was very supportive for both parties.

Such a project enables the children to share their home and
community experiences and to show them in a positive light to

others. It enables the members of the families to see their parenting role in a new context, and to have that role confirmed and supported by the school. The resulting exhibition provides an opportunity for the wider appreciation of the images and poems, and the underrepresented worlds which form their material.

Intercultural art: towards a realization

Some LEAs have worked as partners in the Arts Education for a Multicultural Society project set up by the Arts Council in 1987 and have promoted and supported artists-in-schools projects. But despite the increase in this kind of work, for most classroom teachers such opportunities are unusual. It is more likely that individual schools may have to take the initiative in instigating and seeking funding or support for particular projects. Working with issues is a demanding field and the possibilities of producing only token gestures and perhaps of reinforcing stereotypes are very real.

The following account, of an attempt by a primary school in the south of England to run a special 'Arts Week' which promoted appreciation and knowledge of South Asian cultures, illustrates some of the possible pitfalls and some of the successes of such a venture. The week was organized by the two classroom teachers responsible for the development of art and music in the school. Although devised as a way of developing involvement with these subjects, the teachers concerned recognized the opportunity to develop and strengthen their school's commitment to intercultural education:

> We had lots of aims – probably far too many. We saw this as a golden opportunity not only to stimulate intercultural awareness but also as a chance to look at the areas of gender and social class and assess what we offer the children.

The children and staff were mainly white, the children drawn mostly from an estate of mixed public and private housing, and also from a nearby naval base and a small rural community. The decision to focus on South Asian cultures was an attempt to broaden the knowledge and awareness of the whole school community and develop some positive attitudes. The organizers saw it as important to provide the staff with information and resources, and preparations began early.

> We presented each member of staff with a pack which contained background information on the area, religions, customs, languages, artefacts, musical instruments and so on. In retrospect this was a very large area to choose, and could have been a reflection of our ignorance. However, individual teachers did focus on particular cultures within this very broad framework. We are extremely fortunate in Hampshire to have the Intercultural Resources Centre based in Southampton. It runs an advice and loan service, and the curator visits schools as well. We used the material we borrowed in several ways. We thought the setting up of displays was important, and we wanted the children to be able to contribute to these and handle objects. We borrowed musical instruments, posters, wall hangings, embroidered pieces, clothing, dance sticks, ornaments and religious artefacts and displayed them. The children all contributed a piece of art work, so the school looked as if it was ready for a huge celebration, before the week began.

This 'setting the scene' and involvement of the school community in preparing the building provided a welcome for the many visitors who were to take part in the following week. For the Trishul Dance Troupe, who came for a day early on in the week, the welcome was extended by the fact that all members of the school community had dressed in saris or shalwar kameez for the day.

> The Trishul Dance Troupe gave a performance for the whole school, which was spellbinding. The troupe consists of two female dancers: Camilita and Christina Devi, and a male musician. They performed dance in the Kathak style, from several regions. What was so good was that they explained the narrative and the significance of each dance and of the costumes. Our children took it very seriously.

At this particular school dance is quite well established and an equal commitment is expected and achieved from boys and girls. The Dance Troupe was therefore able to extend the children's knowledge and experience of dance by running workshops for the children and their teachers.

> The workshops explored the musical instruments and taught children some dance movements. Boys and girls enjoyed demonstrating their newly-acquired skills to others. The dancers built up an extraordinary rapport with the children in a very short time; some of the children so enjoyed themselves that at the end of the session they cuddled the dancers.

During the course of the week there were seventy visitors, many of whom contributed to the Arts Week. They were all welcomed, and invited to sign the visitors' book. Two workers from the local Bilingual Language Support Service came and ran a mehndi hand-painting workshop and illustrated a Bangladeshi wedding. Children had written many letters of invitation to the extended school community and visitors included parents, governors, the school-crossing patrol officer, the Mayor, the local clergy, the head of the Naval base, advisory staff and the Chief Education Officer. All of these visitors were invited to bring a favourite piece of music and a picture to share with some of the children:

> We did end up with more people than we had expected! However, the children met lots of people who demonstrated how art played an important part in their lives. So perhaps some of the less familiar arts we were studying were put into a context. Some local artists came in to school and set up their easels to work alongside the children, or ran, for example, printmaking workshops. They seemed to really enjoy working with the children, and some of the children were very struck by their commitment.

This challenge, to consider how the arts can function for different individuals or groups, was posed again by the exhibition of young British Asian artists at Southampton City Art Gallery. Here was an exhibition curated with the exploration of cultural and personal identity in mind. This exhibition challenged stereotypes about 'Asian culture', using video, computer art and installation work.

> We arranged for every class to visit the Gallery, including this exhibition. Not all of the teachers could go to the preview evening, and some of the staff reacted negatively to the work, and didn't want to use the teaching material provided by the gallery staff.

For many children it was the first time they had heard of a gallery. One group of 5-year-olds spent a great deal of time investigating one sculpture. It was called 'Vahana', by Anuradha Patel, and consisted of a peacock boat filled with women. The experience seemed very significant for some particular children: the powerful presence of the sculptures, their rich colours and imagery, seemed to hold these children's attention for an unusually long time. For the group of 4-year-olds who went, the experience was very memorable: they are still talking about it, a term later.

Pitfalls and successes

Supporters of this kind of 'arts week' claim that it extends the knowledge of the school community and engenders respect and appreciation for the cultural production of particular groups. In the account above, this was clearly the intention of the organizers, and of the headteacher, who wrote:

It provided an excellent opportunity for promoting understanding of another culture, and – for want of a better term – the children's spiritual response to the world around them.

The event also provided a vehicle for bringing the community into the school and promoting equal opportunities. It gave the children an understanding of how the Arts have had an important role in the religious beliefs, working lives, leisure time and learning of the numerous visitors and performers.

Last but not least it offered the school the opportunity to learn something of value together, not constrained by subject orders, attainment targets and key stages. This is the strongest argument for an annual whole school theme week that I can think of.

This kind of approach and evaluation is very much in the tradition of liberal multiculturalism. It places great value on the sharing of experiences and on collaborative ventures. It is often described as providing 'positive experiences', and indeed it seems to promote a feeling of community and to function as a kind of rallying activity. One of the problems, though, is that it tends to present a world without conflict, that is it functions to provide a gloss on experience, a seamless picture. Thus it has its limits. To avoid the danger of generalizing cultural diversity and supporting stereotypes, any study of a culture needs to be particular;

voices from within that culture need to be heard strongly and these voices should take up different positions.

The very association of 'arts' with 'another culture' invites an assumption of exoticism. The concern of the headteacher, then, that the Arts Week should be seen as part of a school policy which seeks to promote an understanding of how art functions in the lives of many different people is a very important one. A multicultural perspective in other curriculum areas is necessary to counteract this invited assumption.

The claim should not be made that this is anti-racist work. There were some opportunities in the Arts Week for issues to be explored and attitudes challenged, but it is interesting to note that, for example, the work of the artists with South Asian connections working in Britain was offputting to some teachers. This probably has more to do with a very common and under-standable reaction to the apparent incomprehensibility of contemporary gallery art than with the content of the work. Encounters with this kind of work also need much preparation, but in this case would provide some excellent material through which to engage with some of the conflicts, contradictions and possibilities offered by an intercultural existence. It is this kind of critical looking which will be discussed in the next section.

CRITICAL LOOKING

There has been a revival of critical studies in the Primary art curriculum, largely as a result of the introduction of the National Curriculum. For equality education, this is an area which offers many opportunities. It can, as we have seen, extend experience of particular artefacts, processes and cultures. It can also offer the opportunity to develop an interrogatory approach to those products: that is, an approach which acknowledges and examines the context in which meaning is made.

Extending experience of art and artefacts

There are many general teaching strategies which encourage engagement with art and artefacts and these have been well documented (for example, in the work of Clement and Page,

1992) or worked into direct teaching materials for children's use (for example, Norman Binch, 1994). These strategies will be familiar to teachers of young children and can be used across the curriculum. Here are some examples:

- putting children in the role of detectives;
- approaching images in a descriptive, then an analytical, then an evaluative way;
- extending from personal experience;
- imagining one is in the painting;
- developing narratives;
- revealing part of the work at a time;
- exploring sculpture or other 3D work through touch, before looking.

These approaches invite and prolong children's engagement and can kindle interest (Jack and Sang, 1989). They provide many opportunities for connections to be made between their own work and that of other artists. These approaches which privilege the individual's response to the work empower the viewer and provide successful ways of entry into the work and into the idea of being a critical viewer.

However, for this kind of work to intersect with equality issues it is necessary for such approaches to be accompanied by addressing the source and the function of the work being studied. This opens up issues and avoids some of the pitfalls of appearing to speak from a privileged position. In the case of the primary school, such contextualization is very demanding for the teacher and, as noted earlier, needs as much as possible to involve real people and situations.

Interrogating the image

It is also the case that images, art and artefacts represent the world to children, and that these representations may support and perpetuate the inequalities which are the subject of this chapter. As well as an approach to looking at paintings that offers the possibility of an illuminating experience, it is the responsibility of the teacher to engage young children in the business of interrogating the images through which the world is represented to them, and these include images from fine art.

This kind of interrogative approach draws its methodology from media and cultural studies and seeks to deconstruct the construction of images and their reception (Allen, 1994: 133–45). This approach does not prescribe a correct reading, but acknowledges that images are made with reception in mind, while at the same time recognizing that the significance of images will be different in different contexts: that is, that images can be continually returned to and reread in the light of different perspectives. What the viewer brings to the image or artefact is acknowledged.

A small project, using material from the Development Education Centre in Birmingham (1989) illustrates this kind of approach in action. A young teacher working with 8-year-olds, explains how she began:

> I insisted on the functions of photographs being addressed. Why were particular photos taken? Who were they taken for? How did a photo taken in a studio differ from a snapshot, and so on? I found that children were sophisticated viewers, but that as with adults, they needed to develop strategies of looking and questioning which unpacked their responses and their knowledge.

Some of the work she did helped the children to confront issues of veracity. For example, the strategy of revealing images gradually was used not so much to encourage imaginative involvement, but more in order to illustrate how cropping can direct the viewer's interpretation in ways which are dishonest if a larger view is considered.

Similarly, the teacher asked children to select a photograph from their personal collection at home and these were shared around in a group. Individuals were invited literally to extend a photograph, using drawing. Then the drawings were compared and discussed with the owners of the photos, who had memories of the occasion depicted, or had discussed versions of the occasion before:

> This exercise involved the children in making and then discussing alternative readings of the same image. They noticed how much information can be present in a photograph, because they had to discuss visual evidence for the readings they had made. But they also learnt how ambiguous an image can be.

There was also an opportunity here to debate the authority of those readings and whether the photographer or the owner had any more authority than anyone else in claiming a 'right' interpretation.

This attempt to encourage children to be critical about representations has important applications in education issues. In addition, the teacher was able to encourage more exploration of the interaction between the work and the viewer, when she got the children to pose themselves in photographs:

> I was interested in how some of the children took the opportunity to construct visual representations of their interests. Some of the girls adopted poses learnt from images of women in circulation, apparently actively adopting particular versions of femininity. However others used the photographs as a site of resistance, apparently deliberately defying dominant stereotypes.

This work is fascinating not only in how it reveals the sophistication of young children's viewing abilities, but also in illuminating the strength of teaching strategies which empower the learner and offer opportunities for examination and debate.

LOOKING TO THE FUTURE

In this chapter we have argued that a close reading of *Art in the National Curriculum* can identify opportunities for equality education. First, a notion of entitlement remains, although in practice it is under attack from the increasing demands on curriculum time from core subjects. Second, there is an emphasis in the Programmes of Study, on the range of art, craft and design which children should encounter and use. This remains an opportunity to select material which offers an engagement with equality issues, although the potential of this emphasis is weakened by the absence of examples. Third, the development of the requirement for the children critically to evaluate cultural products, including their own, is potentially empowering.

We have also, however, argued that there are, concealed within the text of the curriculum, ideas about the nature of art and artists, their function and the function of art education, which contradict or militate against the development of the curriculum's potential for equality education. We have tried to identify some of these ideologies by listening for some of the curriculum's silences. Our discussion of some examples of recent practice suggests that teaching for equality demands strategies which counter these silences, which structure accessibility, not merely provide availability, and which enable children to control an art medium in order not only to organize a response to the world, but also to take action on it.

We end this chapter with some suggestions for teachers, which we hope will be helpful in guiding practice in this direction.

Finally, it is the statement, prefacing each Programme of Study, which offers the key to the curriculum's most radical reading. What this seemingly rather bland statement points to, is the connection between the two ATs:

> Pupils' understanding and enjoyment of art, craft and design should be developed through activities which bring together requirements from both Investigating and Making and Knowledge and Understanding, wherever possible.
>
> (DFE, 1995)

However, we can make what is a crucial interpretation of this request, that is that connections should continually be made between practical investigations, knowledge of the contexts in which art is made and critical comment. It is the making of these connections, in the form of visual or verbal comparisons, appropriation and reworking of material, which constructs the opportunity for a dialogue. And it is this dialogue which holds the potential for the participants to critique, redefine and develop control over art as a medium and a subject.

CHECKLIST OF ACTIONS

As a primary teacher trying to provide equal opportunities in art do I:

For AT1: Investigating and Making

- Provide opportunities for children to use art to celebrate the cultural production of their own and each other's communities?
- Provide for a range of ways of experiencing the physical

world by, for example, providing tactile experiences when children are involved in investigating and making?

- Develop and adapt work surfaces and levels, equipment and tools, to provide equal access for children with particular needs?
- Allocate time to engage with and monitor the progress of children with speed and language difficulties who may be using art for a wide range of intellectual and social functions?
- Monitor, structure and organize the use of art materials and equipment, where appropriate making special provision so that children are offered equal access as opposed to free choice?
- Encourage children to challenge stereotyping in their own art work by using strategies to avoid them restricting themselves in their selection of themes and content?

For AT2: Knowledge and Understanding

- Contribute to the development of a whole school policy, in which art is one of many curriculum areas used to promote appreciation of cultural diversity?
- Explore with the children the functions of particular art and artefacts in the context of the societies, including the context of the school, in which they are made and used?
- Seek out examples of art by minority or under-represented groups to use in the classroom?
- Invite members of such groups who use art in their work into the classroom to talk about their working lives?
- Use examples which illustrate how influences in art can work across and between cultures, making explicit the power relations involved?
- Look for opportunities to challenge stereotypes by using and talking about examples of women who have developed particular skills, who use tools to work with resistant materials, who combine computer-aided design with traditional skills, who are successful in their field?

ACKNOWLEDGEMENTS

We should like to acknowledge: Joanne Lear for material for 'Critical Looking'; the headteacher and staff of Red Barn Primary School, Portchester, for material for 'Intercultural art: towards a realisation'; Judy Harrison and Portsmouth City Arts, for material for 'Working with Artists in Schools'.

REFERENCES

Allen, D. (1994) Teaching visual literacy: Some reflections on the term, *Journal of Art and Design Education*, 13(2).

Atkinson, D. (1991) How children use drawing. *Journal of Art and Design Education*, 10(1).

Atkinson, D. (1993) Representation and experience in children's drawings. *Journal of Art and Design Education*, 12(1).

BBC (1992) *Artshow*. Schools TV recording.

Binch, N. (1994) *Oxford Primary Art*. Oxford: Oxford University Press.

Clement, R. (1994) The readiness of primary schools to teach the NC in art and design. *Journal of Art and Design Education*, 13(1).

Clement, R. and Page, S. (1992) *Primary Art Pack*. Harlow: Oliver & Boyd.

Department for Education (DFE) (1994a) *Final Report on the National Curriculum and its Assessment: the Government's Response* (the Dearing Report). London: HMSO.

Department for Education (DFE) (1994b) *Art in the National Curriculum: Draft Proposals of the SCAA*. London: HMSO.

Department for Education (DFE) (1995) *Art in the National Curriculum (Revised Statutory Orders)*. London: HMSO.

Department of Education and Science (DES) (1990) *Art Working Group Interim Report*. London: HMSO.

Department of Education and Science (DES) (1991) *Art for Ages 5–14: Proposals of the Secretary of State*. London: HMSO.

Department of Education and Science (DES) (1992) *Art in the National Curriculum: Statutory Orders*. London: HMSO.

Development Education Centre (1989) *Get the Picture: Developing Visual Literacy in the Infant Classroom*. Birmingham: Development Education Centre.

Gardner, H. (1980) *Artful Scribbles: the Significance of Children's Drawings*. London: Norman.

Gardner, H. (1990) *Art Education and Human Development*. Los Angeles, CA. Getty Center for Education in Arts.

Jack, M. and Sang, J. (1989) Using original paintings with young children. *Journal of Art and Design Education*, 8(3) 257–73.

Sharp, C. and Dust, K. (1990) *Artists in Schools*. London: NFER.

Wolf, D. and Perry, M. (1988) From endpoints to repertoires. *Journal of Aesthetic Education*, 22(1).

CHAPTER 13

Physical education

Gill Clarke, Ray Leigh and Sara Reed

INTRODUCTION

If we are to have equal opportunities within physical education
(PE), it is important from the outset to acknowledge that
children will bring to the subject differing experiences of
physical activity and also differing expectations of 'appropriate'
gender behaviour. It is likely that due to early socialization
patterns boys in general may have greater physical literacy,
in terms of motor co-ordination and physical skill, than girls
who may not have had access to the same sporting opportunities. Thus, girls may be not only less skilled but also their
self-confidence and self-esteem may not be as high as boys.
Simply to offer boys and girls access to the same curriculum
may not lead to equal opportunities when they are not starting
from the same place. Consideration may therefore have to be
given to providing girls only or boys only sessions where
each can receive experiences which they have not previously
encountered. In association with this there may also be a
need to subject to critical scrutiny our own beliefs and values
about what we think boys and girls can do in PE, since we
may be guilty of perpetuating gender and racial stereotypical
expectations and assumptions about children's physical capa-

cities and aptitudes. If this seems to imply that only issues of 'race' and gender are prevalent it is not the case, but the weight of evidence would suggest that these are the main areas that need addressing at this stage.

In order to facilitate equality of opportunity within PE we believe that it is important to examine and monitor the following:

- curriculum content;
- policy for children with special educational needs (SEN);
- teacher attention, interaction and expectation;
- language usage;
- assessment;
- clothing and changing facilities;
- resources;
- extra-curricular activities.

CURRICULUM CONTENT

It is vital that the activities on offer to pupils are drawn not only from a variety of cultures but also from games and sports that have been traditionally associated with both genders. Otherwise there is a danger that we will continue to promote and sustain the view that sports are for the boys. Indeed there is much evidence that indicates that sport culture is deeply embedded in traditional notions of masculinity (Whannel, 1983). It is against this backdrop that pedagogical practice must be scrutinized if we are to challenge rather than reinforce such damaging and limiting situations. Games should be included that are neither Eurocentric nor ethnocentric. Pupils need to recognize that games are universal, accessible to every child and that we have much to learn from exploring and celebrating others' cultural traditions. Within health-related exercise activities it is also necessary when talking about diet or lifestyle to refer to a range of cultures and traditions. It is important then that the curriculum content selected is appropriate and accessible to pupils of all cultural backgrounds and that cultural norms and religious observances are taken into consideration when planning the programme. Suitable provision should be made for pupils who are fasting or celebrating particular festivals (Runnymede

Trust, 1993). Specific curricular examples will be described later in this chapter.

In recognizing the rights of all children to a PE curriculum devoid of racism, sexism, classism, homophobia and ableism, it is essential that this programme includes children with special educational needs. Indeed, while it may seem unfair to single out a particular group of children, both the Statutory Orders and the Non-Statutory Guidance (DES, 1992) do make specific reference to children with special educational needs. It seems therefore appropriate to begin by examining their provision.

CHILDREN WITH SPECIAL EDUCATIONAL NEEDS

The Physical Education Interim Report (DES, 1991:15–16) stated that children with special educational needs (SEN) are as entitled as all other children to the full National Curriculum. The authors of this Report commented further that equal opportunity requires that teachers treat all children as individuals with their own abilities, difficulties and attitudes. Thus, while it is acknowledged that this will present difficulties for some schools, it is essential that the focus within the lesson is on what the child can do and needs rather than cannot do. The emphasis should be on improving movement skills and changing possible feelings of dissatisfaction, underachievement and low self-esteem (see DES, 1992: E1 on SEN). We endorse the Physical Education Proposals (1991b:35) to the Secretary of State which suggested four principles that should underpin a PE programme for children with SEN: entitlement, accessibility, integration and integrity. In the light of these statements it is essential that the teacher is aware of the implications of the impairment or disability on learning and physical activity. We recognize the difficulties that this may entail but would wish to offer some brief general guidelines for teachers in mainstream schools (see Table 13.1).

Table 13.1   PE guidelines for children with special educational needs

Pupils with visual impairments	Pupils with hearing impairments
• Clear verbal instructions are necessary. • Auditory signals should be given for the end of an activity. • Brightly coloured equipment or balls with bells inside may be useful. • Pupils need to comment on their own performance rather than that of others if they are unable to observe their peers working.	• Instructions should be clear and slow. • Background noise should be reduced. • Visual demonstrations will help clarify communication. • Visual signals should be given for the end of an activity.
Pupils with learning difficulties	**Pupils with emotional and behavioural disorders**
• Complex instructions may need breaking down into smaller achievable tasks. • Allowance for the completion of tasks needs sensitive consideration. • Successful performance requires reinforcement and praise to build up confidence.	• Access to creative opportunities is essential. • Encouragement should be given to move to more independent work. • Working in pairs and groups is to be encouraged. • Emphasis should be on personal and social skills development.
Pupils with physical impairments	**Gifted pupils**
• Modifications may be needed to the task set through alteration of all or some of the following: equipment used (bigger bats/balls, lighter rackets), the rules (bigger/lower targets, shorter distances), and/or the response expected (a ball may be dribbled using the small front wheels of a wheelchair).	• Appropriate challenges should be available through the balance of activities offered and the learning approaches employed.

TEACHER ATTENTION, INTERACTION AND EXPECTATION

It has been well documented how boys receive more teacher attention than girls (Stanworth, 1983) – thus how the curriculum is presented is also important if equity is to be achieved. Teaching methods may require close scrutiny, for example, to check whether there is an over-emphasis on one teaching style (Mosston and Ashworth, 1986) or competitive activities at the expense of more co-operative activities. How activities are delivered and organized will affect children's sporting perceptions, as will the allocation of leadership roles and responsibilities, selections for demonstrations. Who teaches the activities is also important; do female teachers teach soccer, do male teachers teach dance? Equally we need to consider whether we have different physical expectations for boys and girls; do we look for opportunities to praise boys and girls for achievements in activities that are often stereotypically considered to be more appropriate for one sex than the other?

Do we racially stereotype with respect to athletic abilities? It should be noted that there is no biological evidence to support the beliefs that African-Caribbeans cannot be high-level performers in swimming because they are 'natural' sinkers, or that Asians cannot play professional football because they are too small, or that African-Caribbeans are 'natural' sprinters and not likely to be good middle- or long-distance runners (Sports Council, 1994:18).

In terms of groupings we may also want to consider whether for some activities it is appropriate to allow children to work in single sex groups or whether it might be appropriate to group according to skill level.

LANGUAGE USAGE

It may be argued that language is central to all social actions and that through this medium a vision of the world is both constructed and conveyed (Clarke, 1992). Hence it is incumbent upon the teacher to ensure that the sporting vision conveyed to pupils through the medium of speech is one which is devoid of

Table 13.2   Words to avoid

Avoid	Use
he (when used to refer to both sexes)	the pupil, or a neutral noun
last man in	last person in
man to man	one to one, or person to person
sportsman	sportsperson, athlete
sportsmanship	fair play

Table 13.3   Phrases to avoid

Avoid	Use
man-to-man marking	one-to-one marking or person-to-person marking
you throw like a girl/you throw like a boy	you throw correctly
girls' push ups	bent-knee push ups

(hetero) sexist and racist images and terms. Abusive language and homophobic comments should be challenged and countered. It is essential that the language used is inclusive and respects both gender and ethnicity. We must be aware of the power of the spoken word to convey to children messages about the way they perceive not only PE and sport but also how they view themselves and others. Thus, with regard to sexist language, certain words and phrases should be avoided and be replaced by others. See Tables 13.2 and 13.3 for examples which are merely indicative and in no way comprehensive.

ASSESSMENT

Evaluation of children's progress in PE needs careful consideration if teachers are to avoid the promotion of male standards as the norm. Thus, we need to ensure that assessments are neither gender or racially biased and that they are free from comparisons between boys and girls. For example, is flexibility valued as much as strength, is balance and agility as important as speed and strength, and are our testing, recording and reporting systems free from any other biases? It is important that inappropriate encouragement for achievement in PE is not given to pupils to the detriment of their overall educational attainment. We should not assume that skill in PE is determined by ethnicity or gender (Runnymede Trust, 1993). Peer assessment and evaluation needs careful handling so as to avoid the perpetuation of stereotypes with regard to performance; any name calling or racist abuse must be challenged and pupils must be encouraged to be sensitive and respectful of each other's work.

CLOTHING AND CHANGING FACILITIES FOR PE

Clothing needs to be safe and facilitate movement rather than being associated with traditional gender conventions. Pupils should be allowed to wear appropriate clothing that does not cause embarrassment and does not create distinctions between boys and girls (Harris, 1993). It should be affordable and accessible to all pupils (Wilkinson and Hunt, 1992). Attention should also be paid to cultural practices when considering the type of clothing that is considered appropriate; for instance, Muslim pupils should be permitted to wear clothing that safeguards their modesty and decency. In connection with these aforementioned points, if possible, changing facilities should be single sexed.

RESOURCES

The equipment that is available should reflect equal value placed on female and male participation (CAHPER, 1994). Women's sport has traditionally been underrepresented and marginalized by all forms of the media; there is considerable evidence that supports the negative impact of this on girls' and women's participation in sport. Hence, teachers need to analyse resources to check that there is an equal display and portrayal of female and male athletes. It is important too that the images presented are non-stereotypical (i.e. male dancers, African-Caribbean swimmers, female footballers, etc.) Noticeboards and school bulletins need to be monitored for equity. Children need to see sporting heroes and heroines if they are to be encouraged to pursue active leisure time – there are many examples at national level, but it is also worth using local sports personalities.

EXTRA-CURRICULAR ACTIVITIES

Examination should be made of the activities on offer to pupils after school to ensure that there are equal opportunities for participation and that the school policy goes beyond the delivered curriculum. The activities on offer should be open to all pupils, regardless of their sex, ethnicity, class or ability. Pupils should have equal access to equipment, teaching resources and facilities. In connection with this, it is essential that all pupils are encouraged to adopt a healthy and active lifestyle, for it has been well documented elsewhere how girls continue to be in the minority in terms of participation in sports in later life. It is evident that girls are far less likely than boys to participate in team games. We must therefore ensure girls and boys are given equal encouragement to want to continue to participate in sports. It may be necessary to explain to parents/guardians the value of their children participating in extra-curricular activities. It is also clear that access to sport for many Asian, black and other minority ethnic individuals is still disproportionately restricted (Sports Council, 1994). Participation in extra-curricular activities needs careful and sensitive monitoring and where appropriate positive steps need to be taken to ensure that there is access for all.

PROGRAMMES OF STUDY

This section offers various suggestions for providing PE for all. The new 1995 standing orders for PE indicate a reduction of activity areas to three at KS1, namely games, dance and gymnastics, while the original 1992 list still applies at KS2. This does not mean that those areas that may be excluded from KS1, namely athletics and outdoor and adventurous activities, will not be taught, as the expectation is that they would be absorbed into other areas which include the development of complementary activities. For example, jumping skills, which are a part of athletics, would also be frequently found in many games activities and are, in addition, fundamental to both gymnastics and dance.

GAMES

Games at this stage may be seen as a development of play, educating the children in the fundamentals which constitute the structure of all games:

- objectives;
- rules;
- co-operation or competition.

The 1995 Programme of Study (POS) does not refer to any particular game forms so the teacher can have access to a variety of activities which transcend cultural boundaries. It would be appropriate therefore to use children's games from a variety of cultures and not merely to rely on those founded on a predominantly Western culture.

At KS1 children 'should experience elements of games play that include chasing, dodging, avoiding and awareness of space and other players' (DES, 1992:5). Children's play includes many elements that relate to parts of 'major' games. For example, from games like 'tag' or 'tick' comes practice of quick changes of speed and direction fundamental to many games. It is only necessary to identify these elements from within any particular children's game to be able to find value in the activity. Because the choice of content is in the hands of the teacher, then activities should be adopted on the basis of non-gender specificity (Green, 1993).

The main requirement at this stage is to give pupils the opportunity to handle the variety of equipment that they are likely to encounter later when their PE diet will move towards those traditional activities with which games have become associated. This experience is largely intended to be undertaken on an individual basis and provided enough space is available for all pupils to practise (Williams, 1989), there should be a reduction in the tendency for boys to dominate the working area (Green, 1993).

Some activities could be undertaken individually within a large group setting and this would provide an opportunity for both sexes to be encouraged to 'share' working space. In order to 'experience, practise and develop a variety of ways of sending, receiving and travelling with a ball' (DES, 1992) children are now required not only to work alone but by implication to work with a partner or in small groups. A number of writers (Uttley and Sugden, 1994; Nelligan, 1991; Harris, 1993) comment on the importance of grouping pupils along non-gender-specific lines, although it must be recognized that the teacher's grouping strategies will vary from task to task depending upon the objective to be achieved, for example:

- setting according to ability (which will allow for differentiation according to task/difficulty);
- friendship groups (which will allow pupils to work with particular friends chosen by themselves);
- random groupings (which will ensure groups associated on no particular basis).

It is this last area that often brings about undesired results in terms of the way children form into groups. The general tendency is for the groups to form on a gender basis. There are some games like 'numbers' that can help to bring about mixed sex groups. In this game get the children to run about the work area. Tell them that you are going to call out a number and they are to get into groups of that number as quickly as possible.

Children not in correct groups should sit down. Vary the numbers in order to reduce the participants. The competitive nature of the game forces pupils to take the nearest 'partners'. Once the nature of the game is understood by the children it may be used to determine random groups of varying sizes.

Adult traditional games have a tendency to exclude some children. When children are given the opportunity to 'make up and play games' (DES, 1992) they approach the task differently from adults. Their games are often based on their experience of what they can do. Consequently, where pupils with special needs or disabilities are involved in the experience, the game can become inclusive in that everyone is capable of participating. At KS2 children will be moving towards 'small-sided simplified versions of recognised games covering invasion, net/wall and striking/fielding games' (DES, 1992). This brings with it both problems and possibilities; problems in the sense of those that derive from the traditional stereotypical views held about games. Some of these may be overcome by utilizing a variety of strategies of which the following may form part:

- Increase the number of women staff as PE curriculum co-ordinators. This will send messages not only to the pupils but also to parents.

- Promote games activities which are non-gender specific or to which children attach no gender specificity. Many of our games have traditional gender links; for example, rugby for boys, netball for girls. There are new games, such as Korfball or Handball, which have been specifically designed for anyone to play and many governing bodies have developed adaptations of traditional games to include both sexes. Examples of the latter are New Image Rugby, Pop Lacrosse and Mini Soccer ('Mini Soccer is for all youngsters regardless of ability. It is intended for girls and boys, and young footballers with disabilities and learning difficulties' (Russell, 1992:6).
- Condition games to reduce boys' tendency to dominate.
- Concentrate more on the skilful nature of the game rather than its aggressive side.

However, it must be noted that this is not an endorsement for skill-based lessons which have a tendency to focus on the skill being taught and neglect the importance of the game itself.

- Allocate time to all pupils and not merely those who are most demanding.
- Project more positive active images of girls. Display a balance in posters illustrating both males and females.
- Identify female role models to whom pupils may aspire.
- Identify role models from a variety of social or ethnic backgrounds. Oliver Skeet, the show jumper, would fulfil both of these requirements without being stereotypical, although there is nothing wrong with using examples of black/Asian athletes, basketball players, soccer stars or cricketers.
- Avoid comparisons in performance related to gender.
- Use boys and girls equally for demonstrations.
- Examine the provision of extra-curricular activities.

Does it reflect sufficient opportunities for all pupils regardless of gender, class, ability or ethnicity? Some parents of ethnic minority children may attach a low value to extra-curricular activities, particularly since games may clash with the child's need for academic study or religious worship (Daley, 1991).

GYMNASTICS

Gymnastics has attached to it many of the organizational problems associated with games.

- Grouping problems are similar and may be overcome by utilizing similar strategies.
- There must be an alteration in the traditional views regarding the capabilities of boys and girls in gymnastics (Williams, 1989; Green, 1993). Boys should be used to demonstrate movements requiring artistry and flexibility just as you should use girls to demonstrate those movements demanding of strength characteristics.
- Be aware of ethnicity issues relating to contact between pupils of different sexes and the same sex with some religious groups (Daley, 1991).
- The use of teacher or pupil demonstration can greatly assist pupils with special needs to understand the nature of tasks. This can be allied to a breaking down of skills into easily digestible portions and the provision of only sufficient guidance to ensure progress (Beaumont and Gutteridge, 1993).

SWIMMING

This is an activity area which has distinct advantages over others but also contains some problematical features which need to be taken into consideration.

- Swimming is a non-gender-specific activity. It has traditionally been accessible to children of both sexes without problems and can be taught at either KS1 or KS2.
- In a public facility changing would be undertaken on a separate basis, but in a school with its own pool it would not be unusual to see children at KS1 changing together. This ought not to be happening at KS2 where at the top end some children would be pubescent and therefore would require separate changing accommodation.
- Muslim children, in general, may have difficulties coping with communal nakedness, a concept alien to their culture (Sarwar, 1991).

- The question of the removal of jewellery is one that may affect Sikh children who, for example, would not be permitted to remove bangles.

The water-borne environment is one that is particularly helpful to many disabled pupils who have the opportunity to perform to the best of their ability here. This is not to say that all children will feel comfortable and there are some factors that will make the experience even more worthwhile.

- Do not make general assumptions about ability. Beware of putting children at risk.
- The 'buddy' system of working in pairs can be of benefit both to the disabled child and partner.
- Teacher positioning is important when dealing with some special needs both for general safety reasons and for effective communication to take place in an environment that is traditionally difficult.

ATHLETICS

The requirements for athletics identified in the National Curriculum for both KS1 and KS2 speak only of athletics in its most basic forms, namely those activities that involve the skills of running, jumping and throwing. At KS1:4 pupils should: 'experience and be encouraged to take part in running, jumping and throwing activities, concentrating on accuracy, speed, height, length and distance'. These are further broken down so that running may be divided into activities that promote the development of:

- running for speed;
- running for distance;
- running over obstacles;
- relay running.

We can determine jumping as meaning:

- jumping for height;
- jumping for distance;
- combination jumping.

Throwing will involve activities that promote the use of a variety of equipment being handled in appropriate ways in order to send it both over distance and with a modicum of accuracy. This will then approximate to the athletic requirement of keeping implements within the confines of a sector.

It should be noted that none of the requirements specifically mention individual, traditional competition events (the only reference to competition in fact comes in KS2:6, where pupils should 'experience competitions, including those they make up themselves'), and therefore are to be seen as non-gender specific. The issue of which is the most effective way to deliver some of these activities, whether through mixed-sex or single-sex groupings, is not really a vexed one at this stage but it should be noted that there are conflicting views (Millar, 1992; Evans, 1989) regarding this topic as children move out of KS2. It should also be recognized that the very general nature of the requirements would also mean that the vast majority of experiences could be undertaken by all children regardless of ability. However, thare are some activities that children would find difficult to undertake. For example, wheelchair users would find obvious difficulties with certain activities and some might be precluded, such as jumping.

OUTDOOR AND ADVENTUROUS ACTIVITIES

Within this area there is a recognition that traditional activities do not suffer from particular problems of gender specificity and there are many instances of the benefits to be gained by both special needs and disabled pupils from involvement in associated tasks. Indeed, there are societies established such as Riding for the Disabled that espouse the positive value of these.

The Programmes of Study do not seek to promote particular 'hazardous' activities, but rather seek in a general way to develop a feeling for the possibilities available within the 'immediate surroundings' (KS1:4) and a variety of 'different environments (such as school grounds and premises, parks, woodlands or seashore)' (KS2:6).

Should this involve the undertaking of a residential experience, then there may be some problems relating to the value of the experience as perceived by parents, particularly by those of certain religious groups, irrespective of their ethnic background. There may also be a problem of 'ability to pay'. While this should not figure, where schools have available funds to cover those who are unable to help with the 'voluntary contributions' essential in most cases for this type of experience, there is the problem of the stigma that may be associated with having to accept assistance in this matter. Hence some parents may be reluctant to seek help.

DANCE

Equal opportunities are a fundamental right of all children and should be promoted through dance education as part of a whole school policy. The dance policy may be based on the following principles (ACGB, 1993:9): entitlement, accessibility, integration and integrity. To these ends it should address issues of social class, 'race', gender, sexuality, disability and special needs. Dance has a special contribution to make within this context. It offers an alternative method of communication and a different language that has been available to all children at some level. Movement is a common starting-point and one through which children can learn about themselves, others and the world around them (ACGB, 1993).

Children come to dance lessons with different degrees of experience, ability and interests. To treat them all the same does not necessarily constitute equality; it may ignore the very differences from which they can all benefit.

Multicultural education offers an ideal opportunity for teachers in primary schools to explore a multitude of different dance forms. Likewise, dance in the National Curriculum offers teachers the chance to explore different cultures through their various dance forms. Clearly the opportunity exists for children to learn about and understand other cultures apart from their own. However, how many teachers are fully aware of these opportunities and the resources available to them? The updated statutory orders for dance, under physical education, state at KS1 that children should 'perform movements or patterns, including some from existing dance traditions' (SCAA, 1994).

This can be interpreted in the widest possible sense to embrace any traditional dances performed within the British Isles, including those from different cultures. Similarly KS2 states that children should be taught 'a number of dance forms from different times and places, including some traditional dances of the British Isles'. The requirement that children are taught dances from different cultures is much more explicit than in the previous orders and it offers a clearer sense of equality if interpreted in its widest sense.

Dance can offer a very positive move towards combating racism among children which is so often fuelled by ignorance. Stereotypes associated with particular ethnic groups should be challenged, for example, preconceptions about natural ability or rhythm in certain people can negate true achievement (ACGB, 1993:10). Within the local community, there may be people of different ethnic groups already involved with the school who would be willing to share the dances of their culture; examples may be the role of rhythm in African, Asian or Flamenco dance. The use of 'Mudras' (hand gestures) in Indian classical dance may be explored in relation to story-telling; the importance of music in Flamenco dance or the significance of myths and legends in some African dances, may be used as starting-points for lessons or units of work. Dance on video can be helpful in demonstrating different dance forms. If possible, a visit by a professional dance company can provide positive role models as well as an exciting and memorable introduction to a particular dance form. Opportunities for working with dance companies and artists are outlined in the Arts Council's booklet *Dance In Schools* (see Resources). When choosing starting-points for dance, it is important to explore the wealth of music, art, literature and artefacts available from different cultures as a stimulus for creativity. Exploration of a variety of dance forms need not emphasize their differences but rather their similarities and the fact that people of all ages, abilities and backgrounds have always danced, still dance and will continue to dance.

For many years, children with special needs have been part of mainstream education; some will have formally recognized difficulties and others will not. Uttley and Sugden point out that teaching PE to children with special needs is 'an extension of good practice rather than the acquiring of new and distinctly different skills and techniques ' (1994:12). All children can and should be integrated into dance activities. Particular care needs to be given to some children, for example, those with spina bifida who may not have any feeling in their legs; limbs can be easily bruised and skin damaged, sometimes taking weeks, if not months, to heal (Groves, 1994). However, this should not prevent these children from taking part in dance lessons which can give them a rare chance to participate in a physical activity on an equal basis with their peers. Some asthmatic children may feel nervous about taking part in physical activities but encouragement to join in dance classes can lead to an improvement in posture, breathing and self-esteem. Adequate warm-up activities and changes in the pace of the class and methods of delivery are important in any dance lesson, but they are particularly pertinent for children with disabilities, whether these are due to physical and/or learning difficulties.

Wheelchairs can be included in dances and may be used as a focal point for a dance; a partner to help move the wheelchair at certain times is just as important as a partner in any duet. Tasks relating to such things as balance, travelling, turning, stillness and most other areas of the Programmes of Study for KS1 and KS2 can be included in any integrated dance class, whether children are in or out of wheelchairs. At any stage, starting with the capabilities of the individuals in the class is the key to accessibility; using familiar movements builds confidence, trust and competence. Exploring movements on the floor, for example, rolling, stretching, curling, rising, sinking, feels safe to begin with and helps to develop control, co-ordination, balance and poise. For children with physical disabilities the exploration of pair and group work is particularly valuable in helping to build confidence and increase the range of movements that are possible. For example, trust exercises in pairs and tasks based on balance, which can be developed into interesting duets or small group dances, provide suitable material for all abilities at KS1 and KS2.

Sensitivity needs to be shown by the teacher in relation to cultural practices, when children are required to touch and work in close physical proximity to each other. Patterns may be explored by travelling around the space alone or in pairs and rhythm can be developed by using different body parts as a response to music; working on a sprung or wooden floor may be helpful to children with a hearing impairment. Children with learning difficulties may find dance an area where they can 'shine' and develop their ability to communicate, providing them with a sense of satisfaction and achievement that may have been very limited in other areas of their school lives; often they respond particularly well in this area of non-verbal communication. Dance companies, for example Candoco, who have disabled dancers in their company and Green Candle, who work with disabled dancers, are excellent role models for children and both companies tour around the country performing and giving workshops. Companies are usually happy to provide information for schools on request and sometimes leaflets/posters illustrating their work for display on notice boards.

Dance can be used to change the status quo by challenging the myth of its being essentially a female activity. Because feminine practices are rejected in the development of masculinity, dance is seen, by many, as problematic for boys, by boys and by some girls, teachers and parents. Many of the problems associated with boys and dance at the end of KS2 and the beginning of secondary education in particular, and beyond, may be greatly diminished by sensitive and informed teaching in the primary school. The place of dance in the social construction of masculinity, femininity and sexuality needs to be carefully considered in the planning and content of lessons. The new emphasis on traditional dances of the British Isles in the revised Programme of Study for dance at Key Stages 1 and 2, although a positive move in relation to ethnic dances, may increase the potential for problems in these other areas.

Traditional partnering, as seen in some British folk dances, may need to be challenged, for example partners could be numbered 1 and 2 rather than labelled as boy and girl, in order to discourage gender stereotypes and reluctance to join in by some children. Teachers should be prepared to challenge any other stereotyping of male and female roles. Dance at this stage provides an ideal opportunity for teachers to dispel those myths associated with femininity and masculinity. Stephens (1991) points out that negative attitudes towards dance, by children, parents and teachers, because of ill-informed and preconceived ideas should be a thing of the past. Meiners (1993) reminds us that the issue in relation to boys dancing is not one of gender but of masculinity. The inclusion of positive role models at this stage is extremely valuable and may be achieved in various ways, for example, by looking at male and female dancers on video or in live performances and giving children the chance to discuss their roles and performance styles.

There are various contemporary choreographers whose work is particularly accessible and available on video, for example: Richard Alston, Siobhan Davies, Jiri Kylian, Shobana Jeyasingh, Adzido and Lea Anderson. These choreographers' works and others also offer a vast potential for cross-curricular activities which may be topic linked. Other ways of providing positive role models may be to include male teachers in dance activities within schools and by inviting dance companies who can provide a male dancer/teacher to work with children.

CHECKLIST FOR GOOD PRACTICE IN DANCE LESSONS

- Are the ideas/movements you teach equally accessible to all?
- Do you use a wide range of examples of different dances with positive role models for both boys and girls?
- Do you use both boys and girls to demonstrate and show work?
- Do you use boys to demonstrate good work in relation to sensitivity, grace, gentleness?
- Do you discourage gendered movement ideas and boys' and girls' roles within dances?
- Do you use girls to demonstrate strength, agility, power?
- Do you use a variety of warm-up activities appropriate and accessible to all?
- Do you use a wide variety of starting-points for dance lessons drawing ideas from different cultures and backgrounds, for example, artefacts, stories, poems, pictures, music, video?
- Do you question your own assumptions in relation to dance? For example, who dances? What is their role in dance? How do they dance? How important is their body shape?
- Do you recognize that teachers and children can both bring prejudices to the classroom?

- Do you encourage children to work in mixed-sex groups?
- Do you differentiate in order to establish equality of access within your lessons?
- Do you encourage all pupils to watch and discuss each other's work and to listen to each other?

CONCLUSION

The issues raised in this chapter have highlighted the need for teachers to monitor carefully their own actions, perceptions and pupil expectations if PE is to become open to all regardless of ethnicity, sex, ability, and/or social class. Without this critical self-examination and reflection, PE is likely to remain a subject on the sideline for the able few.

RESOURCES AND USEFUL ADDRESSES

Academy of Indian Dance, 16 Flaxman Terrace, London WC1H 9AT.
Arts Council of England, 14 Great Peter Street, London SW1P 3NQ.
Cheshire Dance Workshop; Laurie Grove, London SE14 6NH.
Dance Books Ltd, 9 Cecil Court, London WC2N 4EZ.
English National Ballet, Education and Community Unit, Markova House, 39 Jays Mews, London SW7 2ES.
Green Candle, Room 309, 22–24 Highbury Grove, London N5 2EA.
The Laban Centre for Movement and Dance, Laurie Grove, New Cross, London SE14 6NH.
National Dance Teachers' Association, 29 Larkspur Avenue, Charetown, Walsall, Staffordshire WS7 8SR.
National Resource Centre for Dance, University of Surrey, Guildford, Surrey GU2 5XH.
Race Apart, 19b Albert Road, Teddington, Middlesex TW11 0BD
Sports Council, 16 Upper Woburn Place, London WC1H 0QP.
Women's Sports Foundation, Wesley House, 4 Wild Court, London WC2B 4AU.

ACTION

For a comprehensive list of resources, addresses and other relevant information see The Arts Council booklet *Dance in Schools*, available free of charge from the Arts Council.
Join the National Dance Teachers Association to receive their termly journal *Dance Matters*.
Contact the National Resource Centre for Dance at the University of Surrey for extensive information on resources including, books, videos and information packs.

REFERENCES

ACGB (1993) *Dance in Schools*. Spring, ACGB.

Arts Council of England (1994) *Dance in Schools*. London: Arts Council of England.

Askew, S. and Ross, C. (1989) *Boys Don't Cry: Boys and Sexism in Education*. Oxford: Oxford University Press.

Beaumont, G. and Gutteridge, K. (1993) Physical Education and Children with Learning Difficulties. *Bulletin of Physical Education*, 29(3):18–22.

Canadian Association for Health, Physical Education and Recreation (CAHPER) (1994) *Gender Equity Through Physical Education*. Gloucester, Ontario: CAHPER.

Clarke, G. (1992) Learning the language: Discourse analysis in physical education. In A. C. Sparkes (ed.) *Research in Physical Education and Sport: Exploring Alternative Visions*. London: Falmer Press.

Daley, D. (1991) Multicultural issues in PE. *British Journal of Physical Education*, 22(1):31–3.

Department for Education and Science (DES) (1991a) *National Curriculum Physical Education Working Group, Interim Report*. London: DES.

Department for Education and Science (DES) (1991b) *Physical Education for Ages 5–16*. London: DES.

Department for Education and Science (DES) (1992) *Physical Education in the National Curriculum*. London: DES.

Evans, J. (1989) Swinging from the Crossbar. Equality and Opportunity in the PE Curriculum. *British Journal of Physical Education*, 20(2): 84–8.

Green, K. (1993) Primary practice and the gender bias in PE. *Bulletin of Physical Education*, 29 (2): 31–6.

Groves, L. (1994) Specific Disabilities 2. *Primary Focus*, Autumn.

Harris, J. (1993) Challenging sexism and gender bias in physical education. *Bulletin of Physical Education*, 29(1):29–36 Spring.

Meiners, J. (1993) The dancing man. *Animated*, Summer, 6–8.

Millar, B. (1992) The National PE curriculum and femininity: Breaking the mould or continuing the trend? *British Journal of Physical Education*, 23(1):31–3.

Mosston, M. and Ashworth, S. (1986) *Teaching Physical Education*. New York: Merrill Publishing Company.

Nelligan, C. (1991) Equal opportunity in PE. *Bulletin of Physical Education*, 27(1):12–14.

Runnymede Trust (1993) *Equality Assurance in Schools*, Stoke-on-Trent: Trentham Books.

Russell, R. (1992) *Mini Soccer Handbook*. London: FA Publications.

Sarwar, G. (1991) *British Muslims and Schools: Proposals for Progress*. London: Muslim Educational Trust.

Schools Curriculum and Assessment Council (1994) *The National Curriculum Orders*. York: SCAA.

Sports Council (1994) *Black and Ethnic Minorities and Sport Policy and Objectives*. London: Sports Council.

Stanworth, M. (1993) *Gender and Schooling*. London: Hutchinson.

Stevens, S. (1991) Current issues in dance education. *British Journal of Physical Education*, 22 (4), Winter.

Uttley, A. and Sugden, D. (1994) Special education needs and primary physical education. *Primary Focus*, Summer:12–14.

Whannel, G. (1983) *Blowing the Whistle: The Politics of Sport*. London: Pluto Press.

Wilkinson, S. and Hunt, M. (1992) *Equal Opportunities and Special Educational Needs in Physical Education*. Hereford: Hereford and Worcester Education Department.

Williams, A. (1989) Equal Opportunities and Primary School Physical Education. *British Journal of Physical Education*, 20(4):177–81.

Williams, A. (1991) Foundation subject: physical education. In P. D. Pumfrey and G. K. Verma (eds) *The Foundation Subjects and Religious Education in Primary Schools*. London: Falmer Press.

PART 4

RELIGIOUS EDUCATION, SEX EDUCATION AND CROSS-CURRICULAR ISSUES KEY STAGES 1 AND 2

CHAPTER 14

Religious education

Ruth Mantin

Religious education (RE) is in many ways, and in many senses of the word, 'peculiar'. It was the only subject designated as compulsory by the 1944 Education Act. This was largely to do with the 'compromise' reached between the Church and State, as the latter took over responsibility for education, especially primary education, from the former. A quotation from one of the first Agreed Syllabuses[1] conveys the function of religious instruction (RI), as it was then called.

> The aim of the syllabus is to secure that children attending the schools of the country ... may gain knowledge of the common Christian faith held by their fathers for nearly 2,000 years; may seek for themselves in Christianity principles which give a purpose to life and a guide to all its problems; and may find inspiration, power and courage to work for their welfare, and for the growth of God's kingdom.
>
> (Surrey, 1945)

This extract demonstrates the view that the attempt to nurture children into the Christian faith was regarded as an appropriate exercise for state schools to undertake. There was some dissent from this view, for instance from the British Humanist Association, but the majority of post-war British society agreed with it (Wedderspoon, 1966:19–20). The phrase 'common Christian faith held by their fathers' reflects the relationship between the teaching of religion in schools and an attempt to convey a sense of 'cultural heritage'. This is just one small example of the many ways in which religion has been and still is used by those in power to legitimize a particular view of society, often to perpetuate situations of injustice and oppression. Some of the most obvious examples of this are the roles of religion in maintaining slavery, colonialism, apartheid and the caste system. As one writer puts it so succinctly: 'The easiest and most efficient way for small numbers to oppress large numbers of people is to sell them a religion' (Christ and Plaskow, 1979:271).

Religion has also been the inspiration for those challenging the power structures which maintain oppression, for instance liberation theologians[2]. However, justifying the role of RE in the primary curriculum poses a considerable challenge to those advocating an education which promotes equality. This chapter argues that RE has a contribution to make towards an education for equality because an alternative approach to the aim of the subject has emerged in the last twenty years. The multi-faith and multi-cultural nature of this new approach is the most obvious aspect of its role in an education for equality, but I wish to argue that its implications are wider than this and relate to all forms of inequality and discrimination.

By the 1960s changes in the nature and understanding of society and education led to more questioning of the suitability and ethics of the 'confessional'[3] approach illustrated by the quotation from the Surrey Agreed Syllabus. Developments in the theory of education, as illustrated by the Newsom Report in 1963, challenges to traditional expressions of theology, and the changes in society introduced by the increased numbers of members from Asian, black and other minority ethnic communities led to a reassessment of the role of religious education in schools. In 1971 the Schools Council Working Paper 36 provided a comprehensive critique of the confessional approach to religious education and argued that the only legitimate criteria for the inclusion of RE in the school curriculum were educational ones. The report was chaired by Professor Ninian Smart who had just introduced the first 'Religious Studies' (as opposed to Theology) degree at Lancaster University. He applied the same approach to RE in schools as was practised in the Religious

Studies degree at Lancaster (i.e. that the aim of the subject was not to convert pupils or nurture them into a faith but to help them understand the phenomenon of religion as an aspect of human experience). In 1969 the Shap Working Party was formed, which helped to develop resources and teaching strategies for the teaching of multi-faith RE. This 'phenomenonological'[4] approach or 'world religions' approach is reflected in the aims of RE stated in the Agreed Syllabuses produced after 1970, for example:

> The principal aim of religious education in schools within the public sector is to enable pupils to understand the nature of religious beliefs and practices, and the importance and influence of these in the lives of believers.
>
> (Hampshire, 1978)

Within the world of specialists in religious education, therefore, there was a radical change in the perception of the aims of the subject. As the world religions approach developed, its role in contributing towards a multi-cultural and anti-racist education was emphasized. In 1985 the Swann Report, *Education for All*, stated that RE has:

> a central role in preparing pupils for life in today's multi-racial Britain and can also lead them to a greater understanding of the diversity of the global community ... R.E. can also contribute towards challenging and countering the influence of racism in our society.
>
> (Swann, 1985:496)

The potential role of RE in promoting a respect for a diversity of beliefs and cultures was specifically stated as part of the aim in some of the Agreed Syllabuses produced just before the 1988 Education Act. For example, the Brent Agreed Syllabus of 1986 states that the aim of RE is:

> To acquire knowledge of and gain understanding of, and respect for, the beliefs of others.
> To help to develop positive attitudes towards, and a sensitive understanding of, the demands of living in a multi-faith society.
>
> (London Borough of Brent, 1986)

One of the paradoxes of religious education is that although specialists believe a 'revolution' to have taken place in the understanding of the nature of the subject, this revolution has not reached the majority of classrooms, especially primary school classrooms, more than twenty years later. On the one hand, religious education was a pioneer of multi-faith and multi-cultural education, on the other, the reality of what actually takes place in the classroom very often reinforces sexist and ethnocentric, if not racist, attitudes. The 1988 Education Act presented a golden opportunity to remove the anomalies surrounding the role of religious education and confirm its educational aims. Once again, however, the statements about RE reflected a compromise, this time largely between right-wing politicians and educationalists. The subject remained locally, rather than nationally, agreed and the right of withdrawal for pupils and teachers remained, suggesting a 'confessional' element. There was, however, some hope given to the educationalists by the phrase: 'New local agreed syllabuses must reflect the fact that religious traditions in Great Britain are in the main Christian whilst taking account of the teaching and practices of other principal religions in Great Britain' (Education Reform Act, 1988:6).

Furthermore, when the Schools Curriculum and Assessment Authority (SCAA) produced their model syllabuses in 1994, they confirmed the need for pupils to encounter all the 'principal religions' of this country by the completion of their education. This document does not have the legal standing of an Agreed Syllabus but, nevertheless, has considerable status. Its introduction includes a summary of the aims of RE – compiled from a survey of all the country's Agreed Syllabuses. It includes the claim that RE should help pupils to 'develop a positive attitude towards other people, respecting their right to hold different beliefs from their own, and towards living in a society of diverse religions' (SCAA, 1994:4).

The debate about what is meant by 'in the main Christian' still continues, but the fact remains that the legally enforced statements about RE should play a key role in helping children to live in a diverse society and in consciously countering racist attitudes. Even with this opportunity, however, teachers committed to an education for equality are faced with a dilemma. If they are to adopt the 'phenomenological' or 'world religions' approach to religious education, they have to reconcile the process of helping children understand a variety of religions – on those religions' own terms – with the fact that many of those religions, implicitly or even explicitly, provide teaching on issues such as the nature of women, homosexuality and mental and physical disability which run counter to the aims of an education promoting equality. Furthermore, primary school teachers especially have to consider how they are going to lay the foundations of understanding in their approach to RE on which their pupils can build in order to reach a later stage at which they can discuss the relationship between religious teaching and issues of feminism, sexuality, disability and of social class and social justice.

In this chapter I am going to argue that an open, child-centred and multi-faith approach to religious education can present pupils with a celebration of diversity. Children can thereby be provided with an environment in which their individuality is acknowledged and affirmed, in which differences of belief, practice and lifestyle are not considered threatening and in which they can learn to understand and respect the world views of others without feeling that they have to agree with them. In this way, pupils are being educated to suspect definitions of the causes of inequality which attribute them to the teaching of 'someone else's' religion. They may, for instance, often hear that Islam is responsible for the oppression of women in some Muslim countries or that Hinduism is the reason for poverty and social discrimination in parts of India. Not only are these over-simplistic definitions a convenient cover for racist attitudes, they conceal the fact that situations of inequality are created by the exercise of power by the dominant group over those they oppress. This is true regardless of faith or culture – religion is used to legitimize such oppression.

If primary school teachers are going to join their pupils in a celebration of diversity, they need to introduce them to a variety of religious traditions from the very beginning of Key Stage 1. There is considerable resistance to this idea among many teachers, and even more so among right-wing politicians. The infamous phrase 'mish-mash' was constantly used in the debate surrounding the place of RE in the 1988 Education Act, suggesting that children received a great deal of 'disjointed' information about many religions, so that they failed properly to understand any (Hull, 1990:121). In reality the OFSTED Report on Religious Education, published in March 1994, claimed that many pupils were not provided with sufficient teaching about religions other than Christianity – especially at Key Stages 1 and 2.

Another common argument against a multi-faith approach to RE at Key Stages 1 and 2 is that children are unable to cope with the concepts necessary to understand a variety of religious positions. This is, however, true of every area of the curriculum. It is, of course, necessary to approach the material in a way which is appropriate to the relevant Key Stage. This chapter will explore some of the relevant teaching strategies and learning experiences. The experience of this writer is that young children have a greater ability than most adults to 'celebrate diversity'. Indeed I would argue that it is the 'hidden curriculum' of most primary school education which teaches children to find diversity threatening and unacceptable. If a school does not include a variety of religious traditions in its religious education and collective worship, it is condoning racism 'by omission'. If only one culture is acknowledged by the school, the message being given is that no other culture or faith is worthy of the school's attention.

The truth of this situation was confirmed for me through my work in primary schools when I first became a lecturer, ten years ago. I worked with a class of 6-year-olds in a first school in a rural area. It was the first time that multi-faith religious education had been introduced into the school. There was only one child who came from a minority ethnic group; he was not in the class I taught. He came from Sri Lanka and the school had not tried to discover his religious background. They sincerely believed, as so many primary schools wrongly do, that the best way to counter racism was to 'treat him just the same as everyone else'.

With my class, I explored the concept of 'celebration'. We began with celebrations with which they were familiar and quickly moved on to birthdays. We discussed the fact that each child's birthday was a 'celebration' to remember the day they were born by all those who considered them 'special', their family and friends. I then introduced the idea that some people were considered so special that their birth was celebrated by not only family and friends but also by people all over the world, even though they were born a long time ago. As it was the summer term, I used the celebrations surrounding the birth of Krishna and of the Buddha as examples.

The children could respond easily to the stories and art I presented from Hindu and Buddhist traditions. They had an instinctive appreciation of symbolism. To them, if someone was blue, or surrounded by rainbows, this conveyed the fact that they were considered 'special'. The children often introduced what they knew about the birth of Jesus into the discussions. On a memorable occasion, one child posed the question: 'But who is the most special – baby Jesus or baby Krishna?'.

As my educational life flashed before my eyes, I took a deep breath and prepared to tackle this awesome question. Before I had a chance to speak, another 6-year-old replied: 'Baby Jesus is special to some people and baby Krishna is special to others'. The rest of the class nodded their agreement and the discussion continued without the need for my intervention.

Our work on 'celebration' culminated in a class assembly, in which the pupils proudly shared their work with the rest of the school. As the class returned to the area, a little boy came charging through the open-plan school to speak to them. He was the boy from Sri Lanka, normally very quiet and shy, but on this occasion so excited that he could hardly get his words out fast enough. 'You were talking about the Lord Buddha – and no one has ever talked about him before – and I follow the Lord Buddha's teaching – and last year I saw the Festival of the Tooth.'

The joy on his face brought home to me just how much it meant to him as an individual to have his tradition acknowledged, affirmed and celebrated by the school. Even more, it exposed how powerful was the message conveyed by silence and by the absence of this acknowledgement – not only to him but also to every child in the school.

Furthermore many of the topics popular in the First School can help to reinforce this message. Unless handled carefully, topics such as 'Ourselves' or 'Homes' can present a stereotypical view of what 'home' or 'family' means. Not only does this reinforce social 'norms' with regard to concepts such as the patriarchal family, heterosexual relationships, middle-class values and the 'invisibility' of people with physical or mental disabilities, it also often alienates children in the class whose own experience does not allow them to identify with the 'norm'. Instead multi-faith religious education allows the teacher to present a celebration of diversity through which children can see

---

Religion in the Hindu Home

By learning about the shrine and daily puja in many Hindu homes, children can appreciate the function of ritual and symbol in religious expression. The teacher needs to convey the fact that murtis (the representatives of the divine) are not being worshipped themselves but are the focus for devotion. The Hindu family treats the murtis as honoured quests in order to express their devotion to the Supreme Reality. Ask children to imagine that their home was to be visited by the person they would most like to meet. How would they welcome them? Show that the same respect is shown to the murtis.

Religion in the Jewish Home

An exploration of the significance of the weekly welcoming of Shabbat also introduces children to the function of symbol and ritual. It also conveys the distinctive emphasis on family and community in the Jewish tradition.

Figure 14.1   Homes (Lower Key Stage 2). Examples of the ways in which the RE element of a topic on 'Homes' can help children understand religious concepts in general and the perspective of a specific tradition in particular.

that 'home' and 'family' can mean different things to different people and learn to respect those differences (see Figure 14.1).

As with all areas of the curriculum, it is of course important that children encounter these ideas in a way which is appropriate to Key Stage 1. The teacher needs to start with an explanation of ideas which are within the children's own experience. For instance the concept of 'specialness' (see Figure 14.2). Children can discuss the places, people, times and objects which are special to them and from there learn to appreciate and respect what is 'special' to others. In doing this, teachers need to avoid using terms such as 'us' and 'them' and using Christocentric or Eurocentric examples as the norm (for example, 'our Christmas' or 'Arabic is written backwards'). One of the most accessible ways into understanding a religious tradition is through a focus on an individual child. Videos or books can be used to 'introduce' the class to a particular child and thereby to the particular places, people, times and objects which are special to 'him' or 'her'. (The 'My Belief' series are particularly suitable for this exercise: see Resources.)

Terms such as 'Hinduism' or 'the Jews' may be meaningless to

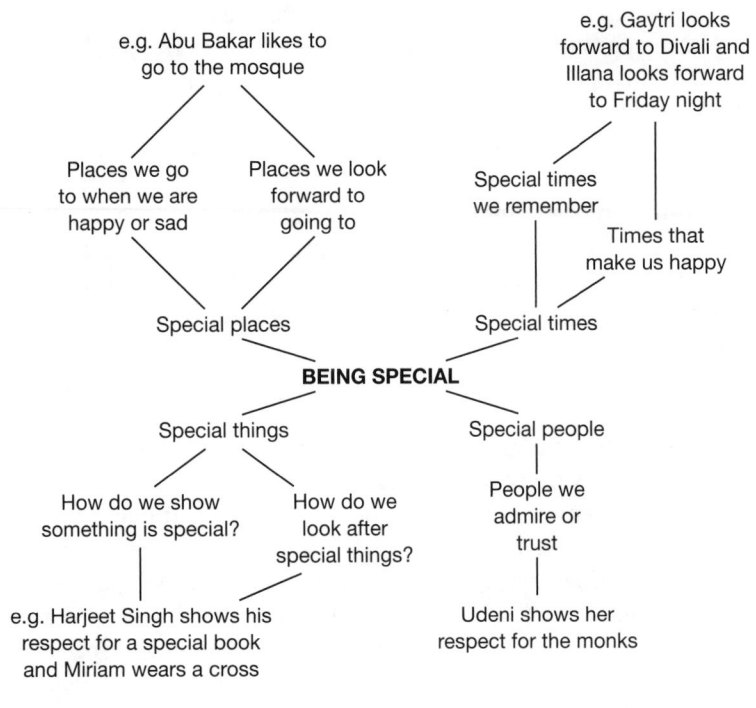

Figure 14.2 Being special (Lower Key Stage 1). An RE focused topic to help pupils develop an understanding of religious concepts, respect for beliefs and concerns of others, and their own self-esteem. This could be part of a larger theme such as 'Ourselves'.

Key Stage 1 children, but they can identify with 'Gaytri' or 'Illana' who is a child living in Britain. On no account, however, should children in the class be used as 'examples'. Children should not be 'spotlighted' and expected to explain their religious tradition to others. This is a difficult task to expect of an adult, let alone a child. More importantly, however, children should not be made to feel that they are being used as an example of something which is not relevant to the class as a whole. The teacher and the class are together learning about a religious tradition because it is worthy of attention, irrespective of the belief or otherwise of the teacher or pupils. When a religious tradition is explored in this way, it is very likely that individual children who identify with it will want to express this and provide an invaluable contribution to the lesson.

These approaches are, of course, as relevant to the teaching of Christianity as of any other world religion. Despite the claims of the political right, until recently, Christianity has not actually been taught in schools but has been transmitted as an assumed 'cultural heritage' (Cole and Mantin, 1994:7–11). As part of an education which promotes equality, religious education needs to show that Christianity is a multi-cultural religion. It needs to challenge the message that Jesus was a white European and counter the message that Christian values are by necessity the values of the middle class or of those in power.

A method by which to meet these aims and which is appropriate for the primary classroom is the use of Christian art. It is possible to acquire posters and artefacts which depict Jesus as belonging to a variety of cultures. Two sources for such material are the Christian Education Movement and Traidcraft (see Resources). In this material, Jesus is also shown as identifying with the political struggle of the 'under class' against oppression in areas such as Latin America and Haiti.

Another approach to Religious Education which is especially appropriate to Key Stage 1 is through an exploration of religious festivals. The celebration of diversity presented in Key Stage 1 can then be explored further at Key Stage 2 (see Figure 14.3). Many of the topics used to present the curriculum at this stage reflect aspects of human experience such as 'Journeys', 'Buildings', 'Clothes' (see Figure 14.4). The central elements of life such as 'Food', 'Water' or 'Light' are also used as the subjects for exploration. There is a religious dimension to all of these for millions of people. If teachers omit this dimension, they are not only missing the opportunity of some excellent religious education, they are also failing to explore fully the subject of the topic. Unless children appreciate the symbolic, ritual and celebratory use of food, for instance, they do not fully understand the place of food in the experience of millions of their fellow human beings.

When RE exists in the curriculum in the way described, it has a very important role to play in countering racist attitudes and other forms of discrimination. The approach advocated here demands that religions are understood on their own terms. Hinduism must be presented from a Hindu perpsective, Islam from a Muslim point of view, and so on. At primary school,

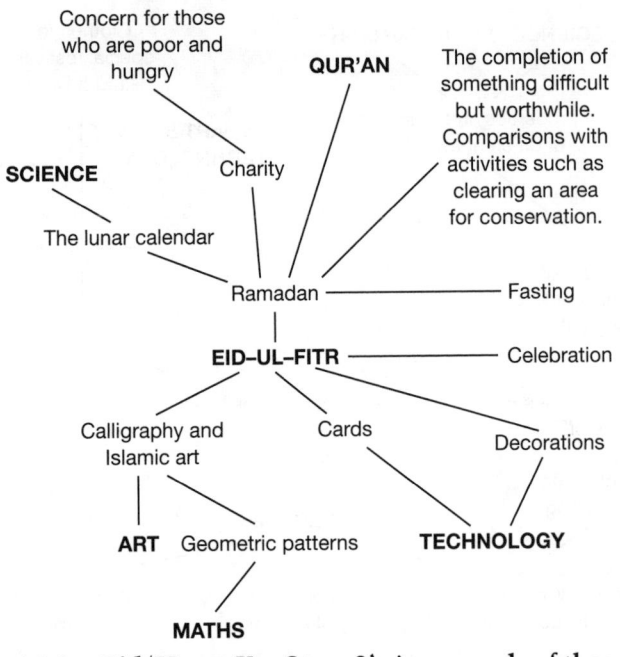

Figure 14.3 *Eid* (Upper Key Stage 2). **An example of the way in which an RE focused topic can provide cross-curricular links. It is important that the significance of the festival of** *Eid* **for Muslims is conveyed, in order to provide an understanding of the Muslim world view and to avoid superficiality.**

therefore, children need to be given a positive picture of these traditions and provided with positive role models of members from Asian, black and other minority ethnic communities. In this way, religious education can help to counter negative messages conveyed by the media about them. This does not mean that as they reach a later stage in their education, pupils cannot exercise a critical analysis of the teachings or practices of different religions, indeed such a preparation lays the foundation for an understanding of the relationship between social and ethical issues and religious belief.

Furthermore, I have argued that to create an environment in the primary school in which religious diversity is celebrated is to lay the foundations for an education in which all forms of difference and individuality are respected. This does, however, leave those who advocate both religious education and an education for

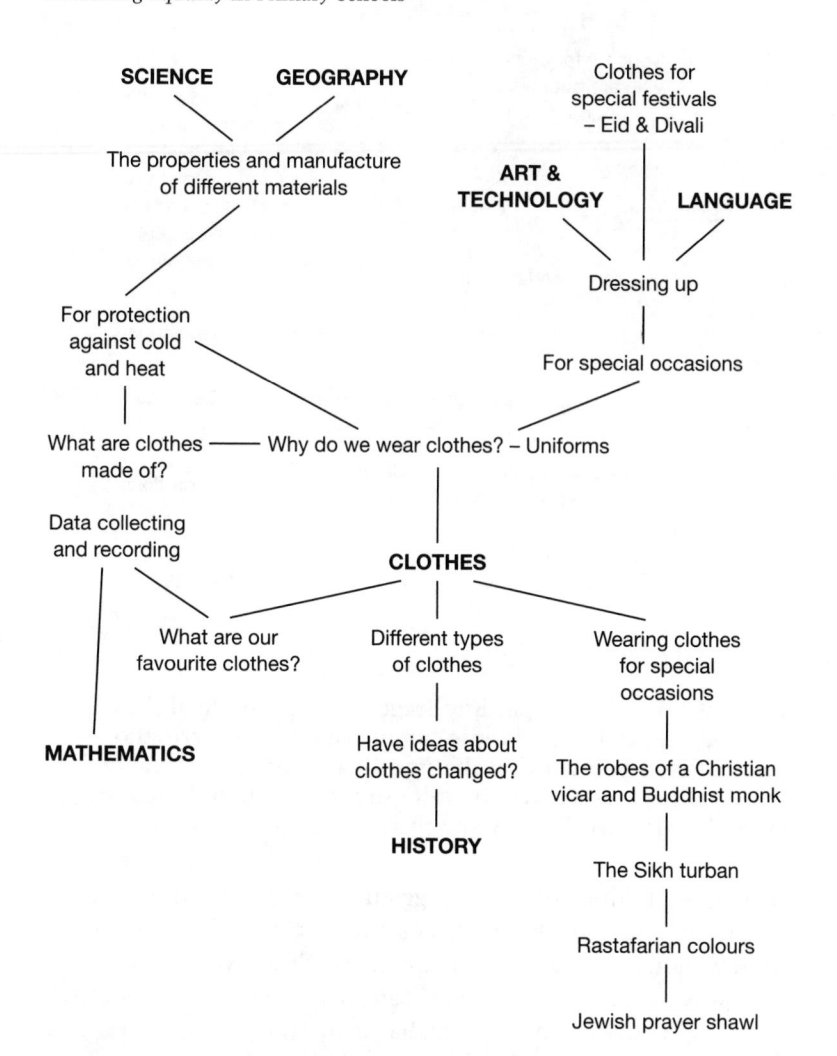

Figure 14.4   Clothes (Upper Key Stage 1) An example of how RE can contribute to a cross-curricular theme.

equality with something of a dilemma. If religions are to be presented 'on their own terms' does this mean we must condone attitudes which present the natures of men and women as fundamentally different, and homosexuality as an 'aberration' or a 'sin', attitudes which present disability and poverty as the objects of 'charity' rather than issues of civil rights and social justice?

First, I would want to argue that attempting to understand a belief is not the same as 'condoning it'. I have already argued that the attempt to understand someone's 'world view' is the first step towards enabling a meaningful discussion with them. I would, nevertheless, go further and argue that religious education in the primary school can play a more positive role in presenting an education for equality. This can be achieved through the use of story.

An important aspect of understanding religion is understanding the role of story as a means of expressing truth as it is understood by the storyteller. Storytelling is a powerful and central aspect of human experience in religious cultures. Our post-Englightenment secular culture does not, however, value 'story' in the same way. Most Key Stage 1 children would ask the question 'is it true or is it just a story?'. In this world view, 'truth' and 'story' have become mutually exclusive. 'Truth' is defined as 'historical accuracy'. This is a rather limited view of 'truth' compared to other cultures, where the 'truth' of a story lies not in its historical accuracy but the extent to which it expresses 'the way the world is'.

Religious education therefore needs to help children realize the power of storytelling, in order to understand the function of stories, such as creation of narratives, in a religious tradition. In helping children to appreciate the power of story, however, RE can help them to understand the ways in which power operates in society to create and sustain inequality. An explanation of story can help children to appreciate that there are many different ways of seeing the world, expressed in different stories, expressing different 'truths'. The story which is told most determines the way in which the world is understood – 'history is written by the winners'. Those who have the power can prevent others from telling their stories and so render them 'invisible' or 'demonize' them. The reclaiming of their own stories, history and 'world view' is therefore a vital aspect in the struggle of all marginalized groups to claim their right to equality.

The reclaiming of story is a central issue in the feminist study of religion, for instance:

> We have learned that our stories have been dominated by the fathers, Augustine, Moses, Muhammad, Shiva – and that we must reclaim the mothers too: Hildegard, Vashti, Rabia and Devi, if those stories are to be complete.
>
> (Harris and Moran, 1989:45)

Another writer argues, therefore, that because women have been denied access to the process of telling stories,

> there is a very real sense in which the seemingly paradoxical statement 'Women have not experienced their own experience' is true.
>
> (Christ, 1980:4–5)

The feminist study of religion is therefore proclaiming the women who have been rendered invisible by religious history and reclaiming the power and authority of women which has been demonized by religious stories.

There are many picture books available for use with young children which can prepare them for an exploration of these issues. At Key Stage 1 a book which tackles 'head on' the effect of society's 'stories' on sexism and racism is *Amazing Grace* (Hoffman, 1991). The book begins with the words 'Grace is a girl who loves stories'. Grace is a clever, talented Afro-Caribbean girl who loves to hear stories and then re-enact them. She notices that most of the best parts are male – but she plays them anyway. Her mother and grandmother support her view that she can do anything that she sets out to achieve. She finds however, that her wish to play Peter Pan in the school play forces her to confront the assumptions of others about her suitability to be the hero of the story. Her fellow pupils tell her that to be Peter Pan you have to be male and white. In the end, however, her grandmother's support and Grace's own ability and determination ensure that she gets the part and goes on to make a wonderful black, female Peter Pan.

A book suitable for Key Stage 1–2 which also deals with the power of stories and their effect on 'world views' is *The Whale's Song* (Sheldon, 1990). This is a picture book with excellent illustrations by Gary Blythe which begins with the central character, Lily, listening to the stories of her grandmother. She learns that 'once upon a time' the ocean was filled with whales who were the most wondrous creatures you could imagine. Her grandmother tells her that she used to see and hear the whales. If she gave them something special they would give in return, sometimes they would sing to her. Grandmother's story is interrupted by the angry remarks of Uncle Frederick who gives a very different view of whales and tells her not to fill Lily's head with nonsense. 'Whales were important', he says, 'for their meat and blubber.' Lily goes on to find out for herself. Her own encounter with the whales, in which she hears them sing and call her name, confirms for her which story is 'true'.

This story presents two different stories which reflect very different ways of viewing the world. The story told by Uncle Frederick has had the most impact on human history – with disastrous results for the whales, if not the entire planet. Grandmother's alternative story is one which is being discovered by more and more who are willing to listen. In presenting children with stories about 'story', RE can help them learn that it is not only whales who have suffered from a world view in which the domination of one group by another is presented as the 'truth'.

In the same way, a book like *Brother Eagle, Sister Sky*, an interpretation of the words of Chief Seattle (Jeffers, 1992) presents children with a chance to understand how the rejection and suppression of world views such as those of the Native Americans have brought the world to the brink of ecological disaster.

It is the argument of this chapter that as a celebration of diversity, religious education can help primary school children develop attitudes which welcome and respect a variety of faiths, cultures, lifestyles, abilities and sexualities in society. Furthermore, it provides opportunities for the teacher to convey an understanding of the means by which dominant groups can disempower and oppress others. In order to do so, however, it has to make a conscious effort to counter the message and methods of a more traditional approach to the subject. The latter often uses RE to transmit a notion of 'cultural heritage' and social norms which help to create and maintain situations of inequality. The debate surrounding the definition of RE in the 1988 Education Reform Act demonstrated that such an approach was staunchly defended by right-wing politicians (Dodds, 1991:169–71). Like religion itself, religious education can be a powerful force for good or ill in the creation of a just and anti-oppressive society.

RESOURCES

Books for the classroom

Celebrations series: A. & C. Black: *Sam's Passover*; *Dat's New Year*; *New Baby*.

Growing Up series. Longman: *Judaism*; *Sikhism*; *Christianity*; *Hinduism*; *Islam*.

My Belief series. Franklin Watts: *I am a Buddhist; I am a Greek Orthodox; I am a Jew; I am a Hindu; I am a Muslim; I am a Rastafarian; I am a Roman Catholic; I am a Sikh.*

My Class series. Franklin Watts: *My class at Divali; My class at Christmas.*

Our Culture Series. Franklin Watts: *Buddhist; Hindu; Jewish; Muslim; Rastafarian; Sikh.*

Religions through Festivals series. Longman: *Judaism; Sikhism; Buddhism; Hinduism; Islam; Christianity.*

Artefacts and posters, suggested suppliers

Articles of Faith, Christine and Leslie Howard, Bury Business Centre, Kay Street BL9 6BU. Tel: 0161 705 1878.

Jewish Education Bureau, 8 Westcombe Avenue, Leeds LS8 2BS. Tel: 01532 663613.

Pictorial Charts Educational Trust, 27 Kirchen Rd, London W13 0UD. Tel: 0181 567 9206.

Christian art in a multi-cultural context

The Misereor Lenten Veils from Haiti and Latin America. These cloths depict Jesus at the centre of the political struggle against oppression. Explanatory leaflets available. They can be ordered from some branches of Traidcraft or from: Misereor, Mozartstrasse 9, D-5100 Aachen, Germany.

Jesus Worldwide is a set of six A3 posters depicting Jesus through Philippino, Cameroons, Haitian and Chinese art. They can be ordered from: Christian Education Movement, Royal Buildings, Victoria Street, Derby, DE1 19W. Tel: 01332 296655.

SUGGESTIONS FOR FURTHER READING

Bastide, D. (1992) *Good Practice in Primary Religious Education, 4–11*. London: Falmer Press.

Cole, W. O. and Evans-Lowndes, J. (1991) *Religious Education in the Primary Curriculum*. Norwich: Chansitor.

Erricker, C. (ed.) (1993) *Teaching World Religions*. London: Heinemann.

Grimmitt, M., Grove, J., Hull, J. and Spencer, L. (1991) *A Gift to the Child: Religious Education in the Primary School (Teachers' Source Book.)* London: Simon and Schuster.

Hammond, J., Hay, D. *et al.* (1990) *New Methods in RE Teaching: An Experiential Approach.* Harlow: Oliver and Boyd.

Jackson, R. and Starkings, D. (1990) *The Junior R.E. Handbook.* Cheltenham: Stanley Thornes.

King, U. (ed.) (1990) *Turning Points in Religious Studies.* Edinburgh: T. and T. Clark.

Rankin, J., Brown, A. and Hayward, M. (1989) *Religious Education Topics for the Primary School.* Harlow: Longman.

Rankin, J., Brown, A. and Hayward, M. (1991) *Religious Education across the Curriculum.* Harlow: Longman.

Read, G., Rudge, J. and Howarth, B. (1992; 2nd edn) *How do I teach R.E.?* Cheltenham: Stanley Thornes.

NOTES

1   The 1944 Education Act made it obligatory for every education authority to draw up a syllabus for RE. It was determined by a committee which had to include representatives of the Church of England, 'other denominations', the local authority and teachers. The 1988 ERA continued this local basis for religious education, distinguishing it from the rest of the National Curriculum.

2   The term 'liberation theology' was first used by Roman Catholic priests in Latin America whose identification with the struggle of the oppressed led them to understand Christian concepts such as liberation in terms of political action. They applied a Marxist analysis to an understanding of the causes of poverty and oppression and rooted their theology in praxis. For further information, see L. and C. Boff (1987) *Introducing Liberation Theology,* Tunbridge Wells: Burns and Oates. Their ideas have been adopted by other Christian groups involved in political struggle, for example in South Africa and Asia.

In this country, the report by the Church of England on Urban Priority Areas argued that it was appropriate to apply liberation theology in order to oppose the power structures which perpetuate inequality and poverty in Great Britain. See *Faith in the City* (1985) Church House Publishing, pp. 63–4.

3 This was a term used by the Schools Council (1971) to describe approaches to RE which understand its aim as the nurturing of pupils into Christianity.
4 This term describes the approach to RE pioneered by Ninian Smart which understands its aims as understanding religion as a phenomenon and as an aspect of human experience.

REFERENCES

Alves, C. (1991) Just a matter of words? The religious education debate in the House of Lords. *British Journal of Religious Education*, 13(3).

Christ, C. (1986) *Diving Deep and Surfacing*. Boston: Boston Beacon Press.

Christ, C. and Plaskow, J. (eds) (1979) *Womanspirit Rising – A Feminist Reader in Religion*. San Francisco: Harper and Row.

Cole, W. O. and Mantin, R. (1994) *Teaching Christianity*. London: Heinemann.

The Education Reform Act (1988) London: HMSO.

Hampshire Education Authority (1978) *Paths for Living: An Agreed Syllabus for Religious Education*. London: HMSO.

Harris, M. and Moran, G. (1989) Feminism and the Imagery of religious education. *British Journal of Religious Education*, Autumn.

Hoffman, M. (1991) *Amazing Grace*. London: Frances Lincoln.

Hull, J. (ed.) (1990) Editorial. *British Journal of Religious Education*, XII.

Jeffers, S. (1992) *Brother Eagle, Sister Sky. A Message from Chief Seattle*. London: Hamish Hamilton.

London Borough of Brent (1986) Brent religious education: Now and tomorrow. Wembley: London Borough of Brent Education Department.

Schools Council working paper 36 – religious education in secondary schools (1971). London: Evans/Methuen.

Schools Curriculum and Assessment Authority (SCAA) (1994). *Religious Education Model Syllabuses*. SCAA.

Sheldon, D. (1990) *The Whale's Song* (illustrations by Gary Blythe). London: Hutchinson.

Surrey County Council Education Committee (1945) *Syllabus of Religious Instruction*. London: HMSO.

Swann, Lord (1985) *Education For All*. London: HMSO.

Wedderspoon, A. G. (1966) *Religious Education, 1944–1984*. London: Allen and Unwin.

CHAPTER 15

Sex education

Terry Brown

In recent years, there has been much public and political debate about sex education. The legal obligations of schools in this area have changed and the Department for Education (DFE) has issued advice and guidance to all schools. The National Curriculum has been slimmed down (with a reassurance of no changes in the next five years). The Office for Standards in Education (OFSTED) will be inspecting schools on a regular basis, sex education policies being specifically mentioned in the inspection Handbook. The cross-curricular themes seem to have lost their importance, with no intention to reprint the curriculum guidance documents for them. The content and methods of primary school sex education have been questioned by the media, both in response to the publication of resources and to particular aspects of delivery. This chapter will consider the impact of all these issues on the equality of opportunity for primary pupils in the area of sex education, and suggest ways to limit this impact.

THE LEGAL OBLIGATIONS OF SCHOOLS

The Education Act 1993, section 241(4) prohibits 'the teaching as part of the National Curriculum in Science, of any material on AIDS, HIV, and other sexually transmitted diseases, or any aspect, other than biological aspects, of human sexual behaviour (DFE, 1994, para. 16).

> All maintained secondary schools are required under section 2 of the Education Reform Act 1988 (as amended by section 241(1) of the Education Act 1993) to make provision for sex education for all pupils registered at the school.
>
> (DFE, 1996, Annex A)

Section 17A of the Education Reform Act 1993 (inserted by section 241(2) of the Education Act 1993) provides that:

> if the parent of any pupil ... requests that he may be wholly or partly excused from receiving sex education at the school, the pupil shall, except in so far as such education is comprised in the National Curriculum, be so excused accordingly until the request is withdrawn.
>
> (DFE, 1994, Annex A)

Previous enactments, with minor recent adjustments, also apply to primary school sex education. Section 18(2) of the Education (No.2) Act 1986 requires that it is the duty of the governing body:

> a. to consider ... the question whether sex education should form part of the secular curriculum of the school; and
> b. to make, and keep up-to-date a separate written statement:
> i. of their policy with regard to the content and organisation of the relevant part of the curriculum; or
> ii. where they conclude that sex education should not form part of the secular curriculum, of that conclusion.

Section 241(5) of the Education Act 1993 also requires schools to:

> make copies of the statement available for inspection (at all reasonable times) by parents of registered pupils at the school and provide a copy of the statement free of charge to any such parent who asks for one.

The Education (School Information) Regulations 1993 require all maintained schools to publish in their prospectus a summary of the content and organization of any sex education they provide (DFE, 1994, Annex A).

Section 18(6) of the Education (No.2) Act 1986 also provides for it to be the duty of the head teacher: 'to ensure that that curriculum so far as it relates to sex education, is compatible with the governing body's policy (as expressed in their statement)'.

Section 241(2) of the Education Act 1993 inserts in section 114(1) of the 1944 Act a definition of 'sex education' which includes education about HIV and AIDS and other sexually transmitted diseases. The law does not, however, define what else is included in sex education; and the Secretary of State has no statutory power to prescribe, by subordinate legislation, the content or organization of sex education (DFE, 1994, para. 16).

The final legal obligation on schools directly related to sex education is section 46 of the 1986 Act which requires the governing body and the headteacher to 'take such steps as are reasonably practicable to secure that where sex education is given to any registered pupils at the school it is given in such a manner as to encourage those pupils to have due regard to moral considerations and the value of family life (DFE, 1994, Annex A).

Equality of opportunity for primary pupils to be provided with sex education may be restricted by these legal obligations in a number of ways.

Some governing bodies may decide to offer no sex education outside the National Curriculum, so that whether a pupil receives any will depend on which school they attend and the composition and concerns of the members. Governors are unlikely to be fully representative, may not understand the issues and current good practice in this area, and may have views and perceptions based on their individual experience as parents and in their occupations, or on their religious or political convictions. Decisions made by governing bodies may be affected by these factors and not result in equality of provision between schools. The protection of young children's innocence is often quoted as a reason for not providing them with information. However, keeping them ignorant does not keep them innocent, and may mean that they make decisions based on lack of information or on myths and misinformation.

If a decision is reached to provide sex education in addition to the National Curriculum, since there is no detailed guidance, each school will decide for itself on the content and organization of its programme. This leads to another layer of inequality of provision between schools. The interpretation of the encouragement of regard for 'moral considerations and the value of family life' is also likely to reflect current media and political values around abstinence before heterosexual monogamous marriage for life, rather than the range of supportive family structures currently existing. Fulfilling and supportive relationships outside this apparent value system may not be regarded as appropriate for inclusion, and may even be denigrated or criticized, thus reducing pupils' perceptions and views of the breadth and variety of sexuality and relationships. 'Sex is dirty, save it for the one you love' is often used to describe one aspect of this approach, and offers what is clearly a very mixed message.

If a governing body decides to provide sex education in addition to the National Curriculum, any parents may withdraw their children from relevant lessons, meaning that there will be inequality of provision within the school, and that those withdrawn are likely to receive a garbled version from their peers in the playground, not an accurate one from the teacher.

While the recent changes in legislation may mean that more schools feel the need to attend to this issue, there is no additional funding dedicated to support the development of sex education. The scope, but not the amount allocated, for basic curriculum and assessment has been extended to include education, but schools can use this how they wish. In addition, expert and experienced support and advice and training is not available in all LEAs since the ending in 1993 of Grants for Education, Support and Training (GEST) funding to support the posts of Health Education Co-ordinator.

The secondary school to which pupils transfer has to provide sex education for all its pupils. However, those who have attended a primary school which has no sex education may be at a disadvantage with regard to the starting-point of the programme.

The legislation only applies to schools maintained by the DFE, leaving independently funded schools to decide on their own curriculum.

The legislation on primary school sex education therefore creates a broad context of inequality of provision for young people in England.

CIRCULAR 5/94 EDUCATION ACT 1993: SEX EDUCATION IN SCHOOLS

It is made very clear on the cover of this document, and in the Introduction that 'this guidance does not constitute an authoritative legal interpretation of the provisions of the Education Act or other enactments and regulations; that is exclusively a matter for the Courts' (DFE, 1994). However, many governors, headteachers, teachers and parents may follow the advice and guidance in order to develop a policy covering the content and organization of sex education in their schools. This advice and guidance includes:

* consultation with LEAs, health authorities, parents, religious groups and minority ethnic communities;
* choice of teaching materials;
* dealing with particularly explicit issues in class;
* advice to individual pupils;
* in-service training.

Special schools are informed that 'children with learning difficulties are entitled to the same opportunity as other children to benefit from sex education' (para. 12) but may need additional support.

Most of the advice in this circular about primary school sex education is sensible, but the media stories prior to its publication appear both to have affected its content and to have led a variety of primary schools, and those involved with sex education in them, to be extremely cautious about delivering any at all for fear of adverse publicity.

In itself, the circular does no more than the legal obligations to limit the scope of sex education, but those who wish to will be able to cite it to support the restrictions they may wish to impose.

THE NEW NATIONAL CURRICULUM

The Programme of Study for Science Attainment Target 2, Life Processes and Living Things (SCAA, 1994) makes a possible contribution to sex education. It indicates that pupils should be taught:

- *At Key Stage 1*:
that animals, including humans ... reproduce;
to name the external parts (e.g. hand, elbow, knee) of the human body;
that humans can produce babies and these babies grow into children and adults.

- *At Key Stage 2*:
that there are life processes, including reproduction ... common to animals, including humans;
the main stages of the human life cycle.

These statements are open to a wide variety of interpretations, some of which could leave children with no understanding of sexual matters whatsoever. For example, how many schools will encourage the naming of the external parts on the human body usually covered by swimwear? It would easily be possible to teach pupils that reproduction is a life process and what the main stages of the human life cycle are without going into any depth or detail about the reproductive organs, let alone how they work. The level descriptions are equally unspecific and do nothing to encourage this depth and detail.

The school governing body is responsible for ensuring the delivery of the National Curriculum and for determining the policy concerning the content and organization of sex education. The headteacher has a duty to ensure that the sex education curriculum is compatible with the governing body's policy (DFE, 1994; Annex A). It is therefore possible for a primary school, while keeping to its legal obligations to deliver the National Curriculum, to offer no real sex education to its pupils. On the other hand, it is also possible than an enlightened governing body and headteacher could interpret the above to offer a very broad programme of sex education, as long as it dealt only with biological aspects of human sexual behaviour, from which parents could not legally withdraw their children.

However the programme of study is interpreted, the main point is that the provision of sex education, even within the National Curriculum, will vary considerably from school to school.

In total, the statutory obligations of primary schools in relation to sex education lead to no uniformity, and therefore no equality, of provision. Some commentators would go further and interpret recent developments as a concerted effort to reduce the amount and openness of sex education in all schools.

CURRICULUM GUIDANCE FOR SEX EDUCATION

In parallel with the original subject-based National Curriculum, the National Curriculum Council published guidance for five cross-curricular themes, one of which was health education. This detailed appropriate areas of study at each Key Stage for nine components of health education, which included sex education, family life education and psychological aspects of health education. (The others are substance use and misuse, safety, health-related exercise, personal hygiene, food and nutrition and environmental aspects.)

The document was distributed to all maintained schools, and while some are blissfully unaware of its existence, others use it as a framework for their health education, with the three components mentioned as the basis for the content of their programme. It includes, at Key Stage 1, naming the parts of the reproductive system, the concept of male and female, good and bad touches, valuing oneself and others, and dealing with emotions. At Key Stage 2, the physical, emotional and social changes at puberty, the basic biology of human reproduction and relationships are covered (NCC, 1990).

The guidance is out of print, and there are no plans to reprint or update it, which is likely to reinforce the variety of provision and perceived lack of support already mentioned.

OFSTED INSPECTIONS

It is the intention that primary schools are inspected every four years. One current evaluation criterion for pupils' welfare and guidance is 'the effectiveness of the implementation of the governing body's policy for health education and sex education'. (OFSTED, 1994, Part 2:34). While DFE Circular 5/94 encourages schools without a policy to 'put its development in hand' (DFE, 1994, para. 45), this aspect of inspection is the only attempt to monitor the situation. There are at least two factors which may limit the meaningfulness of this monitoring. First, there are very few registered inspectors and team members who have any relevant experience of sex education policies and practice which will enable them to understand and assess the policy they receive in advance. In addition, anecdotal evidence indicates that the lay inspector, who is least likely to have this experience, is given the responsibility for this area. Second, schools are unlikely to choose to deliver this sensitive, and possibly contentious, area of the curriculum during an inspection, making evidence of the implementation of the policy difficult to find.

It would seem to be fair to say that OFSTED inspections are unlikely to promote equality of provision of sex education in primary schools. At the time of writing a proposed revision of the *Handbook for the Inspection of Schools* has been distributed for consultation. It is considerably reduced in comparison to the previous version and cuts down the areas required to be inspected, and has less references to sex education.

THE PRINCIPLES AND PRACTICE OF GOOD SEX EDUCATION

> Sex education provides an understanding that positive, caring environments are essential for the development of a good self-image and that individuals are in charge of and responsible for their own bodies. It provides knowledge about the processes of reproduction and the nature of sexuality and relationships. It encourages the acquisition of skills and attitudes which allow pupils to manage their relationships in a responsible and healthy manner.
>
> (National Curriculum Council, 1990)

This approach can form the basis for a broad and open sex education programme, which as well as benefiting all young people can contribute to the current Health of the Nation target of reducing by at least half the rate of conceptions among under 16s by the year 2000 (Secretary of State for Health, 1992). International studies have concluded that sex education does not result in earlier sexual activity, and may lead either to a delay in the onset or to a decrease in overall sexual activity. Countries with greater availability of sex education and birth control for young people have the lowest rates of teenage pregnancy, abortion and child-rearing (National Children's Bureau, 1994). There is evidence that chastity education may encourage sexual experimentation. Young people want practical information and help, rather than didactic approaches emphasizing anatomical or moral aspects of sexual behaviour, and in a context sensitive to the realities and constraints of their lives (Oakley *et al.*, 1995).

There is a 'broadly based consensus that sex education has an important role to play in equipping young people with the skills to communicate effectively within relationships, to resist abuse and unwanted sexual experiences and with the means to protect their own and others' sexual health when sexually active' (National Children's Bureau, 1994). The lives of girls and young women may be affected or restricted by abuse and pregnancy. Boys also require more sex education at school, as, among other factors, including abuse, they have less access to health professionals and are less likely to seek information from them as young men (National Children's Bureau, 1994).

Appropriate and relevant sex education can develop all of the above while promoting gender and other dimensions of equality by putting into practice some basic principles.

Development of a comfortable, open learning environment

It is common practice in personal, social and health education to negotiate ground rules, particularly for sensitive areas like sex and drugs. Curriculum Guidance 5 (NCC, 1990) quotes a set negotiated by a group of 11-year-olds for health education:

- listen to what other people say;
- don't be nasty to each other;
- no talking when someone else is talking;
- be kind to each other and give support;
- if all you can say is something unpleasant, don't say anything;
- if people don't want to say anything they don't have to;
- don't laugh at what other people say;
- think before you ask a question.

These can be supplemented for sex education with, among other aspects, some reference to confidentiality. This must include reference to the fact that the teacher has no option, under current codes of practice, but to pass on information about abuse, regardless of the consequences. The use of ground rules promotes the valuing of all contributions and the opportunities for all to participate in the way they feel comfortable.

Start where children are

Before embarking on a programme of sex education, it is important to find out what the pupils know, think, feel and understand, and what issues are relevant to them. This offers a sound starting-point for development, rather than making presumptions or following an imposed and prescribed syllabus. A small survey in three primary schools in Enfield used the 'Draw and Write' technique (developed by Noreen Wetton of the Health Education Unit at the University of Southampton) to elicit how much primary pupils knew about the sexual parts of the body, the sexual differences between boys and girls, the changes that occur at puberty and how people use their bodies to show others they love them. A variety of lack of information, misinformation and stereotypes emerged, which then formed the basis for suggested content for the next part of the sex education programme (Brown, 1995).

Consulting pupils gives them all the opportunity to be involved in the content and process of sex education, making it more meaningful and relevant, regardless of their gender, class, ethnicity, sexuality or ability.

Attend to attitudes, values and skill development

As well as providing accurate, unbiased and comprehensive information, attention should be given to attitudes and values and skill development. Giving people information only makes them better informed. If the development of behaviour is intended, then the underlying attitudes will affect how the information is assimilated. Therefore these need to be considered and discussed before new information is offered.

Myths and misinformation abound in the area of sex. Some are propounded by adults who are unable or unwilling to talk openly about the subject (e.g. storks and gooseberry bushes).

Some are as a result of children trying to make sense of new information in relation to their experience (e.g. 'If I plant my penis in the garden will it grow?' – that's what you normally do with seeds!). Others are used to justify behaviour (e.g. you can't get pregnant the first time you have sex, or standing up).

Some information is withheld under the misapprehension that keeping children ignorant preserves their innocence and may discourage them from involvement in particular activities. There is no evidence to support this view and withholding information that young people feel is relevant may confuse them or reinforce misinformation, stereotypes and prejudices about, for example, homosexuality.

Consideration of one's own and other people's attitudes and having accurate information are insufficient to deal with relationships, especially sexual ones. The development of appropriate skills, both general ones like assertiveness, making and keeping friends, and specific ones such as responding to unwanted touches and communicating with parents and doctors about changes and concerns, should form part of a programme to enable young people to deal with the situations in which they may find themselves.

This three-pronged approach to sex education can facilitate the breaking down of gender and ethnic stereotypes, dispel myths and misinformation on which some of these are based and promote skills to enable people to treat others and to be treated on an equal footing in relationships and sexual matters, regardless of perceptions of status and power.

Sex education as part of a broader programme

Sex education is best delivered as a part of a broader programme of personal, social and health education, in the context of the health-promoting school. Mixed messages are an unfortunate element of modern Western life. If pupils receive them in school, they will be at best confused, at worst they may ignore the important ones and lose trust in those communicating the messages. Simple practical examples include exhorting pupils to wash their hands after going to the toilet, but without hot water, soap and towels as the budget does not stretch to these. In relation to sex education in the primary school, menstruation may be dealt with in the curriculum, but feminine hygiene materials and disposal equipment may not be available, nor may there be a demonstration of sympathy for those girls who may be severely distressed about its onset.

What messages do the boys and girls receive if menstruation is dealt with for the girls by a visitor from a company which sells tampons, while the boys play football? Where do the boys get information about menstruation and do they get a visit from the 'wet dream' man? An approach based on equality would ensure that each gender has relevant information about the workings of their own and the other's bodies, which will demystify certain aspects of sexual functions and limit the development of misinformation and prejudice.

Active pupil involvement

The methods used in sex education should be based on the active involvement of the pupils. Traditional methods of imparting information by mini-lecture, reference books and videos, while they may play a part in a sex education programme, may presuppose a level of understanding and sometimes literacy, may distance all participants, including the teacher, from the subject matter, and may remove some responsibility for the level of learning from the pupil. Currently available resources offer a variety of pupil-centred, often small group activities which counter this and give the opportunity for all pupils in the class to be involved at their own level of experience and understanding.

PROMOTING EQUALITY IN SEX EDUCATION

The following strategies concerning policy development and the practice of sex education may be considered by those teachers wishing to promote equality in their school both in and through sex education.

Policy development

Governors have responsibility for the interpretation of the National Curriculum, and defining the content and deciding upon the organization of any additional sex education offered. Raising their awareness of the relevant issues would enable them to make appropriate decisions not based on myths, misinformation and prejudices. Many local education authorities and governor organizations offer sex education training for governors.

Co-operative working and perhaps training with the secondary school which the pupils will attend and with the other primary schools who feed it may help to develop a situation in which the opportunity for sex education for all pupils in the area is the same.

Parents, who have the right to withdraw their children from sex education offered in addition to the National Curriculum, can be involved in the consultation process, in order to reduce the numbers who may consider this option. Local religious leaders may be important allies in this process.

The practice of sex education

Teachers who will be delivering sex education need to have considered the issues and information, and perhaps confronted their own attitudes and prejudices, in order that these are not passed on to the pupils or restrict their learning.

The principles mentioned above can be applied, and materials and methods selected, at least not to reinforce stereotypes and prejudices, particularly related to gender, and perhaps to confront them and contest their reality. The hope is that primary school pupils will then have a basis of a consideration for the feelings and concerns of others before they embark on sexual relationships.

REFERENCES

Brown T. (1995) Girls have long hair. *Health Education*, 2, March: 23–9.

Department for Education (DFE) (1994) *Circular 5/94 Education Act 1993: Sex Education in Schools*. London: HMSO.

National Children's Bureau (1994) *Highlight No. 128 Sex Education*. London: National Children's Bureau.

National Curriculum Council (NCC) (1990) *Curriculum*

Guidance 5 Health Education. York: National Curriculum Council.

Oakley, A., Fullerton, D., Holland, J., Arnold, S., France-Dawson, M., Kelley, P., McGrellis, S. (1995) Sexual health education interventions for young people: a methodological review. *British Medical Journal*, 310:158–62.

OFSTED (1994) *The Handbook for the Inspection of Schools*. London: HMSO.

Secretary of State for Health (1992) *Health of the Nation. A Strategy for Health in England*. London: HMSO.

School Curriculum and Assessment Authority (SCAA) (1994) *The National Curriculum Orders*. York: SCAA.

CHAPTER 16

Information technology
Tarsem Singh Cooner and Avril Loveless

Information technology (IT) capability in the National Curriculum is a very good vehicle for thinking about many issues for teachers – from 'how do children learn?' to 'how do we promote equality in the classroom?'. In considering the implications of appropriate and effective use of IT across the curriculum, teachers can address the ways in which IT can empower or limit children's experience in learning (Loveless, 1995).

This chapter will consider a number of issues associated with equality and IT in the National Curriculum:

- the meaning of the development of IT capability in its broad sense;
- the impact that IT has made in working with children with special educational needs;
- the effects that different ways of working can have on girls' and boys' experience of and aspirations with IT;
- the implications for different groups on the degrees of access to information available to the technological 'haves' and 'have nots', locally, nationally and globally.

Finally, there will be ⌐ detailed account of one particular multimedia package, CRMKB. The rationale which underpins the package will be described in relation to the design, which promotes access across the curriculum with positive images of all cultures, not just the male, Western European, English-speaking market of most computer products.

IT CAPABILITY AND ACCESS TO RESOURCES

IT in the National Curriculum is described by Dearing as a 'basic skill', with oracy, literacy and numeracy, developed through a range of subject content (Dearing, 1994, 4.12, 4.14). It is also described in the National Curriculum Orders as a 'capability' – the ability to use effectively IT tools and information sources to solve problems, to support learning in a variety of contexts and to understand the implications of IT for working life and society (DFE, 1995a). The framework for IT capability is presented as 'strands' which run through all curriculum areas (although not definitively in PE).

- Communicating and handling information.
- Controlling and modelling information (Key Stage 1).
- Controlling, monitoring and modelling information (Key Stage 2).
- Controlling, measuring and modelling information (Key Stages 3 and 4).

Throughout these experiences pupils should be encouraged to 'examine and discuss their experiences of IT and look at the use of IT in the outside world' (DFE, 1995a:2).

The notion of 'capability' is important in that it extends the use of IT beyond particular skills with particular systems and includes an involvement in the context in which IT is being used.

> Awareness of the reasons for using IT and the effect it has, both on the context and on the participants involved, is an important aspect of IT capability and one that can be transferred to new situations with new resources.
>
> (Loveless, 1995:12)

The interest in IT capability as a desirable goal in the education of children for their lives in society has a number of elements – economic, social, intellectual and pedagogical – and many writers have highlighted the need for this broad view (Underwood and Underwood, 1990; Beynon and Mackay, 1993; Loveless, 1995). Teachers need to think carefully about how to develop an understanding of the appropriate use of IT, as it can be argued that it is not a neutral tool, but reflects the context in which it is used. Participants in the development of the 'information society' need to have technological literacy in order to be aware of the issues of access, control, choice and production (Beynon and Mackay, 1993).

A key issue to be addressed by students and teachers concerned with equality is that of access to resources which enable the development of IT capability. The technology in terms of hardware and software develops and changes quickly and, in many ways, is becoming more accessible to more people in its design and in the variety of applications in personal and professional spheres. The cost of the technology, although dropping in terms of the value of the processing speed and memory size and the facilities these make available, is still an important factor for schools and individuals wishing to make full use of IT and provide access for all the children.

Most classroom-based resources provide facilities to support the general strands of IT capability and specific areas of the curriculum. A school may have PC, Apple Mac or Acorn computers, all of which will provide software for communicating and handling information (word processors, graphics packages, desktop publishing, databases, spreadsheets); modelling (adventure games, simulations, spreadsheets); monitoring and measuring (datalogging and graphical representation); and controlling (from Roamers and Pips to control technology and robotics). There will also be subject-related software to support a range of activities, from maths and language games to historical simulations of time travel and geographical mapping packages. Jean Underwood's book *Computer Based Learning: Potential into Practice* (1994), has an interesting and useful focus on different areas of the curriculum; identifying issues relating to IT and describing classroom case studies of the use of particular IT resources.

Many schools, primary and secondary, will also have the technology to use CD ROMs as information sources, from talking books to encyclopaedias. CD ROMs provide access to multimedia presentations of information, using text, sound and visual images – both still and moving. The design of material presented on CD ROM influences the ways in which the user can browse, search and make connections between elements of information. The next stage after being an observer of information presented by others, like reading a book from the library shelf, is that of being the author, designer and presenter of information.

The development of 'multimedia' with IT is important in that it enables children to be participants in and producers of information as well as consumers (Heppell, 1994; Sefton-Green, 1994). Working with these resources enables pupils to make decisions about the media in which information can be presented; the ways in which it can be collected, manipulated and transformed; the connections that can be made between different elements of information and the nature of the interaction with the user or 'reader' of the presentation. Software such as Hyper Studio, HyperCard, Guide, Genesis and Magpie are currently used to enable children to handle and communicate information in this way.

There has been much media coverage and discussion of the impact of the setting up of the 'Information Superhighway' – a network capable of transferring large amounts of information, text, audio and visual images, at high speed. Such a superhighway would have the potential to deliver a wide range of services, from electronic shopping to video conferences with people around the globe. This includes, of course, the potential to provide a wealth of educational resources. In the USA, the Clinton administration challenged industry to connect all the country's classrooms, libraries, hospitals and clinics by the year 2000. In Europe there are moves to develop policy to encourage market mechanisms, rather than substantial public subsidy, to develop European Superhighways. The Department for Education in the UK produced a consultation document, *Superhighways in Education* (1995b), to promote comment, discussion and collaboration between the educational sector and the industrial providers of the telecommunications technology required. Some of the implications of the provision of such technology and the access available to different groups of people, nationally and globally, will be discussed later in this chapter.

While waiting for the development of the Superhighway, many

universities, libraries, companies, individuals and, increasingly, schools, have had access to the Internet – a worldwide network linking numerous smaller networks and with many millions of users. This 'narrowband' network does not transmit data at the speed and volume possible on the 'broadband' Superhighway, but is used for electronic mail, bulletin boards, conferencing and accessing remote sources of information from around the world. This information can include text, audio and visual images, but the transmission times are slower and the quality of images is not as high as on 'broadband' networks. There are a number of pilot projects in UK schools evaluating the educational potential of network communications across the curriculum and the skills and capabilities required by learners and teachers.

IT AND SPECIAL EDUCATIONAL NEEDS

> Technology should be used to magnify abilities that are there, bypassing as much as possible cognitive, emotional, physical and sensory disabilities.
>
> (Hawkridge and Vincent, 1992:28)

It is in the area of SEN that IT has been able to make a unique contribution to children's learning experiences, empowering them with wider access to the curriculum and with a variety of means for communication and interaction with others. The National Curriculum Orders state common requirements and specify that:

> appropriate provision should be made for pupils who need to use:
> – means of communication other than speech, including computers, technological aids, signing, symbols or lip-reading;
> – non-sighted methods of reading such as Braille, or non-visual or non-aural ways of acquiring information;
> – technological aids in practical and written work;
> – aids or adapted equipment to allow access to practical activities within and beyond school.
>
> (DFE, 1995a:1)

Children with physical disabilities or sensory impairment are able to bypass the usual means of communicating and handling information. They can express their responses and ideas with standard IT applications by the adaptation of input and output in order to meet individual needs.

If their co-ordinated movement is constrained or not easily controlled, a variety of switches and sensors is available for particular situations. These can range from a flat concept keyboard which can be pressed with fingertips or the palm of the hand, to sensitive switches which can detect small movements of the head, face and eyes to indicate a response. Children are therefore able to interact with IT resources, whether they be an adventure game or a word processor using a speech synthesizer to communicate scanned, edited and finished text. Rahamin (1993) describes some powerful uses of IT giving children with physical disabilities access to words and images, which include that of a pupil using a word processor attached to his wheelchair to prepare a number of sentences to be read by a speech synthesizer. These enabled him to participate in conversations with such phrases as 'I'd like to say something now' and 'I haven't finished yet!' (Rahamin, 1993).

It might seem that the visually impaired are disadvantaged by the very visual designs of the screens of many personal computers. There are many ways, however, in which recent developments in IT can provide access to sources of information usually restricted for the visually impaired. Talking word processors and speech synthesizers are increasing in sophistication in 'reading' text from the screen with appropriate pronunciation and intonation. The storage capacity for text, visual and audio information on CD ROM has led to the development of a range of talking books which can be read aloud in a more flexible way than a cassette tape, allowing non-linear selections of and connections between elements of the text. The Grolier Encyclopaedia can be made available in this way as one CD ROM, where it would have 'normally taken up 21 volumes of printed text and 350 large Braille volumes' (Loveless, 1995:96).

Of course, the visual medium of many IT resources enables the hearing impaired to have access to different levels of information, communication and interaction. Conversations with electronic mail and video phone allow an immediacy and informality in the structure of colloquial communication usually experienced by the hearing on the telephone. The NCET have outlined the ways in which IT could meet some of the learning needs across the curriculum of hearing impaired children:

- the development of literacy skills, vocabulary and language extension, with more direct reinforcement of selected aspects than is needed by hearing peers, can be achieved though word-processing, with the help of symbol systems and voice synthesis
- improved expression and communication, with enhanced receptive language skills, can occur through the use of age-appropriate listening and reading programs
- improved general cognitive and communication skills can be developed through collaborative decision-making and problem-solving programs, including simulations and adventure games.

(NCET, 1991)

Children with cognitive learning difficulties, whether mild, moderate or severe, can also be supported and given access to the wider curriculum by the use of IT. The characteristics of learning with IT are particularly important in developing the self-esteem and success of children who have experienced learning difficulties. The animation, feedback, patience and interaction of a computer program can promote children's sense of independence, autonomy and choice in their work. For many children with special educational needs in a mainstream classroom, IT can provide access to alternative ways of representing their ideas and ways of working, as individuals or with their peers.

Word processors and graphics packages allow children to save, revisit, check, edit and develop their ideas in words and images in order to print work of good quality which is attractive and presented appropriately for an audience – a piece of work to be proud of in process and product, perhaps after many experiences of hurried, untidy, unco-ordinated and frustrated work. The use of predictive spelling checkers and talking word processors provides a multi-sensory experience for children who might need the reinforcement of integrating sight and sound and the encouragement of being able to develop their ideas without the anxiety of errors which cannot be deleted or edited.

IT AND GENDER

Girls and boys in the classroom can have very different experiences of the use of IT – they may have different attitudes and may work in different ways with the resources and with each other. It is important that the teacher is aware of and sensitive to these experiences in order to plan and manage the use of the resources effectively for all the children's learning. Although access to IT resources is a key factor in building confidence and competence, attitude and approach also affect the ways in which boys and girls interact with and develop their learning with IT (Loveless, 1995).

There has been concern that the proportion of girls and young women entering the IT industry or taking related courses in higher education has declined, from 24 per cent in 1979 to less than 10 per cent in 1989 (Kirkup and Keller, 1992:269). This decline in interest seemed to occur in the secondary school phase, as girls and boys in the primary sector seemed to express equal interest in using IT. What is it in the nature and quality of pupils' experience that has such a powerful influence and how can teachers address this in their classrooms?

The image of IT in our society has long been associated with males and considered inappropriate or unappealing to females. The culture and jargon of the IT world is as distinctive as that of any other technical area and serves to baffle and exclude, reinforcing social networks and expressing power and prestige. Much of the jargon is unnecessary and can be expressed in other ways, but teachers do need to reflect on the role and use of such language in developing children's understanding and expression.

Traditionally computers were regarded as part of the male domain of 'hard' mathematics and science. The historical links with military developments were extended into the market of home computer games, where the resources for action and adventure games were sold as boys' toys. More home computers were bought for boys than for girls, even when the girls expressed an interest in owning them (Culley, 1988). A quick glance at popular computing magazines in the high street newsagents will also illustrate the narrow culture of much of the marketing for computer games and activities. Most of the advertising and images used in the games represent males in action, often militaristic and violent. The games targeted at girls reflect the general toy industry in its focus on dolls and princesses, pastel colours and 'cute' cartoons.

There are encouraging indications that these patterns may be changing in recent years with the growth of multimedia computers in the home market. These provide access to a wider range of applications and resources which have a less gendered image and purpose. Multimedia applications enable boys and girls to work in more open-ended ways. They may still express their ideas in the gendered forms of the culture surrounding them, but the more visual and user-friendly design of the resources does not necessarily exclude or discourage groups in the early stages of their involvement with IT.

The children's attitudes to themselves as users of IT are an important element in the quality of their interaction with the resources and each other. Boys seem to regard computers as 'more for boys', whereas girls seem to hold less stereotypical views (Eastman and Krendl, 1987). Newton and Beck noted that secondary school girls described how the boys would take over the computers, push them off and brag about their knowledge (Newton and Beck, 1993). Beynon and Loveless both observed that in working with mixed groups, girls were often marginalized, bored and frustrated (Beynon, 1993; Loveless, 1995).

The role models presented by teachers can play an important part in pupils' perceptions of the potential and use of IT. When computers were first introduced into schools they were often associated with mathematics, science and technical subjects and IT co-ordinators were usually represented by male teachers. It is therefore important to reflect upon the presentation of positive role models in which children see the equal responsibility and competence of male and female teachers in dealing with IT and the variety of contexts in which it can be used.

Although there does appear to be a significant gender difference in the use of IT by boys and girls in school, the reasons for those differences cannot be described as a straightforward connection between images, attitudes and access to resources. The nature and quality of the experiences that children have when working with IT can have significant effects on the children's learning – both cognitive and social.

There has been a series of studies of the interaction between learners working with computers, leading one researcher to remark that 'boys, girls and computers are a dangerous combination' (Underwood, 1994:9). The purpose and context in which children work with IT make a difference to the responses made by girls and boys, girls being more affected than boys by the level of engagement with and relevance of the activity (Barbieri and Light, 1992; Littleton *et al.*, 1993). There are also differences in the ways in which single sex and mixed sex groups perform with IT and a number of interesting studies conducted by Underwood and others highlighted the significance of the nature of the discussion underlying the activity (Underwood, 1994).

Groups working with IT performed most effectively when they collaborated and shared each other's ideas in negotiation and reflection. The most effective groupings were girls' single sex groups who seemed to be able to work collaboratively without too much input and encouragement from the teacher. Boys' single sex groups tended to co-operate or compete with each other, needing more support in developing the skills of full collaboration. The least effective groups were mixed sex groups which were characterized by tension and a lack of co-operation and communication.

These studies have far-reaching implications for students and teachers wishing to provide equality in the learning experiences of the children. Not only does there need to be an awareness of the impact of cultural expectations of girls and boys on their attitude and access to IT, there needs also to be a closer and sensitive consideration of the ways in which teachers provide children with the opportunity to develop a variety of styles of working and interacting with each other. Girls can be disadvantaged by the lack of access to and self-esteem with IT – boys can be disadvantaged by the lack of support in developing collaborative ways of working with IT.

IT, SOCIAL CLASS AND ECONOMIC ACCESS TO INFORMATION

The access that people have to the technology of information has been seen to be an important factor in their development of IT capability in its broad sense, that is an informed and critical approach to the impact and influence of IT in educational, social and economic life. Research in the USA has indicated that the microprocessor 'revolution' in primary education actually exacerbated previously existing inequalities. Access to the Internet and related networks through home computers was biased towards the educated and upper income households. The study also showed that computer ownership was least likely in Black African/American households yet more likely in the Pacific/Asian than white households. Those who had studied beyond the equivalent of A level were eleven times more likely to own a computer than those who had studied only to high school level (Cotterill, 1995).

Although family income is not a direct predictor of computer ownership – neither as it is with video players and recorders – the cost of powerful and flexible multimedia computer systems for home and school is still a considerable factor when resources are scarce and there are many competing priorities. Within a classroom, there may be considerable variation in the access that children have to home computers which not only play games, but enable them to use word processors or graphics packages in open-ended ways or give access to information sources over the Internet.

Nationally, there is also great variation in the amount of money that schools spend on IT resources in their schools. The DFE 'Survey of Information Technology in Schools' in 1995 indicated that there were differences in the capital expenditure on IT resources which were reflected in the prosperity of the schools' catchment areas as well as the age phase. Primary schools in relatively prosperous areas reported expenditure of £53 per pupil, in economically disadvantaged areas an expenditure of £34 per pupil, and in areas described as neither prosperous nor economically disadvantaged £14 per pupil. Secondary schools in prosperous areas indicated £29 per pupil, in economically disadvantaged areas £22, and in areas neither prosperous nor economically disadvantaged £21.

The degree of involvement of a PTA or parents' group in the different areas is very variable in the primary sector. In relatively prosperous areas, the percentage of expenditure for information technology was met by 51 per cent from school budget, 8 per cent from LEA or central government and 40 per cent from a PTA or parents. In economically disadvantaged areas the proportions were 52 per cent from school budget, 35 per cent from LEA or central government and 12 per cent from a PTA or parents. Areas which were neither prosperous not economically disadvantaged distributed the IT capital expenditure 52 per cent, 10 per cent and 35 per cent in those areas. This is in contrast to the expenditure on IT resources by PTA and parents in secondary schools, where the percentages of expenditure range from 1 per cent in the prosperous and disadvantaged areas to 3 per cent in areas neither prosperous nor economically disadvantaged. Fisher has stated that, 'It is difficult to think of any other kind of basic educational resource where such wide variations between the best and worst equipped schools would be likely to occur' (Fisher, 1993:77).

Globally the unequal distribution of wealth and technology is perfectly illustrated by the number of access points that countries in Africa, South America and the Far East have to the Internet. Although the net connects more than 150 countries, those unconnected tend to be from the world's poorer countries. The effect that this situation has is to widen the gap between rich and poor countries in having the infrastructure to carry out international business, access information and communicate. To get these systems up and running incurs a penalty as most of the infrastructure is rooted in North American technology and the use of English as the language of communication. If the countries that do not have access to the Internet are not able to build in their own unique identity and character then the diversity of cultures and forms of communication will be very limited. This inevitably means that most of the information and services carried on the Internet are heavily biased towards Western needs.

What effect does this national and global inequality have? It is difficult to predict the future, but we can assume that the 'information revolution' will continue and that those with access to these forms of information will have the advantage over those who do not and those that control or constrain that access have further advantage and power.

IT IN A MULTI-CULTURAL SOCIETY

The notion of preparing pupils for living and working in a multi-cultural society has gradually disappeared from the documentation in the National Curriculum. Any wording conveying the idea of a pluralist society has been erased. 'British' seems to be viewed as synonymous with 'white English' once again and British values have become synonymous with conservative values. Racism, in this right-wing view, has been reduced to nothing more than individual prejudice which will disappear, no doubt 'if you don't go on and on about it' or by 'celebration of difference'. Anti-racist education, discredited by the Right, has little or no place in many school policies for equal opportunities. While a good many of these schemes have begun to take cognisance of the diversity in society in that they use names and illustrations of people selected from a wide variety of backgrounds, they are sometimes misguided or select contexts which bear little or no resemblance to the real and lived dimensions of children's lives. It has always been difficult to bring the experiences of the outside world within the confines of the classroom; pupils and teachers alike find it difficult to share their communities' experiences with each other. School Development Plans, however, need to consider resources which address the wider issues of a diverse society.

Where pupils do have access to IT it is important to ensure that the programs used are sensitive to the issues raised in a diverse society and that the current inequalities are not perpetuated through the purchase of inappropriate material. Most of the material produced reflects the male, West European and US English-speaking market. To try to redress that unequal bias there are now products produced by people who are becoming more aware of the global and national inequalities created within the information technology sphere. One of these products is the Cultural Roots Multimedia Knowledge Base (CRMKB).

Cultural roots multimedia knowledge base (CRMKB)

CRMKB is the product of a group of professionals from a variety of backgrounds who are committed to promoting positive images of all cultures with the specific aim of enhancing the cultural identity of Asian, black and other minority ethnic group children through the medium of computers. This package also actively helps to promote the contributions made by females to the development of the subject areas covered. It is a CD ROM package which has been developed to meet the requirements of IT in the National Curriculum, while engaging pupils in challenging perceptions of the diversity of cultures around them.

The basis of the program has been to introduce, through the use of multimedia, a cross-curricular program that allows access to and makes connections between history, geography, English, music, science, religious education and the arts. While pupils model, handle and communicate information, they glimpse the real-world experiences of other communities which most computer products have not addressed. It is a timely, much needed development. The creators of the package realized the motivating power of interacting with IT. The creators of CRMKB have researched and found through the development of the knowledge base that there are not many children who fail to be engrossed by the fascination of graphic images and the capability of manipulating them and being able to interact with and control them.

CRMKB enables the user to access pictures, sound and text in a flexible manner, unlike the linear form of a video. The user can therefore interact with the information, controlling not only the direction of the subject matter, but also the medium used to present it. The package can be used in a non-directive way in that pupils can be allowed to explore the subject areas contained within the program while becoming familiar and confident in the use of IT. Discussion, project work and further research can arise from using the program, teacher and pupil learning together. The theoretical rationale and interpretation of the material can develop from understanding the principle of value accorded to the diversity of faith, language and cultural practices.

CRMKB uses the latest technology, is teacher and pupil friendly and can be updated to keep up with ongoing developments. It can be used as a knowledge base for teachers preparing for particular topics and a research tool for children. For example, white teachers who shy away from introducing Guru Nanak and his teachings because they feel ill-prepared to do justice to such a topic can use the CRMKB as a knowledge base from which to learn about him and the Sikh religion. They can use popular contemporary and current pictorial representations of Guru Nanak and ensure that they are able to pronounce his name accurately through the use of the pronunciation checker which uses digitized sounds of real-life pronunciations which are captured, stored and repeated for the user.

It is felt strongly by the designers that certain principles underly the package: respect; accessibility; nurturance.

Respect

It is the hope of the contributors that teachers using this program will do so in a manner that does not in any way disrespect the many faiths, history, cultures, societies and people portrayed within the knowledge base. Each may be used as a stimulus to extend any appropriate work as well as their own knowledge. There is the opportunity to choose from four broad subject areas, or 'segments', each accompanied by a quiz section:

1 *Punjabi* – a basic introduction to the pronunciation of colours, numbers, shapes, face parts and the calendar (see Figure 16.1).

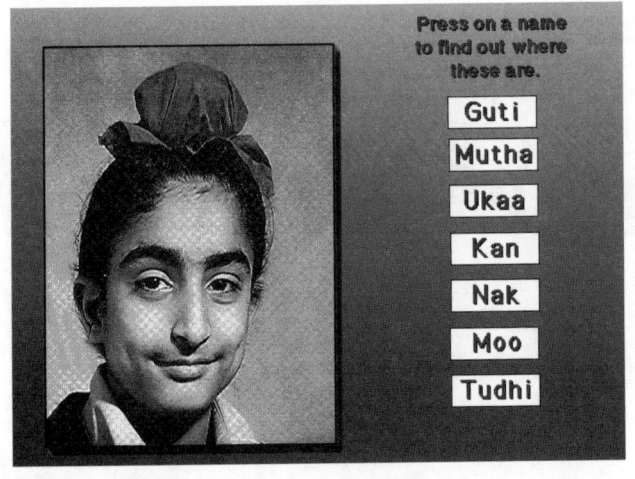

Figure 16.1 Punjabi
Source: CRMKB

2 *History of Sikhism* – This segment is offered on two levels, light and heavy. The light segment introduces the ten Sikh Gurus using text, pictures and sound, which reads the text

Figure 16.2   History of Sikhism (light level)
Source: CRMKB

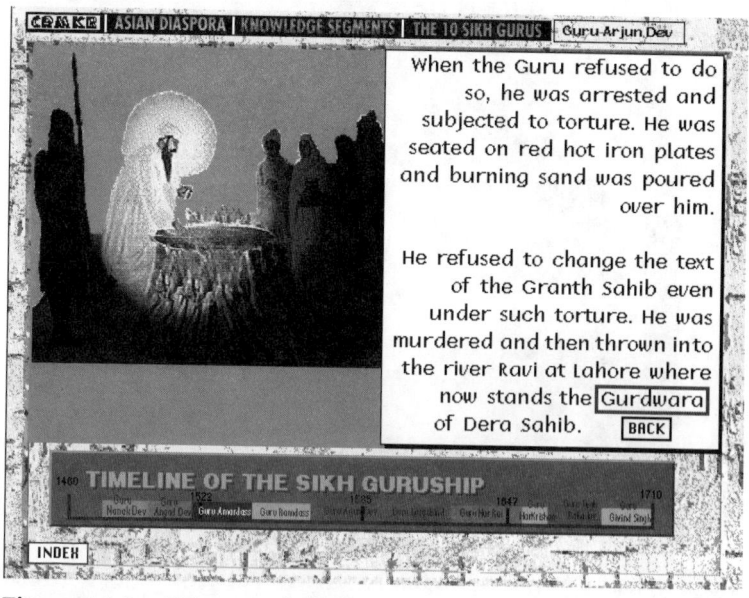

Figure 16.3   History of Sikhism (heavy level)
Source: CRMKB

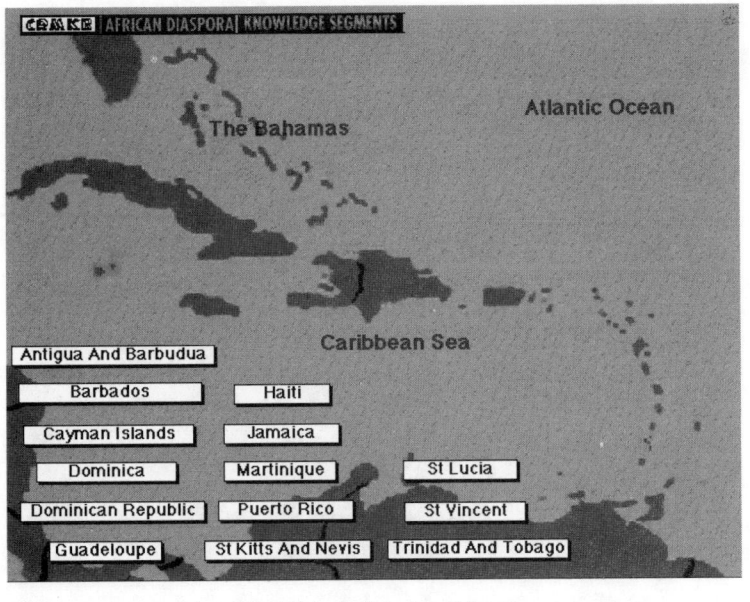

Figure 16.4   The Islands of the Caribbean
Source: CRMKB

aloud. The heavy segment goes into further detail and encompasses the main progress of Sikhism from its introduction to the succession of the Guru Gobind Singh. This also includes pronunciation checkers (see Figures 16.2 and 16.3).

3   *The Islands of the Caribbean* – this introduces the user to fifteen of the islands in the Caribbean. With the use of maps, the precise locations of the islands and the information of the flags, main languages, population and capital cities are shown (see Figure 16.4).

4   *The Black Pioneers* – this looks at the contributions made by people of African/Caribbean descent to the areas of science, medicine, art, literature, presented on two levels of detail (see Figures 16.5 and 16.6).

Accessibility

Experience shows that many Asian, black and other minority ethnic group children go through their school life shying away from their home culture, unable to identify or link their home

379

Figure 16.5   The Black Pioneers, Mary Seacole (light level)
Source: CRMKB

Figure 16.6   The Black Pioneers, Mary Seacole (heavy level)
Source: CRMKB

background to the classroom and school. For example, a large number of children enter the nursery or reception classes speaking, making meanings and connections in two or three languages. They often leave the primary school with little or no communication skills in their home language. CRMKB presents the information, where appropriate, in a multilingual or bilingual mode, allowing pupils to accept and use their home languages as a tool for learning. White pupils' perceptions of their classmates are closely tangled with their impressions and internalized negative images of the 'Third World' – famine- and flood-ridden and overpopulated as projected by the media. Much of the curriculum reinforces this by treating cultures other than English as aliens – subjects of study rather than real-life experiences.

Nurturance

The concept of the 'whole child' and of holistic development is central to the CRMKB package. Positive role models will no doubt enhance the pride and meaning of ethnicity for Asian, black and other minority ethnic group children around the issues of history, 'race', culture, language and religion, while correcting misconceptions of the same for white children. They can learn about the suppressed history of the contributions made to humanity by people from the African Diaspora, such as Mary Seacole (Figures 16.5 and 16.6) and Ida Wells. Portrayals of Asian languages and religions as being inferior in Western societies can be countered by accurately providing insights into these subjects from a non-Eurocentric perspective. This can be done in a way that connects with children from those backgrounds as being authentic because it is something that they can recognize as passed on to them by their parents and not a product of Eurocentric academic research with all its interpretations and possible innuendo. One of the biggest contributions made by the package is the positive nurturance of Asian, black and other minority ethnic group children in an education system where the majority of curriculum content is geared towards a majority white audience (Milner, 1983; Clark, 1955). The package sends the intangible message, 'If something like this is created for me, then maybe I am worth something and those in

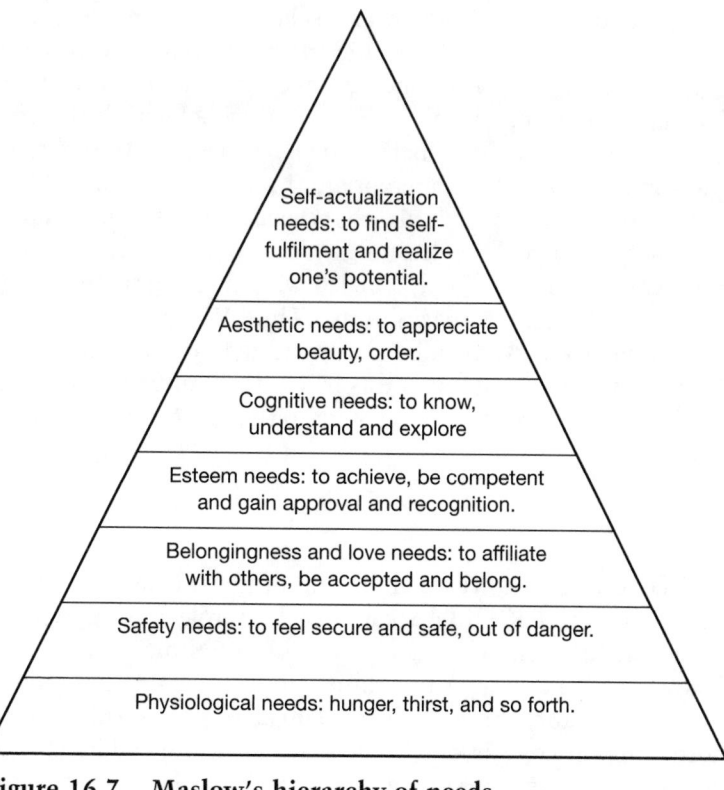

Figure 16.7   Maslow's hierarchy of needs
Source: Maslow (1954)

my communities are worth something.'

Although policy-makers in Britain state that they accept Britain is a multi-cultural society, too little is being done within the school curriculum and hidden curriculum positively to reflect the different communities that make up the populace of Britain. Although many school policies aim to promote good 'race relations' and use diversity for raising standards, Burns (1982) states that these aims have not been realized in the curriculum and that young minority ethnic group children often show more negative feelings about their ethnicity when compared to American research. Exposure to the forces of racism will have negative effects on identity and self-esteem of minority ethnic group children, particularly if they are a small minority in a school which is dominated by a racist ethos.

Maslow's hierarchy of needs (Figure 16.7) identifies the importance of being accepted and belonging (Maslow, 1954). If children do not experience this level they cannot begin to meet the needs of positive self-esteem and positive self-concept – important higher order needs required for healthy psychological development. To compensate, the child will develop complex psychological processes to avoid having to come to terms with this reality and the consequence is a great deal of psychological damage.

CRMKB is essentially a multi-faceted tool that covers a great deal of the National Curriculum needs. The move away from a Eurocentric perspective means that some of the needs of minority ethnic group children are met by providing information that will help to enhance and build on their cultural identity in a positive manner and provide white teachers and children with the information that will help them to re-evaluate the negative images of minority ethnic group people portrayed throughout British society. The product ensures that IT capability is approached through a range of curriculum activities.

HOW CAN TEACHERS PROMOTE LEARNING WITH IT FOR ALL CHILDREN?

The Role of IT: Practical Issues for Primary Teachers (Loveless, 1995) highlights three areas in which students and teachers can address issues of equity – access to resources, images of IT, and the role of the teacher – and asks a series of questions (Loveless, 1995:116).

Access to resources

- Do the tasks asked of the children reflect different cognitive styles and contexts?
- Is there flexibility in the organization of groups to allow for single- and mixed-sex groups in different situations?
- Are the children actively encouraged and supported in collaboration and co-operation?
- Is IT capability being developed across the curriculum to avoid association with particular subjects?

- Is there a relationship between expectations in the classroom and the general equity policy in the school?
- Are the children given the opportunity to relate IT experiences to wider issues of the impact of IT in society?
- Are software and supporting resources selected with the consideration of different interests, languages and ways of working?

Images of IT

- Has there been thought given to the role models presented by the teachers and IT co-ordinator in terms of gender balance in confidence and expertise?
- Is the expertise of girls and boys recognized throughout the school, or are the IT monitors always Year 6 boys?
- Are the children given the opportunity to discuss their images and expectations of themselves and IT – both positive and negative?

The teacher's role

- Do you take time to listen to the interaction of different groups?
- Do you consider a range of appropriate interventions for social and cognitive interactions?
- Do you challenge bullying, sexism and racism?
- Do you encourage and help to develop collaboration skills?
- Do you encourage 'computer-shy' children to experience a range of activities to help them find a comfortable context?
- Do you attend INSET courses to extend your own confidence and competence with new resources?

Having access to IT for communication and learning can be positive and enabling, but can also reflect the stereotypes, expectations and influences of society. Children must be given the opportunities to challenge inequity in the ways in which they gain competence and capability with new technologies and use them to work together and express themselves with confidence and empowerment.

RESOURCES

CRMKB is priced at £35 and will work with any Macintosh with a CD-ROM drive, or any IBM compatible computer that has multimedia level 2 (MPC2). To purchase the product please contact: Trilby Multimedia, 148 Poplar Avenue, Edgbaston, West Midlands B17 8ER. Tel: 0121 420 1482. Fax: 0121 429 2943. e-mail on the Internet: Tarsem@cooner.demon.co.uk.

REFERENCES

Barbieri, M. S. and Light, P. (1992) Interaction, gender and performance on a computer-based problem solving task. *Learning and Instruction*, 2, 199–214.

Beynon, J. (1993) Computers, Dominant Boys and Invisible Girls: OR 'Hannah, it's not a toaster, it's a computer!'. In J. Beynon and H. Mackay (eds) *Computers into Classrooms: More Questions than Answers*. London and Washington: Falmer Press.

Beynon, J. and Mackay, H. (eds) (1993) *Computers into Classrooms: More Questions than Answers*. London and Washington: Falmer Press.

Burns, R. (1982) *Self Concept Development and Education*. London: Holt Education.

Clark, K. (1955) *Playing in Harmony*. Glasgow: Save the Children.

Cotterill, K. (1995) *Guardian Online*. 30 March:4.

Culley, L. (1988) Girls, boys and computers. *Educational Studies*, 14, 3–8.

Dearing, R. (1994) *The National Curriculum and its Assessment: Final Report*. London: School Curriculum and Assessment Authority.

DFE (1995a) *Information Technology in the National Curriculum*. London: HMSO.

DFE (1995b) *Superhighways for Education*. London: HMSO.

Eastman, S. T. and Krendl, K. (1987) Computers and gender: differential effects of electronic search on students' achievement and attitude. *Journal of Research and Development in Education*, 20, 41–8.

Fisher, E. (1993) Access to learning; problems and policies. In P. Scrimshaw (ed.) *Language, classrooms and computers*. London and New York: Routledge.

Hawkridge, D. and Vincent, T. (1992) *Learning Difficulties and*

Computers. London and Philadelphia: Jessica Kingsley.

Heppell, S. (1994) Multimedia and learning: normal children, normal lives and real change. In J. Underwood (ed.) *Computer Based Learning: Potential into Practice*. London: David Fulton.

Kirkup, G. and Keller, L. S. (eds) (1992) *Inventing Women: Science, Technology and Gender*. Cambridge: Polity Press in association with the Open University.

Littleton, K., Light, P., Barnes, P., Messer, D. and Joiner, R. (1993) Gender and software effects in computer-based problem solving. Paper presented at the Society for Research in Child Development. New Orleans, March.

Loveless, A. (1995) *The Role of IT: Practical Issues for Primary Teachers*. London: Cassell.

Maslow, A. H. (1954) *Motivation and Personality*. New York: Harper and Row.

Milner, D. (1983) *Children and Race – Ten Years On*. London: Ward Lock Educational.

Newton, P. and Beck, E. (1993) Computing: an ideal occupation for women? In J. Beynon and H. Mackay (eds) *Computers with Classrooms: More Questions than Answers*. London and Washington: Falmer Press.

NCET (1991) *The IT Needs of Hearing Impaired Pupils and their Teachers*. Information Sheets 1 and 2. Coventry: NCET.

Rahamin, L. (1993) *Access to Word and Images*. Coventry: NCET/CENMAC.

Sefton-Green, J. (1994) Unpublished presentation at Catching Up With The Kids conference, 1 October.

Underwood, J. and Underwood, G. (1990) *Computers and Learning: Helping Children Acquire Thinking Skills*. Oxford: Blackwell.

Underwood, J. (ed.) (1994) *Computer Based Learning: Potential into Practice*. London: David Fulton.

CHAPTER 17

Drama

Tig O'Hearn

*In life, experiences do not come in separate packages
with subject labels.*

(DES, 1989)

When the present government invented the National
Curriculum, it decided that the educational experiences of children from 5 to 16 years of age should be divided into ten separate
subject packages.

Each package was given its own subject and colour to distinguish it from other packages. They fitted nicely on a shelf or two
in every staff room throughout the country.

Conscientious teachers could use these tomes to find out
whether they were delivering that which the government
deemed important. They could also check which subject they
were teaching and so avoid the confusion of what the radical
Right saw as 'outmoded, leftist', cross-curricular links.

There was one package that was missing. It could have fitted
anywhere along the shelf, quite comfortably wedged between
History (purple) and Geography (brown), English (yellow) and
Art (orange), or Music (pink) and Physical Education (blue), for
example. It would have been very happy next to Personal, Social
and Health Education, but alas, that did not warrant its own

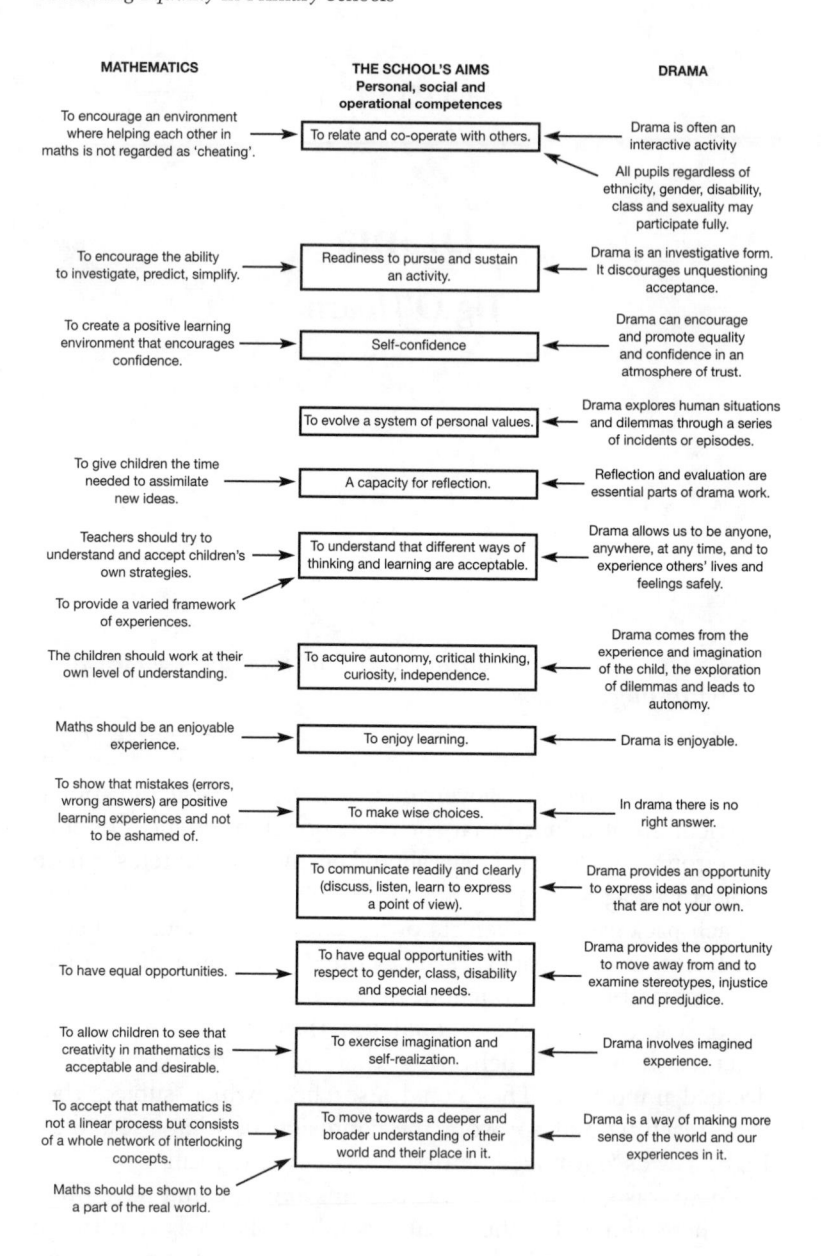

MATHEMATICS

THE SCHOOL'S AIMS
Personal, social and
operational competences

DRAMA

To encourage an environment where helping each other in maths is not regarded as 'cheating'.

To relate and co-operate with others.

Drama is often an interactive activity

All pupils regardless of ethnicity, gender, disability, class and sexuality may participate fully.

To encourage the ability to investigate, predict, simplify.

Readiness to pursue and sustain an activity.

Drama is an investigative form. It discourages unquestioning acceptance.

To create a positive learning environment that encourages confidence.

Self-confidence

Drama can encourage and promote equality and confidence in an atmosphere of trust.

To evolve a system of personal values.

Drama explores human situations and dilemmas through a series of incidents or episodes.

To give children the time needed to assimilate new ideas.

A capacity for reflection.

Reflection and evaluation are essential parts of drama work.

Teachers should try to understand and accept children's own strategies.

To understand that different ways of thinking and learning are acceptable.

Drama allows us to be anyone, anywhere, at any time, and to experience others' lives and feelings safely.

To provide a varied framework of experiences.

The children should work at their own level of understanding.

To acquire autonomy, critical thinking, curiosity, independence.

Drama comes from the experience and imagination of the child, the exploration of dilemmas and leads to autonomy.

Maths should be an enjoyable experience.

To enjoy learning.

Drama is enjoyable.

To show that mistakes (errors, wrong answers) are positive learning experiences and not to be ashamed of.

To make wise choices.

In drama there is no right answer.

To communicate readily and clearly (discuss, listen, learn to express a point of view).

Drama provides an opportunity to express ideas and opinions that are not your own.

To have equal opportunities.

To have equal opportunities with respect to gender, class, disability and special needs.

Drama provides the opportunity to move away from and to examine stereotypes, injustice and predjudice.

To allow children to see that creativity in mathematics is acceptable and desirable.

To exercise imagination and self-realization.

Drama involves imagined experience.

To accept that mathematics is not a linear process but consists of a whole network of interlocking concepts.

To move towards a deeper and broader understanding of their world and their place in it.

Drama is a way of making more sense of the world and our experiences in it.

Maths should be shown to be a part of the real world.

Figure 17.1   School development plan – mathematics and drama

388

package either (perhaps they ran out of colours). The colour of this package should have been gold, bright, reflective and universally valued. Its subject would have been Drama.

At present, Drama is squeezed into the English National Curriculum. The Arts Council *Guidance on Drama Education* states:

> The Statutory Order for English in the National Curriculum shows that Drama, as a component of a Core Subject is required to be taught by law. The component is largely identified within the Speaking and Listening Attainment up to and including Level 6.
> (Arts Council of Great Britain, 1992)

Despite the fact that schools are legally required to teach drama, I believe the subject is underused in many primary schools, partly due to its low status in the National Curriculum. Whether the slimmed down Curriculum remedies this, remains to be seen.

In this chapter I intend to examine the power of drama as a vehicle for the exploration of issues of (in)equality, and to show that, if it is delivered by open-minded, flexible teachers, it can enable children to experience equality in their own education.

I discovered drama about four years ago when I attended a twilight course run by West Sussex Education Authority. I believe that it has, at the very least, as valuable a role to play in the education of our children, as any subject in the present National Curriculum. To begin to convince my overworked and pressured colleagues of this, I used our school's Development Plan and its Mathematics Policy to show how the (egalitarian) aims and philosophy of our school, can be reflected and delivered by subjects as seemingly diverse as mathematics and drama (see Figure 17.1, which I have adapted slightly).

WHY DRAMA CAN HELP THE PROMOTION OF EQUALITY IN THE PRIMARY CLASSROOM

- Drama should enable children to share and examine experiences from the different perspectives of class, gender, ethnicity, sexuality and disability.
- All pupils, be they gifted or with other special needs, physically or educationally, or with little or no English, may participate fully in drama. No one is excluded.

- Drama is appropriate for the whole age and ability range in our schools since its emphasis is on the individual perception of each member of the group, including the teacher.
- Drama allows children safely to adopt attitudes that are not necessarily their own and so they can explore human situations and dilemmas from other points of view.
- Drama is an effective tool in enabling children to recognize and explore racism, sexism, social class discrimination, stereotyping and injustice.
- Drama helps children to develop the skills to challenge these issues whenever they arise.
- Drama helps develop the children's ability to think quickly and to be adaptable.

I have talked to many teachers who feel that they 'can't' teach drama, that they would feel too exposed and vulnerable, especially when going into role. Even excellent, experienced practitioners have said that they worry about drama lessons disintegrating into an orgy of silly behaviour.

Primary teachers do not, in general, recognize and value their skills sufficiently. We should remember that questioning, especially open-ended questioning, is second nature to most of us. We use it all the time, in every aspect of school life, social or academic, to encourage the children to think for themselves. In drama, the questioning is an important skill for the teacher in role. We do not impose our ideas yet we can direct, and so still have control over what happens. We might say:

- What would happen if ...?
- Where do you think ...?
- When did it ...?
- How did we know that ...?
- How can we change this ...?
- Can you help me ...?

It takes time and practice to play in role convincingly but it does not require the ability to perform, as a professional actor might, using different voices or accents, for example. Successful teacher role play allows the children to do the talking, thinking, responding and decision-making. It provides an opportunity for the teacher-in-role to encourage the quiet, shy ones to contribute and to keep a balance between the genders so neither is too dominant. As the drama/story evolves, so aspects of the role will develop in response to the story. It is necessary to be flexible and to think quickly. These are skills which every competent teacher possesses, and yet we tend to undervalue our talents.

I suggest that teachers who are wary of drama should try going into role for a short time: ten minutes would do. Also they should remember that the drama can be stopped at any time. It does not have to drag on painfully until playtime.

When working with a new group I introduce ground rules that need to be established before the drama begins.

- The drama must be believable. For example, it would not be believable if a child in role as a medieval peasant spoke in a silly voice and started to strangle the local Lord of the Manor.
- There are no right answers – just responses that may be more or less appropriate to any given situation.
- When we sit in a circle (usually at the beginning and end of sessions) the class must sit girl/boy/girl/boy as far as possible. I find that this begins to break down gender barriers, creates new working groups, and the resulting drama is generally of a much higher quality than if the working groups are single-sex.
- When we are working in the hall we use only half of it. It is easily divided by using benches. This makes it easier to gather the children together at any point. Drama lessons can just as easily take place in the classroom, as in the hall.

I always explain that in drama we can be anyone, go anywhere and go backwards and forwards in time, but it is a pretence. It is vital that the children understand the difference between what is real and what is drama – that we are starting a 'fiction', an imaginary situation and adopting a 'fictional role' – we are not ourselves. A sign of when the drama begins is useful. Statements like:

- 'When I roll up my sleeve ...'
- 'When I put on this shawl ...'
- 'When I hold this book ... I am in role as ...'

will aid the children's understanding and increase their sense of security and trust, which is an essential element of drama. In order to explore new ground and take risks confidently in drama, the group needs to work in an atmosphere of trust and security. A close partnership between the teacher and children, and between the children themselves is especially necessary when working with drama.

I agree with Jonathan Neelands when he writes:

> Spontaneous drama work cannot be imposed. You cannot set drama, or worse coerce groups into it. A group has to move to a point where they are willing to work at a subjective level of involvement in open ended pretending situations. Successful drama does not stem from silent obedience to a teacher's authority and status. (You can shout and scream that maths has to be done, or that spellings have to be learnt – but unless a child willingly enters the drama on her own terms, nothing will happen.)
>
> (Neelands, 1984:27)

The nature of drama lends itself to encouraging questioning, openness to ideas and the acceptance of the right of all individuals to hold and express a viewpoint. As a teacher of drama, I accept all the answers and opinions given by the children when in role. I may ask the group if the role play is believable in the given context and encourage an open discussion. Alternative outcomes are often suggested. The fact that no response is 'right' in the sense of representing the only way someone in that role would react and therefore by the same token none is 'wrong', gives the children a sense of security in which to experiment. They become more inclined to explore different perspectives, grow in self-esteem when they know their views and interpretations are valued and thereby move towards a greater autonomy.

˙ HOW?

Drama, certainly at primary level, is essentially a group activity. For both the children and the teacher in the group to experience equality, a feeling of unity and trust needs to be established.

Warm-ups and games can play an important part in this. I was fortunate enough to be involved in a project organized by West Sussex County Youth Theatre. English and Spanish students aged between 15 and 24 were brought together for two weeks on a production of *A Midsummer Night's Dream*. Only a few of the students knew each other and time was at a premium. It was important to break the ice very early on by overcoming language and cultural barriers.

We played introductory games, group games, exercises that involved physical contact and non-verbal communication. By the end of the evening, all of us felt we were part of a group identity and were united in our aim of producing a performance. From that evening on, I noticed that during and between rehearsal, members of the 'Dream Team', regardless of nationality, gender, acting experience or age could be found heaped together in comfortable piles like sleepy puppies. I am sure that the 'games' fostered this sense of unity and trust.

Many very useful exercises can be found in Augusto Boal's (1992) book *Games for Actors and Non-Actors*, some of which I have used successfully with primary age children.

SAMPLE LESSON: *JYOTI'S JOURNEY*

Stories are useful for exploring social issues. I have used *Jyoti's Journey* (Ganley, 1986) with a group of 28 children in Years 4 and 5. Two of the group were Asian, the rest were white. This picture book, which is beautifully illustrated, tells the story of a young girl, Jyoti, who lives in a small village in India with her mother, sisters and grandmother. Jyoti's father has been in England for two years. One day the family go to a cousin's wedding, where there is much joy and celebration. On their return home, Jyoti's mother finds a letter from her husband asking her and Jyoti to join him in England. Grandmother and the two youngest children go to stay with friends in a nearby village. Jyoti and her mother fly to England where they are met by Jyoti's father and taken to a flat in a tower block. Everything feels cold and bleak to Jyoti.

My aims for these four drama sessions were:

- To introduce early drama strategies and to encourage their use as a form of expression and interpretation.
- To encourage empathy with others – to emphasize the similarities between Jyoti and themselves.
- To examine life from another viewpoint.

- To encourage the children to look beyond the pages of a book and examine the possibilities of expansion – and alternative outcomes.

The children did not know each other well as they came from six different classes and had never worked as a group before. Because of this, I felt it was important to get to know each other and to establish a group identity. I used the following exercises with this aim in mind. I did not use them all for every session. It is important that the teacher joins in all the activities wherever possible.

As the group becomes familiar with the exercises, different members can introduce the games and the teacher becomes part of the main group and is redundant as a leader.

Introductory games

Everyone stands in a large circle:

- The first person says her/his name and makes a gesture to show how s/he is feeling at this moment. The whole group repeats the name and gesture, – then the next person says her/his name with a gesture, and so on round the circle.
- The first person introduces the person on her/his left using their name and their gesture, 'This is my friend ...' and the whole group repeats this.
- One of the group throws a ball to someone s/he knows and says her/his name.
- Pass the magic – number one turns to the person on her/his left (or right), makes eye contact and claps – number two quickly makes eye contact with number three and claps, and so on round the circle as fast as they can go. (This requires immense concentration and is very satisfying when it goes right.)

Blindfold exercises

These exercises are useful for raising questions about trusting and being trusted. It is best if the partners swop over so each can experience what the other has been through.

Working in pairs

- A is blindfolded. B leads A around the room touching A and describing their journey.
- A and B work out a signalling system to enable B to guide A around without speaking (e.g. tap on the back means 'stop', etc). No sound can be made.
- A and B devise their own particular sound for B to make and A to recognize. B moves away from A and makes the sound, directing A to find her/him.

Working as a group

The class is put into groups of four or six.

- Each group is divided into two. Group A is blindfolded and B makes a group sculpture. A feels Group B and then tries to make an identical sculpture. The moment of truth when A removes their blindfolds can be quite amusing!

Afterwards we discussed the feelings the children had during these exercises. Did they feel vulnerable, dependent or uneasy when blindfolded? Did they trust their partner and feel cared for? Did the 'sighted' group feel powerful, responsible, aware of their partners' needs. With experienced children this can be done with much larger groups.

Working with the story

I began by reading the story from beginning to end, showing the pictures. I did not encourage any discussion of the story at this point. I wanted ideas and thoughts to develop as they explored the story.

During the sessions we examined parts of the story that existed in the book and explored events that could have happened.

Mime

Jyoti had jobs to do at home in India. Individually members of the group mimed a job that s/he might do at home. They showed a partner and discussed what they were both doing.

Frozen image and thought tracking

In groups of three or four the children imagined a scene at their homes or Jyoti's, just as they or she arrived back from school. They made a frozen image. Each voiced the thoughts of their character.

Discussion

We brainstormed the question of what sorts of things make a home a home, rather than just somewhere to live? (I recorded the suggestions and kept them to compare later on with Jyoti's reaction to her new flat.)

Flashback

With groups of three or four we made a frozen image of the moment that Jyoti learned that her father was leaving. They brought the scene to life. We heard the actual words that were spoken and then the thoughts of those in the scene. We asked were they different? Why?

All the groups actually decided that Jyoti's father was emigrating so that he could earn more money for the family. This raised the question of why people move and emigrate – is it always voluntary? What about refugees? Who are refugees? Where do they come from? What about those seeking political asylum? Through discussion the groups became aware that people from all over the world regardless of ethnicity or wealth, may emigrate or become refugees.

Hotseating

Initially this was the teacher in role as Jyoti's father. The class asked how he felt about leaving home, his reasons for doing so and what it was like in a strange place. As they developed in confidence they took it in turns to be in the hotseat. Time to change was indicated by a member of the group gently tapping the hotseat on the shoulder and taking her/his place. This can also work with a group of children in the hotseat acting as one character. This provides a support framework for the less confident.

Frozen image

The whole class moved on to an image of the wedding photograph and froze on a count of three. We discussed what had made Jyoti happy that day. The group felt that to be happy it was important to be surrounded by family and friends.

Defining a space

We moved, by contrast, to Jyoti's father's flat and, by defining a space, created the room in which he was sitting when he wrote the letter in which he sent for Jyoti and her mother. One member of the group was placed in the room, in role as father.

Soundtracking

Using our bodies and voices we created the sounds that he may have heard while he was writing this letter: a radio playing in the flat above; rain on the window, pigeons cooing; traffic passing on the road many storeys below; the fridge humming; clock ticking; footsteps approaching his door, but passing by, etc.

We discussed the contrast between Jyoti's life and her father's at this time.

A moment in time

In groups of three or four the children re-enacted the scene where the letter from England arrives. The reactions and thoughts of the individuals in the family were explored and discussed. We talked about how long two years is (the length of time since Jyoti had seen her father) and what can happen in that time. They looked back in their own lives to see what they were doing two years ago.

In a circle we expressed the grandmother's feelings about going to stay with another family when Jyoti and her mother left. Many issues were raised: Will the younger children listen to me? Will I lose my independence? Will I ever be with my whole family again?

A parting gift

The group stood in two equal parallel lines. Line A represented grandmother, Line B represented Jyoti. Each person in line A presented their opposite partner in line B with a gift and spoke one line of dialogue. A stepped forward to receive the gift and also spoke one line as a response to the gift. This was repeated but with their thoughts expressed. In most cases Grandma and Jyoti were seen to be concealing their true feelings of fear and sadness, by putting on a brave face.

Final scenarios

The final scenarios included going through immigration at the British airport where half the group, as airport officials, devised a sinister intimidating march and chant. The other half, as tired immigrants, responded in a cowed and frightened way.

We used *Forum Theatre* to examine how a different response from the airport officials may have elicited a more positive reaction from the 'immigrants'.

Finally we hotseated Jyoti to find out what she felt about her present situation and what hope she had for the future.

Anything can be used to start off the drama: a poem, an extract from a book or newspaper, or an artefact can lead to complex and meaningful insights.

FORUM THEATRE

The technique of Forum Theatre is an excellent means of encouraging children safely to explore issues that they find threatening. In my own teaching, the areas that most frequently arise are bullying in all its shapes and forms, racism and conflict at home.

Forum Theatre is a form within the movement of the Theatre of the Oppressed, developed by the Brazilian director Augusto Boal. This form of theatre has been used all over the world for over twenty years, so inevitably there are many manifestations of it in use today. Ali Campbell writes that:

> the principle philosophy of the work is that everybody can and does act out a role in real life, often playing to a script which isn't under their control. Through theatre which is a language of action that all can easily use, we can, however, not just talk about but act out other ways of living and being, more beneficial to our selves. Boal calls this 'a rehearsal for reality'.
>
> (Campbell, 1994:1)

In Forum Theatre the spectators become active spect-ACTORS. They have the right to intervene during or at the end of a scene, and to substitute themselves for any of the actors and lead the action in their chosen direction. The other actors in the group have now to respond to a new situation. The power to change the outcome of a situation is equally in the hands of each individual in the group.

I deliberately withdraw from my role as 'joker' (a Boal term for facilitator) as the children become more confident and adept at implementing their own changes. With enough experience the Forum should become peer led.

IMAGE THEATRE

A useful way in to Forum is Image Theatre. As with Forum Theatre, there are many different ways of using Image Theatre. One method that I have used with primary-aged children is as follows.

After some warm-ups which focus on co-operation and physical trust, I ask the class, in groups of five or so, to make a group body sculpture of forms of transport, a room in a house, or a piece of furniture, for example. They then dynamize it, bring it to life, using sounds and actions. Each group shows their image. This often causes much hilarity. A clap of the hands is a signal for the action and sound to stop and for the sculpture to freeze. We look again at each group and I change their perception of the sculpture by asking the question, 'If this image is at the shops/in the playground/classroom/cloakroom, *what can you see?*'

The children suggest what is happening. The 'joker', whether teacher or child, chooses a scenario to be explored. Using thought and speech bubbles, the whole class starts to build up the story. The 'joker' will ask 'What is this person actually saying? Now, what is this person really thinking?' The action of the scenario continues and Forum Theatre takes over when anyone who thinks they have a solution to the problem shouts 'Stop!' and substitutes her/himself for the person with the problem and tries out something else. Always the question 'How did it feel?' is asked of the victim(s) and perpetrator(s). As different solutions are tried out and the outcomes change even slightly, the responses change too. Often the victim is offered strategies that could possibly relieve the situation.

THE GREAT GAME OF POWER

This exercise is simple but thought provoking. It can be used as another way into Forum, or devising a story, or exploring issues.
Six chairs are set out round a table (see Figure 17.2).

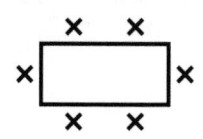

Figure 17.2   The great game of power

The group is told which chair represents the most power and which the least. They then sculpt the furniture in such a way as to show this. You can have the whole class working on one sculpture, but I prefer to divide them into smaller groups of five or so, each with their own table and chairs. We look at each sculpture in turn and interpret them. Many interesting ideas start to flow. For example:

- This one is trapped under the powerful one and is being held in by the others;
- This one has been pushed away from its friends because it is weak;
- The powerful one has its back to the others.

We discuss the similarities and differences between the groups' ideas. They begin to understand the concept of different interpretations. I then ask each member of the group carefully and slowly to become part of their sculpture. This is done in silence and with no conferring. They have to be aware of the rest of the group.

Some stand on chairs, some support those chairs, others crouch under the table, some cover their heads, some exude power, just by the way they hold themselves. We then look again at each sculpture. I ask:

'Where could this be? What is happening?'

The children begin to buzz with ideas and stories begin to emerge:

- This is a bully. No one wants to look at her. She has kicked this one because he told on her.
- This is a boy and his mum and stepdad are having a row.
- This is the King and these are his servants. This one is in the dungeon.

The possibilities for follow-up are numerous. I have used this exercise recently as an introduction to some work on medieval realms, with a Year 7 group. I used drama to help the group to look at the class structure of those times, its effect on people's lives and to compare it with society today.

If children are given the opportunity to experience equality in their own education and are encouraged to recognize and explore inequality within and beyond their own experiences, they will be empowered to challenge issues of discrimination when they encounter them.

While running a Forum Theatre training session for teachers in West Sussex, Ali Campbell asked us to think about whether equality is something that we fight for or something that we allow to happen.

I believe that as teachers, responsible for the education of the future generation, we should fight for equality and also let it happen.

REFERENCES

Arts Council (1992) *Guidance on Drama Education*. London: The Arts Council of Great Britain.

Boal, A. (1992) *Games for Actors and Non-Actors*. London: Routledge.

Campbell, A. (1994) *Report on Phase One of West Sussex Health Education Through Drama Project January/February 1994*.

Department of Education and Science (DES) (1989) *Maths Non-Statutory Guidance*. London: HMSO.

Ganly, H. (1986) *Jyoti's Journey*. London: Andre Deutsch.

Neelands, J. (1984) *Making Sense of Drama*. London: Heinemann.

CHAPTER 18

Promoting and monitoring equal opportunities

Sheila Humbert

Equality of opportunity in education plays a small but significant role in the wider provision of equality within British society, the historical progress of which has been inconsistent and closely linked to both the economic and social climate. The 1975 Sex Discrimination Act and the 1976 Race Relations Act were not only a response to growing public awareness and concern for equality issues, but also required considerable public funding. The progress of equal opportunities in education is undoubtedly influenced by social and economic circumstance and has therefore followed a similarly disrupted path. Its current position, perhaps due to lack of recognition and funding, remains somewhat unco-ordinated.

This chapter considers four connected areas, under the following headings:

- Where are we now? – a view of the current position of equal opportunities in primary education.
- Monitoring and attitude surveys – identifying areas for development at school level.
- Classroom resource packs – facilitating an equal opportunities approach in the classroom.
- Further school initiatives – examples of some successful equal opportunities initiatives.

WHERE ARE WE NOW?

Despite the fact that the complete school curriculum provides numerous opportunities to promote equality, major research has tended to address issues within specific areas. Subject-based research has intermittently produced evidence and recommendations which have contributed to equal provision within curriculum subjects; for example, the GIST (Girls into Science and Technology) Action Research Project, which commenced in 1979 and investigated the underachievement of females in science and technology. Through the use of classroom intervention strategies it succeeded in developing a more positive attitude towards science and technology in female pupils. In mathematics the Cockcroft report (1982), noted concern for the achievement of certain social groups. Similarly, the Swann Report (1985) promoted the multi-cultural aspect of equal opportunities. These government-funded initiatives raised awareness in specific curriculum subject areas, while a cross-curricular and holistic approach to equal opportunities appears to have been accorded less status.

Within this chapter, the interpretation of 'cross-curricular' extends beyond the limitations of curriculum subjects to include the full range of school activities, both in and out of the classroom. An holistic approach to equal provision must embrace every school-based activity. Teachers also need to recognize the effects of external influences on the pupils and the school itself, both of which are products of our society.

While many local education authorities now proclaim themselves to be equal opportunity employers, few have comprehensive policies for the provision of equal opportunities in their schools, despite the fact that many authorities developed policy statements on 'gender' and 'race' in the social climate of the 1980s. Furthermore, financial devolution, within the introduction of Local Management of Schools, has placed funding for equal opportunities in the hands of governing bodies. There is therefore serious cause for concern that, in the absence of clear guidelines from local education authorities, the importance of both equal provision and education for equality may fail to be recognized.

However, it is encouraging to note that the explicit requirements of the Office for Standards in Education (OFSTED) provide some leverage to promote equality of opportunity. OFSTED makes reference to the implementation of school policy, establishing the legal requirement to develop a policy, a need previously contested in some schools. However, the content, implementation, monitoring and review of such policies will be the subject of continuing debate. While the requirements are clearly outlined, individual schools are left to determine how those requirements are best met.

The following extract from the OFSTED *Handbook for the Inspection of Schools* (1993), gives some indication of the degree of equal opportunities organization and planning now required from schools.

7.3.(ii) Equality of Opportunity

Evaluation criteria
The school's arrangements for equality of opportunity are evaluated by the extent to which:

- all pupils, irrespective of gender, ability (including giftedness), ethnicity and social circumstance, have access to the curriculum and make the greatest progress possible;
- the school meets the requirements of the Sex Discrimination Act (1975) and the Race Relations Act (1976).

Evidence should include:

a   standards of achievement of individuals and groups;
b   assessment of pupil's needs within the curriculum;
c   the school's stated policy for equal opportunity;
d   admission policies, intake, exclusions;
e   curriculum content and access;
f   class organisation and management, teaching and differentiation;
g   the use made of support teachers, bilingual assistants and other provision under section 11 of the Local Government Act 1966;
h   pupils' relationships.

OFSTED (1993)

Despite OFSTED requirements, equal opportunities promotion in many schools remains controversial, with one of the main areas of debate focusing on the practical definition of equal provision. The two most commonly held views can be summarized as follows:

Standardization

This approach standardizes the delivery of education to ensure that all pupils receive identical opportunities. It is concerned with establishing practices and procedures that avoid overt and covert discrimination, but it is less concerned with the preparedness or achievement of pupils, in other words, with more equal outcomes.

Compensation

In this approach the emphasis is on the input and output rather than the system itself. It recognizes that some pupils enter the educational system heavily disadvantaged and seeks to compensate in order that certain disadvantaged groups may improve achievement. This approach seeks more equal outcomes.

Although these opposing views are primarily an educational issue, it inevitably reflects personal opinion and invites comment on our social system, which is inextricably linked to our educational system. I would suggest that advocates of standardization are not sufficiently dissatisfied to attempt to change the status quo, while those who support compensation envisage only minimal progress without reconstruction of our social system. It is my view that equal access can be more successfully achieved through the use of compensatory activities, to counter some of the disadvantages of pupils' formative experience. These might take the form of additional support for language skills, or the use of practical equipment or ensuring equal access to playground space.

National and educational press coverage undoubtedly contributes to classroom teachers' perceptions of equal opportunities issues and perhaps therefore influences its promotion within schools. There continues to be regular, if limited, coverage in the mainstream educational press, focusing primarily on 'race' and gender but less so on disability and special needs and with very little reference to social class and sexuality. Subject-based research into equality issues is usually featured in journals and reviews, but these have limited accessibility. Unfortunately, there is little representation of a cross-curricular approach to equal opportunities, a reflection of the subject-dominated National Curriculum. Although wider media coverage includes discussion on many important aspects of education, such as curriculum legislation, funding or public examinations, the development of equal opportunities currently appears to have little status.

Past research into equal opportunities provision has successfully identified areas of concern and raised the level of awareness. As a practising primary teacher it is my experience that overt sexual and racial discrimination are no longer considered acceptable and that teachers now tend to have a better understanding of the subtle nature of discrimination and counter-discrimination – for example, the lack of positive role models for particular social groups or the positive/negative influence of classroom interactions and management. Although much literature emphasizes the importance of a cross-curricular and holistic approach, there is still a distinct lack of advice and material with which to convert theory into practice. It is hoped that this book successfully addresses the problem.

School discussion on the provision of equal opportunities will no doubt include the choice between a subject-based approach on the one hand and a cross-curricular approach on the other. A 'whole school' approach should provide a degree of consistency across the formal curriculum, the wider curriculum and the hidden curriculum. As with all school provision, the delivery of equal opportunities will be most effective when carefully planned and undoubtedly facilitated by the appointment of an equal opportunities co-ordinator. In a large school, particularly, this will allow a degree of co-ordination otherwise unachievable if responsibilities for equal provision are allocated to subject consultants. Although the development and implementation of an equal opportunities policy will of course require whole staff discussion and agreement, its promotion and progression may depend on the understanding and skill of an equal opportunities co-ordinator, as well as the active support of colleagues. In this, the legitimating role of the school management is also crucial.

MONITORING

Before an effective development plan for equal opportunities can be drawn up it is essential to establish the current individual school situation. This necessitates close monitoring of school practices and pupils' responses to them. The reality of what is really happening in school may not match very accurately with what staff perceive to be happening. Nevertheless, impartial monitoring can be achieved through two means: (a) statistical and (b) observational.

Statistical monitoring

The following extract, from the Equal Opportunities section of the OFSTED Handbook (1993) illustrates the requirement both to monitor the academic progress of groups of pupils, although limited to gender and ethnicity, and to use the results to inform future planning.

> Monitoring
> Inspectors should establish whether the school monitors outcomes by gender and ethnicity; whether examination or test results are compared with earlier assessments of ability or attainment; whether the destinations of different groups of pupils on leaving school are analysed and whether teachers are aware of the results of such monitoring and use it for planning and guidance purposes.
> OFSTED (1993)

The main social groups within the school must first be identified. It will not be possible to monitor statistically unless pupils are represented in sufficient numbers. Within my own school, although pupils from Asian cultures represent 20 per cent of the number on roll, the vast majority of all pupils, regardless of ethnic origin, are drawn from the immediate community and share a similar socio-economic background. The two main divisions for monitoring purposes are therefore 'race' and gender. Each pupil can be classified by a simple code as follows:

FA = Female Asian FE = Female European FO = Female Other
MA = Male Asian ME = Male European MO = Male Other

Subdivision, by religions, for example, may be useful, but consideration should be given to the likely provision that can be offered following the identification of need correlated to social groups. Can the school consider providing additional support to subdivided social groups? Or is it more realistic to concentrate on larger groups? It is not my suggestion that this administrative identification of social groups should disregard the needs of individuals or small groups. Nevertheless, where time and funding limits provision it may be necessary to incorporate them into larger groups, while still recognizing their specific needs. Monitoring pupil achievement along such lines will not only enable a more accurate provision of support, but also serve to justify equal opportunities initiatives when necessary.

Observational monitoring

This type of monitoring can be applied to a wide range of school practices and activities. Classroom interaction has been the subject of much educational research and, as a well recognized research tool, several formats of observation have developed. Such close observation does require a high level of confidence and co-operation among staff, but will offer a valuable insight into classroom reality, and therefore the opportunity to redress the balance where necessary in favour of certain pupil groups.

Monitoring of classroom interaction and monitoring of play areas and other shared space can provide a surprising amount of relevant information on which to base equal opportunities intervention. However, in order to gain a more complete picture, monitoring could be extended to cover some of the following, as appropriate to individual schools:

- Participation in extra-curricular activities, both initial response and persistence (i.e. who joins and who stays?).
- Adult attendance at consultation evenings: are certain social groups less well supported and if so what can be done to encourage greater support?
- Allocation of responsibilities and tasks, participation in public events, contributions to assemblies, etc. All contribute to furnishing a clearer picture of the school reality, which must be established in order to provide an accurate starting-point and a higher standard of equal opportunities provision.

ATTITUDE SURVEYS

Advocating a cross-curricular and holistic approach to equal opportunities does not imply adopting the 'standardization' philosophy. Standardization treatment of equality issues within school will not make best use of the type of detailed evaluation previously outlined. For example, allocating equal time and resources to each curriculum subject may only perpetuate the existing differences. As science and technology are well documented as subjects in which females underachieve, there may be a case in many schools for a greater input in these areas in order to redress the balance. The use of attitude surveys, in specific areas, will enable a more accurate assessment of need. It will give access to information that will contribute to an understanding of some underachievement, or of certain patterns of behaviour in pupils. Areas for intervention can then be more precisely identified. It is widely accepted within the teaching profession that pupils' attitudes, related in part to the attitudes of teachers and peers to them, do influence their achievement and their level of participation. Educational research does support teacher experience, while acknowledging that many other factors also contribute to underachievement. Despite the fact that some factors contributing to the underachievement of some social groups are beyond the influence of primary education, such as social and economic circumstance, changes in attitude can be achieved.

While the following examples of the use of attitude surveys refer to science, the principles and methods can be applied to other subjects or cross-curricular areas. The Manchester-based GIST project of 1979 was an action research programme, investigating the causes of female underachievement in science and technology and attempting to instigate change. It employed attitude surveys with 11-year-olds and analysed the results by gender. The following quote from the GIST Final Report (1984), indicates its success.

> The specific focus of intervention was the stereotyping of science and technology as masculine, and in this respect the children's attitudes were considerably modified.
>
> (Kelly *et al.*, 1984)

My own school-based science research supported the GIST findings, and gave a valuable insight into the science and gender issue in my school. Pre- and post-intervention attitude questionnaires were employed with Year 6 pupils, and analysed by ethnicity and gender, as these were the two most significant social groups within the school.

The pre-intervention attitude survey showed that responses correlated more closely to gender than to ethnicity, with girls displaying a less positive attitude than boys to science. The classroom intervention covered five weeks and consisted mainly of providing 'hands on' experience, for the whole class, in a range of science activities. The post-intervention results showed a 60 per cent increase in positive attitude in girls, despite the limitations of such a small-scale study.

While intervention strategies of this nature may not always be possible, the use of attitude surveys should be considered as a means of collecting detailed information to better inform any assessment of a whole school situation. They need not be confined to curriculum subject areas, but could be extended to investigate attitudes to 'race', gender, religion, culture, disability, sexuality, class, or indeed any area which raises issues of equality. Needless to say, assessment of such sensitive areas should be a whole school decision and would probably require the support of the governing body. Devising a suitable questionnaire will need careful consideration and should take cognisance of past research. The information gathered will have the advantage of being specific to your school and free you from depending on the assumption that what has been documented elsewhere is relevant to your pupils. The more specific information you have about your pupils the more accurate and effective your equal opportunities provision will be. I include a copy of the science attitude survey used in my school research, together with an outline of the method used to analyse the results. I hope that this might be usefully employed in other schools (see Table 18.1)

Table 18.1   Attitude survey (Science)

Name _____

Class _____   Girl _____   Boy _____

1 Tick three things you would like to know more about

Space Exploration __	Painting and Drawing __	Music and Dance __
Homes and Families __	Electricity/Magnetism __	How Things Fly __
Kings and Queens __	The Human Body __	How Machines Work __

2 Do you think building sets like Lego are

Good fun __   O.K. __   Boring __

3 Tick the three most interesting jobs

Driver __	Sales Assistant __	Atomic Scientist __
Receptionist __	Chemist __	Hairdresser __
Doctor __	Electrician __	Teacher __

4 Do you think your science lessons at school are

Good fun __   O.K. __   Boring __

5 Tick the three presents you would like best

A Board Game __	A Microscope __	Clothes __
Sports Equipment __	Books __	A Painting Set __
Music/Video Cassette __	Lego Technic __	A Chemistry Set __

6 Do you watch science programmes on TV such as *Johnny Ball* or *How To* or *It'll Never Work*?

Often __   Sometimes __   Never __

7 Tick three jobs you might do when you are grown up

Plumber __	Drugs Researcher __	Teacher __
Telephonist __	Driver __	Beautician __
Inventor __	Sales Person __	Doctor __

Is there any other job you might do? _____

8 Do you read children's books about science experiments?

Often __   Sometimes __   Never __

Thank you.

Results

The questions were designed to reveal pupils' attitudes to a range of scientific activities and were given the following titles:

```
Q1   Topic subject preference
Q2   Construction kits
Q3   Job interest
Q4   School science
Q5   Gift preference
Q6   TV science
Q7   Job aspirations
Q8   Science reading
```

The questions were of two main types:

1   The graded question, in which the children selected from three responses graded from positive to negative.
2   The multiple choice question, in which the children selected three from nine responses.

In order to focus more clearly on the significance of the results, in their role as a measure of attitude, the 'positive' science responses were considered separately. In the multiple choice questions, three of the nine choices were designed to reflect a positive attitude to science and these are identified as follows:

```
Q1 Topic subject preference   Choice E  – Electricity and Magnetism
                              Choice H – How Things Fly
                              Choice I  – How Machines Work
Q3 Job Interest               Choice C – Doctor
                              Choice E – Chemist
                              Choice G – Atomic Scientist
Q5 Gift Preference            Choice D – Microscope
                              Choice F  – Lego Technic
                              Choice I  – Chemistry Set
Q7 Job Aspirations            Choice C – Inventor
                              Choice D – Drugs Researcher
                              Choice I  – Doctor
```

In the graded questions, in order to focus on the 'positive' indicators, the negative response is simply discounted. Pupils were given an ethnicity and gender classification code and a simple frequency count was made of the number of positive responses from each social group. These results were recorded on a class results sheet, on which the 'positive' responses were asterisked for ease of reference. The format could of course be adapted to accommodate different social groupings.

CLASSROOM RESOURCE PACKS

A cross-curricular approach to equal opportunities is facilitated in schools where teaching is topic based as opposed to subject based. Fortunately, although under assault from the government, topic-based work appears still to be the norm in most primary schools. It cannot be denied that availability of resources plays a crucial role in determining not only what is taught in the classroom, but also how it is taught. The resources for cross-curricular topics are often selected from a wide range of available materials, a practice which although time-consuming does allow teachers the opportunity to develop a specific focus and meet the interests of the pupils. Some equal opportunities material may well be included within subject-based publications. The equal opportunities content of a topic frequently depends on the knowledge and commitment of individual teachers, but even the most committed teachers cannot succeed without adequate provision of suitable resources.

Equal opportunities work can be facilitated through the introduction of classroom 'resource packs'. Such resource packs, topic based where appropriate, would provide the class teacher with a ready-to-use and 'user-friendly' equal opportunities option. Some equality issues may not be easily topic linked but can be separately addressed. Packs could be developed to cover, for example, racism, sexism, disability, bullying, sexuality or social class discrimination, following whole school agreement. More confident teachers might expand and extend the contents of resource packs, while others rely on them to provide a coverage of equal opportunities which might otherwise not exist. Of course, staff training in equal opportunities to provide skills and knowledge should not be neglected, nor the need for teacher support groups.

Access to the curriculum would be improved through the provision of equal opportunities resource packs, which could fulfil the following aims:

- to present classroom work in a way that certain social groups could relate to more easily;
- to challenge stereotyping and counter discrimination;
- to achieve the first two aims through differentiation by ability.

Access to the curriculum is given a high priority in the OFSTED requirements, as illustrated by the following quotation, from the

Equal Opportunities section of the OFSTED Handbook (1993): 'The core task is to assess the influence of the school's practice and policies on pupils' access to the curriculum and their achievements.'

The specific contents of an equal opportunities resource pack will depend on the resources available within individual schools, but does not have to be limited to a selection of worksheets from published materials. A list of a range of activities should be provided and might include suggestions for role play in drama, use of video material, use of parents and/or visitors, or suitable theatre visits.

The following example is suggested for a topic based on Food and Farming, which lends itself naturally to an egalitarian approach. For reasons of copyright and because each school will have different resources from which to select, it is not possible to include a wide range of worksheet examples. It is hoped that the resources listed at the end of this chapter and familiarity with individual school resources will provide a suitable selection of classroom material.

AN EGALITARIAN APPROACH TO A FOOD AND FARMING TOPIC

1   A selection of information/activities on inequalities in global distribution of food and environmental issues.
2   Who owns and controls food production in Britain? Large landowners, smallholders, crofters?
3   A study of food/cooking from another culture (preferably represented within the school). Perhaps a parent could be invited to cook.
4   A selection of information/activities on the role of food in cultural traditions.
5   Drama to explore prejudice about other cultures (food would provide a useful starting-point).
6   Challenging stereotypical roles. Who cooks in the family?
7   Gender socialization. Looking at packaging of 'cookery toys' and their target audience.
8   Class survey to identify any group with less experience of preparing and cooking food. One teacher or classroom assistant could give a compensatory lesson.

Before such resource packs can be compiled, a good deal of resource investigation and collection will need to be done. Here the work of an equal opportunities co-ordinator may be invaluable, both in expertise and time.

So where are all these resources to be found? Many subject-based publications contain suitable material. Geography books that deal with world studies or developmental/environmental issues are a useful source. Religious studies, home studies and personal and social education publications also contain relevant material. However, some publications, while addressing important issues, may inadvertently reinforce negative stereotypes. Many commercially produced equal opportunities books limit themselves to one particular dimension of inequality and are therefore useful to include in a classroom pack focused on a specific issue, but not so helpful for a topic-linked approach. Charity organizations such as Oxfam, and organizations interested in the promotion of equality, for example, the Equal Opportunities Commission and the Commission for Racial Equality, will provide resources inexpensively or sometimes even free of charge.

The provision of equal opportunities classroom resource packs does not, of course, guarantee their usage, but a continued absence of classroom resources will probably contribute to a continued failure to address many equal opportunities issues.

FURTHER SCHOOL INITIATIVES

Without question, there are many areas beyond the National Curriculum where equal opportunities need to be considered, many of which I have mentioned within the scope of monitoring. The breadth and depth of the subject can appear daunting to those committed to equality in education but unsure about where to start, how to prioritize and which initiatives will prove most effective. Therefore, in closing this chapter I include some examples of equal opportunities initiatives which have proved successful within my own school in the hope that they might be applied with equal success elsewhere.

Bewbush Middle School has 450 pupils on roll, of whom 20 per cent are from Asian cultures. The majority of pupils are drawn from the local community, which consists mainly of low-cost housing and a predominately young population. The intention is that all relationships within the school are based on the premise of mutual respect, with pupils expecting and receiving recognition of the value of their opinions and contributions.

The provision, implementation and review of an Equal Opportunities Policy has not only established the importance of equal provision, but has also focused attention on specific areas for development. The creation and publication of an Anti-harassment Code has clearly defined all forms of harassment and established accepted procedures to deal with incidents. These two public statements indicate the importance the school attaches to the concepts of equality and respect.

The formation of a School Council, which meets half-termly to discuss issues raised from any source, and at which elected pupils represent the views of each class, is a further reflection of the school's commitment to equity.

Playground observations raised the issue of domination of space and, via School Council discussion and agreement, a 'girls only' weekly football session was introduced. Perhaps this contributed to notable success in the local girls' football league.

A Better Classroom Practice document, based on equal opportunity principles and agreed by teaching staff, now influences classroom management and interaction.

More careful consideration is now given to such issues as the content of assemblies and displays; compensatory activities in the use of woodwork tools or cooking equipment, where certain pupils lack formative experience; parental and community involvement, where ethnicity and gender imbalance might exist; distribution of responsibilities, among both pupils and staff; public image and the influence of role models.

The development of a whole school, cross-curricular approach to equal opportunities has been achieved through consultation and agreement involving staff, governors, parents and pupils, the combined support of whom is vital.

The promotion of equal opportunities in education is still controversial in many schools and the task is not an easy one. Progress can sometimes be frustratingly slow, but realistic aims can be achieved through careful planning. I hope that some of the ideas in this chapter will facilitate progress for others.

RESOURCES

Food and farming topic

Button, J. (1989) *The Primary School in a Changing World*. London: Centre for World Development Education.

Fisher, S. and Hicks, D. *World Studies 8–13*. London: Oliver & Boyd.

Hutchinson, G. (1985) *Home Economics for You, Book 2, Yourself and Others*. London: Blackie & Son Ltd.

Hix, P. (1992) *Kaleidoscope*. Southgate Publishers & Hampshire Education Authority.

Oxfam (1987) *World in a Supermarket Bag*. Oxford: Youth and Education Dept., Oxfam.

Pergamon Educational Productions (video). *Looking at Faith*. Exeter: Pergamon.

SUGGESTIONS FOR FURTHER READING

Adams, C. (ed.) (1986) *Primary Matters*. London: ILEA.

Blatchford, P. (1989) *Playtime in the Primary School, Problems and Improvements*. Windsor: NFER NELSON.

Clark, K. (1955) *Playing in Harmony*. Glasgow: Save the Children Fund.

Department for Education (DFE) (1994) *Bullying, Don't Suffer in Silence*. London: HMSO.

Hughes, P. (1991) *Gender Issues in the Primary Classroom*. Leamington Spa: Scholastic.

Rieser, R. and Mason, M. (1990) *Disability Equality in the Classroom*. London: ILEA.

REFERENCES

Cockcroft, W. H. (1982) *Mathematics Counts*. London: HMSO.

Kelly, A. Whyte, J. and Smail, B. (1984) *Girls into Science and Technology, Final Report*. Manchester: Manchester Polytechnic.

OFSTED (1993) *Handbook for the Inspection of Schools*. London: HMSO.

Name index

Subject index